ONCE UPON A PARABLE...

A JOURNEY INTO LIFE

by Dr Steven L. Hairfield, PhD

with Christian M. Kamerer, Editor

When thy intelligence shall cross the turbidity of delusion, then shalt thou become indifferent to what has been heard and what is yet to be heard.
When thy intelligence, which is bewildered by the Vedic texts, shall stand unshaken and stable in spirit, then shalt thou attain to insight.

The Bhagavadgita (52-53)

Library of Congress Catalog Number
Txu 1-012-867
under the title: "Once upon a Parable – A Journey into Life"

ISBN 0-9720080-0-4
I.A.O.M Publishing, 550 E. Plumb Ln, Suite 305, Reno, NV 89502

DEDICATION

This book is dedicated to all the spiritual people everywhere. It is dedicated to those who are striving to climb the ladder that leads to the one called God, or Spirit, or Jehovah, or YHWH, or Allah. By whatever name you may know the Creator, It is always within you, ready to help guide your life on a wondrous path to eternal joy. May this book be a humble inspiration to those who wish to bathe in the glow and warmth of our collective Father.

ACKNOWLEDGEMENTS

You could not guess the tribulations brought on by the mischievous literary muse until you sit in front of a blank computer screen or a blank piece of paper, either begging for your creative input. A book is usually the culmination of a long trek, the beginning of a new life, or the tiny period at the end of a sentence. Let it be said, however, that for the most part, books may be inspired by only one person, but the writing is another matter.

This book is wrapped in the teachings, love and care of hundreds of people who crossed the path of my life, of my search for spirituality. If I were to make a list, I would have to publish a thank you volume the size of a telephone book. Each individual brought me words and actions that allowed me to compose this work about the acceptance of self and others. These teachers, friends and acquaintances gave me a deeper understanding of life.

Human kind is on the edge of a great evolution, and we must be ready. This process began in 1992, yet I read about it while studying with the Tibetans. It was on a document that, I was told, was thousands of years old. This shift is to bring us to the higher levels of understanding about life, spirit, and the subsequent union of both. What you are about to read is the sincere expression of my thanks to all those in my life who have found or are seeking the wondrous effects of Spirit.

In that vein, I would like to thank each and every person for the lessons of life they taught me. In my mind and heart, there are a few who have made a huge impression on my life and my own level of comprehension: **Master Hahn**, a Zen Master and my first teacher, who taught me how to enjoy my emotions and to focus them, to use them as a source of power, to not give the emotions away, but allow them to flow for what they were; **Master Lobsang and Master Tolku**, for their kindness and teachings on the power of the mind, and for introducing me to St. Issa – Jesus, for sharing the records kept on Issa and John – among other disciples who were also in that part of the world, namely India, Nepal and Tibet. Those biblical personalities were there to learn from the seat of ancient knowledge, from the original Masters of the Kashmir region.

There are many people in this country who have helped me in their own way, from my parents and family to the friends I met along the path of enlightenment. There are some who do stand out for their kindness and unwavering support. My thanks to **Ray and Nancy Smith, Zach Flores, Rena and Omer Petty, Don and Andrea Moss and Jean Read**. If anyone were to meet these fine folks, they would be in for a real treat, for they are very loving and kind. They are always willing to help – even the stranger on the street.

My greatest thanks go to **Chris and Connie Kamerer**. As you can see, Chris edited the entire text. He became a combination student, amanuensis, editor and dear friend. Connie was a contributing inspiration and practiced the fine art of gentle constructive criticism. This book would not have been completed without their dedication and the expertise they offered in the finessing of the written word.

My thanks also go to the most dynamic physical teacher I have ever known, my friend **Lisa**, who showed me myself and brought me to fruition in this life.

These types of people make life a pleasant and exciting adventure, even in the face of adversity. Bless all of you for your love and support through the years.

I cannot forget to thank Spirit, the greatest teacher of all. It is there for all of us if we but ask, or knock so that the door will be opened. Bless you all, and in some small way, may this work shorten the journey to a better understanding of life and spirit, so that your higher state of vibration and energy will be there to help others along the path of life.

Dr Steven Hairfield, PhD

PREFACE

After thirty-five years of research, while being submerged in the experiences of everyday life, it was time to produce this book. Through the years, there have been innumerable interactions with many people, but only one conclusion: They are indeed the greatest teachers one can inadvertently discover. They provide a magnificent diversity because of their varied backgrounds and personalities. If we allow it, each of them can teach us something about ourselves. Whether it is something we should or should not do, we all offer each other valuable lessons in life and how to live it to the fullest extent of our being. We should learn to share these lessons with others, free of opinions and judgments. We are all special in every way possible. We are as unique as a single snowflake in the midst of a winter storm. We were created to share the experiences of life rather than own or control them. Through this concept, we are meant to show who we are, and not what we are. We were designed not to hide our inner selves for any reason. Once we hide part of our nature, we no longer offer the truth of self. We offer only deception to those that we encounter on the path of life. We are then unable to live a full life in an honest state of mind. If we act in that fashion, we begin a process of physical and spiritual reclusion. We eventually become resistant to the prospect of living a better, loving life, even if we originally wished it.

This is a book designed for deep inner reflective thinking about ourselves and our interactions in all matters. It is a self-help guide from a spiritual point of view. Its purpose is to get a person to see that life itself can be transformed by a simple change of thought or act, or most of all, a change of feeling. Any of these alterations will bring a shift in our overall lifestyle. It is that simple. The words found in these pages have been designed to result in a potential shift of the psychophysical attributes of the readers, including their personal lives. It is conceived to rid ourselves of the heteroclite nature of the mind. This is not easy reading and yet it is. We must take a moment to reflect on what is offered, and its relationship with our own being. It has been written in as straight forward a manner as possible. The only requirement is to carefully think our way through each word and paragraph.

We need to don our thinking cap and peer into our own circumstances, in order to bring about spiritual growth and understanding in our lives. Spiritual growth is not that much of a mystery. It is the act of moving into higher forms of thinking and feeling. We hope this work will create a deeper comprehension of life in general. The most important key is the journey into and through life upon which we have decided to embark. It is the only path we may take, and no matter how doubtful we may be, it cannot be avoided. We must learn to confront our inner selves in order to grow, and we must persevere to the end. It is the path toward the self-mastery of life and it all begins within each of us.

Our contemporaries and life itself are our teachers through the experiences presented to us. Each of us has a different level of understanding and sees these events in various perspectives. We will attempt to avoid many of these experiences, and we should not. This work will lead to a better appreciation of personal growth and give you an insight as to what these events can be. On the surface, some of it will not be enjoyable, but if we do not decide to avoid such events, it will indeed add to our knowledge and wisdom. It is about the cycles of life, why they are cyclic and how they can be broken if we so choose.

"Once Upon a Parable" is not intended as a religious work. However, it has been devotedly composed to give us a deeper comprehension of the book known as the Bible, and how we can live it spiritually. It is the largest belief system known through all of humanity. It is full of ancient messages about life and how to live it. The book you hold in your hands is written as one very large parable in the fashion of a Zen Kuan. A Zen Kuan is intended to produce deep abstract thinking in a person, to induce deep meditative inner reflective thoughts leading to the understanding of self. This can be achieved by using all attributes of the human mind, thinking with both sides of the brain. This will lead us to see ourselves as we truly are, and not as we think we are. The purpose of this book is to induce each reader to reach for his/her higher spiritual nature. The readers may of course reach their own conclusions and hopefully glean enough information for their own spiritual growth. We cannot avoid life, therefore we hope to furnish enough guidance to help you live it to the fullest.

This book is written in two parts. The first one covers relevant scriptural texts and could be considered a metaphysical interpretation thereof. In the second part, we strive to show you how to live a spiritual life – not a religious one. However, it is not our intent to move people away from their chosen denomination. We simply wish them to have a greater level of flexibility within themselves toward religion, and to read the Bible under a different light. We do not need to follow a "one size fits all" pattern. As individuals, we must fit our own. No matter what we think or believe, we each walk a different path. We may be all here, together, and we are traveling in the same direction but not on the same road, because of individuality.

You will discover that parts of this work may appear to be repetitious. In some respects, they are, but we are dealing with the same basic data on four separate and distinct levels of life. The same subject may be studied under the realms of the physical aspect, the mental, the emotional, and most importantly, the higher spiritual aspect of being human. This allows us to see the subject in the full light of self.

It is truly my earnest desire to see an end to personal struggle, greed and domination of life, to lead us to a more peaceful and loving way of living, a life of sharing and enjoying what it holds for us. Imagine a world free of discrimination on all levels, everything being in a state of true equality. Imagine a life of happiness, one of trust and devoid of deception. It is the truth of life and the direction in which we must travel, and it is a matter of time.

We hope you will read and enjoy this book, and allow your lives to unfold in grace and beauty in all respects. We must seize the moment we have, for this is all that we truly have.

Dr Steven Hairfield, PhD
Reno, 2001

A NOTE FROM THE EDITOR

It has been an honor and a privilege to help Dr Steven Hairfield in his efforts to propagate the Truth. This terminology, commonly used by many guests and Masters of Ceremony, is offered to you with a fundamental difference: I sincerely mean it... It is indeed an honor to know the man who, in the midst of a cruel war, retained his sanity and his pride by seeking spiritual solace in the local religious retreats, rather than destroying his being through drugs and readily available, vile human distractions. It is a privilege to have been chosen as the editor of his book. It has given me invaluable insight into the true meaning of Jesus' teachings.

I must confess that I was born a Catholic and raised as a Catholic. At age 71, I still try to live my life by the doctrines well anchored in me by Franciscan brothers, in a poor district of Paris. The beliefs are still there, but since meeting Dr. Hairfield, they have been enriched, refined in the soft glow of Truth. Jesus told His disciples that He would speak in parables to satisfy past prophecies, and so He did. For almost two millennia, millions of people have read these metaphors, and most accepted the literal sense while remaining spiritually perplexed. During the editing process, I suddenly realized that the light at the end of the tunnel was not a locomotive... It was the light of an awakening consciousness turned on by Dr Hairfield's logical symbolism, by his acquired wisdom in the Far East and within his inner self. It was extremely gratifying, after all these years, to finally ingest the words of Jesus in their true form.

Our eternal Creator loaned an outer shell to each of us for an undetermined finite period. It added a brain and various attributes to insure the proper mechanical functions of our physical body. Most of us have a limited understanding of its internal gears, but we all are fascinated and even obsessed by the exterior looks. We pamper them, modify them, paint them, decorate them and abuse them in the process. We seem to forget that we also have a mind that begets thoughts that beget action that beget dharma, but we would rather kowtow to an obnoxious ego rather than the inner peace of our spirit. We do not see spirit, therefore: out of sight, out of mind. Our materialistic environment makes us impervious to the fact that a union of our physical and spiritual self would indeed bring us a better life, as compared to the continuous illusions we create. That is what this book is about!

I have not changed my religious denomination, nor have I donned the saffron robe. The words in this book, however, have enlightened what I must have known all along but never wanted to reveal to myself. The material side of life indeed seems to stifle our inner thoughts and provides a certain driving force in the acquisition of finite objects. We are caught on this physical merry-go-round and have developed the art of defining ourselves by our wealth and possessions. And when is the last time you conducted a "retro-inspection" of your conscience? For many of us, it appears to be covered by layer upon layer of superficial materialism, and perhaps, we are afraid to take a peek. This wonderful book will help clear that dilemma. It will peel those unnecessary layers, and in the long run, it will make you a better person. It will make you see what Jesus had in mind. It will depict His vision of a world of peace and understanding. If you go beyond the words and genuinely put the ideas set forth into action, you will indeed attain your own peace of mind. You may even find out that you are capable of appreciating your boss, your family and children in general... Unfortunately, you may also suddenly realize how low our society and our culture have sunk. If enough of us can comprehend what Dr Hairfield is saying, and if we have the courage to act it out, perhaps we will help mankind get on the right path again.

Christian M. Kamerer, Reno, 2001

TABLE OF CONTENTS

PART 1 – ONCE UPON A PARABLE

PART 2 – A JOURNEY INTO LIFE

APPENDICES

oꞃce upoꞃ a paꞃaꞰle...

INTRODUCTION

"Constancy in the knowledge of the Spirit, insight into the end of the knowledge of Truth – this is declared to be (true) knowledge and all that is different from it is non-knowledge.
The Bhagavadgita

This book is written with the sincere belief that it will convey the necessary level of knowledge conducive to further growth in this thing called life, and how to live it spiritually. An inspired, personal quest has taken me around the world, seeking a deeper knowledge of God and the One known as Jesus. It is my earnest desire to share with the reader the fact that there is more to the Bible than has ever been said or written, and to bring forth the Truth from a metaphysical point of view.

My journey began in the late 1960's. The purpose was simple: I wanted to learn why there were 18 years missing out of Jesus' life, especially since so many other biblical facts were revealed on the subject of this holy man. *The search for those lost 18 years was the turning point of my life.* The more I studied, the more was perceived that He left a path a mile-wide, so that anyone could follow, if one wanted to seek and find what He knew. It is my personal belief today that any human being can join me on that spiritual path, by merely looking for the information. It is my hope that this work will provide a shorter route to the Truth, the true nature and the wisdom of Self.

As mentioned earlier, my actual studies in metaphysics began when I became associated with the Zen philosophy of life, at the Zen Buddhist Monastery in Quang Ngai, South Vietnam. The Zen masters mentioned many times that I should focus on an individual named **Issa**. I eventually had to ask who Issa was. To my surprise, this name – in any of the English translations of the Bible - is loosely translated as **Jesus**. This old Asian culture knew of Him! This fascinated me, and I had to know more. My own Christian upbringing was whispering to me that such revelation was just not possible. It was this new knowledge that changed everything I had been taught. From that point on, and the journey that ensued, I had to understand more! I simply had to know how the Zens knew of this man, because I was under the impression that they only knew of the Buddha and Bodidharma. What a pleasant surprise it was to discover that they were familiar with many Masters, including Issa, and that they had incorporated all of their teachings.

After I achieved my degree in Psychology, I had an urge, a calling, to travel to India, to quench my thirst for enlightenment. Once there, I began to learn about the Tibetan Philosophy. It started in Patanjali Province, in northern India, into Nepal, and into Tibet on two different occasions. Amazingly, the Tibetan masters told me the same thing as the Zen monks. I was to study about Issa, learn what He did, and most importantly, understand it all. In that part of the world, in the spectrum of time, it seems that these eastern civilizations have been there forever. They have much in recorded history, in the form of tablets and scrolls. Those invaluable documents tell stories of events during forgotten times, and about people such as John the Baptist and of course, the man we call Jesus. My research with those learned masters lasted two years, after which I once again continued my education in the United States, this time in religion and theology. I simply had to understand the belief system, and in the process, I began to have even more questions. Just having faith did not work. Here is an example:

First, there was Adam, and then God gave him Eve as a mate. They had two sons, one of which killed the other. Cain, the survivor, was banished and later took a wife and settled in Nod. Question: whence did the wife come, if indeed Adam and Eve were the "original" human creations? How many of you asked yourselves the same question? As another example, and according to the historical side of the Bible, the appearance of mankind on this planet only took place 3,500 to 4,000 years ago. This time frame is geologically impossible. We know there are human remains and even buildings and monuments that are much older than that. Those are only two of many queries, and it led me to realize that so much had to be missing from biblical texts. Somehow, hearing the words "YOU MUST HAVE FAITH, MY SON" just does not give the knowledge sought. It pushed me to study all religions, in an attempt to locate the missing parts. The majority of our known religions are extremely similar in nature. They relate the same story, or at least their version of it. The names of the main characters are changed, and that is about all. Granted, some of them get into – they believe – the "how to be" teachings. Yet, none of these religions gives any instructions on attainment of these teachings, except for the external trappings, with no real inner substance being offered. It certainly is not my desire to downplay or to judge any religion whatsoever, as each does have its place – thank God. My point is that, in all religions, there appears to be a great deal of missing information. My quest is indeed for what was "left out", and why. Suffice it to say that many disclosures were in store for me on this journey of enlightenment.

My next attempt to understand it all and explore the deeper side of our spiritual being led me to the field of metaphysics, since it encompasses that which is behind any principle or subject - the unseen of things. Why this field? Simple. Jesus, among other religious figures, kept referring to the inner nature of the Self. "The Kingdom of Heaven is within you", "Know thyself". Those are just two of the many other references to this "inner nature". My inquisitive side just had to grasp those meanings, and my journey continued. Many revelations were presented to me. This work is my attempt to present this information and share it with all who seek the Truth of Self, Life, Relationships, Soul nature, and most of all, God. We all think we know who we are. If this is the case, why do we respond to others the way we do? We are seldom ready to take a progressive risk, as long as we are willing to point our finger at another. That progressive risk is one of forward movement – or growth – and our growth is held in place while we blame others for our very own dilemmas.

Once more, I must reiterate that it is not my purpose to point the finger at anyone or anything. To some, it may seem that way. Let me assure you that it is not. Many great people have walked upon the face of this earth. Each of them has left us a certain legacy in the way of knowledge, and these great ones all appear to be so ancient. Through time, we have written numerous great works on religion, and religion is based on old knowledge. Modern society has interpreted it and printed it in its "approved" version. We have to consider the state of the various civilizations when the texts were written. Example: If all the facts had been offered then, no one would need the churches, for we would all know the Truth – and not just a few... It is interesting to me that so much time passed before anything was written about any of these great people. Do you realize that we did not have an American version of the Bible until 1901? That is one thousand nine hundred and one years after the birth of Jesus and 125 years after the Declaration of Independence! What took so long? Once again, it was interpreted, and the number of "interpretations" is absolutely incredible. Originally, it was written in Aramaic, Hebrew and Sanskrit. Then it was translated in Greek, English, and finally, there came the American version. In the process, much has been lost or removed, and it may never be recovered at all. What I have sought all these years is all that is missing – and why. The key, in my judgment, is those 18 missing years in Jesus' life. Even the men that prepared most of these texts wrote them on hearsay. They were not even associated with any of the Masters when they walked.

To cover every facet of the Bible would take a couple of lifetimes, hence, we will limit our discussions to certain vital biblical areas. I will open for you the aspect of the birth of the soul and its chain of events, to wit: **Genesis**, along with Old Testament excerpts and other works for support. We will then move to the New Testament and will cover the books of **Matthew, Mark, Luke and John** and the **Book of Revelations**.

The beauty of all these ancient texts is that all of the information necessary to understand self and the interactions of life is in the veiled words of these texts. These works also state that at some time, this information will be made plain, for all to understand. After all my studies, I found that what is really being said is, in truth, still contained in the books themselves – if one knows how to read them. In all my searching the world over, I believe that the greatest book of all time on the subject of **spiritual enlightenment** is the Bible. It tells us what our own experience is going to be, and the best way to handle things within ourselves as they occur. After all, the "Kingdom of Heaven is within You", and all of these texts clearly explain how to live a better physical and spiritual life. On some levels, you may find it very uncomplicated, yet, what it brings forth within us may create somewhat of a dilemma. Why the dilemma? The answer is really quite simple. Our real struggle in life is balancing our material world with our spiritual self. The material side is seen, and the spiritual is not. Our belief systems are based on our material world and not the spiritual nature of the Self – which is the real or inner Self.

The reason for the selected books mentioned above is rather simplistic in nature. Matthew is about the physical self, Mark the mental, Luke the emotional, John the spiritual, and the Book of Revelations is about the awakening of Self, and what such experience will be. If we know how to read the different texts, they will give us a wonderful understanding of our lives. They will let us know what to expect, and how we will – or will not – handle the course of life necessary for us to continue to grow. Religion, at this point in our contemporary society, is equated to a belief outside of our own Self rather than within, and that is God. God is love, not vindictive, as portrayed by the religions. If God was so vindictive, why is it that Jesus never begged His Creator? He commanded, for He had a deeper realization of His Father, and no harm came to Him. Yes, Jesus was different, but only in the sense of His education and His understanding. He changed the dispensation of the Covenant – or understanding between the physical and the spiritual – from the erroneous concept of superstition to a spiritual reality. He showed us how to work with God, and not against Him. It is time for a new level of understanding, and acceptance of what God means to all of us. This is not really a religious work. It is one that offers and shares that understanding to all who wish to work with the energy of spirit, so they may grow in the spiritual aspect of life. We have greater influence over life than anyone could ever imagine, as we, like Jesus, are the first cause of physical reality

If we were to really understand the work and the studies of the Master, we would realize many things in life. These thoughts, words and actions are what we create for our own learning experience. We organize these, more times than not, through our subconscious nature which has much to do with our higher Self. This higher Self is not something separate from our physical Self. It is the reason we do have a physical body. Deductively, it is not my desire to further a dual nature, for, in reality, we are singular in our being. The point is that we should pay attention to our subconscious nature, as this is how spirit will communicate to us about our life, and of the events going on around us. Modern psychology is now realizing that there is more to dreams than ever previously known. Had we studied the Bible, we would already know this, since spirit was always, in those days, communicating through our dream nature. Today, we ignore the dreams, if we dream at all. The aspect that is – and will be – attempted to be given is that there is more to us than we may fully realize. There is more to our nature that the eye does not see. Metaphysics is all about the unseen -- what is behind our nature. The greatest piece of knowledge – if one could fully realize it – is that we create ourselves with each passing thought, no matter how small or great we make it. All of these shape our lives from moment to moment, and we may control and channel them to the highest levels of consciousness, thereby giving us all that we desire, as it is stated biblically. Be single in purpose, and all will be given unto you.

It is my desire to assist in bringing forth all that the Masters of old told us we could do or become. It is also my intent to help with a road map that will let you know where in this spiritual journey you will find yourself. Would it not be nice if you had an exact path to follow in life, to know that what you do is the right thing, for you and all concerned? Bless you for having taken the time to read this introduction. I sincerely hope that the next chapters will bring you love for all and peace of mind.

Dr Steven Hairfield, Reno, 2001

PART 1

Once upon a Parable

CHAPTER I

THE BIBLE

"Apart from its being a book of great historical and biographical interest, the Bible is, from Genesis to Revelations, in its inner or spiritual meaning, a record of the experiences and the development of the human soul and the whole being of humankind; also it is a treatise on humanity's relation to God, the Creator and Father."

From the **"Metaphysical Bible Dictionary"**, Charles Fillmore Reference Library

To begin this work, we will have to travel through the paths that led to the creation of the Bible. We will dwell in the contents within its covers when we arrive at the actual texts. We must first build a foundation for this ancient data, and must ponder upon its original intent. History is always about "what was", and we must deal with the attitudes that must have prevailed at that particular time in the history of the world known as the "dark ages". In the first fourteen centuries A.D., one could say that pagan beliefs were rampant, and the Church wanted to rid the world of paganism. Some of the methods used could not be qualified as humane. In some instances, the public's gullibility and naivety were exploited. In fact, on the eve of the second millennium, Pope John Paul II publicly acknowledged such methods, including the Crusades and the Inquisition, and for which he apologized and asked forgiveness. Historically, many kingdoms needed this type of support for control purposes. The power gained by the Church was largely due to mind manipulation of the congregations through fire and brimstone. The people did not wish to be condemned, nor did they want a one-way ticket to hell. The Church originally was selected as the tax-collecting arm for such kingdoms that were fledglings at the time. It was an opportunity to acquire greater levels of power through fear. The ruthless kings had been doing this through force, but now the people could lose their soul along with their homes and lands if they did not yield to the will of the churches. Again, we must understand that in the early days, there was only one Church, with many branches, since they had not yet been organized under the papacy.

Deductively, all Christian religions are in fact based on that original and powerful organization. In the same vein, the different versions of all Christian Bibles have their basis in that same original religion. These versions in turn derive from the first accepted works approved by the religious figures of the day. However, the documents were edited – or left out – to suit the need of the new faith that rose from the old. Frankly, during its forming years, the Church wanted to frighten the populace into its enclave. The masses in 285-400 A.D. were, by today's standards, extremely superstitious and lived in fear of the unknown. As a matter of recruitment, they were told they would surely die, and God would punish them if they did not submit to the will of the Church. The first Bible was intended to manipulate the masses, through the guise of fear, a fear that God would harm them if they did not agree with the Church of the day, or of the region. The initial versions of the churches were not in harmony with each other. In fact, it was a war to determine who had more power, using the old adage that says: "we are right, and everyone else is wrong". As a result, some individuals began to come willingly. Others did not and were forced into it, under the threat of losing their homes and their land.

Even though the first Bible was compiled with ulterior motives in mind, it still contains the essence of the original Truth. It has been asked: why "ulterior motives"? If we change the meaning of a word, or an event, there must be an ulterior motive for this action. In those days, the last thing was for the people to know the real Truth of God and the nature of the true spirit of Self. If one is seeking the Truth, here are just a few points that should be considered. **Genesis 4:17**: "…and Cain had relations with his wife…". How can that be? Who was she? The preceding verses in Genesis clearly state that Cain's parents, Adam and Eve, were God's very first human creations. By these words, we are led to believe that there were only one man and one woman upon this newly created Earth, along with the two sons they begat outside the Garden of Eden. **Joshua 10:13 and II-Samuel 1:18**: both these verses mention a person by the name of **Jasher**, an important, highly respected man who accompanied Moses and Aaron. His writings were preserved and passed through the ages, yet his book is not included in the Bible. In his work, Jasher does not mention Eve, the slaying of Abel or the great flood. His story implies that Adam and Eve stayed in Eden, as opposed to what is told in **Genesis 3:23.** He does relate that Cain "went out and dwelt on the east of Eden, in the land of Nod" without mentioning the fratricide. He writes about Japhet, Noah's son, who asked his father permission to move to the "plain of Shinar", to avoid overpopulation. The reason for these variations is unknown today, other than the fact that it did not support the doctrinal intent of the approved versions of the time. Had there been a flood, how could there now be overpopulation? Jasher was not in agreement, therefore his book was left out. So were the works of Enoch, who was Noah's father. Why was this done? If you were to read these texts, you would know for yourself. With the exception of a few, none of the religions of today will inform you of these works. In fact, they will tell you to ignore them because they are not important. The average mind will accept this argument, but then, why is Jasher mentioned **twice** in the Bible?

The many books that were left out of the Bible are known as the **apocryphal texts**. There are numerous versions, and most are different in nature from the presently printed biblical texts, at least in what they contain. For instance, the Book of Luminaries indicates that March is the first month of the year and January is the last, yet it was changed to the Julian calendar. If we are going to believe in Biblical texts, we should not be selective about it, but we should know all we can about what we believe, and why we believe it. The apocryphal texts are all as important as the Bible itself, since they date back to the same era. If one is truly seeking God or information about God/Spirit, one would believe that all information gathered over the centuries would be carefully catalogued, studied, and made available, yet they are not. For the most part, they are seldom – if ever – mentioned. If you were to bring this up to most religious organizations, their representatives would discourage any further search or study. How can this be, if one is an earnest seeker of the Truth of Spirit? The reason most of us do not read or study any of these dissertations is because we do not know such texts are available or where to look. We must first formulate in our mind what we are seeking, then where to find it. It takes a lot of research to identify what they are, much less where they are. Even though the texts are readily available, the Churches of today are not about to guide us toward them, since it would complicate the established beliefs of said Churches and what they have been teaching us. It could not be explained as easily as "you must have faith"…

There is a movement in today's society to understand more about God and the nature of the spirit within. In most cases, the more we know, the more we desire to know on the nature of spirit and God. There are marvelous texts written to direct us on our journey, but, as an example, how many are aware of the **Nag Hammadi,** or the full contents of the **Dead Sea Scrolls**? These works were all written at approximately the same time period. They tell many of the same stories as the Bible, but from different points of view, and with more expanded information, opened for your interpretation and comparative capabilities. In this first decade of the second millennium, do we still need someone to tell us of God? Are we not competent enough to understand all the meanings? Jesus said: *"Verily, verily, I say unto you, He that believeth on me, the works that I do **shall he do also;** and greater works than these **shall he do…**"* (**John 14:12**). These words recognize the fact that we are indeed capable of great things, and in a way, they give us permission to act accordingly. Today, most churches – not all – would have us believe that we may not do these things, for it is evil. Yet, the Christ gave us permission to accomplish the "works", but **how** to reach these goals is still hidden. How can we learn the inner secrets when all the pertinent information has been removed? Unfortunately, we have been fed only a portion of the required knowledge. It is known that Jesus was teaching the inner understanding of physical and spiritual forms working in union to the Apostles, the Disciples and the people. Each of these groups was given various depths of knowledge depending on its ability, and it is often punctuated in the Bible by: "Let those with ears hear". The old texts would relate in the depth of the teachings, yet not all were to understand at that time. The problem lies in the fact that many of these teachings were either not included or removed from the Bible. Why? The logical deduction is that we would have to depend on the Church for the "accepted" knowledge. In her work called **"Isis Unveiled", H.P. Blavatsky** states that all the teachings not included in the Bible are still today within the enclave of the Vatican, under Catholic control, and will never be shared. Were they ever to be revealed, we would no longer need the Church, at least in its present capacity, and we would then do the works, as the Christ stated we could.

In the early years of our civilization, there were many motivating factors to organize people and to control them. We cannot discard the fact that there will always be that nature to be in control. We have always believed that there must be someone in control since, it would be surmised, we know not what we do. It is my perception that God is indeed in control, and all for a collective higher purpose. We, in our physical nature, get in the way, because of this need to be in control. Perhaps God really did make us in Its likeness... To this day, that purpose is still being unfolded because, as finite beings, we still have to absorb the staggering impact of infinity. Yet, each of us has the possibility to comprehend and enjoy this ultimate experience. The understanding of the power of infinity and the power of Self – in conjunction with God – shall create all things. We must first break those outwardly imposed controls that reach us through our own inner belief systems. They cannot be broken until we realize the Truth of ourselves and our relationship with this power known as God, which is within us. The Bible is all about control, at least in the way it is being presented. It was written and compiled by mortal minds attempting to fathom the immortal self. It has insidiously controlled us ever since its inception. How so? Have you ever heard of a book known as **"Secret Instructions of the Society of Jesus"**? This work contains very specific policies and procedures for the order of the Jesuit Priests of the Catholic Church and is disseminated the world over. It is quite interesting, in that it provides instructions in the various ways to earn money for the Church. Here are a few excerpts from this manual:

- Chapter 2, page 11: *"The manner with which the fathers of the order must conduct themselves to acquire and preserve the familiarity of princes, magnates and powerful and rich persons"*.
- Chapter 3, page 13: *"How the society must be conducted with the great authorities in the State, and in case they are not rich, we must lend ourselves to others"*.

In the same book, you can find these most significant and somewhat shocking quotes: *"Of the mode of attracting rich widows"* and *"System which must be employed with widows, and methods of disposing of their property"*. These are indeed startling revelations in the policies of the Church itself. It depicts a focus that has always been on the monetary value of a person, and not necessarily on his/her spiritual side. If you have no money, we will concentrate elsewhere...

The above information may be surprising to most of us, but we must realize that most religious organizations are very wealthy, even by today's standards. The coffers have grown heavy from our donations, and most of those are not used for the poor and the needy. Much of the funds are used in the construction of buildings and temples with all their external trappings. Not much is offered for the health of the spirit... As a matter of fact, Jesus Himself strongly emphasized the need to separate ourselves from the hold the material world can have on us, usually at the detriment of our spiritual selves. Several examples of His wise words can be found throughout **Matthew 13**. Are we not still doing today the very same thing the Pharisees of the times of the Master did? Are we still showing the people the wrong, which is the way to the external Self? Are we still attempting to control through ridicule and the use of love as a weapon? We are accepted as long as we go along with what is being taught, without question. Yet, the moment we begin to ask, we can sense the ridicule as a "non-believer". What is faith if we do not have enough belief to test it out?

Anyone familiar with our contemporary Bible, or even the earlier translations, is aware of the way it expresses its teachings. In comparing its several versions, we find that changing the wording can change the entire meaning of the verse. An example of this appears in **Joshua 24:2-3**. In older Bibles, the key word is "flood". In newer versions, the word "river" is used. One must admit that a quite different message is being conveyed by the switching of the words. In those times, metaphors and allegories were very much in use and appear throughout the texts. If one metaphor is changed, it alters the understanding completely. The fault may lie in our modern language, as it can be very limiting in its definitions. This tends to lend some flexibility to the message being conveyed. It was done for several reasons. First, it was assumed in that era that not everyone would understand, thus the statement by Jesus: *"He that hath ears to hear, let him hear"* (**Matthew 11:15**). The other reason is that, since we all have individual natures within us, the texts had to be written so that they could be applied to all people. Hence, flexibility was a necessary aspect of the work. Much is steeped in symbolism, metaphor, allegory and prophecy. The parables used by Jesus are by far the best examples of this style. There are many others, such as analogies referring to water, shepherds tending flocks, etc…

To certain readers, it may appear that some of my remarks are some-what disparaging. That is not my goal, but the premises or basis of this writing is that these things must be pointed out, so that we may all know the truth. Jesus said in John 16:25: *"…but I shall shew you plainly of the Father"*. Every-thing written thus far is very accurate and is copiously documented, so that the readers can locate the quotes for themselves. Most of us allow the ministry to explain to us the meanings of biblical texts. Perhaps it is the reason why I find quite startling the number of people who have never read the Bible. Possibly, it is what Jesus meant when he said: *"For many shall come in my name, saying, I am Christ; and shall deceive many"* (**Matthew 24:5**). He also said: *"…Can the blind lead the blind? shall they not both fall into the ditch?"* (**Luke 6:39**).

Next, we shall look into the eighteen missing years of Jesus' life, as most of us do not fully realize that He was taught all He knew. He had traveled to different areas of the then known world, to learn from the ancient Masters. He went to attain the wisdom of life and, for the most part, it is the very reason why the Bible does not contain this information. If He was "taught", what value would religion have, since we could all learn this knowledge and become what He was? Hence, it was removed – or hidden from us. He left us a trail to follow, and ways to institute what He was showing us about our very own na-ture: the nature of Self, working with spirit. We will offer what I discovered, along with others who journeyed to find this information. This knowledge is still available today for those who are willing to seek the truth. They can also find it on certain television networks, as viewed and produced by theological and metaphysical scholars. The biblical texts foretold this would happen, and so it is. It is asked that you read with an open mind and heart. Consider the possibilities of what we could become, should we know the real Truth. The Bible also confirms that God is us. We are told this twice: once by the Creator, and the other by Jesus Himself. Be open unto your own being, for the true grace of Spirit will be before you. Some of the information will surprise and even shock you. It will shake the very foundation of your belief system. In the book of John, we are told that all will be made clear, and so it shall. Of course, the most asked question is: what is the Truth? We may never know, but by the same token, things will become clearer so that we can work with them. Consider this: does religion truly wish the return of the Christ? If He does return on earth, will He be pleased at what He sees? No one knows for sure until that time. We all know there are things that are hidden from us merely by the way the Bible is written. The omissions hide the truth, but if we were to discover it, would it not change our very lives for the betterment of all? It would offer a greater reliance on the spiritual side, because our eyes would be opened and we would truly see greater things. It would be so, for the mystery would be removed for all to behold.

The next chapter will give you a glimpse of the one known as the Christ. To know that He was taught is a revelation unto itself. As have others, I have confirmed this for myself. I listened to biblical advice: "Knock and the door shall be opened…Ask and ye shall receive". If they were not put to the test, neither would be of any value, would they?

CHAPTER 2

THE LOST YEARS

"Through Knowledge of Truth all evils are destroyed. The true Enlightened One stands firm, scattering the clouds of deceit like the sun shining in a cloudless sky"

Buddha

The most fascinating person still living within the pages of the Bible is that wonderful teacher and master of all things called **Jesus**. Be assured that it was no accident. His coming was known by many, specifically the Wise Men. The power of the spiritual realm did this with great intent, and that intent was to raise the spiritual level of understanding of all of humanity, and to renew ancient knowledge out of the Garden and the old lands. It was only partially successful. Why this conclusion? Because Jesus did not want to become a religion onto Himself, and if it came to pass in that manner, the full message would be lost. This request was given to the Apostles by the Master Himself. Of course, the rest is history.

The only way to explain this aspect is to begin just prior to the birth of the Christ. Immaculate or not, that birth was the travail of a woman. Joseph did not want to marry her, as she was already with child, and in those days, a birth out of wedlock was an extremely negative event. Had others known, Mary could even have been put to death. The prospective husband was indeed undecided, until an angel appeared in his dreams and told him that the child was the Son of God to come. The couple was from the community of Mount Carmel, among the Essenes of Qum Ran. In those days, being members of this sect made them, to a great degree, both outcasts and gentiles. While we are on the subject of the birth, may I suggest to the readers that Jesus was not born on December 25th, as we have been taught. This theory is shared by many biblical researchers and theologians. As mentioned earlier, all references to shepherds do not necessarily adopt a literal sense. They were tending their flocks at night, in the fields, something that is not done in the winter, due to cold and inclement weather. Springtime has been suggested, around the month of May. Some tablets and scrolls indicate the 15th to the 25th of that month. If you were to read about other religions and myths, you would find that most great people mentioned therein were born on December 25th. That is why this particular date was chosen. It was common to the period, a special day of festivals. Jesus' birthday is in alignment with the likes of Odin, Hercules, and many other personages with whom we are familiar. Again, concerning the birth, there seems to be a minor discrepancy in its biblical reporting. **Matthew 2:11** mentions a "house", while **Luke 2:7** places the birth in a "manger". The other two gospels do not mention the birth at all. However, the locale of this event is not important, but the fact that He was born is. The reporting was done after the fact and was magnified, to show us that the greatest among us may come from humble beginnings. That was the purpose, and it is ultimately the Truth.

Jesus came upon this earth with a mission, as we all have, and in that regard, he was not special. Yet, at the same time, there were people who were looking forward to His birth. In fact, they sought Him out on the day of His birth, for ancient prophesy had foretold of His coming. The three "Kings" were not kings at all. They were wise men, or Magi – Mystics as in the time of Moses. They were alchemists – teachers, if you will – teachers of the higher spiritual nature of life in the great school of Helios, in Heliopolis (Egypt). Even today, the Tibetan monks seek out the reincarnated Dalai Lama, in order for them to perpetuate and extend the teachings. In that search, they perform certain tests to insure that the chosen one is indeed the Dalai Lama. That is essentially what those three wise men were doing. They wanted to verify the prophesy. They had traveled great distances from India, Egypt and Syria, to see if this was the One they were told would be born – the Savior, the teacher. Jesus passed the tests and would become a student. The Magi left their gifts and instructed Joseph and Mary as to what they should do in the early years. When Jesus was born, His name in Hebrew was **Yoshesh Ben Yoshesh**, which means Joseph, son of Joseph. The teachings began with the Essenes, when He was one to two years old. When He was about seven or eight years old, He earned the name of Jesus, a name that actually stands for a level of accomplishment, of understanding. With His newly acquired knowledge, the young boy began to be heard publicly. He did not become known as the Christ until after his 18-year disappearance. By the time Jesus reached the age of thirteen, the Bible no longer quotes Him. The last comments concerning Him can be found in Luke 2.

However, the tablets and scrolls not easily available in the public domain do place Jesus in Egypt, whence Moses departed, the land of esoteric teaching, the land of the first Magi, in a place known at the time as **Heliopolis**. These documents mention the Mystery Schools of Egypt, where He studied with His cousin John, later known as John the Baptist (See the book of John). John left the Mystery Schools a few years before Jesus did. He journeyed into what is now known as Pakistan, India, Nepal and Tibet – the ancient lands of

Eden or Kashmir – to learn the knowledge of the ancients in order to carry it forth in its renewal. The second Magi had come from this part of the world, and Jesus followed that same path where the teacher was **Chetan Nath**. These events were indeed recorded on scrolls and tablets, along with several of the Apostles' travels in later years. For those in search of the Truth, they can be found in the same place where they have been for centuries.

In the countries mentioned above, Jesus was known as **Issa**. His accomplishments were well recorded, including the fact that He almost had his life taken in India, because He was telling all people that the cast system was wrong. He was in the Sind region first, and he settled among the Aryans, the land of God, Northern India. His intent was to become more perfect in His nature and to learn the laws of Buddha and the Vedas. He then traveled to the area now known as Punjab. Later, he went to Jagannath, where He studied Brahma and the deeper aspects of the Vedas. He began to teach this to the people, but the Brahmans were displeased, as they began to feel threatened. Jesus was teaching equality and the fact that they should serve one Master and not many. The Brahmans could lose stature and wealth if this were to continue. He could ruin their system and usurp the power they had among the people. He was no longer welcome in these lands. So, after six years in Jagannath, He had to flee. What He began to teach is quite similar to the Gospels, but in different words, and these words were to be written by a scribe. *The law was made for Man, to show him the way. The eternal judge, the eternal spirit, who forms the soul and individual World-Soul, will go against those who arrogate His rights to themselves. The miracles of our God have been ever since the first day, when the Universe was created; they take place every day and at every moment. Those that cannot perceive them are robbed of one of the most beautiful gifts of life. So long as the people had no priests, they were ruled by natural law and they preserved the flawlessness of their souls. Their souls were in the presence of God, to commune with the Father. They had no need to resort to the meditation of an idol. You say the sun is to be worshipped. I tell you your doctrine is false, for the sun has no power but through the will of God, who has willed it to be the star to light the day and seed time of man.*

Once more, He was warned of this event and was asked to leave. He traveled to Nepal and Tibet for further study. This is confirmed by the words of **Nicolai Notovitch**, in his work on Saint Issa. Many since have seen these works, including myself, and know that they exist. Notovitch even approached the Church with his revelations. He was told not to tell anyone about them, to keep it to himself. The Church of the time even went as far as offering to buy his silence. While in Tibet, Notovitch stayed at several monasteries, Lhasa and Hemis among them. Their records show his visits. These orders are meticulous in their record keeping. They have been doing it for centuries, and they do not allow just anyone to read them. One must be extremely patient to see them, and they must also prove their worthiness, so the information is not misused again by the masses. These policies have been in place for the convenience of those who are in the position of power. They intend to maintain them and will, at all costs.

After his long sojourn in Jagannath, and upon passing further testing, Jesus traveled to meet with his third and last teacher: the third Magi. He was located in what is known today as Syria and Iraq. Here, after the ten years of study, much was brought to fruition. Two years later, He returned to Egypt for the final phases that would determine who He was to become: Jesus Christ, the perfection of the Spirit in human form. His studies ended with His graduation, after which he was to return to Israel, to begin teaching what He had learned to the multitudes. It included the inner teachings, but much of it was removed from today's Bible. Unbeknownst to those who assembled the biblical texts, they are still there for us to read, if we know where to look.

What Jesus studied and learned in his travels has always been of interest to most, but especially how He did what He did... Following are some of the areas that are known, not only to myself, but to many others in this world who decided to seek the Truth for themselves. His studies in Egypt were on the subject of alchemy, and there are Biblical indications of this, especially in the time of Moses: **Exodus 4:3 and 7:10.** You may recall that Aaron had turned his staff into a serpent, and the Pharaoh called forth his alchemists to do the same. It was done, magic against magic, and Aaron's serpent devoured the others, to demonstrate superior magic. Hence, they knew something about vibration manipulation in that part of the world. They knew about rearranging material reality. Jesus also studied life and death, and the processes of physical life. He learned about higher realities after physical life has ceased, the *Vedas and Tibetan Book of the Dead*, the spiritual realms. He learned their religious philosophy and deities and especially the power of mental symbolism, as the mind thinks in symbols and images, and not in words. Upon completion of these studies, he began the third leg of his journey of understanding, to further his knowledge of enlightenment and the more subtle aspects of Self and of God. He not only studied about Krishna, but also about the teachings and philosophy of the Buddha. He focused on compassion and the love of humanity, on the gentler outlooks of life, learning the power to merge His emotions with the energy of God in order to heal others. Most of all, He learned to override his own ego. He left India to study the aspect of vibration and the power of His thoughts, as well as to further His knowledge of symbolism. He learned to be single in purpose, no matter what may have been happening around Him at any given moment. He learned to take the energy of His emotional body and combine it with the mental ability to focus with the intent of manifestation, producing what was needed at that moment in time. Once again, at the conclusion of His studies in Tibet, the next segment of His education was to begin in Syria with one of His last instructors, the third Magi.

His mission then was to learn sacred geometry so that He could truly comprehend all that He had been studying, to be aware that what He was doing was a very exact and sacred science. This was one of the last subjects He had to know. At the same time, He began the study of the stars – astrology – for it was written in the book of Genesis that our times and seasons were written in the stars (**Genesis 1:14**). He had to know of the cycles of life. There is further evidence of this in two books removed from Biblical texts. They are the Book of Luminaries written by Enoch, and the Gospels According to the Stars, both spelling this out very clearly. Upon the completion of his studies in Syria, He returned to Egypt, where all His teachers waited to proceed with His final testing in the seven virtues of life that He had studied for so long. It must also be said at this point, that during each step of his education, Jesus studied Prophesy as well. It was a focal point, since He was aware that everything He was meant to do had to be in accordance with what all the prophets had been saying for centuries. This path had to be followed to the letter, in relation to each prophet's vision – and there were many in those days. If you are familiar with the Biblical texts, you must agree that there are numerous references to prophecies. Quotes such as: "As it was told", "..to fulfill what the prophets said", are repeated many times, and one had to know them by heart…

Once Jesus graduated, He returned to his own land to bring about the conclusion of the prophets, and to close out all the prophecies of His coming. Yet, one more important event had to take place. It was the union of His higher and lower selves, his commitment to the purpose. It culminated at the river Jordan with His Baptism by water performed by His cousin John. Water is the metaphysical term for spirit, or spirituality.

Jesus gave us everything He had, simply to show us a different way to live our lives. Apparently, we did not hear or pay attention! Look at the way the world is today. Is it really any different? Can we do things differently, yet better? The answers are found in this book. The chapters that follow are being offered in the hope that it will explain what He meant in all that He said and did, for He gave His **being**, not just His physical body. His **being** incorporated His "I AND MY FATHER ARE ONE". We include only the "I" in any of it, and that is not enough. The "I" incorporates only the physical, physical mental and the material world. No wonder we are filled with such greed! We believe that "physical" is all there is... After all, that is all that we can see and feel, hence, what else could be involved in the cycle of life? The "physical" is only the tip of true reality. Jesus knew this through all His studies. He attempted to teach this knowledge and share it with all that could "hear" or understand. He also knew then – or now – that not all would understand or believe the messages.

The greatest reason for His sojourn in these lands is because they were the birthplace of physical knowledge, and as was already pointed out, the birthplace of humanity. His purpose was to absorb the highest level of ancient knowledge He could attain, so He could bring it forth to the people. His goal was for all of us to understand the ancients and the messages they left for us to know and apply. He passed on this knowledge in the purest form. We had to selfishly change much of it, and as the changes took place, the meanings were lost. It was stated earlier that He did not desire a religion to be made of Him. He did this because he had no ego involvement in this journey, and only the ego would want glorification for His actions. The message was not about Him. It was about US and what we are able to become within our own selves. He wanted to demonstrate the way to the higher Self, as in "I am the light and the way", to promote the right use of understanding. Knowledge of Spirit is the most important characteristic we could have, and He knew this. He also knew that we would get caught up in idols and external trappings to assist the outer Self. The message clearly indicates that the "outer" is not important, as it is only a shell, an outpouring of what we think of ourselves and life external.

The next chapter will cover the Book of Genesis, after which we will focus on the four main Gospels of the New Testament. You will discover that the Bible itself does support the subjects that we will point out for the reader's comprehension. We will cover the metaphysical interpretation of the text and explain the terms used. Some of them are strictly metaphorical and should not be taken literally. Let us take the word **Israel** as an example. In those days, there was no country by that name. Christ lived in Palestine. Explanations and definitions will be furnished to help the reader understand. When you know the meaning of the words, you will see the differences. It will ease the growth of spirit toward the merge that is biblically foretold. We are all to experience it for ourselves, for a union with Spirit.

CHAPTER 3

GENESIS

"Then God spoke to him, saying: 'Oh Brahma, I command thee: again create the world, as thou hast often done in times past. To create is to thee not new. Whatsoever is to be created is already within me, as thou well knowest. Creation is only the projection into form of that which already exists'".

Bhagavatam

What if God woke up one morning and said: "What am I?". Its consciousness had no **experience** of **Self** whatsoever. It realized that experience is what It required to know Its own true nature of **being**. It had no **definition**, only theory, for it was not yet aware of being. It did not know Itself. In that moment of realization, It knew that It had become an individual nature onto Its own self. It could be called the true birth of the **Soul**. It had independent aspects within Its own being and was pure and ethereal in Its thinking. No substance, no form. At that instant of cognizance, the process that we know as **physical reality** began to take place. In the darkness – which was not yet defined – there appeared points of light and patches of firmament. It started the process of definition, giving life to Its consciousness. Darkness is the reference to the absence of understanding and because of that, did God, in the beginning, truly understand as It does today? The appearance of light is an indication of understanding taking place within the Soul, the soul of self. Reference to the firmament is reality becoming tangible in Its thinking. If one would wish to read more on the subject, a Jewish work called the **Haggadah** [1] makes mention of it.

These points of definition were originally not of a physical nature, but rather more vaporous at first, until they drew together through swirling centers of energy, creating gravity and becoming more compact – in truth, a more defined form of thinking. As these points became firmer, God began to have a definition of Its own nature. It started to gain understanding of Itself, a simple comprehension from pure intelligence, as we know and perceive it. As Its knowledge grew, Its thoughts and Soul began to feel the desire for creation. It

---

[1] Haggadah (Haggada or Aggada): In Judaism, a complement to the Halakah in the Talmud. The body of non-legal rabbinical lore, comprising legends, anecdotes and parables, which exemplifies the religious and ethical principles of the traditional law compiled in the Talmud and Midrash during the first centuries of the Christian era.

wanted life and form for Its consciousness. **Genesis 1:26:** *"And God said, let us make Man in our image, after our likeness...."* This was for the advancement of knowledge, for wisdom's sake. Since knowledge and wisdom are attained through experience, and if we are truly in the image of God (**Genesis 3:22:** *"....the man is become as one of us..."*), then the principle holds true for each of us. The experience is necessary for our purpose: the true learning – even about the inner soul self, and It has brought us to that point in creation. This is why there is so much struggle and strife in the world today. God wants us to work on the inner self, because the outer is already perfect in its nature. During Its own process, the sublime consciousness began to realize that all It had was pure intelligence. That must have seemed incomplete, as pure intelligence would be cold, without feelings. A deeper awareness began to evolve. We all believe that God knew all things, even in the beginning. How could this be? If we are indeed like God and we must learn, it stands to reason that It too must learn. It needed experience to understand Itself. Therefore, we must do the same, as all metaphysical laws would apply from the highest to the lowest. Experience is the only real path to knowledge, and that knowledge would apply to both inward and outward aspects, as Spirit created the inner nature first and the outer second. The Alpha and Omega meet where we ourselves are – the true temple of Spirit.

God discovered that pure intellect was not enough. It envisioned Its intelligence, Its individual concept of thought, within Its creation of a physical being. It now had expanded Its own independent nature, of Its own accord, and It wanted to know more, to bring Itself to another level of awareness. Pure thought alone did not have enough depth as Its consciousness had grown. It realized It needed to **feel** what It knew, to add to Its intelligence and Its wisdom, allowing for a more meaningful experience. Yet, being pure spirit and without a physical nature of its own, It had no way to accomplish this task.

We can assume that the **sense** system was in the process of being formed, as the intellect was already present in the soul. This growth would deepen mankind's experience. It would have feelings. Thus, a desire of the true **physical** was beginning to take shape. It had to be evolved to a greater level, as It wanted to know Itself in the purest sense. It had to be able to feel what It knew, for a more consequential experience. What if God, in that moment, wanted to experience Its own concept? What if It wanted to fathom that which we call "love"? It could not, for it had no feelings to achieve this. So, from pure thought came the concept of independent **feeling**. There was no connection to the thought in any way, as they were intended to be both equal in nature. Once more we mention the Haggadah, in which the first attempt of feelings, independent of thoughts, is portrayed as **Lilith** [2] (Adam's first companion). These concepts were too separate, too rebellious. There could be no alignment between the two, since they were autonomous and fragmented. Emotion was then taken away, and Spirit began to reconsider. What if feelings were created out of thought, as a part of thought - which was Adam's attribute? What if feelings worked in conjunction with thoughts, as an individual nature, yet with an inner connection? And so, from the purest of thought came the concept of feelings as an integral part of the thinking process. It was called **Eve**. This amalgamation began to deepen even further the knowledge that It desired to comprehend – Its own being and form in motion. Spirit knew the ethereal or soul part of self, and because creation had already begun and ether was condensing, God knew then that It could take this process further and bring all things to material form. It knew that Its thoughts were gaining life and motion. Thoughts began to set into solid form.

Entered the **serpent (Genesis 3:1:** *"Now the serpent was more subtle than any beast of the field which the Lord God had made..."*). The idea of the serpent is very complex and will be intertwined in this work, due to the variety of interpretations of its meaning. However, it seems inconceivable that God would tempt Itself, unless temptation itself had a greater meaning than what has been presented so far. The concept of temptation was directed more toward the attainment of knowledge through the principle of learning. Such an education must be acquired through the physical aspect of life or the experience of it. We were meant to learn as spirit in physical form. Religions in general have us believe that God created us to worship It. If this were true, would it not be extremely arrogant? Would it not be a gesture of control? In that case, temptation may be our very teacher of Life. After all, was it not temptation that induced God to create all things? In many other texts, you will find that the "serpent" alludes to the rising spirit energy housed within the physical being. This is contained in all of our very own spinal columns. If you wish to study this allegory further, you can find it in The Vedas [3], some of the oldest known spiritual writings, and Buddhism, among other references. It is also confirmed in **John 3:14** (*"And as Moses lifted up the serpent in the wilderness..."*), as Moses was raising the spiritual nature within him. This tempted our independent nature to create a physical illustration (**Genesis 3:14:** *"And the Lord God said unto the serpent, Because thou hast done this, thou art cursed above all cattle....."*). "Cursed above all cattle" implies the importance of the serpent to

---

[2] Lilith: in post biblical Jewish literature, Lilith came to be identified as Adam's first wife (See "Alphabet of Ben Sira", written between the 7th and 10th centuries). She is namelessly mentioned in Isaiah 34:14, as a demon of the desert.

[3] Veda (Sanskrit: "knowledge". Also called the "Samhitas"). The most ancient sacred literature of Hinduism.

the human form. This temptation is merely thought pressing itself into physical reality. We were about to take on physical form. God needed an opposite of Itself, as an anchor, to hold things in place. Now Its thought could press itself downward into material form, since It had found that anchor. **Lucifer** (meaning: "bright shining morning star" in Sanskrit) volunteered for the work, since all things need a polar opposite for existence.

This was the Spirit's first perception of the law of opposition. Alone, it could not truly produce life, since it was only one side of the concept. Realization was becoming much deeper. Spirit started to recognize that It needed a positive and negative pole – as were Adam and Eve. The experience It had begun to seek was gaining in knowledge and depth. The symbol of infinity is the perfect expression of polar opposites, stretching them into existence for reality to become physical, so that we may have the experience we call **life**. This stretching effect was creating a finite form, since there was nothing but infinity at first. What would God be without Lucifer, man without woman, night without day, water without land and earth without atmosphere? Infinity, as in God, recognized that an opposite action had to be used to give foundation to life, and to give certainty to physical reality. For every action, there is an equal and opposite reaction. Harmony in Truth is the action of polar oppositions, working in union with one another, and we, as humans, are in the center, being pulled simultaneously in opposite directions. We are the epitome of the law of polar opposition in action.

We see that Adam and Eve did not even have a truly physical form until **Genesis 3:21**: *"Unto Adam also and to his wife did the Lord God make coats of skins, and clothed them"*. They received bodies because they wanted to understand themselves in the expanse of infinity and because God had given life to independent thought. This is confirmed in **Genesis 2:5**: *"And every plant of the field before it was in the earth, and every herb of the field before it grew: for the Lord God had not caused it to rain upon the earth, and there was not a man to till the ground"*. Spirit had not yet come upon earth. It was not formed until the reality of man came into existence and was pressed down into the physical form. There was no physical reality until this occurred. God knew that to truly appreciate infinity, one had to be finite in nature, to experience limitation, so we could operate within the power of infinity to understand the process of the laws of opposition. If we are indeed in God's image, then we are to be a God in the making and must learn all the laws of spirit. We do this through the experience of limitation. Now, let us go to **Genesis 2:23** and *"bone of my bones"*. Man and woman were not yet physical reality, as they were still in the Garden, still in spirit. Conclusively, if the original garden had not yet materialized, neither had they. What happened was much more esoteric. It is mentioned in many other texts, such as the Vedas and Buddhism. God did not take a literal rib from Adam. It put Adam to sleep so that It could remove the feminine aspect from him and form it as a separate entity, as Adam was. It was named Eve – for sensitivity – as the mother of all things. She was not fashioned out of the physical nature, but rather out of the spirit nature of Self. In other words, no rib was removed, since there was no rib to remove at that time. The sleep that Adam experienced was not sleep as we know it. He was unaware that Spirit was separating the central atom of the inner soul – spirit – which is located in the heart center of what became the body. It was divided in half and can be considered a "spiritual split". This is one reason we all feel incomplete, and we seek the other half, the soul mate, or the twin flame, our mirror image.

This division created full thought and feelings in both male and female, along with the ability to create all things, together. We are to work as a union for creation purposes, yet we work in opposition. It also created the sense of separation, or a sense of being incomplete which spilled into the journey portrayed by the Bible. Our search for this sense of completeness is why the majority of us struggle as we do. We seek union, as we are the opposite of the concept of God. The full reunion will not occur until we are the perfect image It has already created. We do not realize this perfection already exists. Insecurity blocks this from us. We are only separate in the sense of what we may have given up: the true power of our inner combined nature. Physical life was to assist us in our pursuit to comprehend both our corporeal and spiritual sides. We are becoming that, in spite of ourselves, as Spirit continues to unfold all its mystery, and we will become one spiritual/physical human to reach completion.

When Adam and Eve were formed, they brought another factor in the equation: the serpent. God Itself was not yet aware of that which we call **ego**. Ego is a natural influence of thought and emotion combined. And they tasted of the tree of knowledge... *"...then your eyes shall be opened, and ye shall be as gods, knowing good and evil"* (**Genesis 3:5**). They knew the difference between "spirit" and "physical", as God did. We are in Its image, and we too want to understand, as does the Father. The question is: if God truly created all things, why would It have one of Its own creations tempt another? It would not, unless It had independent development as Its concept and It desired to learn about control of Its own nature. It desires this for us as the human corporeal form. It wanted us to develop in a balanced nature, and to do this, we had to know ourselves as the Spirit does. The tree of knowledge was not a "sin", for we were intended to have knowledge – especially if we are in God's image. The serpent was the ego of the Self, and it now became the very key for us to expand as well as a necessary tool for further development. Today, we have regrettably given it too much influence. We have allowed it to have too much to say in the day-to-day activities of life. The ego now controls most of us. This is why so many people have no sense of humility. They need to be in control. This is not acceptance. It is the seat of greed and selfishness. It will not let people be in service with and for each other. We may believe that someone needs to be in control, but it is not so, as other gospels in the Bible will tell us.

This is the perfect time to introduce you to the symbol of **Yin and Yang** – a circle, half black and half white, meaning opposites, with a small red line down the center that is the symbol of balance between the two. This red line represents the ego. It is the balance point between thought and emotion, the center of infinity. The Self chose to know more about the physical aspect of life. It wanted to be like its creator – to emulate that physically – and they accomplished that task by tasting of the fruit of the tree of knowledge. This knowledge brought about the idea of separation, meaning that they were becoming more of a corporeal nature. They were at a transition point between the physical and the spirit nature. Yet, they were not quite there and not separate, as the spirit was being housed within the physical. They were not yet conscious that they had bodies, nor did they see the true differences between themselves, thus they covered themselves with leaves when they did realize the difference. The reality of thought pressing into the physical was taking hold. The seeming separation between Self and God commenced to deepen, which is why God was searching for Adam while in the Garden. Why did they hide? Were they not the first two people? No one else was going to see them. How could they know shame – unless the body is a bad thing…How could that be? God created it through the knowledge already gained. This is manipulation of information, the same as **Genesis 2:23** is a way to explain creation in a world of superstition. If the creators of the Bible had attempted to explain Spirit to an already superstitious people, the Religion would have been doomed. It needed a physical explanation for physical minds: good is Spirit in nature, and evil is the physical nature, as it is a lower form. So we had this paradox bound within us… That is not to say that we are evil, for evil does not really exist, except in the mind of the individual nature of the human. Evil is a matter of choice that we are to constantly overcome because of our ego. Our option must be the original sin, yet it is a difficult one. We are in Spirit's image, and that must mean in all ways. In this superstitious world, we are "evil", because we are "physical". We believe that everything we do must be physical in nature. Not so, as the Ark of the Covenant travels before you… a point which we will elucidate later. Evil – in the sense that is being applied here – does not mean that we are bad, unless we choose to be. "Evil" is only stated to mean a physical nature that cannot think past that "physical" status. It also means ignorance in spiritual matters, not allowing God in our being. At a later time, Jesus expressed that thought, reported in **Matthew 7:11**. We will cover this matter in that chapter.

The first warning came with the advent of Cain and Abel, and that warning was that we should not allow the physical to dominate life. Cain was a worker of the earth, very physical. Symbolically, it is the first indication that "physical" will become our most important feature, and such aspect will slay the "spiritual" every time, except in few cases. Cain slew Abel, a shepherd who tended the flocks. Biblically, shepherds were traditionally wise men, the thinkers of that era, for they herded their thoughts or controlled them. They were much more oriented in spiritual matters. Today, as it was then, most of us pay little attention to the spiritual. Even in those early days, it was a problem. We now had bodies with which to distract ourselves, by which we became enamored, for it was real. We could touch them, feel things and sense things. God had accomplished Its dream of definition, yet, It did not realize how ingrained It would become in the physical. It did not recognize that when It became totally physical, God could not remember Its own spiritual nature, housed in the individual called human. It realized we would need constant reminders about this arrangement, and It sent many a form to jog our memory. We still have not accepted this. Its inner character began to struggle with Itself, and that struggle still goes on to this day. That tussle is really between dark and light, between understanding and the lack thereof. It is that internal nature of polar opposites that gives us the knowledge we have, through the external experiences of life. In Genesis, we are learning of our own individual nature of Self, and the problems involved in being a spirit in physical form.

The Bible describes our experience of Self, how we are to return to God – or the higher Self, and how we are to trust it always. In reality, how much of it do we trust? How can anyone of us trust something that we cannot see and cannot feel in the physical sense of the word? The mission of this life is to get in touch with that higher Self and it has always been this way. It has been since the dawn of time. From our rudimentary beginnings, the spread of knowledge was set in motion. Thus, we are an accumulation of that knowledge today. Our DNA is our personal history, our own tree of life. It is our "book of life" as mentioned in the Book of Revelations, and we are to open its seven seals. We are still working on bringing it to fruition through the day-to-day events of life. What God had created was a mirror of Its own self-perception, bearing the likeness of Its perfection. We do not seem to recognize that perfection of Self is US. God did not commit any error. We are the ones with that discernment. We were and are perfect in all ways and attributes. We are the individual incarnation of the power of God. In the beginning, we were originally fashioned out of perception and not out of reality, and we could not have known that much.

The genealogical listing of the descending generations in the Bible are the different years of development it took us to grow into more physical reality. You see, we never left the Garden of Eden. We just changed it into something other than what it was originally, and that was esoteric by its very nature. We changed it to match our corporeal selves, thus giving it a physical aspect. This is the true birth of physical knowledge. As it took place, the Garden also had to become "physical" to support us as humans. We have looked for this Garden, but we have been searching in the wrong places. **Genesis 2:10-14** tells us *"And a river went out of Eden to water the garden; and from thence it was parted, and became into four heads…"*. It is located in the Kashmir region of the Far East, the northern part of India today; this is why it is the cradle of true ancient knowledge, and why so many masters come from this area of the world. It is also why Jesus Himself journeyed there. Beside Biblical texts that verify this location, there are other works that confirm this theory, such as *"Jesus Lived in India"*, by **Holger Kersten**. Each book of the Old Testament is a record of our experience at that time. We see that in who begat whom and how long each one lived. They were different levels of experience through which we were developing and how long that level lasted – given in the age of each descendant.

It must also be stated that all souls were created at the same time with all of creation. Individual aspects were unleashed and began to grow: the "big bang". This would explain why Cain was able to find a wife – or companion, and the physical took over, as it won the original struggle portrayed as life. Life started as a reality of thought, to attain the experience necessary for further wisdom. We reenact the slaying of Abel by his brother day in and day out, with our own selves. We are constantly slaying the spiritual aspect to pursue the physical. It is so, because we give all the importance to the material side and not to the whole self as was originally intended. We see this confirmed in **Genesis 4:6-7**: *"And the Lord said unto Cain, Why art thou wroth? and why is thy countenance fallen? (7) If thou doest well, shalt thou not be accepted? and if thou doest not well, sin lieth at the door. And unto thee shall be his desire, and thou shalt rule over him"*. Does this not sound like the ego? It is also the first sign of jealousy, and he must master it – as do we all. We were whole until the battle between Cain and Abel. There will always be a struggle between what we **feel** and what we **think** about a particular subject. The Master taught us that we should match what we think with what we feel, and not the other way around. On a daily basis, we attempt to match what we feel to what we think, and that has to be quite frustrating because it usually does not match. Thinking is physical and feeling is spiritual, creating a division on inner levels. Very seldom are they in complete agreement on any issue. Adam and Eve were the differences within our own selves, and they became manifest in physical life as the polar opposites of Self. We were to learn to reconcile these natures within Self, and we have yet to do so, since we always give importance to the mindful things of life. In essence, that encapsulates the rationale of the first struggle and its Biblical allegory. We see this same struggle throughout the Bible, yet we do not understand this very simple message. This lack of comprehension is due to the fact that what **we** think is much more important to us. It has to be, since what we think is what makes us who we are. It gives us our viewpoints on issues, and we will do everything to protect them, with great inflexibility. We do not very easily allow for new ways of thinking about issues, since we are repetitious in our thought processes. We believe that old will contaminate the new, as in new wine in old skins, and it shall, for we do not release the old very easily.

Genesis 7:15-19: *"And they went in unto Noah into the Ark, two and two of all flesh, wherein is the breath of life. (16) And they that went in, went in male and female of all flesh, as God had commanded him: and the Lord shut him in. (17) And the flood was forty days upon the earth; and the waters increased, and bare up the ark, and it was lift up above the earth. (18) And the waters prevailed, and were increased greatly upon the earth; and the ark went upon the face of the waters. (19) And the waters prevailed exceedingly upon the earth; and all the high hills, that were under the whole heaven, were covered"*. We are told of Noah, the flood and the deluge of rain for a period of 40 days and 40 nights. Geological science does not truly confirm this, yet many other religions have recorded this event. As was mentioned earlier, metaphysically speaking, water is related to the spiritual nature. The metaphor here is that spirit was coming back into full play. It would seem that for an initial period, earth was deluged by spirit blanketing all things. What happened? A shift of the ages, if you will, occurred to take us from a physical nature back to a more spiritual one. It was a transition after the Garden by several thousand years, and Biblically, the second time it had to occur. Adam and Eve were the first, from spirit to physical. Noah was the second, from physical back to spiritual.

Ancient prophecy tells us that such a period occurs every 3,000 to 4,000 years and we call it a polar shift, a function of electromagnetism. We see a direct reference to this possibility in **Joshua 10:13**: *".....Is not this written in the book of Jasher? So the sun stood still in the midst of heaven, and hasted not to go down about a whole day"*. It must also be stated that the Mayan texts record a period of extended darkness for about a day. This would make sense, and it appears to have happened during that same period of time. The darkness was on the other side of the earth and confirms what took place in the east. From a geological point of view, this shift has been recorded before on six different occasions. No one knows specifically what occurs during such global upheavals. This possibility may also tend to explain the different ice ages that have come and gone. Unless the sun was to diminish its ability to heat the earth, there is no other explanation for our planet to be covered in ice and snow. If the earth was to change its position or shift on its axis, this would then cause the ice caps to be in entirely different latitudes and longitudes. If one is interested, this information is geologically verifiable. The poles are a function of electromagnetism and ironically, so is the human form.

This concept is carried even further by one of the fathers of the laws of physics, Dr. Albert Einstein. He states that time is not truly linear, but rather, it is an arc or curve. We know that an arc or curve is part of a circle – or cycle – and it will return to the point of origination whence it began. We can apply the same concept with the use of the term "wheels" which we find in **Ezekiel 1:19-21**: *"And when the living creatures went, the wheels went by them: and when the living creatures were lifted up from the earth, the wheels were lifted up. (20) Whithersoever the spirit was to go, they went, thither was their spirit to go; and the wheels were lifted up over against them: for the spirit of the living creature was in the wheels. (21) When those went, these went; and when those stood, these stood; and when those were lifted up from the earth, the wheels were lifted up over against them: for the spirit of the living creature was in the wheels"*. During periods of pure material reality, we use the left brain as primary function and logic prevails. After a shift, we predominantly use the right brain which is more metaphysically oriented through such actions as creativity and intuition. The functions of left and right brain are also laws of opposition within, as thought and emotion are. Those assets – creativity and intuition - are more predominant at that point than at any other time, but logic will not necessarily operate at our usual level. It makes sense that we must learn to operate with both sides of the brain at the same time, rather than rely on one side and then the other. To go through life in that manner would bring us an invaluable experience. We would become aware of the illusion of our dual nature and it would open the doors to creation, thus unifying the duality. Indeed, whole growth would take place, and the duality we think is there would disappear. It would become unified as one and the same, and it truly has been and is unified. We separate ourselves. We do this for the obvious reason that we see the one and not the other, therefore one is real, the other is illusion. We have it exactly backward, as we are the fingerprint of the soul, the external.

During the time of Noah, we shifted from physical back to spiritual. This change will be coming again – possibly in our times – and guide us toward the spiritual Self. The Bible indicates that fact which will be discussed later. Today, all we have to do is look around us, and we will see the rise in interest for the spiritual nature. We will see the rise in curiosity for the intuitive senses of Self. These changes may be nearer to us than we care to believe, for as Jesus said, it will come like a thief in the night. During these periods of alternate development, the Bible depicted the changes to which we were subjected each time a shift occurred. Many ancient texts talk about this period of the flood. No one alive today has been affected by this type of experience, so we do not understand the metaphor or accept it for what it truly is. We see much alteration in the way we lived life after Noah. However, if we carefully read and scrutinize the texts, we will discover that from the point of the flood until today, we have been increasingly steeped in the physical aspect of life. We can see this growth period throughout the Old Testament. Now, the pendulum has begun to swing in the other direction, and our technology will not assist us during this shift. The forty days period mentioned in the Bible is merely the adjustment period through which we will have to travel. In this situation, we will have to either adjust or perish. It is foretold in the Book of Revelations, the book that is about awakening to the spirit-self and recognition of what is occurring within us.

It is also believed that the Bible tells us how to work with this shift. If polar opposites are necessary for us to live in an external sense, then this must also take place on the inner level, as the rule of polar opposites is within us as well. We must experience this to continue our growth. After all, is not growth what occurs within – and not just without, or the physical sense? We usually grow most efficiently when we are confronted with our opposites, or the reflection of what we already are. Is this not the reasons for opposition in life? It assists us to increase the level of our understanding of the way things are and what they can be. The Biblical flood was not one of water, but rather one of spiritual inundation. It was a shift being recorded as a road map guiding us to a new way of life. We may see another suggestion of this very same thought in **Joshua 24:2-3**: *"And Joshua said unto all the people, Thus saith the Lord God of Israel, Your fathers dwelt on the other side of the flood* [river] *in old time, even Terah, the father of Nachor: and they served other gods. (3) And I took your father Abraham from the other side of the flood* [river], *and led him throughout all the land of Canaan, and multiplied his seed, and gave him Isaac"*. Depending on the version you may be reading, you will find the word "river" where "flood" is used (older Bibles use "flood" – newer ones use "river"). If we were to read it as "river", it makes sense only if we apply it to the physical. If the word "flood" is used, it gives greater spiritual meaning, providing we accept the concept that water signifies the spiritual nature of life. Two questions arise. First, why was the word changed? Second, what is meant by "the other side of the flood"? Abraham, a descendant of Noah, was spared (Joshua 24:3), to be an observer of the events to come, and to be a further confirmation of the shifting of spiritual nature, as well as a possible shift of the poles.

Did Noah really build the Ark, this ship of great dimensions? To this day, no one really knows for sure. The Ark is truly intended as the symbol of physical life and not necessarily a ship. It was a vessel of preservation and protection for Noah and his family. In reality, the Ark is the physical body. Of course, this lends itself to the question of the animals of the world being brought on board in pairs, male and female. Could this not be the **memories** of the animals, since Spirit also knew we would be returning to the physical at the next looming shift? Could this not also mean that we have to house the memory of the physical, so that the next time the shift occurred, all of it would be brought back? We would need these for all life to continue, and these memories would produce the animals also. We must acknowledge that the physical reality is truly here for our benefit. We are the ones that expand it because as we grow, so does life. The story of the flood relates how the body was buffeted by the changes. It tells how very little in this world survived this period in history, in the physical sense of the word. Those that were prepared, who had the ability to focus, were saved. In the New Testament, Jesus reminds us that we must be prepared at all times: *"Watch therefore; for ye know not what hour your Lord doth come"* (Matthew 24:42); *"For yourselves know perfectly that the day of the Lord so cometh as a thief in the night"* (1 Thessalonians 5:2). Both the Old and New Testaments warn us of this potential situation.

If we are able to focus, our bodies are all that we will need, since they are the temples that house God. Through focus, we will maintain our consciousness and not the body – at least as we understand it. The body must shift as well to a finer aspect and that will be its transformation, much like the butterfly after it rises out of the cocoon. It is similarly mentioned in the Ark of the Covenant and symbolizes the agreement we have between the physical Self and that of the spirit. There is much power in this union to which we, as people, have chosen not to adhere. Even though we accept the agreement, subconsciously, we have shown a tendency to deny the influence of Spirit or God and to execute its concept without the guidance of the Creator. This subject will be covered more thoroughly in another chapter.

Genesis 11:6-9: *"And the Lord said, Behold, the people is one, and they have all one language; and this they begin to do: and now nothing will be restrained from them, which they have imagined to do. (7) Go to, let us go down, and there confound their language, that they may not understand one another's speech. (8) So the Lord scattered them abroad from thence upon the face of all the earth: and they left off to build the city. (9) Therefore is the* *name of it called Babel; because the Lord did there confound the language of all the earth: and from thence did the Lord scatter them abroad upon the face of all the earth.* " Obviously, in our arrogance, we were not working in union with Spirit, but independent of it. I have to ask: would a loving God do this? No. I do not think so. Following the flood, we ascertain that we were strongly believing in our spiritual nature, but only through a physical mentality, logic and self, in a literal, intellectual way. This belief did not reach the inner Self. We were building our lives on the falsehood of the physical - and anything built on falsehood will not last. After all, we built our lives out of slime and brick, and it will not withstand the test of time. As a people, we are never physically great, except in our own minds. We would come to a time when we would live by our technology and through the material sense of things, without incorporating the spiritual values of life and self. We are the ones that separated our own spiritual nature from our physical, through greed and deceit - and we continue this behavior today. We are traveling a path pointing the way to becoming one people, as we should be, since no one is better than anyone else. We need no proof to know that we are all equal, because we are all here at God's choosing. Our burden is to follow the road to spiritual nature, through trust and love of God, self and each other.

We see this concept carried even further in the story of Sodom. We see Abram pleading with God to not destroy a city, an aggregation of life. In this important segment of the Bible, we can deepen the significance of what is being said. Abram is pleading with Spirit about the growth of life, a life to which he himself wanted to hold on. In his mind, it brought him a great deal of joy. At the same time, this very same life, as known in those days, was holding him in place, as his focus was on its material side, rather than its spiritual side. In His fairness and wisdom, God told him that if he could locate extenuating elements within the walls of the city, it would be saved. We know through the Bible that nothing worth saving was found **(Genesis 19:24-26)**. Again, the reference to Sodom is to remind us how physical nature will dominate life and that within its concept, it does not contain real salvation. It is not permanent, and that which is not permanent cannot last. God communicated to Abram that all things of a physical nature could not lead to understanding except through the experience. This is why we cannot afford to avoid them, in order to learn the lessons that will assist us in overcoming life and attain the spiritual reality we seek. When considered, one can easily see that understanding indeed is an internal function. We only comprehend the external and its relationship to us. Yet, we could learn much from the external, as it does expand the inner nature through experience. Hence, the real message is a suggestion in the use of the external to appreciate the internal nature of self.

Unfortunately, we are too busy believing that we are being attacked by all things. It is accepted that this perception is the downfall of most of us, since we are seldom "attacked". Rather, it is a test of our knowledge. Growth occurs after these tests. We experience what could be called a "shake up" from within, and the old values must be released to allow for the new. We fail miserably with the release aspect. After all, we still have the memory of the event, which should give a greater conception of Jesus' statement: *"And no man putteth new wine into old bottles"* (Mark 2:22). We focus on the memory – not the events – and it is the events that assist us in growth – not the memory. This is well depicted in **Genesis 19:26**. Lot's wife looked back and became a pillar of salt. This happened even after being given specific instructions not to do that. What is meant in this verse is all so simple. We can conclude that any time we look back at what was, we become frozen in time, and it holds us in place. We all long for the past, because we see happier days or we see the opportunity to right a wrong. Going back in time is not necessarily possible. It stands to reason that we must accomplish our work during the best time, and that time can only be now – that is, in the moment we have, or the present. No one should be looking back. Conclusively, if you want to tear yourself away from that frozen moment in time, you must look forward. No matter how eloquently you may plead, NOW is the only opportunity you will have to do the work. Our ability to think for ourselves is becoming increasingly difficult. We depend too much on our physical nature for relief, when we should rely on our inner nature to do the same. Case in point: who takes the time to meditate? Actually, very few do, and we do not lack excuses such as: "I do not have time right now", or "I'm too busy"... As always, we are not looking for the answers within. Rather, we seek them without. Meditation was the original form of prayer, a time when we are to go within for clarity and clarification. Instead, we go to the external. This will be emphasized when we get to the messages of the Master in the four Gospels. It is offered because He was very clear in His statements to us, only if we perceive rather than just read and intellectualize them for the physical mind only. We must read these from a spiritual point – not a religious aspect – for the true meaning of the message will be lost.

The Old Testament describes many events. We learn about the many wars and struggles of old, all of which referring to the inner struggles that will affect all of life. We see that the crossing portrayed in Exodus is that journey from the spiritual to the physical and is a record of the third shift. Moses was the leader during that period of time. It was a difficult task, given the fact that he was to guide his people to the Promised Land. There are many references to the Moses odyssey in other religions. In India, it was Manu; in Egypt, it was Manes, and in Crete, it was Minos. All are texts pertaining to the same human, with a similar crossing – namely to assist in the return to physical nature. We can safely say that this journey continues today. We are still meandering in that same wilderness in spite of all that we have achieved. Perhaps it is because we still worship an external God and not the true internal one that is there for us, in the Ark of the Covenant.

Once again, we have forgotten our higher self. This occurs each time we chose to follow the path of the physical. The depiction of this biblical struggle paints the attempt to recover from the last shift, while being able to operate in the physical world on a better scale. When you think about it, how could a group of people that large wander about for a period of forty years without finding a place to settle? In those days, there were a lot of very fertile areas in the Middle East ready to accommodate a large settlement. **Genesis 13:10**: *"And Lot lifted up his eyes, and beheld all the plain of Jordan, that it was well watered everywhere, before the Lord destroyed Sodom and Gomorrah, even as the garden of the Lord, like the land of Egypt, as thou comest unto Zoar"*. It seems that Egypt was an ideally fertile area. Further, the Ten Commandments were brought forth as laws to guide our lives. Incidentally, were we ever to follow these simple guidelines, the world would be a much different place in which to live, and it would bring us to a changed level of being. We were still attempting to work with the aspect of being physical, or "evil" if you will. We were not incorporating the spiritual, a union intended in the original agreement carefully preserved in the Ark of the Covenant. The contents of such agreement are actually in **Hebrews 8:8-12**. In **Hebrews 9:4**, we have a description of the Ark, but it is not the box that one might envision. It is greater than that. It is not just a material object. IT IS US, once we have reached a higher level of attainment within ourselves. The verse reads: *"Which had the golden censer, and the ark of the covenant overlaid round about with gold, wherein was the golden pot that had manna, and Aaron's rod that budded, and the tables of the covenant;"* "Golden" refers to knowledge attained from Spirit about life, thus the incense on the golden altar. The golden sides represent inner knowledge balanced with the outer. The golden jar is the energy of God held within our heart, and with that only, all things will come to fruition, as in the budding of Aaron's staff. The belief within you will give you that for which you search, and that spirit will bless it for you, for it has already been given. We may reach a better understanding of the Ark if we study **Hebrews 8:10-11**. We get an outline of what this Covenant means:

"FOR FINDING FAULT WITH THEM, HE SAITH, BEHOLD, THE DAYS COME,
SAITH THE LORD, WHEN I WILL MAKE A NEW COVENANT WITH THE HOUSEOF ISRAEL AND WITH THE HOUSE OF JUDAH:

NOT ACCORDING TO THE COVENANT THAT I MADE WITH THEIR
FATHERS IN THE DAY
WHEN I TOOK THEM BY THE HAND TO LEAD THEM OUT OF THE
LAND OF EGYPT;
BECAUSE THEY CONTINUED NOT IN MY COVENANT, AND I
REGARDED THEM NOT, SAITH THE LORD.
FOR THIS IS THE COVENANT THAT I WILL MAKE WITH THE HOUSE
OF ISRAEL
AFTER THOSE DAYS, SAITH THE LORD;
I WILL PUT MY LAWS INTO THEIR MIND,
AND WRITE THEM IN THEIR HEARTS;
AND I WILL BE TO THEM A GOD,
AND THEY SHALL BE TO ME A PEOPLE;
AND THEY SHALL NOT TEACH EVERY MAN HIS NEIGHBOUR,
AND EVERY MAN HIS BROTHER, SAYING, KNOW THE LORD;
FOR ALL SHALL KNOW ME, FROM THE LEAST TO THE GREATEST.

Here we see a great deal of the Truth about God. He says He put the laws in our minds and wrote them upon our hearts, to give us the knowledge we need for life – the inner nature of Self. Here we also see something that Jesus states later in the book of Matthew: we will all know, and we need not tell others at all. We need not teach others about God or Spirit, for each and every one of us will know within our own selves. The teachings are as personal as individuals themselves are. In that time, no one will have to explain any of it. We will not have to see it in another's light, as we will know it for ourselves for the experience of it, and in our own light – meaning knowledge.

The only other mention of the Ark can be found in **Revelations 11:19**: *"And the temple of God was opened in heaven, and there was seen in his temple the ark of his testament: and there were lightnings, and voices, and thunderings, and an earthquake, and great hail."* Well, this should be interesting to most, since these natural events are taking place even while I am writing this book. Again, the physical aspect is not the issue. It is the inner nature of Self-awakening to the very concepts that are being exposed, and there is nothing anyone can do about it, except go with it, accept and not expect. Only those that have an understanding of what this entails will be able to use it. Jesus said "let those with ears hear". That means that not everyone is going to understand, but even if we all did, the Bible also says that many will be called, but few will come. This is a direct indication of what will happen during a period of transformation. In fact, the new covenant is about things changing to a new level of understanding, a new dispensation. The Old and New Testaments give us this very same warning in a variety of places. Internal hail? No, not really, except to say we will be bombarded with new forms of thought. But there will be sounds and quite a real shake up will take place in the inner nature. What we have considered as real will be found to be false. This will occur, because we only believe in the physical aspect, and there will be no foundation for it in the future to come. The next swing will be the journey back to more of the spiritual nature, and logic alone will not work. One must be ready in this arena, so they will recognize the signs of Self. After all, do we not think we all know ourselves better than anyone else? Knowing ourselves is the key to Christdom anyway!

We will leave the concept of creation for now and journey through the New Testament, so that we may learn to understand the messages of the Master. Even He told us that we may be like Him, and that we may learn to be the cause in life and not its effect. The entire Bible is on the subject of spiritual attainment and that is why we should not worship idols. This type of worship is another message advising us not to give the external world so much importance or control over us. After all, Jesus told us that fundamentally, what we do here is laying up for ourselves in heaven. This should automatically tell all readers that the physical self is not the most important thing in life. The Bible was – and is – a wonderful road map of life for us to follow. Others have gone before us and have attempted to leave directions, so that all may attain their goals – not just the few who control the information. These same controlling people will tell us that we will be devoured by Satan for even considering the possibilities of other messages hidden within the pages of the Bible. Creation was a necessary aspect to make the Bible workable, and so much was left out. These omissions must be the very reason that the churches – for the most part – will tell you that any other teaching is wrong. How can this be possible, when it is all of God's creation, and all are different aspects of the same thing? There is only one God and one Spirit, by whatever name you may call it. For one to be right and the other to be wrong is fear of loss and judgment.

We will now begin to discover the messages of the Master through the words of the four main gospels of Matthew, Mark, Luke and John. We will also explore the experience of the Book of Revelations, a book that informs us of the unfolding of the soul and spirit, and what we may expect by working with the true nature of life, thus enlightening the soul housed within us.

CHAPTER 4

THE BOOK OF MATTHEW

"In order that all men may be taught to speak truth, it is necessary that all likewise should learn to hear it".
Samuel Johnson, *The Rambler* (1750-52), 96

Let us begin to discuss the four main Gospels of the Bible, those being the books of **Matthew, Mark, Luke and John.** They are the central aspects of the biblical texts upon which most churches have established their basis. Within are some of the most wonderful guidelines one may use on the journey to the higher self. These works are submerged in the truths of life. They tell us what our individual experiences will be, how others will do things to us and why. They let us know how to work with the pitfalls we all will encounter, not just in the religious sense of the word, but in the living sense as well. The only condition – if there is one – is to be a seeker of the higher truths of life, and not just life itself. The following chapters will hopefully bring a deeper understanding of a work not many truly read. If and when they do, it is done out of literary curiosity, without genuine spiritual reverence. This is the real mistake, yet we allow others to tell us what they have interpreted. We should not do this, for it affects our very own beliefs. The Bible does warn us of this, but we fail to heed its message.

What has been found to be most interesting is that only one of these men actually walked with the one known as Jesus, the Christ. He was a tax collector in the ancient Palestinian port of Capernaum, and Mark called him "Levi the son of Alphaeus". When he became a disciple, Jesus called him Matthew (Aramaic: "gift of Yahweh"). Tax gathering is the epitome of the physical demonstration of the corporal form, and how we accumulate material things to burden us in our lives. None of these gentlemen was present at His birth, and none knows what the actual circumstances were. They heard the story from others, or built it out of their own minds – at least the details. Consequently, no one can be absolutely sure.

Most people will comment that these four books are all alike in what they have to say. My humble opinion is that they are very different in nature. Matthew is about the **physical** aspect of life, while Mark covers the **mental** aspect; Luke is the **emotional** one, and John tells us of the **spiritual** nature of the whole being. These books attempt to explain what our experience will be, and how we may eliminate certain tribulations that will confront us, each in our own way. The next four chapters will be about the messages contained in the Gospels, as they probably are the most significant features of the Bible. This selective coverage is not intended to downplay the rest of the book.

Why is Matthew considered to represent the physical aspect of the Gospels and life? We see this in the fact that he was a tax collector, one that dealt in the material side of life. Further, his book happens to be one of the longer books of the New Testament. Its length could be construed to mean that the physical side of life would be the greatest characteristic to overcome. Every great master that has ever walked has said that the physical is the **real illusion of life**. It is difficult for anyone to understand this philosophy, because it is indeed so real. "I felt this" – "It hurts" – "things happen"… On a human plane, it has to be real, and the other side is the illusion. The physical is the greatest challenge to us because of this perception. It only leads us to many misconceptions about life, thus we mistrust the physical.

Do any of us really trust others? I would have to say no, and the reasons are very simple. People merely see and recognize physical actions by which they measure their judgments. It is the reason why Jesus said: *"Judge not, that ye be not judged"* (Matthew 7:1). The action is the illusion, as we will explain later. We will now begin the journey of the physical message contained in the book of Matthew. If indeed this is the Truth, then it should assist people in understanding why we do the things that we do with life and other people.

Our analysis of each of the chosen gospels will begin with the birth of the Master. Because all four are slightly different, we must be aware of all the nuances touching the story of the Master Jesus. We start with the genealogy, which only Matthew recounts. His intention was to show the validation of the prophets of old. In his first three chapters, we find numerous prophecies either fulfilled, or to be fulfilled. We find the first reference to the three Magi from the East, traveling to investigate the birth of the Child. We see their metaphysical aptitude embodied in their dreams, the warnings they received, and the fact that they followed a star. The star can be interpreted in many ways, including a heavenly body totally disobeying the laws of physics… These gentlemen, as well as the shepherds in the fields, are being portrayed as following their inner light, that of spirit. This inner light is the knowing of Self, the premonition of an event. That is simply what these people saw. It is very apparent that not everyone in those days knew this was happening.

Had Herod known, why did not he just have his people follow this same star, instead of using deceit to locate the Christ? Many simply could not see this in the sky. Remember: *"He that hath ears to hear, let him hear"* (Matthew 11:15), so not everyone was going to be aware, and other means would be necessary. The wise men came to see if the child was indeed the chosen one. When they were satisfied that he was, they left no physical gifts – just instructions to Mary and Joseph on his upbringing. Gold, Frankincense and Myrrh can be compared to contributions of Knowledge, Understanding, Peace and Instructions for the parents to follow and pass on to a growing young man who had a very special mission. Nothing else is said about Jesus until His encounter with John the Baptist at the river Jordan, where He wanted to be baptized. These two men met without seeming to know each other. As mentioned earlier, they were cousins, and we will provide the proof later. Again, this event was to fulfill a prophecy.

The baptism of water is the symbol of spirit being unified with the physical form. It would make sense that after the simple ceremony, spirit would descend upon Him and take over in His life. It was a greater alignment than He had had before - a true merging of both aspects into a single nature. What actually flowed into Him was the knowledge being locked in place, the culmination of all His studies in the actual sense of the word. He had become **the Word**, the physical manifestation of the spiritual presence of God. Not until then did this occur.

Next is the appearance of Satan, the tempter. As mentioned earlier in this writing, Satan – in Sanskrit – is nothing more than the ego of a person. We find this in the Nag Hammadi, and in its text, it even sounds like the ego. It has been written that the closer you come to God, the greater the pull of evil becomes. It actually makes sense, because of the counterbalance that must ensue within the person. It is confirmed in the Gospel of St Thomas in the Nag Hammadi. In fact, there are some biblical scholars who believe that Jesus Himself wrote this particular gospel that He had sent to Thomas in the form of a letter. The tempter operated in all sorts of ways. It wanted Him to control people, and He said no. Jesus dealt with His own ego, at first - not others, as we all must do at some point in time.

He dealt with it on the inner level of Self – not outside – meaning He did not place the blame on others. He never said to others: "See! I have changed and have become great,...". With that kind of intensity, He had to be tempted. Temptation reaches us as well, so that we may grow in strength. He survived these temptations with apparent ease and overcame the very thing that, thus far, we have been unable to defeat, and that is: Ego. Our egos were involved when we originally set down the works of the Bible. Why? Because of all the manipulative translations of words and events in the Bible, the need for control and the selfish wish to be the one considered correct. This constant aspiration we have to be always "right" is in error. Not everyone can be correct in all matters, and the lesson about the ego is one of the greatest in the Bible, whereas one should overcome it, since it always shows up in physical life. We may never rid ourselves of it, but we can control it so it does not dominate us the way it does today. The ego tends to stem from insecurities that very few will admit they have. It will hide itself through subtle manipulation of our thoughts, so we can blame others and not assume our own responsibility. The Master experienced those temptations. So must we.

The next message we detect comes to us in **Matthew 5:14-16**, concerning our light. *"Ye are the light of the world. A city that is set on an hill cannot be hid. (15) Neither do men light a candle and put it under a bushel, but on a candlestick; and it giveth light unto all that are in the house. (16) Let your light so shine before men, that they may see your good works, and glorify your Father which is in heaven".* What could the Master mean with this statement? The answer is quite simple. We are to let our good works be our statement and our light, rather than our often empty words. We are not to gloat about our good deeds, especially those revolving around the nature of God, nor should we boast about them. Allow others to see by our light, a light that should not dim because of the insecurity of another. Jesus advised us that we are not to hide it, but to let it shine forth as the house on the hill. To put it in a contemporary fashion, He was saying that actions speak louder than words.

Such benevolent behavior should be accompanied by humility, rather than the arrogance we display today. We demonstrate this condescension by thinking or saying "I am better than you", when we are not. As Jesus put it: *"I am the least among you."*. We let our light shine through the external trappings of religion and not through the real inner nature. The trappings will disappear, but the inner self is permanent. This light is the Knowledge of things and not the thinking of things. There is a distinct difference between these two elements. Knowledge and wisdom are derived from thought and experience, and the experience is to produce the knowledge and wisdom. When we decide to learn about spiritual being, we will experience many things in life which will assist us in our formation for the knowledge. Usually, these things are not necessarily going to be fun, yet we will have to be subject to the experience for fruition purposes. The reason for the experience is because we need definition of the self, and the occurrences show us, shape us and mould us into what we are to become. We can see verification of this philosophy in **Matthew 5:18**: *"For verily I say unto you, Till heaven and earth pass, one jot or one tittle shall* *in no wise pass from the law, till all be fulfilled.".* We will be able to escape nothing that we, ourselves, have created through our thoughts, actions or deeds. Once they are in process, we will follow them to the extent they will take us. Remember, it is self-knowledge that we are here to learn.

How can we do this when we are so involved in thinking we know everyone else? We cannot know another in truth, until we know ourselves first. In this era, we pretend to know others only by comparing them to our own nature. Unfortunately, this practice creates a high degree of misunderstanding. This is what is meant by *"Judge not, that ye be not judged".* It is indeed a mistake, because we will not be able to accept others as they are, only as WE are. We do not allow them to be themselves, except through the way we see them. Does this not make them resemble us? Is this not the illusion we tend to create in life?

Matthew 6 is the most compelling of all. The very first verse tells us: *"Take heed that ye do not your alms before men, to be seen of them: otherwise ye have no reward of your Father which is in heaven".* The Master spoke against what most people do today. They are virtuously attempting to save us, when in reality their words and deeds are about saving themselves, the majority of the time. They are clamoring to us that we are but dead, and God/Spirit is now showing us the reflection of what we create for ourselves. Jesus said: *"For many shall come in my name, saying, I am Christ; and shall deceive many"* (Matthew 24:5). Let this not be a misunderstanding. I very much believe in God and my works will speak for themselves.

Where is it written that God needs our help? We need Its help... In **Matthew 6:5-7**, the Master Himself speaks of this very subject: *"And when thou prayest, thou shalt not be as the hypocrites are: for they love to pray standing in the synagogues and in the corners of the streets, that they may be seen of men. Verily I say unto you, They have their reward. (6) But thou, when thou prayest, enter into thy closet, and when thou hast shut thy door, pray to thy Father which is in secret; and thy Father which seeth in secret shall reward thee openly. (7) But when ye pray, use not vain repetitions, as the heathen do: for they think that they shall be heard for their much speaking."* It is not difficult to confirm that prayer is a very internal deed and not the external function we have been taught to follow.

Prayer has always been a fascinating thing to me, because we are taught to pray to God outside of ourselves, and most people do. To do this in front of others is to Christ the wrong thing to do. It is my perception that prayer is actually very personal meditation, with great reverence, going within one's own being. Why else would the scriptures instruct us to go into our inner room and shut the door? Why would it tell us to proceed in secret with what we are about to do, and not tell anyone of its nature? This is also another message telling us that our journey is not as outwardly as we may think. If our intent and subsequent actions are right, then it would appear that the Father will reward us.

As an example, when we approach God, we ask It to help us understand our own life, or why people treat us this way or that. We suddenly realize that everyone, everywhere, is now doing what we so piously asked. God is answering our prayer and is attempting to demonstrate to us why people act toward us the way they do. Actually, they are merely a reflection of our own self. Those mirror images exist so that we may learn of our own nature, and that we can alter those behaviors by changing what we are to others. The answers can sometimes be difficult for us to carry out. Nevertheless, our prayer was answered, but perhaps not in the way we expected it. Prayer should be a very personal and private affair, but we must also be diligent in its response, to absorb its reason and its consequences.

Once, a Tibetan Monk said to me: "What if God heard everything that you thought and considered what you were thinking as a request to do something for you. Would you change the way you think?" I answered yes, and he said: "Good, for that is the truth of things". If this were indeed the truth, would you also change the way you think? If you did, you might find that your life and circumstances would change very rapidly – all because you began to pay attention to what you thought only. Paradoxically, we may find this in **Matthew 6:8**: *"...for your Father knoweth what things ye have need of, before ye ask him"*. This certainly would imply that Spirit already knows what is on our minds. All forms of thought are in actuality a form of prayer, whether we truly want the thought in our lives or not. We must also accept that whatever one does is returned ten-fold, including thoughts. Philosophically, we should now recognize why we have what we have…We asked for it!

Matthew 6:19-21: *"Lay not up for yourselves treasures upon earth, where moth and rust doth corrupt, and where thieves break through and steal: (20) But lay up for yourselves treasures in heaven, where neither moth nor rust doth corrupt, and where thieves do not break through nor steal: (21) For where your treasure is, there will your heart be also"*. This metaphor speaks of the gathering of treasures on earth. It implies that we have the tendency to place our focus on the material only, an aspect that will dominate us. Of course, He was correct. As mentioned, we put more of ourselves in what we can touch, feel or purchase, rather than where we should place the emphasis, to wit, the inner nature of enlightenment.

The physical is significant in itself, since it is the outer world, the teacher of self. The difficulty is that we hold on to the physical, because the spiritual gives us nothing concrete that we can see or touch, consequently, it cannot be real. Yet, it is very real within us and in the realm of eternity. Perhaps this may be the proper time to introduce the concept of reincarnation, since it would help to explain the process. If we were to analyze **Matthew 17:10-13**, we could easily see the reference to reincarnation, wherein one does not always take on the same appearance as before, making physical recognition an impossibility. Most people either do not believe this concept, or are extremely doubtful. In view of this consensus, please allow me to elucidate. With the exception of the western mind, most peoples believe that we chose to come into life as we know it to continue our journey on the way to the ultimate lesson. If God is indeed a loving God, why would It give us life and realization, only to take it away forever? In my mind, it is not really possible, because we are an energy based vibration, and energy will just become finer or unseen by the human eye. There are people today who speak to the "other side". By the same token, many individuals have experienced it for themselves and believe in that so-called phenomenon. Spirit does not take us after our life span and throws us unceremoniously into some dark corner, never to be seen again.

If we take into consideration the statement clearly written in **Genesis 3:5** (*....and ye shall be as gods, knowing good and evil.*), is it not saying that we are a "God"? Furthermore, Jesus said: *"...Is it not written in your law, I said, Ye are Gods."* (**John 10:34**). Would God kill a God? No! We appear on this earth life after life to learn how to use the total power of being, just like Christ. The "being" in question is in concurrence with a God not opposed to it, for we are just like It. You see, this is a learning experience in which we transform from an infinite being into a finite, to help us understand our development. Conclusively, we are as perpetual as God, for It has given us eternal life already. We shed our body much like a snake sheds its skin, so that we may be renewed for new levels of growth. If we were to follow what the Bible says, we would not have to "re-experience" life so often. In fact, we could do it once and move to many other mansions. However, we hold on to physical life entirely too much, thus we return more often in order to take care of unfinished business. It is unfinished because we avoided it the first time, therefore, we come back to conclude the task. We will most certainly know when our time is near, and at that point, we better hope that we were correct in what we did. Our actions during our finite passage are stored for ourselves in heaven – and that is the other side. It is the most important part of life, real life, and not what we think it to be. Heaven is not a mystical place. It is very real in its nature, even if we do not remember the Garden.

People have asked me: "If we have lived before, why do we not re-member?". According to **Edgar Cayce**, we have all lived an average of 200 to 250 lifetimes. For the sake of this forum, let us suppose he was correct. Let us also say that we do remember these lives. How would you know which life you are presently living, with your mind filled with births and deaths and perhaps filled with regret for those lives you do remember? It would be entirely too difficult for us to manage, hence we are protected until we can handle such knowledge, and until we know how to use the information to assist us. Rein-carnation is also an aspect of Karma or a solution to our own past, whether in this life or another. It can be very complicated, yet it need not be. When we pass on to the other side, what we have done here comes into play. Even Jesus said that we would meet again. What we do here will give us a glimpse as to what lies before us – but that could be another book unto itself.

In Matthew 6:19-21, what Jesus was actually exposing was our greedy nature, and He was telling us to use caution in what we choose to pursue, whether on a physical or spiritual level. The physical would lead us toward the greed aspect of self, or to the dark side of life. Obviously, we have not paid heed at all! Look at us! Are we not a sight to behold, so full of our own selves that there is no room for anything else... This physical pursuit leads us in so many directions that it truly can become confusing. In turn, it leads us to the next aspect of the self, that being **judgment**. **Matthew 7:1-2**: *"Judge not, that ye be not judged. (2) For with what judgment ye judge, ye shall be judged: and with what measure ye mete, it shall be measured to you again"*. You have just read the written expression of the biggest failure in life. We all shower these judgments upon each other, with no exception. Even though Jesus said that nothing is above the law, we apparently consider ourselves above it. After all, we judge all the time and believe there is no harm in it. To the contrary, there is great harm, because we downplay our own selves the moment we judge oth-ers. By our own standards, we should see the truth of the above verses. In real-ity, we measure all according to our own knowledge, not theirs. We judge through what we know of our self, and how we would manage a particular inci-dent, rather than how they would do it. When we judge them, we have to an-swer for that in our own actions. Why? Because if you detect whatever you judged in another, it first has to be in you. It has to be for you to recognize it in another person. You had to have done it first, yet you condemn them for what you yourself had done before. Once we have judged another, we will have many lessons to face.

We will have to understand why we think we are above others, nor will we be able to ignore those lessons. Look at the cycles of your own life, espe-cially those you would like to break, to go on to better things. Learn the lessons of what one has done, and you may go forward once more as the cycle becomes broken. Life can be confusing, and only because of all the judgments we tend to have already set in motion. We are always adding to that stack and never seem to get to it. We let others handle it because "it is not my fault". Contrary to popular belief, it is always the fault of the person who sets it in motion and generates the first cause. The laws of physics state that for every action, there is an equal and opposite reaction, so on it goes. We do not consider this deeply enough as being a cause, and our thoughts carry more weight in life than one would tend to believe. To us, our own thoughts are not all that important, but remember: Jesus said that nothing escapes the law.

We now move to **Matthew 7:11**, wherein Jesus says: *"If ye then, being evil,..."*. Come to think of it, we might just be that. Look at the state of the world, the state of business! It seems that a wave of greed and power-seeking has engulfed the people. How can one control the people when they cannot even control themselves, even in a spiritual sense. What did Jesus mean when he said that? He was stating that we are the densest form of natural matter next to a piece of granite. He was saying that we are quite heavy. If you recall the concept of God and Lucifer in the beginning, polar opposition was necessary for life to begin and for matter to actually take form. Lucifer, being the opposite of God, was concluded to be evil, as evil as God was good. Because Lucifer was the anchor and evil, we now had the propensity toward evil. The truth is that we are not evil in nature, just ego oriented. That can lead to selfishness. Calling us evil somehow verifies the concept of the original sin which in truth was knowledge, a knowledge of self, so we could become what we already are, i.e. a God in the making, with limitless power in conjunction with Spirit.

The definitive intention is for us to know and not ignore what we are. This message has been carried throughout time, and we have shrouded it and hidden it for very manipulative reasons. We can substantiate this in **Matthew 7:13-27**, for Jesus tells us point blank that we should be genuine with each other, and treat each other as we desire to be treated. Further, He says that we should build ourselves a strong foundation, and that strength is what we are, good and loving, and knowing that we shall be guided in all things by our inner spirit, rather than outside ourselves.

He says the gate is wide and the path broad, which means that temptation will be great, and only our diligence will prevail. He reminds us that in truth, the gate is small and the way is narrow, with little room for error, for the natural laws are unrelenting and we are not predisposed to accept them. What we do will be very obvious, says the Master, for we will know each other by our fruits. If we looked, and if we were to follow our conscience, we would have the opportunity to build ourselves a stronger foundation. If our base is not strengthened, it will be destroyed by the obstacles of life that will greet us along our journey. If a person realizes that he/she has a good life, then that person will be protected by that perception, making the journey somewhat easier. The aforementioned foundation is the understanding of life and the nature of how things operate, both within and without.

The within is the first cause – not life, as most of us believe. According to the deep convictions of this author, we will see life as the cause, and not the self. Life is a reflection of our own being. We seem to be perfectly satisfied simply looking at the reflection, rather than realizing that the image originates with us. If we learn to work with this concept, we will have a much stronger foundation, and it will be steadfast.

Spiritual communication is another subject worthy of discussion, one that we all practice or have practiced. We are told that we may not perform such a thing, because it is very evil. Actually, it is quite natural. How else, as an example, would one hear God, were it not in that form? **Matthew 10:19-20**: *"But when they deliver you up, take no thought how or what ye shall speak: for it shall be given you in that same hour what ye shall speak. (20) For it is not ye that speak, but the Spirit of your Father which speaketh in you"*. We all react much too quickly, and the key word is "react". We should "react" to nothing, because when we do, we are not in control. What or whoever created that reaction is the one in control. There is a great deal of difference between act and react, when "act" is what we should do.

It tells you to wait for the instructions that will indeed come, whether it is something to say, or something you must do to resolve a situation. It is telling you that it is not you who provides the answer, but the Father within you. Once we learn this, it tends to allow life to be much easier on us, since it simplifies matters and solves problems. If you experience an inner struggle, it is simply that your ego is obstructing Spirit, not allowing it to clear your path. Hence, this struggle is merely Spirit trying to tell you to step aside so it can guide you. We know that Jesus was the perfect channel of God. It means that He relied on his internal impressions, rather than just His sight, hearing, smell or taste. He listened to the impression of His thoughts extended by Spirit to His physical human self. This is another area in which the churches would lose, as we would discover that we do not need an outside source to tell us about our own inner knowledge of God, a God who knows. This may be the proper time to present the idea of the Father, as in *"I and my Father are one"* (John 10:30).

The "Father" is a very interesting and very sensitive subject for any human to undertake. It is truly quite simple, yet very complex. The Father is that part of each of us that began with Creation itself. It is that part of God that remains with each of us today. This part can never die, for it is God Itself, or possibly a cell of the whole structure. It is that part that wanted to gather knowledge and would gain it through your experience. That part and the soul of a person have a weight value to it, and it can be recorded at the point of passing. It is the element that returns to God, its true nature. It can be called the central atom of a person, that from which everything springs. Jesus and other masters have continually told us to get in touch with this vital inner part, and not to give so much importance to the physical. They told us that the physical would pass while the inner self would remain, and that is the part of God that we seek. This is why Jesus has said so often that the Kingdom of God is within us. Why not look there, instead of trying to find it in a cold, conscienceless material world? Is it not futile for a very personal being to pray to a totally impersonal, external God?

The event that took place at the river Jordan is the true realization of the unification of the physical form and its inner spirit. The knowledge that we and spirit are actually one in the same being - to fashion the whole self - is the reason why our Father does the work, and we just merely carry it out for the spirit within. When we tasted of the tree of knowledge, then we – like God – had to have the experience of this knowledge to assist us in creating the wisdom required within us – not outside of us. It is very surprising that most people do not realize that life, in and of itself, is not personal, yet we consider ours to be. It is one of these "opposites" again! Our own individual lives are personal because we are internal beings, and it is God within that assists us. The illusion of a personal life seemingly makes it the cause and not the effect. Life's journey is the external teacher to show us the way. It is also the source from which we learn and to which we bestow power in order to attain what we want, rather than placing our faith in Spirit within us. Jesus is saying this to us throughout the book of Matthew.

This leads us to **Matthew 12:25-26**: *"And Jesus knew their thoughts, and said unto them, Every kingdom divided against itself is brought to desolation; and every city or house divided against itself shall not stand: (26) And if Satan cast out Satan, he is divided against himself; how shall then his kingdom stand?"*. This is another very important aspect to life, and it further verifies the intuitive nature we all have. Knowing their thoughts, Jesus was speaking to the Pharisees, a group interested only in the external trappings of the religion at that time. Jesus constantly chastised them for their external nature and leading the masses astray through the external teachings of God. The "external" has always been our problem. Because of this outward distraction, we divide ourselves, our focus, for Jesus also said that we should be single in purpose. How can we be "single in purpose" when we are taught to divide our nature? We are taught this even through the simple concept of God and Satan. We are constantly told that we must choose sides and at that point, we are divided.

The chasm of that division can become wider when we approach the spiritual and the physical. The separation is not just tangible from without, but also occurs within our own selves. Any time we are given a choice, we are divided on what to do. We create so much inner chaos within that we are unable to withstand the impact of life, thus generating the stress that most of us experience. To think that we could choose inner peace instead, a place without division…Peace automatically indicates the lack of division and can be experienced only when we are unified from within. If we dared, we could take a look at our own life the way it really is and promptly understand ourselves. How? Simple! If your life is in turmoil on the outside, the turmoil exists as well on the inside. Once the inner self is stable and at peace, it becomes a reflection of yourself externally – without the turmoil. It must be an inner decision in conjunction with the Father, because the statement *"…the works that I do shall he (man) do also"* (John 14:12) was not exclusive to Jesus. He did not have a corner on the market. He said that we too can do it if we but work on it, and we can have all things granted. This is not false hope. The only way you could ever find out is to take that risk, and no one is ready to take a progressive risk as long as they are willing to point their finger at someone else.

If you are able to retract that finger and accept the fact that life is your own personal mirror, then and only then can you effectively change it. The Father made us all equal because Spirit is part of us, and It would not divide Its own self for any reason. If we believe we are all equal, what is our problem? It is simply our differences on the external side, and the fact that we do not accept our inner self. This "house divided" is a very unrelenting process. We are divided in many directions and we do not really allow for differences. Even in our educational system, we are taught to be just like everybody else, and we are not. This is the message that Jesus conveyed to us, a message that we should celebrate rather than downplay. We attempt to live our life for others to view, whether we live it for love or fear. We are always attempting to endorse other people's issues instead of our own. This prompted Jesus to say: *"And why beholdest thou the mote that is in thy brother's eye, but perceivest not the beam that is in thine own eye?"* (Luke 6:41). How can we help another to understand when we do not understand our own self? It is fair to say that we do not have that right until we do comprehend our own inner nature. Many of us, on an individual basis, have started to help others, and we think that we can leave these deeds unfinished. We think that such situations will rectify themselves. They will not. Our help is needed. Jesus mentioned that we should resolve our issues with our brother before we ever pray or ask God for assistance. We do not resolve anything at all, and this creates the division within as we run away. We do this mentally, emotionally or physically.

Have you ever noticed that any time you run, the situation always seems to follow, no matter where you go? It really does not follow at all, because it is within you the whole time in its unfinished form. It has to appear again so you can complete it and gain an understanding of your own inner nature. We run and run, and these incomplete deeds pile up until we become a fragmented person seeking professional help. Today, we look outside of ourselves for the world to save us but it will not, because of the impersonal nature of life. Take a moment to reflect on your own life. Face the reasons why it is the way it is and stop pointing the finger in another direction. Look within for the answers, resolve your issues and/or insecurities, then speak with Spirit and see what happens.

God does not do the things for which It is blamed. We do them to ourselves, for our Father and we are one. It will allow us to do anything we wish to do. Let us examine a negative situation in life, especially if it is someone we love. Something happens between two people and negativity reaches one of the two. It begins to be felt, and it expands. Do you not realize that as this situation festers within, there will come a time when the other person becomes the cause of such negativity? Both will be so entwined in it that you will not know the difference between them and the negativity. One will blame the other for it and will depart, leaving it unresolved. It will then spill over into the next relationship, and so on. Resolve the issues when they happen and do not let them extend themselves any further than necessary in your life. Seize the moment, always, as the moment is all that we have. If we do not, it will be the memory of an event that could affect us for the rest of our lives. It can be either positive or negative within us. The positive is not in the forefront of our mind, but the negative is. The Bible warns us of this attribute. Do not allow the division or fragmentation to continue. Solve the situation with your sister or brother before it reaches a point of non-repair from within, and regrets build up.

THE PARABLES

To most people, parables have always been difficult to understand. Jesus said: *"Who hath ears to hear, let him hear"* (Matthew 13:9). He meant that not all would understand. Parables were offered to bring about esoteric, inner thinking, to provoke the deeper knowledge of the Self. Most parables, on the surface, make very little sense and remain that way, unless we take a profound look within ourselves and at the subject it covers. We naturally look at the physical, literal intent – the external approach – but interestingly enough, when we look at the meaning of the words with our inner self, it will begin to make sense. This segment will be to examine the parables in such a way that we will be able to absorb the guidance given to us. Jesus is actually letting us know that we may be able to accomplish what He did. However, in order to do that, we must comprehend what is being said, and much is veiled in the words offered. Parables, in their literary style, are used to fulfill the words of a prophet, and Jesus confirmed that fact. They are all grouped together. Only seven parables are offered, with variances in the other Gospels. We will discuss the nuances when we come to them, because they present a different significance, as mentioned at the onset of this chapter.

We will study the parables one at a time, reproduce them as they are written, then discuss them with you , to help you understand the true meaning. As mentioned above, only seven parables were offered, and coincidentally, that number appears many times in the Bible. Remember that Jesus studied in India for a period of time. While there, He learned of the energy centers of the body – and there are seven. These centers are there to assist in understanding ourselves. They interact with us to assist in life and are guideposts for self-discovery as well as markers to indicate where we are on our journey. Most parables are found in **Matthew 13**, and one shows up in a later chapter. Before we earnestly begin, we must look at **Matthew 12:34-35**: *"O generation of vipers, how can you, being evil, speak good things? For out of the abundance of the heart the mouth speaketh. (35) A good man out of the good treasure of the heart bringeth forth good things: and an evil man out of the evil treasure bringeth forth evil things"*. What is meant is that our heart will tell the tale of what we are inside. The use of "treasure" is not as in "money". It is the knowledge of what we ourselves already are, and it is up to us to bring that forth. Again, what Jesus is revealing is that life tends to make a person a good one - or not so good. We have the choice to learn, or not to learn, but if indeed we do, we tend to be good people. If we do not, the tendency is to slip toward selfishness and greed. Greed comes out of the insecurity within our own selves, and in turn, it breeds the evil nature within us all. Our experience will be the determining factor, especially if we create an internal division and do not bring understanding to fruition. Everything must be balanced. It is a natural law of metaphysics, and as Jesus told us, nothing is above the law. We are aware that Jesus knew of the energy centers of the body and we can find His reference to this matter in **Matthew 12:43-45**. He implies that if we ignore these centers, even though they have been cleansed, or in our process of learning, impure spirits may enter. The warning is that once we have learned what is necessary, we will relax too much and soon forget what we know. We must be vigilant at all times, so that wisdom can continue to grow within us. We actually reestablish a new level of innocence within ourselves, a new level of acceptance, whereas we may become too trusting and could be led astray too easily.

The Sower

The first parable is found in **Matthew 13:3-9**: *"And he spake many things unto them in parables, saying, Behold, a sower went forth to sow; (4) And when he sowed, some seeds fell by the way side, and the fowls came and devoured them up: (5) Some fell upon stony places, where they had not much earth; and forthwith they sprung up, because they had no deepness of earth: (6) And when the sun was up, they were scorched; and because they had no root, they withered away. (7) And some fell among thorns; and the thorns sprung up, and choked them: (8) But other fell into good ground, and brought forth fruit, some an hundredfold, some sixtyfold, some thirtyfold. (9) Who hath ears to hear, let him hear."* Those words were spoken to the "great multitudes". Once again, at the end of the parable, we have a reminder that not everyone will understand, especially if it is a mystery in the first place. Jesus implies that there is more to life than what we actually see, and that the physical aspect is not all there is. He is telling us that we must be cautious in what we know of ourselves, and that our belief system in the right concepts must be strong. It is also an indication of what God Itself was doing. It was planting the planet, but not all of us would be strong in our nature. Many distractions would befall us, and we would have to make choices in life. These choices would bring many things that would be short lived, while some would lead us in many directions and others would in fact work in our favor. The main point is that most of us will receive that deep seed which will enable us to grow.

Many will be called yet few will come, because we build ourselves on false hopes, and falseness has no depth or belief. Inwardly, we know this, but we will insist on our way even if we do not have to follow it. To follow your conscience is the right thing to do because, if our soil is good, it will increase our knowledge. Indeed, the soil is our own fertile inner knowledge of self.

The Seeds

This is an extension of the first parable. However, it is different in nature and meaning. It is more specific to the individual nature of Self. **Matthew 13:19-23**: *"When any one heareth the word of the kingdom, and understandeth it not, then cometh the wicked one, and catcheth away that which was sown in his heart. This is he which received seed by the way side. (20) But he that re-*

ceived the seed into stony places, the same is he that heareth the word, and anon with joy receiveth it; (21) Yet hath he not root in himself, but dureth for a while: for when tribulation or persecution ariseth because of the word, by and by he is offended. (22) He also that received seed among the thorns is he that heareth the word; and the care of this world, and the deceitfulness of riches, choke the word, and he becometh unfruitful. (23) But he that received seed into the good ground is he that heareth the word, and understandeth it; which also beareth fruit, and bringeth forth, some an hundredfold, some sixty, some thirty.". The evil one will come and snatch it from his heart... Jesus refers to people that are built purely on ego, wherein there is no strength, an ego that throws these individuals in a position of weakness. How many people have we met who cover insecurity with large egos? Take bullies, for instance. Why do they act in such despicable ways? Because of their inner fear that others will hurt them. They had this experience before, and they will strike first to intimidate, even though they are usually filled with fear.

The next example in this parable is a person of no depth. These individuals feel that the word sounds good, but they cannot see it, hence it cannot be the truth. Somehow, they would like to believe it but if challenged, they will quickly relinquish this new knowledge, since it has no firm basis within them. They also have a tendency to follow others, right or wrong, as opposed to doing and thinking things for themselves. Because of their own insecurities, they can easily be manipulated by others.

The third grouping encompasses most of us. We are too enamored with the riches and the external frills of life and cannot grow to a high level with Spirit. The external self will indeed choke and smother the true values within those individuals. This is the concept of Cain and Abel. We focus in the wrong direction and strive for the material side. We do this because we believe it will make life easier for us in some fashion. We must learn that it will then control who we are through our possessions. Unfortunately, that is who we are...

The fourth category are those who not only hear but also understand, and to whom all will be given. Understanding of the word does not pertain to the religious aspect because that particular aspect is part of the external nature. It does not fit with the fourth grouping, whose understanding can reach the deeper levels of self. And so there are differences in these two parables. The second tells us what and who we will be through the choices we make day in and day out. Some of these choices are stronger than others and well founded, while others are based on falseness, for whatever reason. The latter will not last. In fact, the inner knowledge of our relationship to life is the real strength, and anything other than that cannot endure – not even our own self. We do have the choice to either understand and accept or not. Many individuals turn away. Some who are churchgoers offer only a "holier than thou" routine, or they claim that they are the only ones who are right and everything else is wrong. Whatever happened to "Judge not...."? Yet, here they are, on the street corners and praying in churches, believers in the external trappings, hoping that others will see them for their own self glorification. The Master told us we should not practice this because of its false nature.

Perhaps it seems that we discuss the physical a little too much, but one must recognize that it is the greatest dilemma of life. If one were to understand true nature, the sheer length of the book of Matthew should help realize that the physical is the pinnacle of illusion. It is confirmed in **1 Corinthians 3:2-3**: *"I have fed you with milk, and not with meat: for hitherto ye were not able to bear it, neither yet now are ye able. (3) For ye are yet carnal: for whereas there is among you envying, and strife, and divisions, are ye not carnal, and walk as men?"*. We are solid and we seek solid. To us, anything in the physical world is solid, therefore very real, even if the reference to the unseen is of more importance. We must learn to comprehend our full nature and not merely its parts, or we will remain as fragmented as we are now. Forgive me, I digress!

The Wheat and the Tares

Let us go on with the second parable, the longest of them all, and recognize the importance of such allegories as specific instructions on the journey to enlightenment. **Matthew 13:24-30**: *"...The kingdom of heaven is likened unto a man which sowed good seed in his field: (25) But while men slept, his enemy came and sowed tares among the wheat, and went his way. (26) But when the blade was sprung up, and brought forth fruit, then appeared the tares also. (27) So the servants of the house holder came and said unto him, Sir, didst not thou sow good seed in thy field? From whence then hath it tares? (28) He said unto them, An enemy hath done this. The servants said unto him, Wilt thou then that we go and gather them up? (29) But he said, Nay; lest while ye gather up the tares, ye root up also the wheat with them. (30) Let both grow together until the harvest: and in the time of harvest I will say to the reapers, Gather ye together first the tares, and bind them in bundles to burn them: but gather the wheat into my barn"*. This metaphor can be interpreted in many ways, depending on your level of enlightenment. When the Spirit planted us on this planet, Its balanced opposite sowed his own brand. Since we are all equal under God's law, both seeds are allowed to grow at the same rate. Again, our actions and choices over time will determine the final judgment. If you are a tare or converted to that specie, your fate is clearly written. We could say that the reapers will come, in due time, and those who are not clean or righteous will be set aside.

The more esoteric aspect is that there will be many distractions in life and we must stay alert. We were all placed here on the very same footing, and many things will come to influence our viewpoint, thus we must exercise caution. As we grow, we must be assured that it is a clean growth. The blending of the seeds will become a tare, if you will, primarily due to events that have already taken place in our lives, such as things we are unable to let go or forgive.

The Mustard Seed

The third parable in the series is found in **Matthew 13:31-32**: *"...The kingdom of heaven is like to a grain of mustard seed, which a man took, and sowed in his field: (32) Which indeed is the least of all seeds: but when it is grown, it is the greatest among herbs, and becometh a tree, so that the birds of the air come and lodge in the branches thereof"*. The mustard seed is small, innocuous, and no one would even know it because of its simplicity. It is a symbol representing the initiation of spiritual growth at the lower level of the mind. Many will overlook it, yet, metaphorically, it is of vital importance to all of us. If, within our physical nature, we allow this seed to grow, our knowledge will eventually reach the higher level of the mind. In this process, we will rejoice in taking refuge in the branches of Truth.

The Leaven of Truth

In **Matthew 13:33**, we find the fourth parable and, in itself, it is a revealing statement, quite similar to the fourth: *"The kingdom of heaven is like unto leaven, which a woman took, and hid in three measures of meal, till the whole was leavened"*. As usual, it depends on how one interprets the words. Do you remember the Ark of the Covenant, the symbol of that spark of divinity in our physical self? Do you further remember the golden jar within, the icon of our heart and spirit? Literally, leaven – like yeast – is a substance that allows fermentation and expansion when mixed with flour. Metaphysically, when Truth (the leaven) is injected within our existing knowledge (the flour or meal in this parable), it may take a certain amount of time, but our wisdom will eventually expand, the same as the flour would rise. With the understanding of that knowledge and truth, we come closer to the realization of God's law.

Let us set the parables aside for a moment. We will return to their analysis at the conclusion of this work. There is much more to them than the literal sense. They were some of the inner teachings that Jesus offered, and their true meaning was overlooked by the creators of the Bible.

The Concept of Faith

As mentioned in Chapter 1 of this book, it was said that *"the works that I do shall he do also"*. In **Matthew 17**, after Jesus cured a deranged child who often fell into fire and other times in water, the disciples asked Him why they could not cast out that devil. In **Matthew 17:20**, Jesus replied: *"Because of your unbelief: for verily I say unto you, If ye have faith as a grain of mustard seed, ye shall say unto this mountain, Remove hence to yonder place; and it shall remove; and nothing shall be impossible unto you"*. That is another powerful statement, but first, we must understand the CONCEPT OF FAITH. Belief is having enough faith in any subject to test it out, thus the two go hand in hand. Belief is having no doubt, and doubt has been placed within us by the very same belief system that holds us in place. Why?

We are taught that only one human can accomplish such deeds and no one else, because if we did, we would be considered evil. Wrong! According to Jesus, we are all able to do these things if we have faith. Were we mere mortals to attempt it, religion tells us that it would be the work of the devil. Many have said that, in faith, they would recognize Jesus the Christ if He returned. Jesus Himself said we could not, and even His own disciples did not recognize Him at the time. Perhaps this is why "Judge not" is also included in the Bible, for we anticipate one but get the other.

His next words are very explicit: *"Howbeit this kind goeth not out but by prayer and fasting"* (Matthew 17:21). Prayer, if we understand its nature, is the most potent attribute we hold, yet it must be done in secret within one's self, and only God should know. The prayer should be generated from and focused on our inner nature, which means that we do not pray to an external entity, because Spirit already knows what is in our hearts. Now, metaphysically, fasting has nothing to do with not eating. It has everything to do with being clear and focused on what we want. Remember that Jesus said to be "single in purpose" and meant for us to be and do just that. He was most correct. However, to be single in purpose is very hard for any of us to carry out, especially in today's confusion of life. Here is the Metaphysical Bible Dictionary definition of fasting: "Denial; also abstinence from error thoughts, to the end that we may meditate upon spiritual truths and incorporate them into our consciousness of oneness with the Father". We must rid ourselves of our "error thinking" to be one with God, and to be one with God will bring us all that we ask. Still, all will depend on how we treat others. This is a very important principle we must learn to realize. All will rest upon it. Jesus did say that we should treat our neighbor as ourselves, then there will be no error. Of course, it does not confine its meaning to the person next door, but rather to anyone or anything next to you at any given moment. It truly assists us in our clarity and purpose.

Continuing on the subject of faith, we see a certain confirmation in **2 Timothy 3:15-17**: *"And that from a child thou hast known the holy scriptures, which are able to make thee wise unto salvation **through faith** which is in Christ Jesus. (16) All scripture is given by inspiration of God, and is profitable for doctrine, for reproof, for correction, for instruction in righteousness: (17) That the man of God may be perfect, throughly furnished unto all good works"*. This comprises many thoughts, yet some organizations have taken it literally, especially when it comes to the word "profitable". Those sensible words are also wrongly used to play on a person's fears. In a spiritual sense, however, these same words, if properly used, will give us all the wisdom necessary to end personal struggles in our lives. Further proof of what life will bring us can be found in **Galatians 3:3-5**: *"Are ye so foolish? Having begun in the Spirit, are ye now made perfect by the flesh? (4) Have ye suffered so many things in vain? If it be yet in vain. (5) He therefore that ministereth to you the Spirit, and worketh miracles among you, doeth he it by the works of the law, or by the **hearing of faith**?"*. This is truly a wonderful statement. It says much in that we are from the spirit, and that life will test us to give us knowledge of the laws of inner consciousness. Through that knowledge – with faith – we may increase our growth. In this context, faith actually implies the knowledge of the law, and not just faith alone. It advises us that what we believe to be in vain really is not.

To the Tibetan mindset, there is no such thing as an accident or coincidence. The above verse shows that Jesus did study there because it is the only way this philosophy would have been known by Him. He wanted to pass on to us that nothing is ever in vain, including weakness. We suffer a misperception in what we term as weakness, as any monk would teach. Even Jesus substantiated the thought in **2 Corinthians 12:9**: *"My grace is sufficient for thee: for my strength is made perfect in weakness"*. This can only be attained through the experience of the weakness, to understand its reasons and whence it came. Once we have learned this, it becomes a strength. Too many of us attempt to avoid these lessons, because they are too painful, or much in vain. This type of thinking is quite wrong, because lurking under the surface, greatness awaits to come to fruition within you. It is not without a price, therefore, we avoid the lesson and continue to misunderstand our very own God-given nature of self.

Return to Innocence

The next verses may be appropriate at this time. **Matthew 18:3-4**: *"Verily, I say unto you, Except ye be converted, and become as little children, ye shall not enter into the kingdom of heaven. (4) Whosoever therefore shall humble himself as this little child, the same is greatest in the kingdom of heaven".* Jesus was talking about us returning to a level of innocence, openness and humility. This is very difficult for the adults of this world. They tend to hold on to so many memories of dire events that to them, no level of inner innocence can be attained. The events of the past contaminate the efforts.

I find it rather interesting that people will not drive a vehicle while looking over their shoulder, simply because they think that an accident would be the outcome. Yet, allegorically, they live their lives while constantly looking over their shoulder at the past. At that rate, one will obviously walk into something, but not until it is too late. Look forward – not back! Remember Lot's wife, so that you will not become frozen in time as she did. The verses also imply that we must trust, and trust is merely about being open, with no conditions attached. But conditions are part of our way, and not the flow of life. In fact, if a person were to conduct a little retro-inspection, anytime conditions are placed on life, it seems to turn to an act in vain and it becomes more difficult. We are generally a very mistrusting specie. We approach everything with doubt and are quite skeptical, because we place entirely too many conditions. As an example: if you want to love me, love me my way, and not yours. Does this really make sense? It should not, yet it is what most of us tend to do. After all, do we not think we know ourselves best? We should allow others to love us their way and keep expectation out of it. Simply be cheerfully opened to it, and learn trust. Hence, nothing is ever really in vain. It is learning to understand what we do not know about our own self that may be perceived as a weakness. Conclusively, weakness is merely not enough inner knowledge on the subject.

The Weight of Life

If you read **Matthew 22:2-14** – the parable of the wedding feast – you will find that it is another example of the external trappings we have in life, and a further reference to the kingdom of heaven. It depicts how we, as humans, tend to take our spiritual side too lightly. In the biblical sense, marriage is the merging of the aspects of self, and when one seeks and asks for humanity to join in, one finds that people are all too busy. Those who answer the call usually have other motivations in mind. This is depicted in the guest who was not wearing wedding garments. He appeared unprepared, in an attempt to ride on the coat tails of others, as a manipulative person. This behavior is earmarked for failure, because no one may manipulate spirit through ulterior motives. In fact, no one may manipulate Spirit at all. If one would attempt it, it would fail. One must be real and genuine of heart and bear the innocence of a child to receive what spirit has to offer. This is reinforced by the words of Jesus in Verse 14: *"For many are called, but few are chosen"*. Jesus also said that many would indeed be called, but few would come. The Master tells us that we indeed have the right to choose what is truly right, yet few of us will heed the offer, simply because we would rather pay attention to the physical trappings and not our inner nature. This is driven by the egoistic aspect of the person. Must we not appear to be successful for others to accept us?

Matthew 23:2-4 could be said to be the birthplace of our old adage "Do as I say, not as I do". It reads: *"The scribes and the Pharisees sit in Moses' seat: (3) All therefore whatsoever they bid you observe, that observe and do; but do not ye after their works: for they say, and do not. (4) For they bind heavy burdens and grievous to be borne, and lay them on men's shoulders; but they themselves will not move them with one of their fingers"*. In the days of the Pharisees, it seems that religious figures did not do the work, but laid many burdens upon others – guilt trips, if you will, for manipulative purposes. One has to wonder if this still goes on today. When observing the actions of some organizations and their leaders, do we not detect the fact that the burdens of responsibility are placed on other shoulders? During His era, Jesus saw through them. Today, we do not seem to see it, yet He told us that they would influence us into doing things for external reasons, thus leading us away from the true path.

In **Matthew 23:16-17**, we hear Jesus carry this subject a little further: *"Woe unto you, ye blind guides, which say, Whosoever shall swear by the temple, it is nothing; but whosoever shall swear by the gold of the temple, he is a debtor! (17) Ye fools and blind: for whether is greater, the gold, or the temple that sanctifieth the gold?"*. There are several ways that temple and gold have been interpreted. However, the majority refers to "temple" as the body, the physical aspect, and not a building, while "gold" is the knowledge or wisdom and not a currency. We must admit that Jesus made a very specific statement. He has advised us that knowledge is much more important than physical trappings, and calls us fools for misplacing our focus, a focus which leads us in the wrong direction.

In **Matthew 24:37-38**, Jesus says: *"But as the days of Noah were, so shall also the coming of the Son of man be. (38) For as in the days that were before the flood they were eating and drinking, marrying and giving in marriage, until the day that Noah entered into the ark"*. If we look around us, do we not see these events taking place? In the days of Noah and the flood, were we not showered with spirit? Jesus is saying that these days will come again and we must be ready. He implies that we must not waste time getting things we think we need. He tells us to prepare ourselves and stay that way, because the spiritual offensive will indeed accompany the Christ Himself. We will shift to a more mystical purpose generated from within and in that time, we shall all know of the nature of spirit. We will not have to shout it everywhere, because we will all have that same inner knowledge, an impelling instead of a compelling as we have today. This compelling stems from our distraction with the physical or material.

This truth is well depicted in **Matthew 25:1-13** in the story of the ten virgins. *"Then shall the kingdom of heaven be likened unto ten virgins, which took their lamps, and went forth to meet the bridegroom. (2) And five of them were wise, and five were foolish. (3) They that were foolish took their lamps, and took no oil with them; (4) But the wise took oil in their vessels with their lamps. (5) While the bridegroom tarried, they all slumbered and slept. (6) And at midnight there was a cry made, Behold, the bridegroom cometh; go ye out to meet him. (7) Then all those virgins arose, and trimmed their lamps. (8) And the foolish said unto the wise, Give us of your oil; for our lamps are gone out. (9) But the wise answered, saying, Not so; lest there be not enough for us and you: but go ye rather to them that sell, and buy for yourselves. (10) And while they went to buy, the bridegroom came; and they that were ready went in with him to the marriage: and the door was shut. (11) Afterward came also the other virgins, saying, Lord, Lord, open to us. (12) But he answered and said, Verily I say unto you, I know you not. (13) Watch therefore, for ye know neither the day nor the hour wherein the Son of man cometh".* This very simple tale is further verification for the reader to have a glimpse at the changes to come. We must be watchful in all we do, especially in the field of our self-understanding. We must have enough wisdom within to complete our inner self because when the time comes and the door is shut, no one will enter. We are allowed a very narrow margin, and as long as others are inclined to lead, we have a tendency to rely on them when we should rely on ourselves. Jesus advises us to be reliant on our own nature rather than what others may tell us. It has to be strictly our own experience, because it will truly give us the wisdom. To avoid it will give us nothing, and we will miss being ready for the growth that is to come – and it will come whether we are ready or not.

In reading the Bible, we find that Jesus often told us to give away our worldly goods. In the tale of the ten virgins, He distinctly advises us otherwise, wanting us not to share, and that can create a paradox. It really is not the case. It has already been said that in the growth of our inner self, we must rely on ourselves and not others. In that time of shift, others may attempt to distract us with their pleas for assistance in the last hour, but we are told to hold on to what we have. We should not accumulate too much in life, because it is in our nature to save or salvage as much as we can. This would become a distraction. In fact, every Master throughout time has told us of this. Material is the illusion that we should want nothing, because a desire will own us and can control our lives. We are to be like the lilies of the field and the birds of the air. Spirit will provide what we really need. We allow life to be the cause when we should realize that we are the cause and life is the effect.

Life after Death

I am sure that many – if not all – of us have questioned themselves and others about the subject of life after death. There are some indications of this within the covers of the Bible. Whenever I am approached by people on this matter, I usually tell them: "You mean to tell me that we are given life, but then, upon our death, we are thrown into the darkness of oblivion? Would a loving God do this?". No! I think not! Even Einstein, in his theory of relativity, stated that we simply become a different energy. We already know, from a scientific viewpoint, that we are energy-based, and that is measurable. We are merely where the naked eye cannot see us. We have shed our body like a snake sheds its skin. In **Matthew 26:29**, Jesus said: *"But I say unto you, I will not drink henceforth of this fruit of the vine, until that day when I drink it new with you in my Father's kingdom"*. He is saying that He will see us again, and that there is more to life than we may be aware. After all, did He not Himself prove it by rising after the third day? In our contemporary world, we are having more and more people with near-death experiences, and their stories are being told. They all say there is more. I know, because I have had these experiences for myself.

The crucifixion of Jesus has brought on much research and study. The real nature of this event is very perplexing. Not only must one study the religious texts, but one must also examine the history of Rome and the Roman Empire at that time. Even the Koran relates versions of this event. History itself will provide many enlightening statements that we will present here, but only once, to avoid unnecessary duplication. We will look at a few of the points regarding this event, but we will merely relate what the Romans did not ordinarily do during the crucifixion process. Their procedures were never broken, except once, in the case of Jesus.

Whenever they put a person on the cross, the usual routine was to break the knees and remove the condemned from the cross as soon as they had passed, but not in the case of Jesus. The Romans never gave the body to family or friends. Instead, they were thrown in mass graves. They never allowed the condemned men to have anything to drink under any circumstances. These few regimented procedures were broken but once in the history of Rome, and that was for Jesus and no one else. They did not break His knees, gave Him to an Essene healer, Joseph of Arimathaea – a relative - and while He was still on the cross, they placed a sponge on His mouth that was saturated with a type of vinegar. The point is that this sad event was handled differently, and it can bring about all kinds of speculations, even about the sponge possibly being saturated with a strong "knock-out" drug. The Koran indicates this very openly. The reason for this implication is that when the centurion pierced His side, Jesus bled. Any doctor will tell you that once you are dead, you no longer bleed, yet Jesus did. As far as speculations are concerned, there is a possibility that Pilate asked Rome for a dispensation, or what action to take. Word did come from Caesar to release Him, but the Pharisees knew of this and somehow slowed the courier, so as not to interfere with the crucifixion – an attempt that may not have worked.

As for the symbol of Jesus carrying the cross, there are many interpretations. It is not for me to say one way or the other, but it stands to reason that the most logical symbol is about us carrying our own burdens. It implies that we must be willing to crucify our very own physical nature to attain spiritual wisdom and go to any extent for that goal, for He showed us the way. To journey further toward spiritual understanding, we must not be afraid to sacrifice all things for that end and purpose, while we consider the physical aspect as the least important.

Those that work to save their life shall lose it, and those that are willing to give it shall save it. Give all that you have in that endeavor. It may be difficult at the beginning, but after you reach a certain point, it is very easy to do. Indeed, the beginning will be a great struggle, but if one perseveres, it becomes uncomplicated as experience and truth grow. The crucifixion was a demonstration to us all that if one is to ascend, one must be clear within and have nothing holding him in place. To do this, give all of yourself, for it is truly worthy, and nothing is ever in vain. It is all very real, and nothing is taken for granted. Our actions are our own manifestation, and these actions will determine our experience when it is our time to pass or shed the skin. At that point, that experience is written in stone and may not be repaired, hence, it behooves us to repair while we have the opportunity to do so. It is why so many Masters declare that the time is always the present moment, one that should not be put off, as the burdens accumulate heavily on a person. Even at passing, these must be shed, which is why we have the concept of heaven and hell, for what we do here, we lay up for ourselves in heaven. Live life to the fullest, in love and compassion.

Be willing to share our unique beauty with all that are interested. Snub no one for what they appear to be and accept them for who they really are – not for who you think they are. Always allow others to be themselves in their own eyes, and not yours. Spirit loves us all. It does not judge us, but regrettably, we have a habit of judging ourselves and others by what we set in motion in our lives. Deplorably, we do not realize what we do set in motion, because all too often, we are quite busy pointing a finger at others, rather than accepting responsibility for our own self-actions. The only wrong we do is to others, in not allowing them to express their individual nature and to bring it forth in the light of spiritual beauty.

We will now enter the second aspect of life – the mental part. We will do this through the Book of Mark, where we will observe and understand the differences it holds for us. This is the true area of the illusions of life, for as a person thinks, so he/she becomes.

CHAPTER 5

THE BOOK OF MARK

"Our life is what our thoughts make it"
Marcus Aurelius, Meditations (2ⁿᵈ Century)

In the New Testament, Mark is the shortest Gospel of the four main books. It focuses on the mental or thinking aspect of the human form. It is truly the steering mechanism of life. Thoughts are very powerful, since they bring to us the very things we desire, even the adverse ones, or those we do not wish for ourselves. In essence, they are the very foundation of our lives. This is one of the two areas in which we must be single in purpose. It means that if we want success, we should focus on it. If we do this, we will be given the power of thought, thus avoiding what we do not want to have. This was the dilemma portrayed in the Book of Matthew. It is where we hold onto or release the attainment aspects of the self. Even though it is the shortest Gospel, it has the greatest impact on us all. Oddly enough, this is where the learning takes place, whether in books or in experience. Here lies the thinking process of the ego, the seat of the illusion of life. It is where our Spirit-given attributes come together for us to use. Conversely, we seldom use the full capabilities of this very powerful storehouse. For the most part, we overuse our analytical ability which can be necessary only under certain circumstances. If one only analyzes, one does not realize, and there is quite a difference. The thinking aspect is also the seat of consciousness and the crown, or highest part of the human. By its own place in our inner selves, it is the seat of the wisdom we hold. Based on our individual pasts, this wisdom can be solid or faltering.

You will notice that the birth of the Master is not even mentioned in this particular text. If you were to read Mark's entire dissertation, you would realize that the differences also extend in the way the text is phrased. These differences will be introduced as they apply to us, in all four of the main Gospels. The variations are there to show other aspects of the human experience. Each of us must pass through these experiences to reach the level of attainment or enlightenment we seek on the inner plane. Even if we are not aware of this journey, it helps us to know that this is the purpose of life. Let us now follow the logic and usefulness of our greatest physical tool: the steering mechanism of the mind and thoughts.

THE MASTER'S TEACHINGS

As was just mentioned, the birth of the Master is not recounted, nor are the early years discussed. The book of Mark covers the life of Jesus only after the completion of His education and His return to Israel, where He began to convey His message to the people. We open this study with **Mark 1:12-13**: *"And immediately the Spirit driveth him into the wilderness. (13) And he was there in the wilderness forty days, tempted of Satan; and was with the wild beasts; and the angels ministered unto him"*. Looking at Verse 12, we see that Spirit drove Him – or impelled Him to go. We know that Spirit – or the internal nature – will always impel a person. On the other hand, life – or the external side – will compel a person. Deductively, to be impelled is a message from the higher self, while to be compelled stems from the physical. Further, no one, not even Jesus, is allowed to ignore the outward aspect for learning purposes. As already cited, the outer is our teacher, the events of our life. Hence, the wilderness was meant for Jesus to experience the things of life. This wilderness is the mental nature of self and the taunting of the egoistic aspect. With the facts He had gathered during His education and His exceptional abilities, He had to have the external experience of such knowledge and how it was to apply. This would make sense when considering the level of power that was to be bestowed upon Him as a human – as we all are. An interesting point is that Jesus the Christ, we are told, was God in the flesh, thus, the temptation by Satan tells us that God was tempting Itself again, as in the Garden of Eden.

Satan was/is not an evil entity. If we were to study Sanskrit, we would discover that it has an entirely different meaning, in that it is described as the ego, the tempter, or external life. If we were to comprehend that only the temptations of the physical side actually attract us – and how much our ego desires the external, we might truly learn a valuable lesson, as the Master Himself did. Have we not all been taught that absolute power corrupts absolutely? This had to be clarified for Him, so that there would be no question as to how that power would be used. It must be used only in service to and for others, rather than self-serving, and we know we can all get caught in that gear.

Mark tells us that Jesus was with the wild beasts. In this context, wild beasts were not the animals we picture. They were the inner thoughts – produced by the physical ego mind -- with which He had to deal. Imagine what temptation would be with His kind of inner power, especially if the temptation was to change life to match Him forcefully. History proves that He did not. The ministering of angels was more for Jesus to stay focused on the positive rather than the negative. It was His inner battle between good and evil. Remember, He stated that no one was above the law and it applied to all, including Himself. He was the law in the flesh, because He understood it so completely. Spirit impelled Him because it needed to know if He could carry on the works. Spirit will not prove itself to us. It does not need to do so. We are the ones to prove ourselves to it, thus "knock, and the door will be opened". We must show the worth of our own being, because we are tainted with impurities. These impurities stem from having a choice, and we choose between good or evil.

This "good and evil" is almost a natural characteristic of the human mind, especially when it comes to choices. It is actually the positive and negative thinking generated within our minds. Let us look into an interesting theory concerning our mental machinations. We have learned of the value of polar oppositions. They also operate in the mental realm, thus the polarization of thought forms in the mind. Positive thoughts are very easy to accept and offer ease of mind and thought forms. The difficulty seems to stem from the negative style thoughts that we also tend to have. They are more designed to balance the mind than anything else, meaning that if you have the one, the other will surely come. The problem is that we deem them to be a bad thing, when in reality they are the natural forms of thinking we all experience. The truth is that if we act on the negative thought, negativity will certainly follow. The proof is all around us. Simply look at the activities of life. The point is to not resist the negative thought, but rather to allow for it as a balancing measure. If we fight any thought, it has a tendency to become magnified – be it good or bad. The object would be to allow the natural flow of the mind and bypass it by not giving importance to it. After all, it is up to us to choose what to think, and the more we judge the external, the greater the pull of the negative thought. This will produce many struggles with life.

When we find ourselves with an inner struggle, it is usually in our mind. We are filled with the wild beasts and become distraught, losing our own power of self. This is the pull of negativity because we think it is bad, based on our power of choice between good and evil. We then are no longer in focus and are distracted by the physical side, which means that we surrender to other things. If one were to notice, it is usually the physical side that creates our inner struggles. Such struggles occur in our minds, so we must learn to have a better balance with the outer. The wrong approach is to balance the inner nature with the outer. It must be the reverse. One must balance the outer with the inner. When this is done, we are the first cause and life is our effect. The Master had to know how to conduct this careful balance, from the outer to the inner, and He did so during His period of temptation.

The number "forty" is used quite often in the Bible. It rained for forty days and nights; Moses was in the wilderness for forty years and Jesus was in another wilderness for forty days and nights. The relationship of these numerical periods is not completely clear. For Noah and Jesus, it was a test of the ability to stabilize within spiritual nature, while Moses was attempting to stabilize in the physical world. According to the Scriptures, it took them that long to accomplish the task. As many learned scholars have speculated, a day to God is a period of 1,000 years. It begs the question: in whose sight was this being done? God's or ours? Actually, both. The first two, Noah and Moses, were in God's eyes. The second, Jesus, was in ours – or in physical terms. To God/Spirit, this concept of time is irrelevant, as time is linear in its movement, and to Spirit, it is eternal. It would not recognize a day as we do. Time in itself does not really exist, since it is but the reflection of mind from its source – self – which is the reference point of all material things. Only in **Genesis 1** do we see that the sun came up and went down, as a reference to what we know as a day. Nothing more is mentioned on that subject. For that matter, there was no sun or light, because at that time, nothing existed. Deductively, it is a reference to cyclical time, or the cycles of life. We must stabilize and balance these cycles, or we are in continuous turmoil. We do this through what we think, thought streams, as thoughts continue to expand through our very own interaction with life. With our choices, we either expand or detract within.

In **Mark 2:7-11,** we find Jesus once again confronted by the Pharisees on the subject of sins, while He tends to a paralyzed person. In verse 11, he tells the sick man: *"I say unto thee, Arise, and take up thy bed, and go thy way into thine house"*. The man's sins were holding him in place, and he was unable to move forward with his life. He, as Lot's wife, was frozen in time and was living in fear. "Take up thy bed" is a symbol wherein Jesus tells the man to carry his perceived burdens, rather than the burdens carrying him. As I remarked before, there is a wonderful book offered by the Unity Church, called "The Metaphysical Bible Dictionary". I will take the liberty to quote from their definition of sin, since in my own journey, I have attained the same understanding. SIN: *"Missing the mark: falling short of the divine law;....Sin is a departure from the law of our being....The creatures of land and sea represent states of mind and they all are contained in the consciousness of every man. Any failure on our part to exercise this dominion is a falling short, or a "sin""*. The "eternal sin", as depicted below, is the belief that God is the creator of disease or inharmony of any kind. It is called that because that which is eternal is abiding. So long as man stands in the conviction that God causes him to suffer, he closes his mind to the inflow of God's gifts of health, peace and harmony. Man's sins are forgiven when he ceases to sin and opens his mind to the fact that he is heir only to such gifts. This is a very appropriate definition to know and very accurate for all of us. The only burdens that we carry are strictly our own creation and are not placed upon us by God. We must realize that they are the results of our own choices. Jesus reminds us of this in **Mark 3:28-30**: *"Verily I say unto you, All sins shall be forgiven unto the sons of men, and blasphemies wherewith soever they shall blaspheme: (29) But he that shall blaspheme against the Holy Ghost hath never forgiveness, but is in danger of eternal damnation* [eternal sin]: *(30) Because they said, He hath an unclean spirit".*

The individual's mind was filled with negativity, therefore he had an unclean spirit. Most of us have experienced periods in our lives when we carried more negative thoughts than positive. That is what is meant by "unclean spirit" and nothing more. If negative thinking was indeed the "sin", then we would all be in trouble. This is more normal than we tend to believe. We are the ones who make an issue of it, not Spirit. Spirit does not know the difference between positive and negative. It just simply is. We merely need to see things differently.

It is during these times that we should turn things over to Spirit and stop fighting our own selves. Unclean thoughts are the biggest detriment we may have in our lives, and we do not know what to do. We must simply continue the course of our works and realize that we laid these unclean thoughts in place, yet they should not carry us. We are supposed to rise above them, not wallow in them. In the days of Jesus, most believed in this Man for what He showed them, for His works. It was that belief that allowed Him to achieve what He did with and to others. He gave them the necessary knowledge required in that era through most of the healings He performed in His life. They were feats of mind over matter, the power of the self in union with Spirit. His purpose was to convey the understanding of the knowledge he had acquired in the Far East – the old lands – and to extend the teachings of the Ancients. This signified that a major change was necessary for all, and we clearly see what was done with this new information. Those in power at the time were afraid. Today, would this not happen again if Jesus the Christ reappeared? Would He not be challenged? Do we expect Him to look the same as He did? If He did, would you recognize Him? Most would not!

To resume, "eternal sin" is about a person perpetuating its own unclean spirit through thinking that it is God's fault, and refusing to accept responsibility for his/her own experience with thoughts. Please allow me to repeat a story that I told in Chapter 4, a story that profoundly affected the rest of my life and seems to again fit the subject at hand. Once, a Tibetan said to me: "What if God heard everything that you thought and considered what you were thinking as a request to do something for you. Would you change the way you think?" I answered yes, and he said: "Good, for that is the truth of things".

Now ask yourself if you would do the same. If the answer is yes, you would now know the root of the problems within your very own life, problems being perpetuated at every turn. They are being achieved by the continual mental channel the person either does not want to change, or does not know how. All thoughts have life as they have a vibration to them. Because they are vibrating, they are alive unto themselves. It is movement.

In the book of Mark, Jesus' message is for us to watch what we are thinking. The Buddha once said that the mind of the human is much like a tree filled with chattering monkeys and it is up to us to stop the noise by clearing the branches. This is done with one change of the mind at a time, understanding whence the thought came in the first place. It is not easy for us to accomplish this task, because we are usually and erroneously too busy to take the time. In our contemporary life, we hurry from one point to another, claiming to be busy – in our own minds – and attempting to keep up with it all. A mind that is too busy on the physical level will freeze anyone in place, especially if it is focused on the material aspects and on the yesterdays that life already offered. Because of this flurry of external activity, we do not notice...Those are the distractions that entwine us and bind us to where we are in the moments of life.

In the book of Mark, you will notice that the parables begin promptly in Chapter 4 with the story of the sower (**Mark 4:3-9**). **Mark 4:10** reads: *"And when he was alone, **they** that were about him **with** the twelve asked of him the parable"*. This seems to indicate that there were more students than the twelve disciples. We can deduce that many were interested in the inner teachings related by Jesus, after the multitudes were gone, and the Master could be more specific in his explanations. Again, the first parable is about the sower, but you will note that it starts in a way different than the one recounted by Matthew. This shows that Mark is presenting it on a different level, away from the physical. Thought will expand its own self if we allow it, and he is telling us that we must watch how our thoughts expand, and in what direction they will travel. He is actually implying that we are rather indolent with our thoughts and have a tendency to let them overrun us. As an example, when we are experiencing fear but do not know exactly why, this fear can expand into many areas, and it eventually will have us chasing shadows. We are no longer sure of the original reason that caused that fear.

We do this in a variety of ways in our lives, because we never addressed our insecurities in the first place and did not bother to investigate whence they came. They become compounded and we constantly repeat these deeds. The true lessons were not gleaned the first time around, thus they become repetitious in nature. If we do not get the message and we have a cycle that is repeating, do not rush into the same pattern. Now we have the solid opportunity to remove an old groove. We should realize that nothing will change until we change our way of thinking in such fashion that things will multiply as we want them – not as we do not want them to happen, as so often they do. Hence, we must learn to not allow the mind to wander aimlessly without an inner structured form. This is accomplished through understanding the nature of our own form, and not that of others. We must realize that we all have these cycles that come and go in life, until we break them.

We are too caught up in other distractions, like people around us. This is purely human error, mentioned many times in the Bible. In **Matthew 7:5**, we read: *"Thou hypocrite, first cast out the beam out of thine own eye; and then shalt thou see clearly to cast out the mote out of thy brother's eye"*. This means that if you cannot see plainly, how can you assist another to see clearly. This led to the old adage: "the blind leading the blind"… We could say that the appropriate message is that our purpose, in some ways, is to see clearly – to understand. First, we are to understand our own nature and not others'. Once we do and can see clearly, we are much more efficient with others. The big concern is the egoistic thoughts that abound in our minds, as we – most times – have issues with the very person we attempt to assist. This generally will lead to unhappy outcomes, unless we are clear within our own self first. To assist, we must bring those we help to our level, rather than go to theirs. It will lend itself to no confrontation, for we will see plainly and know our own position.

In **Mark 4:24**, we detect Jesus' understanding of the teachings in the Far East, where He had studied with the old Masters of Wisdom. It reads: *"And he said unto them, Take heed what ye hear: with what measure ye mete, it shall be measured to you: and unto you that hear shall more be given"*. The Master is talking about the laws of **Karma** and **Dharma** which are eastern philosophies. "Take heed what ye hear" does not necessarily pertain to the words you hear. It concerns the inner nature of thought triggered by the impressions of these words. Many of us accept the physical, literal aspect of verbal communication. In the process of interpretation, Jesus tells us to be aware of the type of energy that we give these words, and as a result, we are to be careful of what our mind puts forth. The laws of Karma and Dharma are unrelenting in their nature, for no one is above the law. Karma (Sanskrit for "action") is about what we do and what we set in motion through our thinking and type of thinking. It is the law of action and reaction, and the reason Jesus said: *"I am Alpha and Omega, the beginning and the end, the first and the last"* (Revelation

22:13).

What starts with me stops with me... On the other hand, Dharma is the path that one will have to walk because of his/her own karmic actions. It is the path that one has chosen in order to continue learning on his/her journey, through self-created experience. Do we have this much control in our lives? The Masters will give you an affirmative answer. We have control with the realization of Spirit only. We see, sense and think about things and other people by our own standards of measure. However, Spirit already knows what is in our hearts. The intent of the action(s) we set in motion – good or bad – will be returned to us in a form larger than we would expect. It comes to us in the physical sense, or reality, and with that added weight, we now walk the path that we created for ourselves. We see a further confirmation of this concept in the very next verse. **Mark 4:25:** *"For he that hath, to him shall be given: and he that hath not, from him shall be taken even that which he hath".* If we can step away from the materialistic thoughts that assail us on a daily basis, we should realize that it is our belief system that is being discussed. If we are weak in that belief, we will lose all that we may have accumulated thus far. If we focus our thoughts on the narrow singleness in purpose, all will be much easier to accept as true, and we will not concern ourselves with the "what if's". These doubts divide us from within and create an inner fear. In turn, that fear will cause us to lose what we now have. The remedy is to be solid in the belief, yet we will be put to the test. We must assume the responsibility for the equal reactions that return to us, then will we be in control. We will then be working with the messages that Spirit sends us for our guidance.

Jesus reminds us of the importance of control in **Mark 4:39-40,** and that we should realize we are in command: *"And he arose, and rebuked the wind, and said unto the sea, Peace, be still. And the wind ceased, and there was a great calm. (40) And he said unto them, Why are ye so fearful* [timid]*? How is it that ye have no faith?".* The wind and the sea are allegories referring to the constant rushing of thoughts. These thoughts are influenced by a variety of sources. In this particular example, the Master is showing us the conflict between the higher and lower reflections. One must command the stillness of the spiritual mind. If it is not controlled or commanded, it will overwhelm us in times of difficulty. Jesus implies that we should not be fearful or timid and that we should stand firm on our belief, our faith in the outcome. If we want to fulfill a desire, we must command our inner nature to produce the results that we are seeking to experience. Biblically, it seems this is unlimited. We may have all that we desire as long as we stay focused, and as long as we do not listen to our external "no's". If we are subjected to these "external no's", we should take a moment to examine them, to determine what is slowing the reaching of our goal. In that fashion, we are using the external as the guide post to self.

At times, Jesus may have appeared to be confusing. There were times when He said "tell no one", and others when He wanted His actions reported. We see this in **Mark 5:19:** *"Go home to thy friends, and tell them how great things the Lord has done for thee, and hath had compassion on thee"*. This was after He had chased the unclean spirits of a man into a herd of swine. But in **Mark 5:43**, after Jesus had resurrected a twelve year-old child, He said: *"And he charged them straitly that no man should know it; and commanded that something should be given her to eat"*. As you can see, His advice after the deeds in the two verses are quite opposite. The last part of Verse 19 comes after He had worked with many people to give them greater understanding of themselves. He felt that all should know of these deeds.

Further, he had been asked to leave the area. He knew that if all were informed of His works, there would be less resistance to the teachings He was offering for their understanding when He would return. The difference in Verse 43 is that belief was already among the people of this community. In this particular village, He was telling them about fear and belief. Fear becomes a large obstacle for us to overcome and is placed in our path by the lack of knowledge. This is what the Master meant in **Mark 5:36** when He told the church official: *"Be not afraid, only believe"*. Indeed, if the knowledge is present, no fear will exist and belief will prevail.

If one were to possess the implicit belief system that Jesus describes, there could be no fear. We find this principle in the healing of the little girl – His second raising of the dead. Lazarus was the first and Christ Himself would be the third. His intention was to teach us – through deeds that we consider miraculous – that we do not die as we know and comprehend it. The truth is that in Mark 5:36 and 43, He is actually telling us to have complete belief in our nature and ability, a fact that should never be denied. It is confirmed in **Mark 6:51-52**: *"And he went up unto them into the ship; and the wind ceased: and they were sore amazed in themselves beyond measure, and wondered. (52) For they considered not the miracle of the loaves: for their heart was hardened"*. The disciples had not gained insight into the mysteries and had much doubt. It brought on the remark: "for their heart was hardened" because they could not feel it. They only had the mental, or intellectual comprehension concerning what the Master had been doing to this point.

We read in **Mark 6:38-44** the story of the division of the bread and the fishes, similarly recounted in **Matthew 15:34-38**. Again, we seem to be satisfied with the literal meaning of the words. The reference to bread is manna, or the energy of spiritual nourishment being multiplied and shared among the multitudes. The reference to fishes is something of a very different nature. Fish represents the multiplication of ideas. Jesus quite often used the fish metaphor to illustrate His teachings, because He was a living demonstration of ideas in action - spiritual ideas. All that He did was in the realm of ideas rather than the realm of effects. Fish is a symbol of ideas in which the dominion of possibilities may increase. It was used to represent the inexhaustible, vast presence of abundance that we all may use if we so decide. However, this cornucopia of ideas is available to us only if we learn to understand our own nature and work with the Spirit.

This is substantiated in **Mark 6:48**, wherein we see Jesus walking on the sea. It is a demonstration of His ability to rise above the physical and allowing Spirit to lift Him above, thus walking on water. In the same verse, His disciples were straining at the oars because the wind was against them. It indicates that they were fighting life, fighting their thoughts and fears, and the Master was going to pass them by as they had not yet learned. The winds symbolize the struggles within themselves, struggles generated by the fact that they did not fully comprehend the teachings and examples of the Master. In **Mark 6:51**, Jesus got into the boat with His disciples. It clearly implies that He came down to their level, lowering his vibrations to match theirs. It can also be noted how superstitious they were, in their imagining that He was a ghost. The truth is that they could not yet absorb His teachings, in the form of ideas that He had brought forth for them to know and accept. **Mark 6:54-55**: *"And when they were come out of the ship, straightaway they knew him, (55) and ran through that whole region round about, and began to carry about in beds those that were sick, where they heard he was"*. It is a further representation that we have many burdens in life. We carry them with us in our mortal minds, with all the memories and all the events that go on day in and day out. The pallets [beds] were the only things that could carry the weight of the troubles the people had. We seem to have the same troubles today… The problems were being carried to the One who understood and could relieve them of the burdens weighing heavily upon them. It was His wisdom they came to hear so they too could grasp it.

In **Mark 7:15**, we read: *"There is nothing from without a man, that entering into him can defile him: but the things which come out of him, those are they that defile the man"*. The same principle can be read in Luke 7:18-23 and James 3:5-6. Our mouths are the body features used to externally form what we put forth. Jesus is certainly not speaking about food. He is telling us, however, that what God, the spirit, sends us is pure in nature and good. It is what we do with it in our minds after we receive it and how we bring it to reality. Life was intended to be good and not selfish. Our way to work with it is to think that someone must be in control. That control has turned into a level of greed beyond compare, and today, we all operate out of an incredible height of selfishness. Our egocentric speculation is "what will the impact be on me", bringing this insensitivity to a high degree. Some are practicing this moderately, while others are quite submerged by it. This selfishness has led many toward pure greed and the need to be greedy. We see this every day in the obscene profit taking and skyrocketing prices. If this is not greed, then what is it? We are coldly reminded of this plague in **Luke 12:15**: *"And he said unto them, Take heed, and beware of covetousness* [greed]: *for a man's life consisteth not in the abundance of the things which he possesseth"*. In our contemporary lifestyle, our possessions are our outer nature, the way we see ourselves and our "things". We have allowed our minds to lead us to this conclusion, merely because these "things" are touchable. You will note that between Mark 7:15 and Luke 12:15, there is a subtle difference. Following Mark 7:15, we read in Verse 16 that Jesus said *"If any man has ears to hear, let him hear"*. In Luke 12:15, the Master used the true physiological aspect of the matter for those who did not understand the message.

Apparently, while addressing the multitudes, Jesus for the most part did not like having to explain Himself. Still, He would give His students the full clarification of His statements about matters that were hidden from us by those in control. He, as the enlightened one, knew that we could not all fathom His words. Only those with whom He had been working knew the depth of the messages, the inner truth of the words. In **Mark 7:34-35**, Jesus was working with a deaf mute: *"And looking up to heaven, he sighed, and saith unto him, Ephphata, that is, Be opened. (35) And straightway his ears were opened, and the string of his tongue was loosed, and he spake plain"*. Metaphorically, this suggests that we should all listen to more profound subjects, rather than the obvious – as we do. He is discussing the higher truths to life, the true depth of meaning. It tells us to express as plainly as possible that which we do comprehend. It was an example of Jesus clearing a path to a higher understanding of the nature of life, to release the burdens that bind us. Those are yesterday's memories - the true stumbling blocks of life – to which we insist on holding so tightly. Wanting to hold on comes in with the traditional working of our minds, conditioned to think about it in all sorts of ways. Most times, such memories are filled with regrets. Those are negative thoughts that now have power over us. They will eat at us constantly as we attempt to rearrange them in our minds. We should just see them as an event that occurred and not what it could have been. As a result, it would not be a self-inflicted internal torture. Accept things as they are – not as they are not.

Mark 8:4: *"And his disciples answered him, From whence can a man satisfy these men with bread here in the wilderness?"*. Here, the Master had a multitude of people who came to hear His wisdom, and the hour was late. It had been suggested they were all to be fed, and the disciples asked where and who would provide the food. Not enough bread in such a desolate place? This is an interesting statement, when you consider that earlier, in Genesis, we were told that the lands were quite fertile.

The bread represents the scope of the teachings, as put forth by the energy of spirit, and the desolate place is the individual or collective mind of the people in that era. The real question was: "How may we pass on the teachings to all that have come this day?". Jesus was there to bring about the deeper realization of knowledge to those people who had come to find a greater appreciation of their nature. They came to attain growth from the spiritual perspective, as expressed in the next verse. **Mark 8:5**: *"And he asked them, How many loaves have ye? And they said, Seven"*. The number "seven" is the number of progressive levels of spiritual understanding contained within the seven energy centers of the body. This symbolizes passing the teachings onto others, teachings that can be absorbed by all, at whatever level of comprehension each individual has attained. It further implies that such method would be more than sufficient. It could be divided among the multitude, and the people would have the knowledge they came to learn, regardless of their level of consciousness. The division of the loaves is the propagation of the knowledge. The bread represents spiritual food for the mind – not food for the body. The bread may be compared to the energy of manna from spirit. Upon completion of his dissertation, they were filled. They had to be, unless His real mission was to give food to the hungry simply to satisfy their digestive systems. Of course, we know that this was not the case. The crowds came to hear Him speak of the nature of spirit. This is confirmed in **Mark 8:12**: *"And he sighed deeply in his spirit, and saith, Why doth this generation seek after a sign? Verily I say unto you, There shall no sign be given unto this generation"*. With His deep spiritual sigh, Jesus' higher self was releasing energy, while the Pharisees were caught up in the physical and wanted proof. They still did not grasp that Spirit needs no proof or justification, and that God did not have to comply with an outer manifestation.

In **Mark 8:15**, leaven is again mentioned. This time, it is the leaven of the Pharisees, Herod's leaven. *"And he charged them, saying, Take heed, beware of the leaven of the Pharisees, and of the leaven of Herod"*. It was a warning that untruth would appear from these two directions. The warning is as valid today as it was then. We still have our Pharisees and our Herods. We must be leery of the teachings that are offered by these control-oriented individuals and organizations because they could and do lead us astray, depending on our own inner beliefs. They simply perpetuate the concepts they were taught as their accepted doctrine. The Master Himself attempted to offer a different understanding in His day, and it was left open to interpretation. Today, this is being done in a variety of ways. These teachings are esoteric in nature, not exoteric in the way they are taught. Metaphors always allow for interpretation. The conclusions should arrive through our inner ability, rather than the logic that has also been given to us. This is why most biblical meaning is so misunderstood and why it does not seem to apply.

Something must be said about **Mark 8:13**: *"And he left them, and entering into the ship again departed to the other side"*. In His travels, Jesus was always, it appears, going to "the other side". However, no one ever explains the location of "the other side". He was often using a ship, a boat, thus we can assume that he was going back and forth across a body of water. With tongue in cheek, we could say that He would have spent more time in a boat than carrying out His works. Metaphysically, it is perceived that it was not a boat at all. It was His own physical being. We must remember that even the Master came on this earth the same way each of us did. Instead, it was His personal journey inside the knowledge He had been taught. It was a time to meditate and work within Spirit itself. Traveling to the other side means that He was going into His higher self for greater knowledge, and it was a period of self-rejuvenation for His spiritual energy. Those were truly moments of travel through spirit. The majority of references to water pertain to the spirit or higher nature. These allusions are showing us the ability we all have, should we determine to apply all aspects of being a spiritual human.

Mark 8:23-26: *"And he took the blind man by the hand, and led him out of the town; and when he had spit on his eyes, and put his hands upon him, he asked him if he saw aught. (24) And he looked up, and said, I see men as trees, walking. (25) After that he put his hands again upon his eyes, and made him look up: and he was restored, and saw every man clearly. (26) And he sent him away to his house, saying, Neither go into the town, nor tell it to any in the town"*. This can be easily interpreted as a man who was not really blind sightwise, but rather blind in his knowledge and understanding of life. In fact, when his sight was restored, he thought the people were trees moving about. It represents his lack of understanding, but with further enhancement, he was able to see the truth. After that additional nudge, he could see clearly, meaning he understood. He saw the truth of being, the light of life that spirit gives us in all things. He had learned acceptance, had become opened to what was being taught. He now saw very plainly as he was told to go into his house – or inner being – for more of the same. He was also told not to go into town. It would create confusion in others, for they would not accept the changes that had taken place in him. When we go to others with inner transformations, they are reluctant to accept, because they only know us for what we were, and not for what we have become. When this happens, it can become confounding for any aspirant. He/she may become tangled in an attempt to prove or explain the circumstances surrounding the changes. How may we prove this? We know that the physical form does not necessarily generate the change. It is the inner mind that will do this. It is not something that will inevitably be seen. It may be noticed over time, as we will handle things differently. If we try to furnish proof, we are liable to go back to the old way as we inadvertently work to link the inner shift to the outer. Patience is now necessary to allow others to be who they are, so that we may be who we know we are.

Mark 8:29-30: *"And he saith unto them, But whom say ye that I am? And Peter answereth and saith unto him, Thou art the Christ. (30) And he charged them that they should tell no man of him"*. From Peter's answer, we see that the disciples already knew that Jesus was the Christ. The Master, in all humility, was not a person who Himself would shout this fact. He taught by example and in fact, He only related directly that He was the son of man – and not God. He is telling His followers not to spread this very subject, implying that the inner effects are more important than what other people think. Indeed, they will think what they wish and if you fight them, their belief – right or wrong – will grow even stronger. The lesson is to allow others to have their own type of thinking and to not change their minds, because they now have what they know or choose to accept, truth or not.

In **Mark 8:33,** we find a remarkable statement: *"....Get thee behind me, Satan: for thou savorest not the things that be of God, but the things that be of men"*. He was talking to the physical egoistic aspect of self and saying He would not serve the interests of man. This is the only reason why He was crucified in the first place, according to the Bible. Jesus is again teaching us about the higher self. He is advising us to get out of our mortal thinking about physical nature, and to stop giving it the seat of honor at our table. He further confirms this in **Mark 8:34**: *"And when he had called the people unto him with his disciples also, he said unto them, Whosoever will come after me, let him deny himself, and take up his cross, and follow me"*. Today, to deny one's self is hard for any of us to do, but to take up our own cross... Heavens, no! Not another burden to bear... Jesus is telling us something quite different from the written words. He advises us that we must assume our own being and our own nature, and blame no one or anything else for what they are. This is judgment by any other name, as we usually do this from the egoistic mental part of ourselves. Being our own nature is actually not that difficult, and once it is done, we simply look at things differently. We are more apt to accept the events in our lives and do not tend to fight them as hard as we do – at times.

Mark 8:35-37: *"For whosoever will save his life shall lose it; but whosoever shall lose his life for my sake and the gospel's, the same shall save it. (36) For what shall it profit a man, if he shall gain the whole world, and lose his own soul? (37) Or what shall a man give in exchange for his soul?"*. We can plainly see the influence of the old Church in the words: "for my sake and the gospel's". During the time of Jesus, the gospels had not been formed yet. Furthermore, the Master had not shouted or proclaimed His divinity at that time because it would have been out of character for Him. The true message was that if you are willing to give yourself up to the Spirit nature within you, all will be given, and nothing more. This also implies that we should turn ourselves over to life for what it may bring us and not fight so much from the mental point of fear. We do this when we allow our minds to overrun us through the power of the ego. This has its basis in what others have done, and we fight and struggle to not have it happen again. Jesus is telling us to resist nothing, for if we do, it may overpower us. Mental acceptance will be the key. This way, we will have fewer burdens to carry. The next aspect is the price of the soul, and none of us consider the cost until it has already been sold, usually into one type of slavery or another. The term "slavery" is not used in the obvious sense, yet we deliver ourselves to it by the levels of obligation we give to other things or other people. How many rest their happiness in other people? If you do, you have become a slave and sold yourself. By then, and normally too late, we realize that it may have been a mistake. If this is not the truth, why are there so many unhappy people on this earth?

In **Mark 9:1**, we see a very interesting concept begin to unfold, and according to the Bible, it is repeated many times by Jesus. *"And he said unto them, Verily I say unto you, That there be some of them that stand here, which shall not taste of death, till they have seen the kingdom of God come with power"*. He says that in that time, we shall overcome death, but we will cover that point later, when it becomes more relevant. The Master is talking about the disciples, the apostles and His own self. He is referring to enlightenment, how to attain appreciation of the natural laws of life and living them. This understanding is to assist us in reducing the influence of external temptations, with which we appear to be showered. It is the power of the mind and its focus on the outer aspects to which we give ourselves.

It includes the control of vibration – found in all things -- and our management of such control, to help us in overcoming even the experience of death. He spoke of this only to a few, because they were receiving His inner direct teachings. Some of this knowledge is still veiled in the parables and cannot be detected because of the way we have been taught to understand. Jesus reminds us that we are promised eternal life. The knowledge He imparts is that we already have it. That magnanimous gift depends on how we use the power of our belief systems and the information in which we choose to believe. This explains the warning about the leaven of the Pharisees and Herod's leaven. Like yeast, it will rise within us, as the expansion of facts within our own belief system. Hence, we are told to be careful of the data being processed by our minds, because it will shorten all things with the weight that we give it. It may become a burden that will bind us into place.

Jesus the Christ was relieving these burdens from people, through the clarity of His very own being. We too can achieve this, providing we are given the correct information and work to understand it, not just in the intellectual sense, but through the experience of it. You can purchase a book such as this and read it in the intellectual sense, yet you may not really experience it except through my eyes – not yours. As an example, we should all read a work such as the Bible – or any work that is in print – and find out for ourselves. Is this not what we do with mathematics? We study it, then we have to test its applications to see what we have learned. Why could not the same principles apply to this book or the Bible? Jesus is telling us that the intellect will not give us the actual understanding we seek. This comprehension is to lift us above all things – including death – because that moment will depend upon our inner preparation and our knowledge. This is verified in the very next three verses (**Mark 9:2-4**), wherein we witness the appearance of Moses and Elijah, standing next to Jesus. They came into view from nowhere and returned in the same manner.

Let us now discuss **Mark 9:22-23**: *"And ofttimes it hath cast him into the fire, and into the waters, to destroy him: but if thou canst do any thing, have compassion on us, and help us. (23) Jesus said unto him, If thou canst believe, all things are possible to him that believeth"*. It is apparent that the Master is talking about our beliefs, the contents of those beliefs and how we practice them. It implies that within us, we may have beliefs that are very flawed, and our lives are trying to show us the error in our thinking. Our experiences are our guideposts.

Jesus is learning of the experiences of a mute boy, such as the fits he would have, being thrown in the fire and then the water. This depicts the boy's confusion and his inability to express its nature. It also means a shift from the higher and lower aspects of being – material to spiritual. It is indeed bound to create confusion. Because of that confusion, he did not know what to believe, and the Master's message was quite appropriate: "If thou canst believe, all things are possible to him that believeth". The point of the lesson is that we are capable of doing all things, providing we have belief, and that belief must be our own – not that suggested by another. We must believe in our union with Spirit, because it is the wholeness of our being – I AM. We must resist the temptation to separate it from the physical or treat it as a detached entity. **Mark 9:24**: *"And straightway the father of the child cried out, and said with tears, Lord, I believe; help thou my unbelief"*. This was a plea to assist his understanding, that he too may have the knowledge. Even though his statement was very hollow in its nature, he sought to be fulfilled. Is it not what we all seek? We also detect the influence of the ego. When His disciples were trying to figure among them who was the greatest, the Master told them about the innocence of our nature and not the arrogance of it. He taught them that through the innocence of the mind, our nature would allow for the assistance of Spirit in their lives. Innocence in this sense is not naivete. It is about not having the mind so burdened, so cluttered, that we are unable to see and think clearly. It means that we would not be able to understand if our ego were too involved. When ego is extensively involved, it will produce a hard resistance within us and create confusion. This subject is further revealed in **Mark 10:15**: *"Verily I say unto you, Whosoever shall not receive the kingdom of God as a little child, he shall not enter therein"*. Here, we are seeing acceptance, along with the innocence we discussed above. Children generally approach a new thing timidly, or in humility. The Master's words imply that we must approach all new levels of understanding in the same manner. If we do not, turmoil will ensue. A new way of thinking will saturate all aspects in a person, and if it is to stay new, old things must be shed. It is this very shedding that makes the transformation difficult, simply because we resist the new form of thought – a new form that is impacting the actual belief system of our own self. Jesus tells us to be kind and gentle as these changes take place within us.

Mark 10:21-26: *"Then Jesus beholding him loved him, and said unto him, One thing thou lackest: go thy way, sell whatsoever thou hast, and give to the poor, and thou shalt have treasure in heaven; and come, take up the cross, and follow me. (22) And he was sad at that saying, and went away grieved: for he had great possessions. (23) And Jesus looked round about, and saith unto his disciples, How hardly shall they that have riches enter into the kingdom of God! (24) And the disciples were astonished at his words. But Jesus answereth again, and saith unto them, Children, how hard is it for them that trust in riches to enter into the kingdom of God! (25) It is easier for a camel to go through the eye of a needle, than for a rich man to enter into the kingdom of God. (26) And they were astonished out of measure, saying among themselves, Who then can be saved?"*. If we were to interpret this in a literal sense, none of us would be able to enter, since He is talking about wealth. We must examine this by merely asking ourselves where we direct our focus. Obviously, we seem to emphasize the material side of life. Jesus is very specific, and He is saying that we must be willing to give up all physical possessions. We do not have to "give them up", but should be "willing" to do so. His point is that, in our lives, we must have nothing more important than our own being. If we have something more important to us than our own being, we will not be able to be fully free to be ourselves in our day-to-day activities. In fact, if we are owned by something outside our own selves, we cannot be free. We see this confirmed in Verse 22, in the young man who was owned by the many possessions he had purchased.

Further advice is given in **Mark 10:27**, as a balance between spirit and the human: *"And Jesus looking upon them saith, With men it is impossible, but not with God: for with God all things are possible"*. He is telling us that physical nature alone is not enough. We must also allow for the influence of our inner spiritual nature, because we are not able to do things without the power of spirit. If we balance it all properly, we may achieve all things. Elsewhere in the Bible, we are told that if we have enough faith, we can even move mountains, but in Verse 27, Jesus tells us: "With men it is impossible". This is true in the context that we must allow for the influence of the spirit to complete all tasks. Indeed, if we allow spirit to go before us, as the Ark of the Covenant, we may accomplish all things, with much less effort being required by our physical nature, and with less stress. This notion is repeated after each of His discussions on the higher realms.

On the concept of things being impossible, we see in **Mark 11:23-25** very specific instructions on achieving what people want in their lives: *"For verily I say unto you, That whosoever shall say unto this mountain, Be thou removed, and be thou cast into the sea; and shall not doubt in his heart, but shall believe that those things which he saith shall come to pass; he shall have whatsoever he saith. (24) Therefore I say unto you, What things soever ye desire, when ye pray, believe that ye receive them, and ye shall have them. (25) And when ye stand praying, forgive, if ye have aught against any: that your Father also which is in heaven may forgive you your trespasses"*. We are told here that we may command anything and it will be given. "Command" is used due to the graphic picture that He gives us: to cast the mountain. This should not be misconstrued with "demand". Demanding is a desire to control others and this is not the intent. The intent is to command through confident presence of being, not arrogance of being. Groveling will not work. We must be firm and know that it is done. The reason we cannot do this very easily is exemplified in Verse 25, wherein we cannot hold ill will against another. Spirit implies that we must be single in purpose at that moment. The earthly issue with another will create a distraction and burden our minds, therefore not giving us the full capability to work in union with spirit – and dividing our house.

In **Mark 10:46-52**, we have the story of a blind man named Bartimaeus, whose sight is restored by the Master. After he regained his sight, Jesus tells him to go on his way, but the man begins to follow Him down the road. Metaphysically, Jesus helped the man understand, thus he was no longer blind. This occurs many times in the New Testament, because it was His mission: to impart knowledge in the minds of the people, to get them to change their thinking. In other words, He helped the blind to see or, in most cases, He assisted them in their understanding. Sight can then be associated with mind, clarity of mind and our thinking processes.

We now move to **Mark 11:15**: *"And they come to Jerusalem: and Jesus went into the temple, and began to cast out them that sold and bought in the temple, and overthrew the tables of the moneychangers, and the seats of them that sold doves;"*. Why would such a man of peace do this, especially since He told us that when our enemy strikes us on one cheek, we should offer the other. This same individual is now bodily throwing the vendors out of the temple. This great Teacher is actually showing us that we must remove the thought of greed from within us. To do this, we must shift our thinking of self and become more selfless. The temple represents the human being itself, the flesh, the physical housing of the soul. Jesus was casting out His very own greed, and as we have all found out, it is not an easy chore to accomplish. Casting the vendors out is again merely creating a shift in our self-perception, realizing what is important to us and bringing it all into alignment.

It is not until we reach Chapter 12 that we encounter a parable (**Mark 12:1-9**). It is the story of a man who planted a vineyard. The theme of this tale is to be fruitful. In the process, however, we must watch over the crop that we produce or, in other words, we must take responsibility for all the actions brought about by the activity of the mind – our thoughts. By the same token, we must pay attention to our greedy nature and not let it overpower and blind us with the fruits of life. Jesus is telling us that our own thinking will expand, and from very creative beginnings will come all sorts of self-deceptions from within which could kill the creative aspect of self. These processes give us the knowledge to finish the idea that we have generated. Since we request so much of spirit anyway, they are tests of self, to see if it really is what we desire to have in our life at that moment. We will discuss these tests in depth in the chapter reserved for the Book of Revelations and in Part II. We can consider them as points of resistance to the very thing we want to occur in our life. They are our fears of failure, fears that can indeed negate or cancel the initial idea. We become unsure and frozen in our actions toward accomplishment.

We now come to **Mark 12:18-28**, in which the Sadducees discuss the life and death of a woman and seven brothers with the Master. This very interesting dissertation effectively covers reincarnation, a subject that has peaked the public's curiosity for the last few decades. Contrary to popular belief, death is not as we know it to be. Jesus tells us that we have eternal life, and that translates into the continuation of the individual. You will note that the number "seven" resurfaces. As He learned while in India, it represents the seven energy centers of the body, the number needed to attain fulfillment of the inner nature, and as Genesis mentions, the number of days it took for Creation. We must unify our physical, mental and emotional centers to have the full understanding of our nature. When we are successful, we may bring about the spiritual aspect of the physical self. Verses 26 and 27 verify this concept: *"And as touching the dead, that they rise: have ye not read in the book of Moses, how in the bush God spake unto him, saying, I am the God of Abraham, and the God of Isaac, and the God of Jacob? (27) He is not the God of the dead, but the God of the living: ye therefore do greatly err"*. In effect, Jesus is telling us that we do not die. God would not allow it because we are created in Its image, thus no one passes away as we understand it. "And as touching the dead, that they rise": did Jesus Himself not do this? We have read about Lazarus and many others in the Bible, hence we must conclude that this applies to the least among us as well as the greatest. No one is above the metaphysical laws of the universe, not even the spirit that brought forth the laws of being. It will take all that we have and all that we are, and we must be willing to give all we have to attain this understanding. We do not ever really give all we have to life, yet it is the only requirement. We wonder why it does not give to us, and the answer is that we ourselves hold back. After all, should we give everything we have, others will take advantage of us and we will have nothing left. This is conditioning from the experiences of our past. Those memories hold us in place, and nothing more.

This concept is well depicted in **Mark 12:41-44,** where we see the rich people cast only a small portion of their worth into the church treasury. In contrast, we see the poor widow give her two "mites" – all she had, and for which she certainly was derided. What the rich did is what we all do, and it is not enough. Whose standards are we using, anyway? The rich give as if it was all they had, showing concern that they may not have enough afterward. Allegorically, there is only one way to realize this, and that is by giving all we have, then will we know within ourselves. On the other hand, we have no right to condemn anyone according to our own personal standards, still it is what we do. To explain this, we will go back to **Mark 12:30-31**: *"And thou shalt love the Lord thy God with all thy heart, and with all thy soul, and with all thy mind, and with all thy strength: this is the first commandment. (31) And the second is like, namely this, Thou shalt love thy neighbour as thyself. There is none other commandment greater than these"*. We are to see the spirit in our neighbors and consider it as we deal with them. If we condemn them, we in turn condemn ourselves in the process. It has been said that whatever you do will be returned to you tenfold. Deductively, if we condemn our neighbors, they too will condemn us in a resounding fashion – and so it will go on... This is not sound thinking, because we are all equal in the eyes of God, with the same ability and capabilities as anyone else. Spiritually, we are not better or worse than our neighbor. Only the physical actions generated by our inner nature will tell the difference.

Then, we have **Mark 13:14**: *"But when ye shall see the abomination of desolation, spoken of by Daniel the prophet, standing where it ought not, (let him that readeth understand), then let them that be in Judea flee to the mountains"*. Jesus is telling us that nothing is an abomination, and nothing deserves this and that. If we do, we should leave the area. The desolation is in the mind and what we do with it. Life could be so beautiful if only we did not allow our mind to do what it does. And what it does for most of us is run amuck, doing whatever it wishes. It seems that it is used for destructive purposes. Remember that we have the choice between good and bad as our personal experience, using focus of the mind. Whether we obtain desolation or fulfillment through our choice does not matter to God. It gave us that right. We chose. Spirit did not and it gives what we seek.

We have further confirmation of life after death in **Mark 14:25**: *"Verily I say unto you, I will drink no more of the fruit of the vine, until that day that I drink it new in the kingdom of God"*. This definitely refers to life after death. He bore good fruits. He brought Himself to fruition. Each of us is a fruit of the vine. We must ask ourselves: "What is my vine producing?". If it is vinegar, we simply must change our mind and gain a new outlook. This outlook defines how we see or understand things, and it can be either a help or a hindrance, depending on how we gauge our own circumstances.

I will not go through the aspect of Jesus pleading for His life – which ended with "Thy will be done". The Master gave in to the events that had been set in motion by Spirit, and He knew that it could not be changed. If one is to be a demonstration, then the event must be completed to the bitter end. This is true faith in life and spirit. At the same time, I am fascinated with the story told in **Mark 14:50-52**: *"And they all forsook him, and fled. (51) And there fol-*

lowed him a certain young man, having a linen cloth cast about his naked body; and the young man laid hold on him: (52) And he left the linen cloth, and fled from them naked". This appears only in the book of Mark. It is not found in the other gospels. What does it mean? Could they have grabbed the wrong man? It could be symbolism for the truth being exposed to all. The linen cloth is the representation of the pureness of the outer being. The young man's nakedness or exposing thereof was the true nature of spirit coming forth from the clarity of self.

In Chapter 15, after the Master had been taken into custody, we see the real reason He was not only arrested but crucified. It was jealousy, because He had more influence than the chief priests – which is not surprising. The chief priests are illustrations of what greed may do to a person, along with the need to be in physical control. This need really stems from a position of insecurity, and indeed, they were insecure. If they were in total control, all things bent in their direction, but the appearance of an outside influence demanding changes for the better brought them the possibility to lose that control. And in turn, that brought on fear. How many of us have experienced these syndromes? Fear is there simply because not all the information is known, and we must deal with the dreaded unknown.

In **Mark 15:21,** we learn that Jesus did not carry His own cross: *"And they compel one Simon, a Cyrenian, who passed by, coming out of the country, the father of Alexander and Rufus, to bear his cross"*. In the end, after the Master had carried everyone else's burden or relieved them of it, He had the same done for Him. It is further evidence of the unrelenting metaphysical laws of cause and effect. It was now His turn to be relieved of the burdens, because of the envy and jealousy of His ability. The true meaning of the crucifixion is that we must be willing to do this ourselves, in the thinking sense of self, to overcome the ego nature of the physical aspects of life.

Within each of us, we have the concept of Adam and Eve. They are the left and the right side of the brain. Logic and creativity, thought and feel are simple concepts in action. The left is used to assist us in the aspect of the physical that we call life. The right side is the emotional and creative side of our being, helping us to engage with spirit. The left is the first two books of the Gospels, and the next two are about the right side of the brain. We are to not deny either side, and we are to use both aspects in a balanced nature, working in union with one another. At this moment in time, the left is the focus point for all of us, and it is in the process of a higher evolvement. We see this through the struggles of everyday life, and how we interact with the external nature. We will next begin to explore the more esoteric side of living. We will cover first the emotional and then the spiritual nature of the full self-interacting with the spirit.

We have talked about the obvious sides to life. We will now begin the journey into the more subtle aspects of emotion and spirit, through the last two Gospels, the Books of Luke and John. They will carry us further down the path of life, and on toward becoming spiritually enlightened human beings working in a closer union with each other.

CHAPTER 6

THE BOOK OF LUKE

"All emotions are pure which gather you and lift you up; that emotion is impure which seizes only one *side of your being and so distorts you".*
Rainer Maria Rilke, Letters to a Young Poet, 1904

We now enter into the more delicate nature of being human, and it will become more subtle as we progress. We will be showing the emotional body of the person through the text of Luke's gospel. The reason for the emotional side is expressed by the number of references to the heart, and you will find much more passion in Luke's writing than in the other Gospels. The books of Luke and John are the sum of the most exciting aspects of life, the sensate system – or the sense modality - where we supposedly gain wisdom from our greatest allies and teachers of the external world. These allies are our emotional and spiritual states. Of course, they can also be our opponents. This may happen if they collide with the physical thinking part of us. If these two are not aligned, in a positive mode, they will give total power to the fear thoughts that may arise, thus negativity. This is the reason the Master told us to settle our issues with our brother before coming onto Spirit. If we do not, we may suffer adverse effects. It is a result of how we prioritize our power. As you recall, we have mentioned that too often, we give our true power to other external issues. The gain is proportional to its proper use and its faithful application. Most of us tend to do this. This particular chapter will deal with what happens if we do not address our emotional self, how we then interact with life, and what becomes of simple things if we truly recognize our feelings as our experience. We will now discuss Luke's valuable insight in the subtle aspects of our nature.

Luke 1:1-2: *"For as much as many have taken in hand to set forth in order a declaration of those things which are most surely believed among us, (2) Even as they delivered them unto us, which from the beginning were eyewitnesses, and ministers of the word;".* As you will determine for yourself, Luke is a very sensitive man and as mentioned before, he never walked with the Master. In his use of the "WORD", he seems to be filled with admiration for the people who had received the inner teachings. The use of "The Word" is often encountered in modern Christianity. It would be appropriate to share one of its best definitions through the innovative thinking of Charles Fillmore, the founder of the Unity Church. As he said, Truth is ever changeless, and may I add,

Truth stands unto itself. Truth is the only thing that remains changeless. It needs no improvement at all. We will share with you the most relevant opening of Mr. Fillmore's definition of the "Word", and it shall surpass the test of time:

> *"John gives us the following concerning the Word of God: 'In the beginning was the Word, and the Word was with God, and the Word was God.' The Word of God is the divine Logos, God in His capacity as creative power, and includes all the potentialities of Being. It is the idea of God, the image and likeness of God, spiritual man. In it are all the possibilities, all the qualities, of God.*
> *"Being, the original fount, is an impersonal principle; but in its work of creation it puts forth an idea that contains all ideas: the Logos, Word, Christ, the Son of God, or spiritual man. This spiritual man or Christ, the Word of God, is the true inner self of every individual. Man therefore contains within himself the capacities of Being, and through his words uses the creative principle of Divine Mind to create".* We do create through what we think, and we develop the power behind it by what we feel. It is a matter of the choice we tend to give any subject. No importance is given to whether it is positive or negative. To Spirit, all is creativity. It must be stated that both the positive and negative aspects are alive and well in life... We allow our mind to control – or at least influence – what we feel, based on what we believe we know. Judgment of others will heavily influence what we feel about them and our own being.

Our word is our form of creation. It is our thoughts, externalized. Our thoughts are the inner words destined for creation in the outer realm once they are expressed or released. What we feel toward or about something, no matter what it may be, is one of the strongest influencing factors in our life. This feeling has the greater effect on us, while the Word expresses what we sense about it. It encompasses our hurts, our desires, our dreams, the things that will make us secure or insecure in our lives. It ultimately expresses the inner truth of self that, in turn, reflects the inner feelings of separation that we all experience. We must learn to express the truth – and not just ours. If we learn to do this, we have no separation from life, spirit or people. Instead, we have the union that we seek. Separation occurs only if we limit things to self-truth. We are a mass consciousness, and in a way, we feel what others feel. This has not been fully realized yet.

In **Luke 1:6**, Luke tells us of Zacharias and his wife Elizabeth: *"And they were both righteous before God, walking in all the commandments and ordinances of the Lord blameless".* This is about properly using the knowledge of spirit and obeying the natural law of life – and nothing more. These two biblical personages had great faith and belief in the more refined aspects of life and practiced them. Because of the depth and purity of their spirit, they were rewarded by becoming the parents of John the Baptist, even if they were advanced in age. In Luke's first chapter, he discusses the birth of John and that of a quite different being named Jesus. We see the appreciation of the coming of the Master when Mary visited Elizabeth, as the latter exclaimed: *"For, lo, as soon as the voice of thy salutation sounded in mine ears, the babe leaped in my womb for joy"* (Luke 1:44). This is the first indication of emotion in the book of Luke, as love is indeed the greatest expression of emotion from a human. John could already feel the presence of the Teacher, and he communicated it with a burst of love and the excitement of life. Notice also that there is no mention of the Magi in this particular Book. Again, we see the differences in the approach and introduction of each Book in the Gospels.

It is apparent that all who wrote the texts were not present at this singular event and each is presenting the story within the scope of his own being, from what he had been taught. The first chapter also gives us Jesus' lineage and it must apply to John as well, since they were related. We will explore this further in the book of John. The statement that we find in **Luke 1:80** can be relevant to both Jesus and John: *"And the child grew, and waxed strong in spirit, and was in the deserts till the day of his shewing unto Israel"*. The only difference between the two is that the Master did not live in the desert, but they both began to grow in spirit, and that is the main point. They were being taught to understand the deeper nature of our existence. Not much else is being said about John until we reach the Book of John, and even therein, little is revealed about the harbinger of things to come. This is an interesting aspect, since he played a major part in the roles they were to carry out. This may never be known. However, when you read the next chapter, you will discover many things. It may include the reason why this has been kept from us, and you may learn about the conditioning we have been taught to accept as the truth.

At the birth of the Master, we find that the only people who came were the shepherds of the field. A point of interest is the reference to night (Luke 2:8). Watching a flock by night was done only in the summer – not in the winter. This indicates that the Master was not born on the day we all celebrate. The mention of flocks, sheep and the night watch can also be interpreted as a reference to men of wisdom – masters of the day – similar in nature to the wise men themselves, men who had the ability to control their thoughts and keep them focused.

In **Luke 2:25-35**, we see mention, for the first time, of a man named Simeon. This person is obviously a mystic of some sort according to the description that is being offered to us. He was *"waiting for the consolation of Israel" and "the Holy Ghost was upon him"*. It also tells us that if a person reaches a certain depth of feelings, all may work with it. It must be within the parameters of true feelings, rather than the deceptive ones stemming from past experience. The story tells us that he entered the Temple in Spirit and spoke of Jesus to Mary and Joseph who were amazed, seemingly unaware of the importance of their Son. From all indications, Simeon was a prophet of Israel at the time. He blessed them and left them a parting message found in **Luke 2:34-35**: *"Behold, this child is set for the fall and rising again of many in Israel; and for a sign which shall be spoken against; (35) (Yea, a sword shall pierce through thy own soul also,) that the thoughts of many hearts may be revealed"*.

This is the proper time to introduce to you the concept of Israel, and it does not necessarily apply only to the Jewish people or nation. It does imply a "chosen people", but then, why would God choose one race over another? My own perception says that God would not. It created us all equally, did It not? In Revelations, it specifically states that there will be many races and colors. Hence, one could state that all people have the right and the opportunity to spiritual life, based on the individual nature and not the geographical location of one's birth.

Verse 35 contains the greatest point. The word is "sword", or the word that emanates from us. It is what we say to each other about the way we think, the way we feel or "not" the way we feel – and there is a subtle difference. If one has to think about what is being felt, it is a matter of the mind and not the heart. The heart is what generates the feeling and communicates it to the mind – or the right side of the brain. A true feeling rests in the center of the being – not in the head – and it needs no thought. The next sentence is not meant to generate a gender conflict, but ask any feminine aspects, and they can express exactly what they feel.

The last quotation in Verse 35 tells us that "the thoughts of many hearts may be revealed". It depicts the expression of the heart and not the thoughts therein. We know that the heart itself does not think, and that only the mind is capable of thoughts. Thus, it is about what is truly within the heart and cannot be hidden. Today, we see this gradually taking place. We will know the true person and what is contained within his/her heart. It will no longer be hidden from other eyes. In this present era, we are beginning to express what is truly within us, and it is documented by the worldwide disruptions reported everyday. If individual expressions are not exactly in truth, we will be able to gauge those particular personalities, without placing any form of judgment upon them. By simple observation, we will know that there will be deception attempted from within, engendered by ulterior motives. Again, all we have to do is observe and not judge. The heart can only expose the truth of what the person already is.

In none of the Gospels do we see any mention of Jesus' childhood years or what He was doing. We do know that at the age of twelve, He was in the temple after being missed for a period of three days (another reference to the number three). It happened when His parents noticed that He was not in the caravan that was headed back to their home. We see no mention of their first journey to Egypt after His birth. For all intents and purposes, the Bible merely reflects that Jesus was around Israel until his early teen years. In fact, His first biblically recorded statement was made when He was about twelve years old, during the temple event mentioned above. It bears its own uniqueness found in **Luke 2:49**, as He answered His parents' inquiry: *"And he said unto them, How is it that ye sought me? wist ye not that I must be about my Father's business?"*. Jesus was stating that He was learning the philosophies of spirit, and that He was driven by the urges of His inner nature rather than the physical. Both statements were questions – not answers. It means that He had been questioning and learning. It was a reminder of the Magi's words as to what He had to do, for His works. Not another word is written about Jesus, until He suddenly reappears, at about age thirty, in **Luke 3:23**: *"And Jesus himself began to be about thirty years of age, being (as was supposed) the son of Joseph, which was the son of Heli, etc…"*.

In **Luke 4:4**, Jesus is confronted by His own ego, and his reply is: *"It is written, That man shall not live by bread alone…"* In this context, bread is about the spiritual manna, or our finer nature, that must be combined with the physical aspect in order to work in harmony. We see the law of opposition in physical motion. A little further, we read in **Luke 4:14**: *"And Jesus returned in the power of the Spirit into Galilee: and there went out a fame of him through all the region round about"*. "In the power of the Spirit"! He had unified the physical and spiritual natures into one, no longer experiencing that adverse division – one that we seem to sense about ourselves. He had subdued the emotional egoistic aspects of self. He now fully understood His real nature and the union which was His.

In **Luke 4:16**, we encounter a minor conflict. Luke says that Jesus returned to Nazareth where He had been brought up. However, in the book of Matthew, we saw that the majority of His younger years were spent in Egypt, after which the family returned to Nazareth. In Luke, it appears that He is teaching the Jewish law. He read from Isaiah about the manifestation of our inner emotions, so that we will not become heavy in our nature. He read that through the expression of the truth, we would be released of our burdens rather than be encumbered by them. These appear to be what we perceive others have done to us, and how we feel about it. We see this in **Luke 4:18**: *"The Spirit of the Lord is upon me, because he hath anointed me to preach the gospel to the poor; he hath sent me to heal the brokenhearted, to preach deliverance to the captives, and recovering of sight to the blind, to set at liberty them that are bruised".* In this sense, the "poor" is not poor financially. Poverty in this case is to be burdened by life. The "captives" are the unreleased hurts, the unexpressed feelings toward an outer event that has affected us in some way. To heal the blind is to allow us to see through the fog we have placed before us. To free the downtrodden is to let go of the past. When we are in the present, the past is the only thing that affects our thoughts and feelings. These burdens are assisted by our outer nature in the selection of memories, as opposed to the lessons to be learned, and we find ourselves bound by them. In **Luke 4:21**, Jesus even says that this is fulfilled. The Knowledge has come to us, but only if we have learned to release or to express those past memories and what they did to our inner nature.

  Luke 4:27: *"And many lepers were in Israel in the time of Eliseus the prophet; and none of them was cleansed, saving Naaman the Syrian".* That to which we hold on is unclean in nature. It is the lesson in this verse, wherein all were unclean except a man from Syria. This implies that not many will heed the message, or that most will not pay attention to what the emotions are trying to tell them as a reflection of self. It eats at their inner nature and erodes the level of innocence we are to maintain within our own being. It brought about the allegory of the lepers, of things being eaten away, of parts of ourselves being left behind. Exposing these truths undoubtedly triggered the rebellion we see in **Luke 4:29-30**: *"And rose up, and thrust him out of the city, and led him unto the brow of the hill whereon their city was built, that they might cast him down headlong. (30) But he passing through the midst of them went his way".* Taking a deeper look into these events, we see that rejection obviously took place. In the book of Mark, we see a similar reference in letting one's "light shine as a city on the hill", as Jesus was talking about the expression of self and the fact that no one is better than anyone else. His "passing through them" signified that they understood His meaning. They had built the framework of their own being on a foundation lacking the understanding of the true nature of life, and falseness was the physical façade.

  In **Luke 4:33-34**, we find Jesus entering a synagogue wherein there is a man with an unclean spirit, and who says to Him: *"...art thou come to destroy us?".* Apparently, that man was aware of his inner status, thus he understood the presence of the Master. However, there was a resistance to the acceptance of the knowledge of Truth. We all seem to automatically resist anything that is new, even though we seek change – and change is difficult, particularly in the arena of our own emotions. We are too protective of them, and in the process, we limit our experience. We do not allow for new feedback to move us forward. Since its inception, is not forward movement what life is? Yet, emotionally and spiritually, we bind ourselves in our beliefs – beliefs created out of the past.

In **Luke 5:5-6,** we read: *"And Simon answering said unto him, Master, we have toiled all the night, and have taken nothing: nevertheless at thy word I will let down the net. (6) And when they had this done, they enclosed a great multitude of fishes: and their net brake".* The expansion of ideas and growth was in the process of taking place. Until the Teacher arrived, there was none, yet when they went out with Him, the net became so filled that it broke. The symbol of this story lies in spiritual concepts being born, with an abundance of new ideas and thoughts. Further, in **Luke 5:7-8**, we hear Simon Peter cry out: *"Depart from me; for I am a sinful man, O Lord".* He had suddenly realized that he, a man filled with erroneous thinking and feelings about life, had been given new ideas. As a result, it had him take another look at his self-worth and downplay it. Realization is not a bad thing, but the acceptance of it may be, especially if we are filled with regrets about it. It does not have to be that way. We should merely accept it for what it is and absorb it as knowledge of self – and that is good. We all have the opportunity to accept, rather than deny. He knew in that moment that we are all greater than we "choose to believe". He had recognized the error of his thinking because of the new concepts given by the Master. He had accepted them.

Jesus had more to say in the book of Luke than in any other text, and most of it is about the heart, what we feel about things in life. In **Luke 5:10-11**, we read: *"And so was also James, and John, the sons of Zebedee, which were partners with Simon. And Jesus said unto Simon, Fear not; from henceforth thou shall catch men. (11) And when they had brought their ships to land, they forsook all, and followed him".* This allegory represents the fermenting of new ideas and the subsequent surrendering of the physical things in life. They left everything they had behind, the old hurts, the memories, therefore gaining a new level of understanding what was going on within them. We notice also that the types of healing shifted from the deaf and the blind to those suffering from leprosy, being consumed by the dilemmas of the physical life. This is in addition, of course, with the healings accomplished among the multitudes. In **Luke 5:17-19**, the metaphor being offered is actually an introduction to the understanding of emotions: *"And it came to pass on a certain day, as he was teaching, that there were Pharisees and doctors of the law sitting by, which* *were come out of every town of Galilee and Judea, and Jerusalem: and the power of the Lord was present to heal them. (18) And, behold, men brought in a bed a man which was taken with a palsy: and they sought means to bring him in, and to lay him before him. (19) And when they could not find by what way they might bring him in because of the multitude, they went upon the housetop, and let him down through the tiling with his couch in the midst before Jesus".* This implies that there was great understanding, as the energy of spirit was flowing richly among them, but there was also a certain mistrust of the new knowledge. Jesus was speaking to the people, and there were many queries from the Pharisees about what He was doing. He knew what was in their hearts and told them: *"What reason ye in your hearts?"* (Luke 5:22). They were checking their own feelings about what His actions were that day, as He was helping those wanting to learn from a higher understanding, while challenging their belief system. In this allegory, Jesus is telling us that we have greater control than we think we have. He is explaining to us that a human controls, directs, teaches and disciplines the faculties of the Self to create an inner singular nature.

The term "Pharisee" appears many times in the Bible. Perhaps we can once more borrow a definition from the "Metaphysical Bible Dictionary" in order to clarify its true meaning: *"The Pharisees (Matthew 12:24) were the religiously educated of Jesus' day, and to their minds all who claimed to do the works of the Lord were spurious unless they were members of the Pharisee cult. No matter how good the work of the outsider, the Pharisee always attributed it to an evil power. In individual consciousness, Pharisees represent thoughts that arise out of the subconsciousness, binding man to external forms of religion without giving him understanding of their real meaning (John 3:1)".* While we are in a teaching mode, we should look at the word "boat", since the Master often used this type of transportation. In the same cited reference, it is defined as follows: *"A positive thought – a conveyance that is able to float upon the water (the unstable mind), and to bear up the disciples (the faculties of mind). The multitudes are the numberless thoughts that are seeking light, strength, and healing".* These two concepts from the Unity School of Christianity are very sound from a metaphysical viewpoint. Using these two interpretations alone puts a new perspective in the conversations that ensue within one's own nature of mind. If you were to read the Bible with just these two notions, you would receive new levels of understanding within yourself on what you really feel about the outer world.

In **Luke 5:27**, we perceive Matthew's presentation of the physical nature in the scriptures, personified by Levi the tax gatherer. It raises questions about the nature of the human, as pictured by the number and type of people reclining at Levi's table (**Luke 5:27-32**). The subject leads to what is important and how to rectify an error, as the Master says: *"They that are whole need not a physician; but they that are sick. I came not to call the righteous, but sinners to repentance"*. This is about learning the focus of self and to introduce control within the being. Those who had attained these qualities were not the reason for His presence. He was there to give understanding to those that did not – or do not – know the true nature of the human. In the subsequent verses, we learn of a wedding. Symbolically, the Master is discussing a merger of the higher and lower natures of Self in the person of the bridegroom. Fasting is a reference to the control of the mind, no longer allowing it to wander aimlessly through life, without thoughts or at least with a reduction of the prolific thinking process. It also represents the union of the mind and the emotions with clarity, or forgiving the past and letting it go. It is the healing of the emotional wounds we receive along the way.

In the book of Matthew, we find many parables. In the book of Mark, we find only one. In Luke, we again find many. This seems to indicate that the majority of life is occupied by the physical and emotional natures, prevailing over the mental and spiritual aspects. Our mental side prevails because the mind will understand its own nature, while spirit already does. The physical and emotional are the feedback for our thinking and our relationship to life and the events thereof. If we use them, they may actually be our guideposts. Of course, should we attempt to ignore the emotional events that occur within us, we may be in for further lessons. We will undoubtedly mask the pain and in the process, we will disregard the truth and pretend we understand whence the previous emotional anguish came. We will then continue the way we have in the past, faced with a greater upheaval than before. The true nature of life is a feedback to create a sturdy strength within our emotions. If we use them as a positive teacher, our ability to love will grow in value and power. They become the mechanisms we use for the attainment of wisdom and understanding.

We see a deeper elucidation of this concept in **Luke 5:36-39**: *"And he spake also a parable unto them; No man putteth a piece of a new garment upon an old; if otherwise, then both the new maketh a rent, and the piece that was taken out of the new agreeth not with the old. (37) And no man putteth new wine into old wineskins; else the new wine will burst the wineskins, and be spilled, and the wineskins shall perish. (38) But new wine must be put into new wineskins; and both are preserved. (39) No man also having drunk old wine straightway desireth new: for he saith, The old is better"*. Jesus is discussing new ideas and emotions, and the fact that we will not allow for the new concepts, since in our minds, the old is good enough. We feel more comfortable with the old because we have lived with this notion all along. The old has proved itself to us – so we think... In truth, it has proven that life is difficult the way we are living it today. Anytime we attempt to insert new ideas into the old, there always will be a conflict, simply because the old never agrees with the new. If we try to patch the old and the new, that too cannot work. We must learn to live in the moment of events – not after the fact. Remember that the moment you live is the only reality that you may have. If you are thinking of yesterday, you are obviously not in the present, to see what it may give you. If you have a new idea or a thought process working within you, find out where it leads and decide nothing until you see a distinct path. Study and accept the new, while ridding yourself of the old, but do not mix the two. By the same token, you should always greet the new with humility rather than aggression, for you do not know what gifts it may bring you.

In both **Luke 5:13 and 6:10**, we find a wonderful symbol in the stretching out of the hand. It clearly implies that we are here to assist each other in the way we feel. Instead, we pull away because we do not wish to be burdened by another's weight or to be hurt again by another. It tells us that we are to reach out and help one another. Today, many good things are being done, yet they are but a very small percentage of what could be done on an individual basis. Another interesting excerpt is found in **Luke 6:13-16**: *"And when it was day, he called unto him his disciples: and of them he chose twelve, whom also he named apostles...."* It shows that, at that point, the Master separated the multitude into categories: the **Apostles**, or teacher assistants, the **disciples**, and the **multitudes**. It redefines the differences in knowledge and thoughts or thought types. Please note that Luke is not among those named in verses 14 through 16, yet his work was chosen and included biblically as a main gospel. In verse 17, *"he came down with them, and stood in the plain"*, a level place, where He, the disciples and the multitude were all equal, and all came to learn of the inner knowledge. Not only had they come to learn, but they also wanted to be healed of their unclean spirits, as we see in **Luke 6:18-19**: *"And the whole multitude sought to touch him: for there went virtue out of him..."*. Many people were gaining insight into their own understanding, and it was expanded by the Master as He was imparting His infinite wisdom to those who came to hear. Turning His gaze on the disciples, He offered a deeper journey into the emotional realm, how we will receive an onslaught of judgment from others concerning our own feelings, and what people will do to us for our beliefs.

It is expressed in **Luke 6:20-22**: *"And he lifted up his eyes on his disciples, and said, Blessed be ye poor: for yours is the kingdom of God. (21) Blessed are ye that hunger now: for ye shall be filled. Blessed are ye that weep now: for ye shall laugh. (22) Blessed are ye, when men shall hate you, and* *when they shall separate you from their company, and shall reproach you, and cast out your name as evil, for the Son of man's sake"*. This sensible statement is conducive to forgiveness, and it allows us to let others think of us what they wish. After all, it is their thinking – not ours. Conversely, we seem to spend too much time trying to convince others that we are not like they think we are. Whatever they think is their own perception, and we are to let them keep it, simply because it belongs to them – not to you or me. Jesus is also suggesting that we have gained the experience and will be better off for it, because of what we have learned. This induces growth, and we will find satisfaction within our own nature. No one can tear that down, even though they may and will try. It can be said that at times, we work on pulling everyone else down to our level, no matter what it may be. We should lift people, not pull them down. Go to their excitement, and do not bring them to your depression.

Luke 6:23-26: *"Rejoice ye in that day, and leap for joy: for, behold, your reward is great in heaven: for in the like manner did their fathers unto the prophets. (24) But woe unto you that are rich! for ye have received your consolation. (25) Woe unto you that are full! for ye shall hunger. Woe unto you that laugh now! for ye shall mourn and weep. (26) Woe unto you, when all men shall speak well of you! for so did their fathers to the false prophets"*. The above verses plainly tell us to be happy. However, if we do things to satisfy only the physical sense, we can expect to have our day of reckoning because we have but ignored the true nature of our selves and accepted the outer influence as truth. The Master tells us that we should not be celebrating these achievements, simply because they are no accomplishment at all. Those who are suffering are the ones working to understand. Through that experience, they may realize the nature of what they are able to be, primarily to be good and kind to each other. We endure our own kind of suffering today, for this is not the world that Jesus envisioned. We have not yet realized the inner being and have a bad habit of gloating over the physical. How many people have you met who suffer from the "better than you" syndrome?

He further tells us that no matter what may come our way, we are to act and react from one position only, and that is from the position of love, because we are meant to love all things. Unfortunately, we use this position as a weapon against our neighbor and our enemies. We will adopt it if there is something for us to gain. If not, it comes down to "I will not love you". We give this divine attribute one moment and not the next, yet we will take it away from the person we say we love. We are to give only the best of what we are to those who seek us. We are to hold back nothing, still we always hold back because we feel that if we are to give too much, we will have nothing left. It was said in Mark 4:24: *"What measure ye mete, it shall be measured to you, and unto you that hear shall more be given"*. It stands to reason that if we give it all, it will automatically return to us as a greater reward. It will happen only if we hear and accept.

This gift of giving is exemplified in **Luke 6:27-30**: *"But I say unto you which hear, Love your enemies, do good to them which hate you. (27) Bless them that curse you, and pray for them which despitefully use you. (29) And unto him that smiteth thee on the one cheek offer also the other; and him that taketh away thy cloak forbid not to take thy coat also. (30) Give to every man that asketh of thee; and of him that taketh away thy goods ask them not again"*. This is indeed a lesson on how we are to treat others the way we want to be treated (**Luke 6:31**). You should now understand why you have what you do possess. It may also reveal why we put too much emphasis on the physical aspect in the first place. It gives a whole new meaning to the first cause (God/Spirit), does it not?

We now come to **Luke 6:32-34**: *"For if ye love them which love you, what thank have ye? for sinners also love those that love them. (33) And if ye do good to them which do good to you, what thank have ye? for sinners also do even the same. (34) And if ye lend to them of whom ye hope to receive, what thank have ye? for sinners also lend to sinners, to receive as much again"*. If we love only the people who love us, there is no growth. The challenge is to love everyone equally, and not because they will love us in return. The latter is easy, but if we love everyone, then a special relationship becomes very special indeed. Is this not what we all seek? If we hold ourselves back from others, will we not – out of habit – withhold from a special association? Jesus is saying that we base our love of others on our own self. Is it not proven daily that most of us do not love our own selves? We are taught that "loving one's self" is conceit but it is not, unless carried to the point of ultimate selfishness and pretense. We are unable to truly love another unless we are able to love ourselves first. Many appear to retreat from that. It is too easy to downplay our own nature. If we are not good to our own being, who else will be? At the same time, how can others help, if we will not let them? We feel we do not deserve it. The Master is also letting us know that there should be no ulterior motives, and we should have nothing to hide. If we apply the same rule to and for everyone, no discrimination will befall us. We find a gentle message of goodness, mercy and judgment in **Luke 6:35-38**. It ends the same way as stated in Mark 4:24: *"For with the same measure that ye mete withal it shall be measured to you again"*. We receive exactly what we put forth. Only each of us can know this, and it is why we should stop blaming the outer world. We must take a long look at inner nature and proceed in Truth – which means no justification is necessary. It informs us to accept rather than deny what we have done and do to others, when in reality we do this to ourselves. Once we accept, the burdens are released and we truly begin to know our hurts, developing a new emotional outlook.

The next parable is quite lengthy. We will study it one or two verses at a time, to reap the full message being offered. **Luke 6:39-49**: *"(39) And he spake a parable unto them, Can the blind lead the blind? shall they not both fall into the ditch? (40) The disciple is not above his master: but every one that is perfect shall be as his master"*. As was mentioned earlier, Jesus is talking only to His direct students – the disciples – about the inner teachings. The first point He makes is that if one does not have the understanding, the knowledge, how can he teach another? He is implying that it is important they not only hear Him, but comprehend the sense of the inner message. He is telling them that they are, or will become just as He is, through understanding – as can we all. He confirms this in the next verses: *"(41) And why beholdest thou the mote that is in thy brother's eye, but perceivest not the beam that is in thine own eye? (42) Either how canst thou say to thy brother, Brother, let me pull out the mote that is in thine eye, when thou thyself beholdest not the beam that is in thine own eye, and then shalt thou see clearly to pull out the mote that is in thy brother's eye"*. The message is obvious. The Master is telling us to understand our own being before we attempt to understand another. We tend to believe we know others. How can we, unless we first know ourselves in depth? As we have already discussed, we do not let others be themselves because we see them through our own perceptions, and by comparing them to us and what we know. That is not acceptance or appreciation of their uniqueness. We must allow them to be who they are and to experience what they do. Then we can assist them in their search for Truth. Not only are we filled with too much judgment of others, but self-judgment as well.

The Masters in the East tell us that the moment you now have is merely a reflection of your own self, no matter what you think you may see. We must have the ability to help ourselves before we can help another, and that is what is meant by the mote, meaning the unobvious, the small unseen feeling part of the human makeup. Do we truly expect the other people to make us happy? If we do, we shall wait an eternity... It is something that should be within us already. Why should we look outside for it? Here are the next two verses: *"(43) For a good tree bringeth not forth corrupt fruit; neither doth a corrupt tree bring forth good fruit. (44) For every tree is known by his own fruit. For of thorns men do not gather figs, nor of a bramble bush gather they grapes"*. The subject of the lesson was the nature of the being, how we will hold onto an emotional memory, and how anything that has a root will grow to fruition. This growth will take place whether the goal is good or bad. If the intent is good, the outcome will be the same. We should realize that negative memories will release a bad outcome. In any case, we may perpetuate the end result in either direction. "Every tree is known by his own fruit"... What will come to fruition has already been set in motion, yet we seek to gather the fruits from the wrong direction. We attempt to take them from the bad to make them good. This is the process of righting a wrong, but once an event has taken place, the best we can hope to attain is an understanding, and it cannot really be undone. Holding on to it can do us no good since it has already passed. Take the good fruit from the good trees, and let the others lie where they will. Understand it within your heart and it will not bind you.

Verse 45 is another similar message pointing us in the right direction: *"(45) A good man out of the good treasure of his heart bringeth forth that which is good; and an evil man out of the evil treasure of his heart bringeth forth that which is evil: for of the abundance of the heart his mouth speaketh"*. If our basis for feeling is strong, we may produce only good, but this particular nature must be free of regrets. If there are regrets, they too will come forth and be known. We have learned elsewhere in this work that the heart cannot lie. Only the mind can. The combination of the two produces much from us, so we should carefully choose that with which we fill our hearts. When we give it true power, it must return whence it came – to us. In verses 48 and 49, the Master paints a picture of the man willing to hear and the man who is not. *"(48) He is like a man which built an house, and digged deep, and laid the foundation on a rock: and when the flood arose, the stream beat vehemently upon that house, and could not shake it: for it was founded upon a rock. (49) But he that heareth, and doeth not, is like a man that without a foundation built an house upon the earth; against which the stream did beat vehemently, and immediately it fell; and the ruin of that house was great"*. We know by now that the Master spoke in symbols, and in this particular case, He was not speaking of bricks and mortar. If we dig deeply within us and perform an honest inspection, we begin to really understand the very nature of God's presence – our soul. We are to build ourselves on this reliable ground. We will be much stronger for it. It will come from the spiritual acceptance of what we feel and know. It will become unshakable. If we build on the falsehood of the material realm, we have no strength to withstand the flood of the spirit, or of life for that matter, because we will have no real basis within us to hold us in place. Our foundation is what we feel about life from our emotional inner self, not what we think it to be as given to us by the external world. This solid base is composed of the positive attributes by which we see ourselves – not as others see us. If we are single in that nature, no one will be able to pull us out of the relationship we hold with spirit.

Luke 7:22-23: *"Then Jesus answering said unto them, Go your way, and tell John what things ye have seen and heard; how that the blind see, the lame walk, the lepers are cleansed, the deaf hear, the dead are raised, to the poor the gospel is preached. (23) And blessed is he, whosoever shall not be offended in me"*. Jesus is telling John, and all of us as well, to learn to understand what He says, that the words are not alone and have a symbolic meaning, for they are veiled in His intent. The communication itself is a verification. We are told that there is much understanding of the message He is delivering to the people, that much growth is being accomplished by the teachings on both the inner and outer natures of the multitudes. We must also remind you that these two divine personalities were cousins, yet, they acted as though they were strangers to each other – at least in the public sense. Was this their mission? The point is that they were delivering knowledge to people, so the blind could see. They were releasing the pent-up emotions and their expression was becoming clean and clear, so the lepers were cleansed. They were overcoming their fears, so the dead were raised. They were being enlightened and brought to the point of being able to appreciate the higher aspect of self.

We have mentioned the subtle nature of the human at the beginning of this chapter. We begin to see more of this not only biblically, but in the Master Himself. We find Jesus saying in **Luke 7:27**: *"This is he, of whom it is written, Behold, I send my messenger before thy face, which shall prepare thy way before thee"*. He is talking of John the Baptist in a figurative perspective, yet the inner truth is allowing the feelings, in union with the spirit, to go before us as we journey through life. We have seen this revealed in the Old Testament and in Revelations as the Ark of the Covenant going before you. The suggestion is that if we allow our sense system to go before us – as it does anyway – we will know in advance what the outcome may be. We must use this attribute for our feedback – and we do – but we must use it with focus, and it will indeed clear our way at the right moment. When we detect struggle, we are actually attempting to force the issue, but if we were to use all of our innate abilities, we would allow spirit to go before us and clear our path. We should not force it, because turmoil shall truly come. If there is a struggle, find its nature and why it is there. Turn the situation over and allow your own energy to go before you – and it will, as a natural aspect of you. We must learn to acknowledge this. We all tend to think "Turn it over to what?". If we could get it out of our minds and allow our feelings to guide us, spirit could then assist. Our minds actually do the blocking in this situation, and we may be inclined to struggle. Here is where we must relax within and follow the inner guidance.

In **Luke 7:31-35,** Jesus tells the Pharisees that we but play games with each other and shower each other with unkindness in many ways. It is done for what we believe we can get from the other party. He is teaching us to accept others at an honest level of innocence, and to consider them as individuals in their own nature. We should have no preconceived notions of what we think they are, but simply accept them, and *"...wisdom is justified of all her children"*. This concept is again found in **Luke 7:44-47**: *"And he turned to the woman, and said unto Simon, Seest thou this woman? I entered into thine house, thou gavest me no water for my feet; but she hath washed my feet with tears, and wiped them with the hairs of her head. (45) Thou gavest me no kiss: but this woman since the time I came in hath not ceased to kiss my feet. (46) My head with oil thou didst not anoint: but this woman hath anointed my feet with ointment. (47) Wherefore I say unto thee, Her sins, which are many, are forgiven; for she loved much: but to whom little is forgiven, the same loveth little"*. The point is for us to allow others to be themselves, no matter what that may be, and for us to forgive them. If we were to combine our thinking with our feelings, we would produce a conscience within us that we are meant to follow. To let our conscience be our guide will always lead to the rightness of being and to its correct use. It is where we all seem to fall short of the mark. We know within ourselves what is the right thing to do. Subsequently, we either choose right over whatever else, or we do not. Thus, we all experience the consequences of choice. We are speaking about true compassion for self and others. Physical action is not the only expression, yet we seem to base our judgments on this alone, bringing us back to choice.

We are now in Chapter 8 of the Book of Luke. Verses 5-9 depict the parable of the sower, which we also find in Matthew 13. However, there are very subtle differences between the two. In Luke's version, followed by the inner teachings of the Master, we sense another significance. We see the reference to moisture and to the heart – comments not found in Matthew's. Jesus is letting people know that what you sow into your heart with great feeling and emotion will come to fruition. We should realize that this could be good or bad, depending on what we sow and how deeply we plant it within us. Have you ever noticed that when an event happens that hurts you on the emotional level, you tell yourself: "I will remember this so it does not happen again"? By the same token, have you also noticed that it seems to occur quite often from that point on? It is because that memory is upper most in our heart and mind. It recurs as part of the learning process to understand and release. Even though we are told that bad feelings will override, it happens merely because we tend to give them more importance and hold on to them, thus inviting the recurrence. The Master gives a much expanded version of this to the disciples – more so than in Matthew and Mark. The message is different in that He is telling them to think with their hearts and to be genuine with their feelings. **Luke 8:12** reads: *"Those by the way side are they that hear; then cometh the devil, and* *taketh away the word out of their hearts, lest they should believe and be saved"*. The devil is life spelled backward [*lived*] and common sense tells us not to live life backward. Jesus is telling us that when distress arises, we hold on to it. The good feelings about ourselves are destroyed and will be taken away from us, merely because of what we choose to grasp and remember. We should clear ourselves of these past hurts by balancing them within our own hearts, and by not lashing back at its creator.

The lesson continues in **Luke 8:14**: *"And that which fell among thorns are they, which, when they have heard, go forth, and are choked with cares and riches and pleasures of this life, and bring no fruit to perfection"*. We get hurt, and instead of looking within for a resolution, we become absorbed in the outer aspect in order to avoid the inner distresses. Those may stem from childhood, and most of us carry them in the subconscious. It forces us to look to the physical side and it drives us to seek satisfaction in the material world. Regrettably, it appears that we place our worries upon the external, and this is the main reason it controls us. To truly succeed, we must resolve the inner condition.

We may have all the money and toys in the world, but even with these finite things, how do you really feel about yourself? Once these possessions are gone, it leaves only your own nature. Then what? Be pleased with the gift of life and the true value of the art of feeling. **Luke 8:15**: *"But that on the good ground are they, which in an honest and good heart, having heard the word, keep it, and bring forth fruit with patience"*. The good seed will always produce more. It is also from the heart and what we feel about the self, our nature, and not in relationship to the rest of the world. If we seek to balance ourselves with the outer material world, it will remain in control. Yet, if we create that balance with the inner nature, there will be greater ease. We are the cause of life, and life is our effect – not the other way around. We want other people to be like us, and the truth of the matter is – they already are... Their sense system is exactly like ours, but we must allow for their individual natures and not try to make them fit ours. It lets other people be themselves. Enlightenment takes place through the experience of life. Do not avoid it, just because it may hurt.

Wisdom is achieved by the process of knowledge and the experience that goes with it. Once there, the light should shine without one exclaiming: "I have learned! I have changed!". After all, the growth we do attain, by whatever means, is naturally progressive and should be quietly accepted. We see this in **Luke 8:16-17**: *"No man, when he hath lighted a candle, covereth it with a vessel, or putteth it under a bed; but setteth it on a candlestick, that they which enter in may see the light. (17) For nothing is secret, that shall not be* *made manifest; neither any thing hid, that shall not be known and come abroad".* Once our inner selves have acquired the understanding, others will see it without having to shout it. Truth will always come to light in all circumstances because it must balance out. **Luke 8:18** emphasizes that to which we hold on and what is important: *"Take heed therefore how ye hear: for whosoever hath, to him shall be given; and whosoever hath not, from him shall be taken even that which he seemeth to have".* In "how ye hear", the Master is discussing truth, because we have a propensity to shape it so that it fits us, as opposed to us fitting the truth. If we hold truth in the highest regard, then more will be given. Those that do not and choose to live the lie will have to relinquish more and more for the falsehood upon which they opted.

In **Luke 8:19-21**, we find the Master in a synagogue while his family is outside. In reading these verses, you may tend to think that His family is not important: *"Then came to him his mother and his brethren, and could not come at him for the press. (20) And it was told him by certain which said, Thy mother and thy brethren stand without, desiring to see thee. (21) And he answered and said unto them, My mother and my brethren are these which hear the word of God, and do it".* Jesus is telling us that we are all the same, and that no one should be more important than another. The illusion is that we give more importance to family and relatives. We are carefully selecting above others when we should not, because all those around us are our family. We are unable to consider others within this concept due to physical differences – and not much more. Is the cover of a book more important than the words within it? Were we to seek the words rather than the cover, we would find many marvelous stories among the pages.

It was once said by an unknown Chinese author that: "We gain wisdom through experience, and we can gain more wisdom from another's experience". We must not only do it, as the Master mentioned, but we must also listen and observe. He was always prepared for the events to come, by nothing more than being opened to the moment and being aware at all times of the happenings around Him. Nothing in this world could stop us from doing the same. Regrettably, we are inextricably caught up in the yesterdays of life that cloud our vision, and we are unable to see or to accept. If we were more aware, we would not be so drained, so stressed. We can sense this in **Luke 8:45-46**, as He felt His energy drop: *"And Jesus said, Who touched me? When all denied, Peter and they that were with him said, Master, the multitude throng thee and press thee, and sayest thou, Who touched me? (46) And Jesus said, Somebody hath touched me: for I perceive that virtue is gone out of me".* The woman who had touched His robe was healed. The truth is that the Master was not ready, and He felt a drop in His energy. Is this not the way many of us feel, day in and day out? We are not opened or paying attention to what is going on around us at certain times because we are too caught up in ourselves. We are always pouring our energy onto others who feed upon it and we suffer the consequences. We are tired and stressed out within ourselves. Today, you may have noticed that it is getting much more difficult to just relax. Why? Because we give ourselves away to the outer nature that controls us and our circumstances. The Master was educating more and more people, to the point where He was appointing others to assist Him. We see this in **Luke 10:1**, wherein He selected seventy others to travel ahead of him, heal and teach. We already realize that if the mind and heart are healed, the body will follow, will be made whole. Those in that condition were going forth for this fulfillment. We are told that we should not worry, but rather focus on the attributes of the feeling of love and what it holds for each of us. It is indeed the most important thing in life, and if we have it, there is no need for complaint about what another may do with his/her life. What others do is entirely up to them.

We now move to Chapter 11 of the Book of Luke, wherein we see a third version of the Lord's prayer. We must remember that Jesus taught that lesson to the disciples and no one else, or so it appears. Each version having its variance, we see in this one that the Master interrupted Himself to deepen the discussion with His students. Let us bring to light **Luke 11:8-10**: *"I say unto you, Though he will not rise and give him, because he is his friend, yet because of his importunity he will rise and give him as many as he needeth. (9) And I say unto you, Ask, and it shall be given you; seek, and ye shall find; knock, and it shall be opened unto you. (10) For every one that asketh receiveth; and he that seeketh findeth; and to him that knocketh it shall be opened"*. The point of this advice is that Spirit is a great friend, and we must persist in what we seek through the spiritual side. The need for persistence is required because we seek so much in our lives, and this may be distractive in itself. Since we are constantly changing our minds, Spirit has difficulties knowing what we are really asking. We switch from one request to the next, thereby creating confusion and a delay in the final approbation.

To the Tibetan, all thoughts are requests for God to do something for you. If this is true, imagine what God must go through to determine what we consider serious – and what we really want. This is our own doing because we do not honor our thoughts as seeking assistance, yet we only have to ask and Spirit will answer. If we apply the power of creation – our feelings – we will be granted that which we seek. We do not have to look very far for the help, for it is within the center of our being, our heart, and that is where we should be concentrating. As the Master says in **Luke 11:17**: *"....Every kingdom divided against itself is brought to desolation; and a house divided against a house fal-*

leth". We are continually dividing ourselves between the good and the bad, the past and the future, what we think and what we feel. This attitude does not have a uniting effect. We attempt to acknowledge the two, but all that is necessary is to choose the good. Once this is accomplished, only good can happen to you since there is no longer a division of your feelings. Even if it is just a lesson, it will be good in its nature as it is realized. After all, it is the good that you seek, is it not? To life, it becomes the power of focus and singularity in purpose to keep you on the straight path.

We as human are very lazy in our emotional nature out of fear. We tend to not want to analyze feelings, emotionally, because we believe that they will divide us and yet leave us as we were. Memories will not, if we learn to understand them. What were the events? What was their purpose? What did they leave with us to remember? Were they meant for self-improvements? No event leaves anyone unscathed. They all leave their lasting effect, either in a good sense or a bad one. It is up to us to choose such effect. It is further analyzed in **Luke 11:24-26**: *"When the unclean spirit is gone out of a man, he walketh through dry places, seeking rest; and finding none, he saith, I will return unto my house whence I came out. (25) And when he cometh, he findeth it swept and garnished. (26) Then goeth he, and taketh to him seven other spirits more wicked than himself; and they enter in, and dwell there: and the last state of that man is worse than the first"*. Waterless places are those where spirit does not exist. Of course, one may find no rest therein. We are told in this allegory that we must face whatever situation we have either created or encountered and bring it to a conclusion. If we do not, it will return and we will not know why. As the creator of the original feelings, we have forgotten and we think our house is in order. Had we settled the event the first time, it could not harm us a second time. Jesus is telling us to learn from the events of our lives so they cannot return and be greater than the original, especially since everything comes back to us tenfold stronger and so on. Look within your life to see what is unsettled. Settle it for what it is in that moment, and it will not return.

One of the many profound things the Master brought to light is contained in **Luke 11:34-36**, and the words say a lot: *"The light of the body is the eye: therefore when thine eye is single, thy whole body also is full of light; but when thine eye is evil, thy body also is full of darkness. (35) Take heed therefore that the light which is in thee be not darkness. (36) If thy whole body therefore be full of light, having no part dark, the whole shall be full of light, as when the bright shining of a candle doth give thee light"*. It is said that the eyes are the windows to the soul. The above verses definitely give us a confirmation of this. But what did Jesus mean when He mentioned "the whole body be full of light", and "the bright shining of a candle"? It is the realization of our true nature, whereas we are the spirit (or the light) we choose to be, and our body is the material envelope containing our spiritual aspect. It is also telling us that we should not simply look at the physical appearance of others, but rather gaze beyond the outer attributes, and through the window of their soul. We do have a tendency to pay more attention to the visible and tangible side of others – that side we so love to glorify. Only we know our inner self, and the exultations are intended to advertise and enhance it in the eyes of others. This, in itself, is wrong. We should act out our spiritual nature, rather than boasting of it through words. Words reveal what should be done in secret, in union with spirit. Verbalizing it only diminishes the impact between us and the spiritual side. Our eyes are to speak for us – not our tongue. Being filled with light may occur only when there is no longer a personal, inner division on right and wrong and good and evil. There is only the one nature that we need to confirm for ourselves, and this will reduce division. Greater light will come forth from us, and we will only have to deal with good works.

This is carried further in **Luke 11:39-41**: *"And the Lord said unto him, Now do ye Pharisees make clean the outside of the cup and the platter; but your inward part is full of ravening and wickedness. (40) Ye fools, did not he that made that which is without make that which is within also? (41) But rather give alms of such things as ye have; and, behold, all things are clean unto you"*. Indeed! Did not Spirit make our outer and inner natures? All we seem to do is venerate the external side…Does this not leave out the other half which is Spirit? We do not work with the true cleanliness of our nature, but rather with what others see. The inner aspect is left out. In the same vein, we are to allow for our love to flow forth, yet it appears that we are saving it for some unknown cause and do not wish to waste it. How can we waste it when we do not acknowledge it, or distribute it so sparingly? We give it to others, but only to those we feel deserve it. Then we wonder why love is not returned to us… There should be no questions on this subject, yet there are many – or there must be, because we do not let others enjoy our inner light. Only what we think is all that we give.

In **Luke 11:52,** we find Jesus addressing lawyers: *"Woe unto you, lawyers! for ye have taken away the key of knowledge: ye entered not in your- selves, and them that were entering in ye hindered"*. The lawyers mentioned in this verse are not those we call lawyers today, even though they too could fit in this picture. They were the metaphysicians of the era and they knew the spiri- tual understanding, because they had the keys. However, they were not openly sharing the knowledge. They were not honoring it at the time and were work- ing on preventing the masses to know the truth. The Master came to deliver the Truth of the message. Nonetheless, to this day we still do not have the full message. Most religions talk about the Bible as though it could never change, yet God told us there would be another dispensation. It means that it would change. Did Spirit not include change in Its concept of creation? Change is forward movement, and it is what It had in mind. Universal forward movement includes knowledge, does it not?

In **Luke 12:1-3**, we once more come to the subject of truth – the truth of our inner nature, and we are told that the realization of such truth will happen: *"In the mean time, when there were gathered together an innumerable multitude of people, insomuch that they trode one upon another, he began to say unto his disciples first of all, Beware ye of the leaven of the Pharisees, which is hypocrisy. (2) For there is nothing covered, that shall not be revealed; neither hid, that shall not be known. (3) Therefore whatsoever ye have spoken in darkness shall be heard in the light; and that which ye have spoken in the ear in closets shall be proclaimed upon the housetops"*. Eventually, each individual must face his/her personal covered or hidden thoughts, words or actions. If this is done with the intention and willingness to release these burdens and gain knowledge from them, he/she will receive the appreciation of the nature of life that is facing us today. It will also bring understanding to the dark corners of his/her mind. This applies to all of us. We are alone in this quest, except with Spirit. We must remove the darkness with our understanding, so that all things will be ours in the final phases of what we call life. We will have the knowledge, and our inner light will come forth. What we have whispered in the hidden rooms of self will be known to all. It seems as though we will all share this information and will proclaim it, as mentioned in the Ark of the Covenant. We will all know within our hearts that the inner and outer aspects are unified in the same being, or at least we will recognize the God nature within us.

In **Luke 12:16-21**, we find a parable for the general public, followed by the deeper teachings to the disciples. It covers the acceptance of the nature of spirit and where our priorities lie. Once again, Jesus is talking about the importance we place upon physical nature – an emphasis that will do nothing for us in the spiritual aspect. Whatever we choose to work on will buy us nothing at a later time, especially if there is nothing spiritual about what we do. That is the major point. No matter how large a storage facility we may build, it can only hold material goods. By the same token, if all our time is invested in this physical project only, how can we have a relationship with our inner being? The parable ends in Verse 21 by saying: *"So is he that layeth up treasures for himself, and is not rich toward God"*. The Master then taught the inner meaning to the disciples. The meaning of His words is very much the same as the parable itself, to wit: we simply focus in the wrong direction. He confirms it in **Luke 12:22-23**: *"And he said unto his disciples, Therefore I say unto you,*

Take no thought for your life, what ye shall eat; neither for the body, what ye shall put on. (23) The life is more than meat, and the body is more than raiment". Are we not all somewhat anticipatively anxious? Perhaps it is because we live ahead of ourselves and not with our means. Our focus is always on tomorrow, rather than the present moment. In Verse 24, Jesus explains how the fowls work with the spirit and are provided food, but no more than they can handle, eat or store for later use. He also tells us of our importance vis-à-vis the creation and reminds us that being anxious does not buy much.

Luke 12:35: *"Let your loins be girded about, and your lights burning"*. Jesus does indeed express Himself in a mystical fashion. He is telling us that we should always be ready, and the knowledge of the spiritual attributes we all have should go before us at all times. It implies that we will share with and show our lights (understanding) to spirit only, and we will recognize our continued existence. We may never abandon our knowledge, no matter how hard we try. In **Luke 12:41**, we are faced with a mystery: *"Then Peter said unto him, Lord, speakest thou this parable unto us, or even to all?"*. It is assumed we should have been there to hear the answer, and it is the only time this is ever brought up. To whom do you speak? To us? To them? Or are we simply not paying attention...No one knows for sure now. It is surmised that most do not pay attention to their openness, described in Matthew as the mind of a child.

If you read **Luke 12:42-59**, you will find another introduction to karma and the cycles of life. We are what we think we are. We are to carry out the effects already set in motion. The teachings imply that the physical things are very easy for us to determine. Are we not able to read the signs of the sky and predict whether a storm or a dry spell is coming our way? Conversely, the subtle or the unseen is not so easy to read, thus we must be much more discerning because we will be a part of that subtle nature. It warns us of the great divisions within our own being – our human side of life. Verse 59 reads: *"I tell thee, thou shalt not depart thence, till thou hast paid the very last mite"*. That is undeniably a stern and very striking statement, and it is karma. Debts will be paid as all debts must be, from the spiritual, emotional, mental or physical aspects. These are not only financial. It is to balance out the inner nature so that we may continue. Whether we think we can hide those debts or not is irrelevant, because the Spirit is keeping a tab on them. Consequently, it behooves you to settle yours through what you choose to externalize to others. The same lesson is taught in **Luke 13:6-9**: *"He spake also this parable; A certain man had a fig tree planted in his vineyard; and he came and sought fruit thereon, and found none. (7) Then said he unto the dresser of his vineyard, Behold, these three years I come seeking fruit on this fig tree, and find none: cut it down; why cumbereth it the ground? (8) And he answering said unto him,*

Lord, let it alone this year also, till I shall dig about it, and dung it: (9) And if it bear fruit, well: and if not, then after that thou shalt cut it down". This metaphor relates directly to us from a spiritual point of view, since we are to bear fruits out of the subtle nature of our being. Those are spiritual fruits offered by us to life, and the fertilizing is the inner nourishment necessary for the culmination of the growth of knowledge. It is about what we have learned on the spirit level about life. Unfortunately, we fall short of the mark again, because we give very little credit to the nature of Spirit within. The truth of us working from the inner to the outer aspect, the continued outpouring of our feelings and thoughts toward life – those are the fruits being discussed.

In **Luke 13:32-33**, we find another reference to "three days": *"....and the third day, I shall be perfected"* [I shall reach my goal]. In this instance, Jesus is talking about reaching the culmination of His work with the people, and He further states: *"...for it cannot be that a prophet perish out of Jerusalem"*. We must understand that the Jerusalem to which the Master is referring is not the city we know by that name in Israel. It is an allegory and not a location on earth, but rather a state of being that He must attain. We once again borrow from the "Metaphysical Bible Dictionary": *"**Jeru**, the first part of Jerusalem, means founding, constituting; **Salem**, the latter part of the word, means peace, quiet, safety, harmony, prosperity", "Jerusalem means habitation of peace. In man, it is the abiding consciousness of spiritual peace, which is the result of continuous realizations of spiritual power tempered with spiritual poise and confidence"*. It is the balancing effect of the positive and negative forces – the opposites – and it would take the Master three days to accomplish this task. He had to build His energy to withstand what was to come, and this energy is in the heart center of the human as the seat of the soul, the storehouse of the soul.

In **Luke 14:8-11**, we have a valuable lesson in humility. We are taught that we should not praise our own being but allow others to offer the accolades if they wish. If they do not, simply take it in stride. When we do exalt ourselves, we usually overstep our bounds, as seen in the parable: *"When thou art bidden of any man to a wedding, sit not down in the highest room; lest a more honourable man than thou be bidden of him; (9) And he that bade thee and him come and say to thee, Give this man place; and thou begin with shame to take the lowest room. (10) But when thou art bidden, go and sit down in the lowest room; that when he that bade thee cometh, he may say unto thee, Friend, go up higher: then shalt thou have worship in the presence of them that sit at meat with thee. (11) For whosoever exalteth himself shall be abased; and he that humbleth himself shall be exalted"*. The Master is obviously talking about our inner humility. We are being told to not work on outclassing another. Allow others to do this, but not yourself. After all, is it really that important to be "number one"? In reality, how many number ones can there be? Let those who desire to boost their ego do it. Those who do not should not concern themselves with superficial social ranking or where they stand among their contemporaries. This is a form of measuring Self, and the only reference point we have is how others are doing, thus we compare our own nature to theirs. When we do compare, however, we take apart our own unique nature. Are not our fingerprints unique, or the iris of our eyes, or our DNA? These are all individual one of a kind. Accordingly, we are really comparing apples and oranges. Whether external or internal, there are no similarities. Do not destroy yourself through comparison to others because you are unique in all ways and unlike any other.

So why compare in the first place? There will always be a person who has more – or less – than you have. A form of your ego is performing the comparison to expose your own value, and if you have less, you may suffer levels of insecurity. By the same token, if you have more, it may trigger the adverse effects of vanity and self-important arrogance. The moral of the parable is carried further in **Luke 14:12-14**: *"Then said he also to him that bade him, When thou makest a dinner or a supper, call not thy friends, nor thy brethren, neither thy kinsmen, nor thy rich neighbours; lest they also bid thee again, and a recompense be made thee. (13) But when thou makest a feast, call the poor, the maimed, the lame, the blind. (14) And thou shalt be blessed; for they cannot recompense thee: for thou shalt be recompensed at the resurrection of the just"*. It is suggested that we stand on our own, with what is in our hearts, and not do things merely because there is something material to be gained by it. At times, the only return is the fact that we learned a valuable lesson. In today's society, that is not enough. Many feel that a "return" should include fame, fortune and social standing, or it is worth nothing…What price do we put on knowledge, especially knowledge of the true nature of our human selves. Our greatest wealth is there, within us, and how we use it. Jesus is telling us not to make excuses for our self, but rather accept what and who we are and to celebrate that aspect.

In **Luke 14:16-24**, the Teacher uses another dinner party as an allegory. This time, the guests all have an excuse for not coming, and the host sends his servant to invite indigents to enjoy his feast. The parable reinforces the fact that we should not make any excuses on the subject of spiritual growth. The external world will create them for our selves. We will again be distracted from the higher purpose of life and not do what is correct at that moment because we feel that it is more important to finish things we have begun, materially speaking. We must also remember that no one knows when the bridegroom will come. We have enough energy to complete all things, and this energy comes from the subtle nature within the temple – the physical self.

Luke 14:28-29 follows the same pattern: *"For which of you, intending to build a tower, sitteth not down first, and counteth the cost, whether he have sufficient to finish it? (29) Lest haply, after he hath laid the foundation, and is not able to finish it, all that behold it begin to mock him..."*. If you are determined to reach certain goals, you must carefully plan to conquer every obstacle that may be in the path of success. This is as true for spiritual goals as it is for business ventures. You must not let your ego flatter you into something you are unable to complete. This occurs all too often in life, does it not? The only reason it may happen is because nothing is above the laws of metaphysics, and the ego is the tempter. It lures us all into actions related to material gain only and fools us into believing in their importance. It has no feel.

In **Luke 15:4-10**, Jesus tells the story of the lost sheep and the lost piece of silver. He tells us that we should be more appreciative of the things we have. We should concern ourselves with the minor aspect of the whole picture, that being the material world we call life. The material path is wide and easy. The spiritual path is narrow and hides many obstacles. We do have the right, the opportunity to live more fulfilling lives, providing we do not take away from the major influence – our spiritual well-being – to seek the empty minor rewards.

In **Luke 15:11-32**, we find the much quoted parable of the prodigal son, wherein we are told not to downplay our self-worth. If we express whatever we may have done with the knowledge of what was learned, it becomes a release, a new beginning. Our subsequent life will be better, since we have learned from the experience and attained a higher level of wisdom. We should never deny what has been done by us, simply because it is the truth of the matter. It is never too late to grasp the opportunity to know the truth of self, and that truth will be celebrated. This parable is how we look at our own being for what it has done in the past, and not for what it does in the present. And in the present only will we have the occasion to correct our wavering. The past is where we have been, not where we are now.

Luke 16:1-13 is a very complex story about a somewhat unscrupulous steward, or foreman. Perhaps it is best to revert to metaphysical symbolism in order to clarify this important metaphor. The "lord" is the spiritual self that normally guides us through life. The "steward" is our physical nature, while the "debtors" are karma and the "goods" are the knowledge or understanding. In the course of the story, it seems that the steward drained knowledge through unethical accounting methods, perhaps to enhance his own wealth. He had ulterior motives through the knowledge he had attained. The ego had become involved, rendering him arrogant, and leading people in the wrong direction. Eventually, the lord – or spirit – became aware of this and threatened to create changes in the order of things. We can assume that the steward was charging twice the value of the goods, and as an act of redemption, he cut the amounts owed to their original worth. He had to shift direction, back to the path of truth and honesty. Even though a dishonest act had been committed, the redeeming act can be the only reason the lord commended the steward (Luke 16:8) and forgave him (*for the children of this world are in their generation wiser than the children of light*). By the same token, the debtors looked more kindly upon the steward and made his future look brighter. Veiled by the words of this allegory, we can detect a lesson in mutual respect and faithfulness. As long as we act for the higher good of all, we can be filled with attainment, and not deception, since the latter can only delay us. We must also learn to stop doing two things at once, for we are told we cannot serve two masters (*Ye cannot serve God* [the spiritual] *and mammon* [the physical]). We must recognize and then reconcile our inner division, so that it becomes single in nature. This is accomplished only through the focus on the one nature – which should be the spiritual – and not the other. In reality, to "focus" is to converge or concentrate on one point – one area. Conclusively, how can anyone effectively focus on more than one subject simultaneously? If we waste our own selves physically or spiritually, how can we be entrusted with the true nature that, in union, makes us all God's children?

In **Luke 16:14**, we find a character trait pertaining to our friends, the Pharisees: *"And the Pharisees also, who were covetous..."* [Covetous: marked by inordinate desire for wealth]. This is not money in a literal sense, but rather the physical aspects of life. This privileged sect offered the inner teachings of the time – supposedly. They may be known by other names, but today, the Pharisees are still among us. They proclaim their own kind of spirituality for the love of money, but show little love for the true spiritual nature. They are here to lead us further toward the entrapment of the physical body while they constantly remind us that it is the most important part of our lives. They were in error then, and they certainly are today. Unfortunately, because we have a tendency toward the physical aspects, their "teachings" seem to make sense. Because we do not see ourselves as a spirit in the flesh, anything of the spirit is not real.

We must learn to realize that spirit gives us life. It is what drives us into action. These alleged wise persons are always asking us to justify ourselves, so that further judgment may be passed on us. Why should we? In our material world, it is more important for us to do things in the sight of the physical realm. It gives us a chance to puff up our chests and exclaim: "Look at what I have done!" Who cares! Show it to the Father! Let spirit know what has been done by you and see what it has to offer you on the subject. Your consciousness will awaken! When we boast of our earthly achievements, we are merely seeking meaningless accolades. In the eyes of others, we appear as pretentious braggarts – and rightly so. It is obviously for ego purposes, and the spiritual side is left out.

Is the ego that important that it powers us toward what we do, toward the destruction of our inner self? It has led us to centuries of war and mistrust and nothing more – unless it is properly used. The Master went a little further in **Luke 16:16-17**: *"The law and the prophets were until John: since that time the kingdom of God is preached, and every man presseth into it. (17) And it is easier for heaven and earth to pass, than one tittle of the law to fail"*. "Every man presseth into it"... Is this not how the Bible was compiled? It was cleverly done with only the physical aspects in mind. It was designed for control, and much wealth was showered upon those who had an input in this work. Again, we are also told that the laws were set since the dawn of humankind, and we are the law itself. Because of this, we are never above the cycles that go on and create our lives. All must come to balance by the law of cause and effect. This may continue for a very lengthy period or a very short one. The choice is always ours – only through the acceptance of Truth.

Now it appears that those who suffer in the physical realm will not suffer later. However, this may really mean that those not afflicted by physical suffering will endure in the spiritual realm. This may be balanced out at any time by us so that we are spared the suffering. It will come to pass only if we focus on full understanding and do not separate things as we do. We need to be single in nature, and all good shall come from the spring of creation to have for ourselves.

Luke 16:26-27: *"And beside all this, between us and you there is a great gulf fixed: so that they which would pass from hence to you cannot; neither can they pass to us, that would come from thence. (27) Then he said, I pray thee therefore, father, that thou wouldest send him to my father's house"*. We see that there is more to life. We see that we survive death, and there is a separation between knowledge of the physical and the spiritual. We must be cautious of that upon which we focus, as is described in **Luke 16:28**: *"For I have five brethren; that he may testify unto them, lest they also come into this place of torment"*. This confirms the warning. The person wanted to return to warn his relatives about the Truth. Spirit told him that he could not do this since they would not believe him anyway because, to the living, we have nothing left to offer. The living is the physical. Once we have passed and all things are settled, we may not come back to tell others what happened. We have free will to a point. It is the reason we must make our own choices in life, without any outside influences. It is our life's steering mechanism and once we pass on, it is set. Once we experience our transition, what we did on this earth in the physical aspect will determine what we will have to rectify in the spiritual world. That is karma. It indicates that a return may take place to work this debt out in the physical realm since it is where it was created.

Next, we have a lesson in faith and forgiveness. **Luke 17:1-5**: *"Then said he unto the disciples, It is impossible but that offences* [stumbling blocks] *will come: but woe unto him, through whom they come! (2) It were better for him that a millstone were hanged about his neck, and he cast into the sea, than that he should offend one of these little ones. (3) Take heed to yourselves: If thy brother trespass against thee, rebuke him; and if he repent, forgive him. (4) And if he trespass against thee seven times in a day, and seven times in a day turn again to thee, saying, I repent; thou shalt forgive him. (5) And the apostles said unto the Lord, Increase our faith"*. The Master is discussing the act of stumbling. We are told that this is created by what we hold most important to us. Other people will do things we do not like. It becomes a problem only when we, ourselves, make it a problem – a stumbling block. In fact, the entire chapter is devoted to the subject of faith in one's self. Faith is there only if we believe in our own being. That belief is based on how we see ourselves. We perceive this through others' verbal contributions, what they think of us or what they feel about us, and we mistakenly accept it. It is indeed a grave error, because it does not really matter what others think of us. People are inconsistent. Some will like us and others will not. Those that do like us may suddenly change their mind, and vice-versa, thus common sense should tell us that what others think of us is really not that important in our lives. It is also substantiated in **Luke 17:6-10**. *"...If ye had faith as a grain of mustard seed..."*. It is small and knows not what will befall it. We learn that for us to be whole and complete, we must give to spirit what belongs to spirit. It simply means that we must pay attention to it, and it is our only requirement as physical humans. We should never be so arrogant as to believe that we do things of our own accord. In addition, we should be thankful for what we have, rather than focus on what we do not have. Regrettably, it is what we do.

In **Luke 17:17:19**, we have a look into the ways we handle things – and ignore them: *"And Jesus answering said, Were there not ten cleansed? but where are the nine? (18) There are not found that returned to give glory to God, save this stranger. (19) And he said unto him, Arise, go thy way: thy faith* *hath made thee whole "*. Once events happen and are in our minds, we do not, for the most part, learn anything from them. How can we, if all we do is blame others for our circumstances and how we feel about ourselves? When we bring them to resolution, we should let them go. If you have forgiven, do not hold on to the memory, because it will only cause distress. Most people think "I can forgive, but I cannot forget", and they do just that. If you have the decency to forgive, you should also simply forget and allow others this grace. Mistakes are made to learn. Verses 17 and 18 form a statement attesting to the fact that spirit will relieve our pressure if we allow it. We should be thankful for it. No one really is. We walk away after spirit has assisted us, nor do we give thanks. Rather than being grateful, we will exclaim: "I have survived another one!". We did nothing in and of ourselves. Spirit went before us and cleared our path. This is verified in **Luke 17:20-21**: *"And when he was demanded of the Pharisees, when the kingdom of God should come, he answered them and said, The kingdom of God cometh not with observation: (21) Neither shall they say, Lo here! or, lo there! for, behold, the kingdom of God is within you "*. Spirit is within us, in our midst, and there is no need for it to prove itself as to its location. It is not separate from us and it may never be, for without it, we would not be human.

In **Luke 17:27-29**, Jesus recounts how life was during the days of Noah and Lot, when the people were too ingrained in the physical aspect of life. When this becomes more important that the subtle nature, spirit will become directly involved. When it does, there is upheaval in our physical world. In **Luke 17:30**, the Master tells us that it will happen again: *"Even thus shall it be in the day when the Son of man is revealed "*.

We encounter a slight difference between two gospels. In Matthew 19:16, a wealthy young man asked Jesus a question. In **Luke 18:18**, it is a "certain ruler" who asked the same question. In either case, the person asked the Master how he can "inherit eternal life". We are being shown growth, a sign of attainment. Yet, the person has great wealth and is unable to let go. Even though we reach a certain level of understanding, we will still have the distraction of the material. It means that we still must chop the wood and carry the water. We must show some efforts in our lives. It further implies that just because we think we understand, we must live with the knowledge. Events will continue to befall us, but we will have the understanding to help us through the situations, thus we will not be so distraught. We must not get caught up in the world of "things". It is good to have all that you desire, but you cannot afford to let it own you. There is nothing wrong with owning worldly possessions and enjoying them, but we must be willing to let them go. In **Luke 18:34**, we are told that we will not understand these things and they will be hidden from us.

The best place to hide this knowledge is within, because we will not look there. Instead, we will look outside for the information.

We obviously look in the wrong direction to gain support in our lives. We look to the outer, unlike the birds that just trust and are well provided, along with all the animals. We are the thinkers, and life could become much easier if we were to do the same and take a leap of faith. It will be hard, because we do not know what to trust, since it is not seen by the human eye. Still, it can be perceived by our thoughts and feelings, and with the proper attitude and actions, all things are given to us.

We will be exploring even more of the subtle nature of life in the Book of John. This gospel revolves around the spiritual nature. So far, we have discussed the physical and combined that with the mental, further adding the emotional in the Book of Luke. Now we will bring that level of understanding to the spiritual part of us, as John comes before the "harbinger of things to come".

CHAPTER 7

THE BOOK OF JOHN

*"Far inferior indeed is mere action to the discipline of intelligence, O Winner
of wealth, seek refuge in intelligence.
Pitiful are those who seek for the fruits (of their action). (49)
And in that purity of spirit, there is produced for him an end of all sorrow; the
intelligence of such a man of pure spirit is soon established (in the peace of the
self). (65)*
The Bhagavadgita

The Book of John is the most complex work of the four Gospels. It entails the spiritual aspect of the human form and it is the deepest part of the teachings offered by the Master, Jesus Christ. This area may become very confusing to the reader because of its profundity. It will challenge the very core of the human nature. If you earnestly take the time and reflect on what is being offered, you will gain knowledge about the greatest of all gifts: to learn to work with the nature of God – rather than the external one we are taught to seek. You will also discover that God is truly a loving entity and not a vengeful one. Why indeed would It be vengeful, unless we as human are too stubborn to accept the good that spirit can give, or too proud in believing that we must do all things by our selves. This work is to teach the use of all the gifts that were originally given to us by spirit, and not just the body and the logic. These are only the tip of the iceberg. We all seek completeness, and this may offer great assistance, should you choose to reflect and accept.

At this time, we must remind the reader that Jesus and John were related to one another (Luke 1:36). They were second cousins. One would tend to believe that they knew each other when they met at a later time in the course of their mission. Their mothers, Mary and Elizabeth, were cousins and appeared to be very close. It is confirmed by the amount of time they spent together prior to John's birth. Many years later, when John and Jesus met at the river Jordan, they did not seem to recognize each other (John 1:31). Jesus was there specifically to be baptized by the water of life, the baptism of spirit. John is the one that came ahead, preparing the minds of the masses for the Teacher, much like the Ark of Covenant going before us and clearing the way. He was the Harbinger of things to come. John is the representation of the spirit nature in ourselves, yet he is described as a very physical person by his mode of dress and the way he ate. However, regardless of his appearance, his approach is through our inner nature and not the physical or outer nature. It is fascinating that the Book of John is included as one of the four main Gospels. We are told he never walked with the Master, yet he knows much about Jesus and what He had to offer to the multitudes when He spoke. In **John 1:23-30**, John says of himself: *"I am the voice of one crying in the wilderness..."*, and he goes on telling the crowds that *"there standeth one among you, whom ye know not"*. John is described as "the voice in the wilderness" in the other Gospels of the Bible, but we will cover a different way to perceive that voice a little further along in this chapter, for it has a dual meaning.

We will open the book of John in a completely different way than the gospels we have already discussed. We will now begin to unfold our most subtle nature yet, that being the spirit housed within each living human. We will also attempt to show the integration of the spirit all the way to the physical level of being. It will be a presentation of the "Good" – spirit or soul – and the "Evil" – physical or material nature, and how they work in union, with or without our awareness. The Master's mission was to get us to understand and accept this hypothesis. It includes how to work with both aspects to attain what we wish, on either the inner or outer level. In a practical sense, it means that if we are going to clean and maintain the outer, should we not also do the same for the inner. **Luke 11:39**: *"...Now do ye Pharisees make clean the outside of the cup and the platter; but your inward part is full of ravening and wickedness"*.

John 1:1 is dedicated the "the Word". The Word is the inner expression of Spirit. It would explain that what comes out of the human defiles us and it is what we create as "co-creators", because we do not accept the fact that spirit takes us literally along with everyone else. No one else is to blame. The Word was/is thought externalized. **John 1:14**: *"And the Word was made flesh, and dwelt among us..."*. It is the outer expression of what already existed in the concept of Spirit, and It gave life because of that expression. Existence came into being, into reality. **John 1:5**: *"And the light shineth in darkness; and the darkness comprehended it not"*. In its symbolism, it means that not all was understood. The light did not reach all things, because if it did, we would not have recognition any better than in darkness. There could be no individual nature, so balance was achieved between the two aspects. As a result, we have Yin and Yang, with a touch of each housed within, to demonstrate the inner nature in conjunction with the outer. Total darkness or total light would have no balance or comprehension. There could be no definition, and we had to have both to create understanding through difference. It is that difference that we are to celebrate, wherein we do not have everything matching our life, making us independence in motion. **John 1:9**: *"That was the true Light, which lighteth every man that cometh into the world"*. This is saying that the spirit nature will give us the only true understanding, but only if we decide to seek additional levels of knowledge. In **John 1:10**: *"He was in the world, and the world was made by him, and the world knew him not"*, we perceive an indication that our own thoughts create our own reality, that our reality is not supposed to control us, for it will not know us. It confirms that the material side has no concept of thought. Material is what it is, through our own creation, through our thinking. Our original creation was not one of the flesh. It was a much finer design to us: that of the soul. The soul is subservient to nothing physical. To this date, it is still as much a part of the spirit as it has ever been, as John tells us in **John 1:13**: *"Which were born, not of blood, nor of the will of the flesh, nor of the will of man, but of God"*.

In **John 1:15**, we see John exclaiming that Jesus came before him, yet John was indeed born first. He was chronologically older, so he was speaking of the spirit. He was referring to our own finer or higher self that has existed throughout time. It will always come before us for each incarnation, when the soul will pick up the body again for furthering itself and its experience of life. **John 1:17**: *"For the law was given by Moses, but grace and truth came by Jesus Christ"*. This is a mention of the metaphysical laws of the physical aspect, but the grace and truth come through the complete understanding of the full nature of life, thus the reference to the Christ. This Christ – or spirit – nature is the true voice, the voice in the wilderness, as in **John 1:23**: *"...I am the voice of one crying in the wilderness..."*. It is the voice of spirit that works within us all. It is best expressed by **Annie Bessant**: the "still small voice that surpasseth understanding". The wilderness is an allegory of the many thoughts that travel through the mind at a rate of about 2,500 images per minute. It is about the average for a human mind and it may be faster with a higher rate of intelligence. It is no wonder we are unable to hear that still small voice in the back of the mind. It is so soft that most times, we do not detect it. Still, the majority – or all – of us have and do hear it from time to time. It is the voice of conscience – or spirit – talking to us from within, and if we would but listen, things would become much simpler in our lives. **John 1:29-30**: *"The next day John seeth Jesus coming unto him, and saith, Behold the Lamb of God, which taketh away the sin of the world. (30) This is he of whom I said, After me cometh a man which is preferred before me: for he was before me"*. These verses indicate that John did not necessarily recognize Jesus as a cousin, but rather as the Master, as the embodiment of the spirit. Yet, he says in **John 1:31-32**: *"And I knew him not: but that he should be made manifest to Israel, therefore am I come baptizing with water. (32) And John bare record, saying, I saw the Spirit descending from heaven like a dove, and it abode upon him"*.

"He should be made manifest to Israel"... Esoterically, the physical may have the spiritual knowledge of life. It descended as a dove onto the human understanding, the two becoming unified as its true nature of one being.

Life is truly about forward movement. It means things will be constantly in a state of flux in all aspects of our lives. These changes are generated by what we learn of ourselves and others – through life's experiences. In **John 1:42**, Jesus says: *"...Thou art Simon the son of Jona: thou shalt be called Cephas, which is by interpretation, A stone".* The Master had sensed a shift in belief, a deeper understanding on the part of Simon. Bestowing a different name upon him is a clear confirmation of that change. Why did He call him Cephas – the rock? We again quote from the "Metaphysical Bible Dictionary". Cephas: *"An unwavering faith in God. When this faith is established firmly in individual consciousness, it becomes a rock, a sure foundation, unshakable, immovable, upon which one can build spiritually".*

In **John 2:3-11**, John relates the first miracle of the Master – the turning of the water into wine. However, the text takes on a different meaning, as it is one of transformation. Jesus first told His mother that His hour had not yet come, but in the next moments, the spirit took over within Him. He had transformed into the higher nature and as He did, so should we. Charles Fillmore describes the metaphysical sense of wine: "The 'wine' symbolizes the vitality that forms the connecting link between soul and body. It is an all-pervading free essence that is generated from the nerve substance, or water of life. This wine of life or free vitality of the organism must be present in large quantities before a blending of thoughts, or of soul and body (wedding), can be made successfully".

We now come to **John 2:14-22**: *"And found in the temple those that sold oxen and sheep and doves, and the changers of money sitting: (15) And when he had made a scourge of small cords, he drove them all out of the temple, and the sheep, and the oxen; and poured out the changers' money, and overthrew the tables;....".* The story, as told by John, has a very interesting twist. In other Gospels, you may note that the events he described are not recorded until just prior to the crucifixion. However, John does so at the beginning of his book. He believes that the greedy nature of the physical has too much of a hold on us, and it should be the first character flaw to be ousted, even to the point of crucifying one's physical nature from an ego point of view. Primarily, we must force our own being through the maze of the mind. This must be done at all costs to be able to control it, calming the seas of the inner nature, so that we may hear internally and not externally. We generally will not attempt this because the pain is great. We have to look at our own self in the bright light of truth, and we think it may hurt too much. This is not really so, as we will discuss later in this work. Expelling greed from our own self is confirmed in **John 2:21**: *"But he spake of the temple of his body"* – chasing this debilitating trait. He also expressed the fact that the body is indeed our temple in biblical reference. This, of course, applies to all of us.

In **John 3:1-2**, we see the search for understanding through the person of Nicodemus, as he approached by night – the symbol of darkness and ignorance -- so he would not be seen. He was a Pharisee with different beliefs. The concept of being born again was something he did not grasp, especially at an advanced age. Rebirth is an internal transformation. People change the way they look at life in general. They change their mind and thought process to allow for acceptance of the nature of the spirit housed within each of us. We see this in **John 3:5-6**: *"Jesus answered, Verily, verily, I say unto thee, Except a man be born of water and of the Spirit, he cannot enter into the kingdom of God. (6) That which is born of the flesh is flesh; and that which is born of the Spirit is spirit"*. The Master is telling us about the falseness of a dual nature. We are being reminded that our concerns lead us in the wrong direction and that we must cultivate a finer form of thinking about ourselves. Being born again is the realization and acceptance of the two natures as one, ergo "I and my Father are one". It is no easy feat. It means turning ourselves over to an unknown nature, without knowing where we are going or how to get there – like the birds, or the air... We think we should have a greater level of control. As physical being, we believe we have the steering device, and this is the misconception of control. The soul should always be in that position and will be, whether we realize it or not. Of course, this creates turmoil. After all, does not God know where It wants us to be? Deductively, if that were to be true, we are in the way, are we not? That is why we have such inner struggles. Jesus corroborates the principle in **John 3:8**: *"The wind bloweth where it listeth, and thou hearest the sound thereof, but canst not tell whence it cometh, and whither it goeth: so is every one that is born of the Spirit"*. Being born of spirit is turning yourself over and trusting your own inner, intuitive nature, a nature going before you, like the Ark of the Covenant, to clear your way. It is not for you to concern yourself. Would that not be wonderful? We are completely able to do this if we learn to trust ourselves and our conscience. Our outer aspect has been given so much for so long, while the inner still waits for mere recognition. Must we not look good before we appear in front of others? At least, the ego is being well fed. These actions belong to the external realm and to what others may think of us. What if they should think wrongly of our actions? It seems that we are living our lives for the entertainment of others, rather than for ourselves. We plan too much and structure our lives, while allowing very little flexibility. Today, we see rebellion everywhere around us. It is due to our own physiological make-up and how it paints us into a corner so that we may learn. It is due to our limited belief systems and how we establish our priorities.

As we know, in John 3:1-9, Jesus was having a conversation with Nicodemus, a ruler, a law giver of the times. The man had no real understanding of the inner nature of the teachings, yet, by his important position, one would have expected him to be knowledgeable, since people trusted his capabilities. We see in this encounter that he was somewhat inadequate. "The blind leading the blind" is as true today as it was then. **John 3:10-12**: *"Jesus answered and said unto him, Art thou a master of Israel, and knowest not these things? (11) Verily, verily, I say unto thee, We speak that we do know, and testify that we have seen; and ye receive not our witness. (12) If I have told you earthly things, and ye believe not, how shall ye believe, if I tell you of heavenly things?"*. This expands the fact that all we know is what has already been – our previous experience. If we understand what was, then we know now what is, and more importantly, why. The past brings us to the present moment. If the moment is good or bad, the past brought it to us. We must forgive the yesterdays and consider them as blessings. "Our witness" refers to the memories, how we perceive the events of the past. "Heavenly things" are what we have learned from those memories. This is the valuable side of previous events, no matter what they were in reality, as depicted in Verse 11 above. If you like and enjoy your life in the present moment, the past made it what it is. Conversely, if you do not like your present life, you are reliving the bad instants of the past. These are the memories that hold you in place, like Lot's wife, without forward movement. You are trapped and cannot enjoy yourself.

More of the spirit nature is revealed in **John 3:13-14**: *"And no man hath ascended up to heaven, but he that came down from heaven, even the Son of man which is in heaven. (14) And as Moses lifted up the serpent in the wilderness, even so must the Son of man be lifted up…"*. We are being shown that we originate from the essence of spirit, from which we inherit our simple beginnings. Our real strength is the fact that we descended from spirit, and to that we will return. It is also a reference to our belief or disbelief in this matter of ascension or spiritual attainment and that all metaphysical laws apply, even to the Masters. "Moses lifted up the serpent in the wilderness" is part of the action taking place. It is the lifting of one's spirit, the essence or vitality, one's energy – with intent. Allow me to explain:

The lifting of the serpent is an eastern philosophy. At the same time, there are several references offered by the Master, as well as in other books of the Old Testament. We see its origin in the book of Genesis with the original temptation embodied in the tree of knowledge. If one is interested in learning in-depth details of the rising of this serpent energy within the person, there are many works available to the public. These texts range from the Vedas, Buddhism, Tibetan or Zen to many American writers. One merely needs to seek information on what is known as **kundalini**. These teachings have existed for thousands of years. They are older than the Bible itself. They are perpetuated openly in other parts of the world. To have a complete understanding of these beliefs, one must also learn of the energy centers of the body, called **chakras**. Jesus Himself, the Master, was aware of these teachings, since He had studied them in the lands of ancient knowledge, namely Northern India, Kashmir, Nepal and Tibet. His teachers were the Masters of knowledge. The concept of kundalini is merely lifting one's own energy to a higher level, from the baser aspects of sex and greed – the physical nature – to the higher realms of thought. The higher realms are attained through the various depths of our thought process. As an example, pondering the concept of angels is higher thinking than wondering about money. Physical thinking keeps the serpent in the area of the first energy center, while higher thinking allows it to uncoil of its own accord until it reaches the crown. Even in today's world, it may be accomplished by anyone, through the constant formulation of higher thoughts. There are many exercises that can be taught to assist you in the intentional rise of this energy. If you are interested in the entire concept, many books offer you more detailed instructions. For safety purposes, it is recommended that you seek a competent teacher. The chakras are not materially real, but they are indeed with the body. They are necessary for the accomplishment of physical works, whether we use them or not on a conscious level. This energy brings a higher – or spiritual – vibration to us, thereby creating the need for less effort in the physical world. Be it a thought or an action required by you, things would become easier in life, effortless, when working in union with spiritual energy. Some factions even claim that it will extend life if properly used (Nath Yoga, Christ's teachers). The Master Himself has said on many occasions: *"In that time you will overcome death"*. He is offering this concept to what we think of our own limitation – a way of saying we are not as limited as we believe. Are not our mind and our thoughts the creators of the real blocks? Do they not generate this lack of forward movement? It has been said that the human mind can achieve whatever it can conceive and believe. This is a very true statement indeed. Jesus showed us what we can become by His example, and by the power of self in union with the spirit nature. The concept of kundalini is one of the larger keys to understanding, because it opens the complete nature of the inner Spirit we all have with us. It assists us in the attainment of the union of body and spirit.

The true nature of the power of opposition is the real stabilizer of physical life, and knowledge can be gained from it. *"...Behold, the man is become as one of us, to know good and evil..."* (Genesis 3:22). "As one of us" can now be truly invoked by anyone. The union of the bridegroom (Matthew 25:1, Mark 2:19, Luke 5:34, John 3:29) can take place, and "I and My Father are one" becomes reality. We invoke the power of opposition in our efforts to unify our higher and lower natures, accepting the spirit and the physical as one. Higher thoughts generated by the spirit are an invocation that allows the rising of the kundalini, through our inner nature, from the humblest or lowest point to the highest which is the Crown chakra (sahasrara). The "crown" is what we see portrayed as the illumination surrounding the head of the Master. When this crown chakra is in full operation, all centers work in union. At that point, the understanding of life and spirit are united in one being. We all have this birthright, but **John 3:19** also comes to a conclusion: *"And this is the condemnation, that light is come into the world, and men loved darkness rather than light, because their deeds were evil"*. We must consider again that we are "evil" because of the primary importance we give the material side of life. We must admit that everything we do is not exactly pointed toward the higher aspect of being. We are being informed that we will not lift ourselves in spiritual matters, and will remain in the lower energy centers. Not able to rise above the physical realm, darkness will reign within, along with the propensity toward evil deeds.

John 3:19 is often misused by certain factions in the world of religion. Why would we require a guilt trip placed on us by God? God would not do this, since we are Its creation – in Its image. Based on the premise that all laws inexorably apply to all, from the highest to the lowest – as Jesus taught us - does it not make sense that if we were at fault, so would God? The Master expands on this precept in **John 3:20-21**: *"For every one that doeth evil hateth the light, neither cometh to the light, lest his deeds should be reproved. (21) But he that doeth truth cometh to the light, that his deeds may be made manifest, that they are wrought in God"*. This implies that evil is now exposed as lack of understanding. **John 1:5** tells us: *"And the light shineth in darkness; and the darkness comprehended it not"*. We do not work to increase our level of spiritual appreciation, because with knowledge, our faltering will be uncovered, not by anyone else, but by our own self. It is important to know that all comes from spirit rather than ourselves, as expressed in **John 3:27**: *"...A man can receive nothing, except it given him from heaven"*.

John 4:10-14: *"Jesus answered and said unto her, If thou knewest the gift of God, and who it is that saith to thee, Give me to drink; thou wouldest have asked of him, and he would have given thee living water. (11) The woman saith unto him, Sir, thou hast nothing to draw with, and the well is deep: from whence then hast thou that living water? (12) Art thou greater than our father Jacob, which gave us the well, and drank thereof himself, and his children, and* *his cattle?* *(13) Jesus answered and said unto her, Whosoever drinketh of this water shall thirst again: (14) But whosoever drinketh of the water that I shall give him shall never thirst; but the water that I shall give him shall be in him a well of water springing up into everlasting life".* We have the Master at the well, speaking to a woman about the waters of life. The metaphor relates to the depth of the well within us. The thirst we may develop for knowledge and truth will disappear and we will thirst no more if we accept the cup He offers us. The water is the symbolism of the spirit energy flowing forth from us, to match the energy of the real Spirit. It flows forever as we have since the dawn of time, since physical reality began. We find more teachings in **John 4:21-24**: *"Jesus saith unto her, Woman, believe me, the hour cometh, when ye shall neither in this mountain, nor yet at Jerusalem worship the Father. (22) Ye worship ye know not what: we know what we worship for salvation is of the Jews. (23) But the hour cometh, and now is, when the true worshippers shall worship the Father in spirit and in truth: for the Father seeketh such to worship him. (24) God is a Spirit: and they that worship him must worship him in spirit and in truth".* This day is with us now. We sense that there is a movement toward the pursuit of the Truth, and it explains the many struggles going on today in the world around us. There is always a struggle when people are determined to free themselves of bonds. Truth is coming to the surface and now, we would rather have individual recognition – not national. Simply put, we are tired of being a number manipulated by religious and governmental controls imposed upon us. It is brought on by spirit's individual nature. The truth is being revealed to us so that we may shed the old superstitions for a new spiritual value system.

The continuation of this lesson is found in **John 4:34-38**. The disciples show concern as to whether Jesus ate or not, and they are seeking the food satisfying the physical self. The Master replied that He did not need such sustenance because the Spirit gave Him all that He needed: manna. It fed Him all He desired, like the birds in the fields. In **John 4:35**, He strengthens the lesson: *"Say not ye, There are yet four months, and then cometh harvest? behold, I say unto you, Lift up your eyes, and look on the fields; for they are white already to harvest".* When He said "Lift up your eyes", He meant "Lift your being". Recalling His teaching that the eye is the truth of the being, He began recognizing that the disciples were burdened. The Master was advising them to look up, rather than look down, for things are not that much of a burden unless we choose them to be heavy. The reference to "white" encompassed the light of knowledge and is a symbol of purity. Understanding is what is being offered to those listening. With the understanding comes purity of nature, innocence and readiness to accept spirit. If actions are accomplished in purity, they will return in the same condition, ready for harvest.

John 4:36-37: *"And he that reapeth receiveth wages, and gathereth fruit unto life eternal: that both he that soweth and he that reapeth may rejoice together. (37) And herein is that saying true, One soweth, and another reapeth"*. It may sound as though there are two separate people. This is not the case. Metaphorically, the sowing is the original thinking generated by a person. The reaper is the return action of what we have laid into place. In other words, it is our seed for growth, a union between thought and knowledge. The reward is the return, while the wages are a rebalancing of self. However, the reward may not be that at all... If thought, the original seed, is not any good, how can it be a true reward? Jesus says in **John 4:48**: *"...Except ye see signs and wonders, ye will not believe"*. Proof may be a more appropriate word. It is the reverse of truth, since Spirit has no need to prove anything. We are being told that the proof is already there in the form of what was returned to us, simply because it is our creation. If the returns are not as good as expected, we have a tendency to disregard the truth and conjure a multitude of excuses. This is what we do with our own inner self. If the project is a success, we did it. If it failed, it is not our fault because, allegedly, other things stopped us. As if by some miracle, it is the fault of someone or something else. How can this be? This suggests that we take credit only for the good returns and not the others. Was not the action originated by the individual who, in all logic, reaps what he sowed? We must accept responsibility for self and not blame anyone else for the reality we created.

In **John 5:2-3**, we find truly fascinating verses. One must sense the words and not just read them, because words may be very restrictive. By its very nature, any form of external communication is going to be somewhat limiting, compared to the beauty of the thought. The problem increases with the use of metaphors. We must learn to develop more than the five accepted senses, merely because there is more to the sensate system than just the physical. As an example, the ultra-violet shows a different, deeper range of the known colors seen with the physical eye. Technology has made this possible and perhaps, at some point in the future, it will uncover the rest. Do we really need technology, at least in the way we think we do? The answer is no – since all will be made known to those who seek. It may be nice, but it traps us further into physical reality which seems to be our primary concern. We do not question the fact that technology is the physical manifestation of our thought. Why do we question other things that originate from the same place? The answer may be in those two verses: *"Now there is at Jerusalem by the sheep market [gate] a pool, which is called in the Hebrew tongue Bethesda, having five porches. (3) In these lay a great multitude of impotent folk, of blind, halt, withered, waiting for the moving of the water..."*. Earlier, we defined the concept of "Jerusalem". This would already give these verses an entirely different perspective. Again, we must sense the deeper meaning and not just the words. It is like looking into a mirror of life...! It reflects the original, but at the same time, the reflection is backward and is merely a copy of said original. We see what we think is the real thing, but it is not. It is a reflection. With words, we must perceive their unique intent (the original), rather than their literal worth (the reflection). What is being suggested is that we use more than our five senses. Hidden behind the words are many profound concepts if we but look upon the inner reflection of self. The "sheep gate" – or market – is a portrayal of the mouth that expresses our thoughts. Remembering the shepherds, the "sheep" themselves represent our thinking, our thoughts, externalized through the gate by the gift of speech. The "five porches" are the five senses mentioned above. They are the purely physical attributes through which we receive feed-back from the outer aspect to assist our wisdom, our knowledge. The "pool" is in the center, where an angel – the spiritual influence – would come and stir or "trouble" the waters. This suggests a method for higher communication and sensory perception. It is the sixth sense used by spirit, and if we are in union, it can be used by us. The "waters" are the healing elements belonging to the higher nature. We are told we should use them because it will heal the thinking within us that has become sick and lame. Those described as laying around the pool are the memories that we have not faced or settled within us. We must learn to realize that these are not life itself, but rather its paralyzing elements. The sixth sense is a true gift of spirit. Today, more people are waking up to its use and develop a keener intuition. This further verifies that we are approach-ing a higher level of understanding and we are learning the use of spiritual tools. Progress in this matter would advance much faster if we would only ac-knowledge it rather than deny it. We will cover more of this subject later in this writing.

In **John 5:19-21**, Jesus is speaking to the Jews: *"Then answered Jesus and said unto them, Verily, verily, I say unto you, The Son can do nothing of himself, but what he seeth the Father do: for what things soever he doeth, these also doeth the Son likewise. (20) For the Father loveth the Son, and sheweth him all things that himself doeth: and he will shew him greater works than these, that ye may marvel. (21) For as the Father raiseth up the dead, and quickeneth them* [give them life]*; even so the Son quickeneth whom he will"*. Much is revealed in these verses because we are the true Sons of spirit. Since "son" refers to all, we are being reminded that we may all do these things. We are flesh and blood and can think and decide for ourselves, therefore, we must all be of spirit. In addition, did Jesus not say: *"...the works that I do shall he (man) do also"* (John 14:12)? It is reasonable to assume that we are able to accomplish these deeds, for we house the concept of God and we are Its chil-dren. However, there is a condition: we must acquire and use the sixth sense.

"...What he seeth the Father do..." seems to imply that God will be our teacher, and the sixth sense is the only way. We may also learn by observation and do on our own what is being done. Practice is our teacher, and the raising of the dead is something we do not remember from the days we were but a soul without a body. This knowledge was to be incorporated in our lives, but we are too busy looking only outward – which is easy to understand. Our eyes focus on the physical world that can be appreciated by our five senses. A little more insight would not hurt, since corporeal eyes can only look outward.

In **John 5:24-25**, we are being awakened. *"...when the dead shall hear the voice of the Son of God...".* Allegorically, the "dead" refer to those of us who were unable to understand, and we are now just beginning to see. Spirit gives us life and all the capabilities associated with it. We look only at the reflection! We do not see the real truth – just an image of it, and it must be backward since this is what a mirror will do for you. Jesus continues in **John 5:26**: *"For as the Father hath life in himself; so hath he given to the Son to have life in himself;... ".* We are the original reflection of the spirit of life within us. Logically, if spirit has life eternal, so must we within ourselves, but not in the way that we think, as we see in **John 5:28-29**: *"Marvel not at this: for the hour is coming, in which **all that are in the graves shall hear his voice**, (29) And shall come forth; they that have done good, unto the resurrection of life; and they that have done evil, unto the resurrection of damnation".* This means we will all have the knowledge. We ourselves are the graves. We are already dead, at least in the scope of our understanding and the lack of spiritual sensory perception. We do not hear or comprehend that we are the end result of the spirit influence, that it lives through us as it gives us life. We must build our house on Truth so that, as we follow our consciousness, we may only do good things for ourselves and others and be of service to others, no matter what our position may be. We must be good to others unconditionally, not for what we can get from them, but what we may do for them, or give them. These deeds will bring us our resurrection in life. The Master follows this by saying in **John 5:30**: *"I can of mine own self do nothing: as I hear, I judge: and my judgment is just; because I seek not mine own will, but the will of the Father which has sent me".* It is a truly simple concept. In the deeper part of ourselves, we are not alone, for we are all connected in spirit. We should realize that we merely must share who, and not what we are with others. If we allow the good to emanate from us, it will be returned to us as well. If we are **love**, then this is what we have – and nothing else.

Jesus was aware of His own ego and was doing nothing for or of Himself. It was all for others. He knew that if His deeds were of His own initiative, they would have been created by His ego. To turn it over to spirit was His way to acknowledge that His own initiative was indeed of spirit: *I and my Father are one*. He also tells us that we base our judgment on only what we hear, advising us that we should not do this because we are all the same. He further recognizes that the only reason His judgment was sound is simply because there was no ego involvement in it. His judgment was the will of spirit, pure in its nature, and it could not be in error. This is verified in **John 5:31**: *"If I bear witness of myself, my witness* [testimony] *is not true"*. This occurs when judgment is passed upon yourself or others, independent of the spirit. It implies that we should be aware of the ego in our spiritual growth. The ego cannot be denied, ignored or circumvented. We must work through it and identify it as of self only. We can then work outward to become selfless, using the power of ego for the higher good of all. Spirit is our witness. It records each moment of our life, and at some point, we will all have to face this documentation. Most people do not wish to face it because they believe that "it is not their fault". Jesus further says in **John 5:44**: *"How can ye believe, which receive honour one of another, and seek not the honour that cometh from God only?"*. Does this not indicate the ego? Does it not demonstrate that we cannot see the spirit within because we are blinded by our own light, along with that of others in the self-glorification of the body and the physical? In other words, we seek the elevation of the physical being and not the true inner nature of life. It appears that our most important concern is what others see and think. Must we seek the acceptance of our own self through the eyes of others? Obviously, we believe that if they do not approve, we cannot approve of ourselves either. It is a grave error on the part of those who accept this concept. They cannot attain an inner balance because they already gave one side away. They gave it to the others from whom they sought but did not receive acceptance. Once we surrender this into the hands of others, we no longer have the control and we work to change what we cannot, to wit, the others' perception of us. We persist on proving ourselves to the external world, thus we continue giving part of ourselves to life and others. This practice to prove or justify our presence is the true interference of life. It is why so many are so drained. They live their lives for the wrong reason. We must focus on humility and love within ourselves first and allow this to flow forth to others, to elevate their thinking when they need it, but we should not let ourselves down to another's level.

After Jesus fed the multitude with bread and fish, he said to His disciples, in **John 6:12**: *"...Gather up the fragments that remain, that nothing be lost"*. We now see that all things must come to fruition in life, no matter what they may be – for nothing is above the law. All things must return to their creator to balance the records, so we may have culmination in the trinity of the self: body, mind and spirit. Each time we make a choice or generate an act, the balance must be reestablished. This is the cycle to life. It matters not whether it is a thought, a feeling or a physical action. We will reap the appropriate reward for whatever it may be. We reap what we sow, and whatever ye mete brings returns unto you tenfold. We must gather these and clear them so that there is no waste, and nothing may be wasted.

In **John 6:15**, we return to the subject of the ego: *"When Jesus therefore perceived that they would come and take him by force, to make him a king, he departed again into a mountain himself alone"*. The Master did not wish to fill His ego with all the accolades from the people who loved Him and those who did not. He knew that neither He nor anyone else need these tributes, and they were adverse to His own inner core. Somehow, we came to believe that these flattering praises are good for one's growth... As children, we sought approval and acceptance from others, feeling that it would validate us. It may, but only in the eyes of others, and not within us. If they do not approve, our internal fight will begin, and for most of our lives, we will be trapped in this cycle. Keep in mind that John is engaged in the spiritual aspect in which we may not necessarily believe. We need proof, and his gospel provides it. Even then, those attestations were not accepted. Would they be today? Probably not!

In **John 6:16-21,** we find much veiled information. We learn that Jesus was not interested in becoming king of the Jews, to the point where He withdrew again to the mountain. He went into meditation, lifting His being to commune with the energy of spirit so that He could regenerate His physical form. He had become drained. In the meanwhile, *"...his disciples went down unto the sea, and entered into a ship..."*. The ship refers to the journey of the spirit, much like the Ark of Noah. Initially, that journey will cause turmoil. Jesus Himself said that you must be willing to give up your life in order to save it. We are being informed that overcoming the thinking process limited by the physical nature is difficult. Analogically, it is like letting go of the steering wheel of a moving car, knowing that an accident will occur. We feel that we will reach a point when we will lose ourselves, our fear, and we will not have any control or influence with the world. This is a false view, simply because we gain a greater dimension and ability by turning it over to a higher nature. The only thing that can be lost is what we thought we knew about our own being. In **John 6:18**, a new understanding of self will be attained, as *"the sea arose by reason of a great wind that blew"*. This is spiritual awakening stirring within the human form, and it will not be easy at first. However, once we merge with our spiritual self, the seas will become calm and the turmoil will go away. Our hearts will open. To accomplish this, one must trust in turning one's self over to the higher spirit nature. We cannot trust another to do this for us, let alone something we cannot see with our eyes. We see this merger taking place in the Master's students as He said: *"...It is I; be not afraid. Then they* *willingly received him into the ship...* " This is a symbol of the merger, and the ship immediately came to land where they were going. The ship is the symbol of the human form and the water is the spirit, while Jesus is the symbol of the merger. These are all indicators of fulfillment within the Self. The land to which they traveled represents the goal attained by the teachings that were offered and which they understood.

The fulfillment is carried further in **John 6:26-27**: *"...Verily, verily, I say unto you, Ye seek me, not because ye saw the miracles, but because ye did eat of the loaves, and were filled. (27) Labour not for the meat which perisheth, but for that meat which endureth unto everlasting life, which the Son of man shall give unto you: for him hath God the Father sealed".* This is **Truth**, truth because we eat of the energy of spirit daily without being aware of it. We draw it with each breath that we take. The energy of the heavens is before us – and is us. We are continually filled by this substance called manna, which we derive from the air. The difference within us is the mere awareness of this inspired repast, as well as giving it significance. It is the breath of life from God Itself, so we may continue with life and spirit. We are told not to work for earthly sustenance because it spoils, but the energy of spirit is perpetual and fills our souls. Yes, the physical being does require food, but we should not emphasize it as the most important factor. What have we done to what we inhale and ingest? Have we not harmed it and mixed our own egos into it, through greed? And what have we done to the waters that help cleanse, for the sake of the external self? Once they are gone, then what? If we have soiled our various natures, have we not also soiled the energy of spirit by trusting too much what we see and think, and not what we feel? Thank God we are awakening to another understanding! The internal food we mention is of course not bread in the physical sense. It is the energy of the spirit upon which we must rely.

John 6:31-33: *"Our fathers did eat manna in the desert; as it is written, He gave them bread from heaven to eat. (32) Then Jesus said unto them, Verily, verily, I say unto you, Moses gave you not that bread from heaven; but my Father giveth you the true bread from heaven. (33) For the bread of God is he which cometh down from heaven, and giveth life unto the world".* In this lesson, the Master associates Moses with the physical self – thus Egypt and the journey -- upon which we rely entirely too much. We pretentiously think that we do not require a representative to attain this energy for us since it gives us all life as we may see fit. Humanity used to do this for itself, without the confinement of being told how to do it. No intervention was necessary. It was natural law in action and they knew it. They knew how to use this energy for assistance in the material world of life. Today, we are unsure. The lack of confidence stems from mistrust – mistrust of what to understand or to accept as correct. That is actually fairly easy. Trust your feelings rather than your thinking. You will find the difference quite noticeable and when you do, follow your feelings. Trust is being open to the possibilities of life and not the definition of life, because once you have defined, you have confined. You now have your own personal fences that, at some point, you will have to remove. This will cause a struggle. Why a struggle? Simple. You will have to change your mind or beliefs, and when that happens, your life will be altered. Most of us do not change very gracefully... The simple path is being opened to receive from the spirit, and knowing that this transference takes place. Then each breath will be in reverence and respect for our own being, merging with the energy of the heavens and receiving the bread of life.

We may extend this thinking even further in **John 6:47-51**: *"Verily, verily, I say unto you, He that believeth on me hath everlasting life. (48) I am that bread of life. (49) Your fathers did eat manna in the wilderness, and are dead. (50) This is the bread which cometh down from heaven, that a man may eat thereof, and not die. (51) I am the living bread which came down from heaven: if any man eat of this bread, he shall live for ever: and the bread that I will give is my flesh, which I will give for the life of the world"*. Jesus talks about our soul – that part in all of us that comes from heaven – and the faith of a mustard seed seems to become more important. This lesson is not limited to Him only. It includes all of us. He is telling us to shift our focus to the higher nature, because throughout time, the physical distraction has always been an issue for human kind. *"...the bread that I will give is my flesh..."* is the corporeal illustration of us all, from the soul to the material side. The soul wanted the experience of the physical and gave it flesh and blood. We are locked into the five senses and not using the sixth. We are not allowing the merging of the energy of heaven within. When this is achieved, we will realize that we do live forever and are eternal in nature, for we are in the image of God. For too many among us, this is not accepted or understood. It is stated clearly in Genesis 3:22: *"...the man is become as one of us..."* and it carries an enormous realization, coming from an eternal God down to Its human creation. Yet, it seems we are unable to absorb this wonderful characteristic. On the other hand, how may one truly understand infinity as it was once known? It would now be finite, would it not? As we expand, so must all things in our reality. We are told this is to be our experience, because creation is constant – not just at the beginning – and we are still creation in process.

The verses in **John 6:53-58** are further substantiation of the process of the energy of spirit housed within us: *"Then Jesus said unto them, Verily, verily, I say unto you, Except ye eat the flesh of the Son of man, and drink his* *blood, ye have no life in you. (54) Whoso eateth my flesh, and drinketh my blood, hath eternal life; and I will raise him up at the last day. (55) For my flesh is meat indeed, and my blood is drink indeed. (56) He that eateth my flesh, and drinketh my blood, dwelleth in me, and I in him. (57) As the living Father hath sent me, and I live by the Father: so he that eateth me, even he shall live by me. (58) This is that bread which came down from heaven: not as your fathers did eat manna, and are dead: he that eateth of this bread shall live for ever".* The Master is discussing the level of faith necessary for the attainment and acceptance of the bridegroom when he comes. This is the symbol of the merging of our higher and lower aspects, or the union of the physical nature of self-bonding with the higher consciousness. Faith is a matter of perspective within each of us. There is a single definition for this word, yet it will come to each of us in an explanation as individual as we are. What faith means to one will not be the same to another. The reason for this is because of the experiences of our own lives. Each of us tends to qualify it differently. The truth is, faith is being open to our beliefs with flexibility – not the hard, fast position we take. One may easily peer into the Christ energy and can see that this is our own soul talking to us. After all, are we not the temple, or the potential of the temple? We are, but only if we see ourselves in a sacred light rather than the darkness of the body only. We are being taught that we must incorporate the information of the Christ within ourselves, because it is what we all are.

Jesus tells us in **John 6:62-63**: *"What and if ye shall see the Son of man ascend up where he was before? (63) It is the spirit that quickeneth* [gives life]*; the flesh profiteth nothing: the words that I speak unto you, they are spirit, and they are life".* "The flesh profiteth nothing"… We are told beyond a doubt that physical life is not the real focus, and it does not gain a thing. All we do here is in the interest of the higher level, since we will shed the lower and leave it behind. Hence, the physical life is the untruth, the illusion, for the soul withdraws and our physical side is no longer of any use to us. At that time, we will have to own all that we have done in life. The Master warned us when He said that what we do here, we lay up for ourselves in heaven. It is the spirit that gives us life. It is God within us, and it knows our accomplishments – good or bad – since It is with us always. We just ignore it and think of it as a fantasy or an illusion. As mentioned before, our physical selves are just the tip of the iceberg. **John 6:66**: *"From that time many of his disciples went back, and walked no more with him".* When the Master began His dissertation on the food of life, many of His students left Him simply because they considered only the literal sense of the words. It was difficult for them to accept this particular lesson that must have appeared to them as a form of cannibalism. Those intuitive enough did realize that Jesus was not talking about the physical aspect of the body as food. He was talking about our true spiritual nature that must fill every aspect of us through faith. Thus, spirit will permeate the entire physical form, into every cell, and it will allow for a person to be "born again". Jesus was not talking about food as we know it. He was talking about the energy of spirit. How many, over the centuries, have misconstrued the important biblical messages by accepting them only through the mere value of the words? How many have missed the opportunity to decipher the symbolism that could have given them a better life?

In **John 7:1-3**, we catch a glimpse of ancient history. Jesus had just preached in Capernaum and wanted to stay in Galilee because Jews sought to kill him. Some people were attempting to talk the Master into going to Judea which, at the time, was a place of turmoil. In his explanation, John gives us remarkable verses in **John 7:4-5**: *"For there is no man that doeth any thing in secret, and he himself seeketh to be known openly. If thou do these things, shew thyself to the world. (5) For neither did his brethren believe in him"*. We are reverting once more to the subject of ego. If we are interested in being known, we believe that we must gloat or show off on the rooftops. If you look around, you may discover that not many do much in secret. Our culture has become one of vain ostentatious efforts. We are very busy shouting our own greatness, making it difficult for anyone to believe what we are. In fact, it creates mistrust. The next verse tells us that in all humility, Jesus turned the suggestion down. He knew it was not of Him, nor would he show off for the people. He did not want to use His skills for the wrong reason, for it would serve only their ego - and also His own.

In Chapter 7, we see the awakening of the human to the understanding of the higher nature. **John 7:16-17**: *"Jesus answered them, and said, My doctrine is not mine, but his that sent me. (17) If any man will do his will, he shall know of the doctrine, whether it be of God, or whether I speak of myself"*. This is the knowledge that comes with the progressive efficiency in the conduct of our physical life. It does not entail reaching goals in the material world, but rather the attainment of higher understanding, a rising above the pull of life and ego. It is one of cognitive thinking or creative thinking with a willingness to be open. We may do this by initially relinquishing ourselves to the spirit nature, thus discovering our real depth of self. Jesus then says in **John 7:18**: *"He that speaketh of himself seeketh his own glory: but he that seeketh his glory that sent him, the same is true, and no unrighteousness is in him"*. In the first sentence, there is no question that the Master is telling us of our own arrogance. It is quite easy to get caught up in the game of self-glorification, and it appears to be a most important aspect for us. Those who flirt with selfishness and think they know it all only think through their own intellect. As a result, they can only speak of themselves. It also allows them to deal with their external world, but it reflects a limited understanding of life within their inner selves. In the second portion of the verse, we see the "glory that sent him" as an indication of the importance of the person's soul. We must all give it recognition and honor our true selves rather than the body or the physical. It is corroborated in **John 7:24**: *"Judge not according to the appearance, but judge righteous judgment".* If you recall, the Master emphasized "judge not, lest ye be judged", but now it appears to be acceptable. What is the difference? We judge people and their deeds by what we see and hear. We rely only on the outer nature and our five senses. For example, if we encounter a person dressed shabbily, we categorize him/her by whatever name we choose. We would categorize a well-dressed person quite differently. Those are outer judgments, not necessarily correct. In the above verse, we are told to look a little deeper before we come to a conclusion. "Righteous" simply means to let our higher understanding control our physical tendencies. We will see more clearly and will be able to formulate a better determination of the deed or the person. The interesting thing is the enlightenment we will receive, as well as the level of objectivity we will get to assist us in this type of deeper judgment. We must exercise caution, however, because what we judge, we will receive as the reward. If we condemn someone, we will also be condemned by our own nature. We become harsh and critical of our own self, wondering why and how it happened.

John 7:25-27 also deals with physical appearance: *"Then said some of them of Jerusalem, Is not this he, whom they seek to kill? (26) But, lo, he speaketh boldly, and they say nothing unto him. Do the rulers know indeed that this is the very Christ? (27) Howbeit we know this man whence he is: but when Christ cometh, no man knoweth whence he is".* At first they knew Him and whence He came. In the next statement, they did not. We are told that we may know whence a human is, but we do not know whence the spirit is. We must look deeper into those we encounter and if we do, we may know them in the true sense. Most of the times, we do not consider the spirit of the person – only what we see. The true message being offered is: look into the person and not at him or her. If you look into that person, much more will be shown. Look into the eyes, for it is the window to the soul. If you are unable to do so – or dare not – it may be time to analyze your own insecurities and fears, not the other person's. We do not look because we believe that all will be known, and we would rather hide. To a great degree, this is the truth of us. We are reminded of this in **John 7:38**: *"He that believeth on me, as the scripture hath said, out of his belly shall flow rivers of living water".* We are to let our inner selves flow from within to the outside. Regrettably, we do not, because we are concerned only with what others will think and how they will judge us. Consequently, we bind ourselves and do not let the expressive nature of pure self come forth. Imagine the Master acting in such fashion. We would not have the world we have. Judging holds us all in place, whether it is from us or from others. If we were to follow His example, there could be more like Him doing these works. Unfortunately, and incorrectly, we are told that we cannot, that it is of Satan, and that it is wrong. Not so, says the Master. We may do all these works, should we choose to do so. We must learn how to do these things and even greater ones if we have the faith of the mustard seed. But then how can we, with the onslaught by others? This is why Jesus always says to do it in secret and tell no one. Let them see the proof through the actions that will take the place of our words. How can these words be judged if they come from the heart of the sender. Those who do judge will already have their reward.

In **John 8:7**, Jesus said: *"...He that is without sin among you, let him first cast a stone at her"*. In essence, the Master was telling the scribes and the Pharisees: "Do not judge her!". This type of behavior puts any and all of us above others, does it not? The matter of sin is something with which we all deal on a regular basis. According to the churches, we are simply filled with sin... In reality, it is only a confirmation of the fact that we do not focus our own being on ourselves. After all, analyzing another's actions shifts the attention away from our own flaws. Jesus is telling us that we should not place ourselves in such a position. We each have our weaknesses, and we will generally accuse others for our own doings. If you are without sin, cast the stone! However, if you do, you will now have what you did not have before: sin within you. Leave the people as you found them and let your own light shine before you in grace, as He tells us in **John 8:12**: *"...I am the light of the world: he that followeth me shall not walk in darkness, but shall have the light of life"*. His advice is for us to follow our higher selves and be that light. We, of ourselves, are nothing save for what spirit will make of us if we allow it. The light of life is understanding how life itself operates, how we may influence all things.

In **John 8:13-18**, there is real stimulation in the verification of the self. It confirms the two natures being one in reality. If one were to lift himself toward spirit – or the soul of the individual – the two natures would become one when offered for the higher purposes of life. *"The Pharisees therefore said unto him, Thou bearest record of thyself; thy record is not true. (14) Jesus answered and said unto them, Though I bear record of myself, yet my record is true; for I know whence I came, and whither I go; but ye cannot tell whence I come, and whither I go. (15) Ye judge after the flesh; I judge no man. (16) And yet if I judge, my judgment is true: for I am not alone, but I and the Father that sent me. (17) It is also written in your law, that the testimony of two men is true. (18) I am one that bear witness of myself, and the Father that sent me beareth witness of me"*. The testimony of two men is the substantiation of the soul and the physical nature working in union with each other, or the higher and the lower merged as one unit of being. It is in all of us if we make the effort. When properly used, we attain the "I and my Father are one" within each of us. It will produce a knowing and/or cognitive thinking within each person through the acceptance of self. Jesus carries this a little further in **John 8:23** when He says: *"...Ye are from beneath; I am from above: ye are of this world; I am not of this world"*. We have been taught that these words apply only to the Master Himself. This is not exactly the truth. The soul is talking to us, and it is not of this world. It is not physical. The body being the "beneath" is only this world's temporary habitat of the soul housed within. **John 8:24** tells us that we must believe the soul is a part of us, not separate from us. All we have to do is pay attention to this. It will assist us every day, making our lives easier to live and helping us work with each other. **John 8:29** is linked to this subject matter: *"And he that sent me is with me: the Father hath not left me alone; for I do always those things that please him"*. This verse relates that our spirit or higher self is responsible for our lives. No matter what we do, it is always with us. It springs us into life and if we listen to it, we may only do what pleases it. If we were to look around us seriously and impartially, we would know that we do not pay much attention – if any – to where spirit could lead us. It is an inner feeling, a knowing that is always attached to us. It is a voice to which we do not listen. If we did, we would all be in service to each other. In reality, we already are, but we place profit first. We think in term of what can be made off that person, or what we can get from another. Whatever happened to the gift of giving without expecting some sort of return?

John 8:34-35: *"...Verily, verily, I say unto you, Whosoever committeth sin is the servant of sin. (35) And the servant abideth not in the house for ever: but the Son abideth ever"*. Sin is not what we have been taught it is. It is merely erroneous thinking and believing in the wrong things. As Charles Fillmore explains it: *"Sin is a departure from the law of our being"*. An example might be idol worship. It is an extension of our longing for things outside of the self rather than the inside. We have become too dependent on this material gratification. This is the sin we all perpetrate. Because we let the external world own us through this sin, we become a slave to it. This is something that cannot last in our lives, and the Master's reference to the Son is to the higher self, a higher self that is as permanent as God Itself. It can be the solution if we were to believe this of ourselves. It would set us free from all burdens and live an easier life than ever before. In **John 8:38**, we are told of our independent spirit nature: *"I speak that which I have seen with my Father: and ye do that which ye have seen with your father"*. Jesus is advising us directly to listen to our own soul nature, that all of us may do what He does. He refers to "my Father" and "your father" as two separate entities that belong to each of us individually. It is our unique nature of self that no one else may have. It is you and nothing else. It is soul communication.

John 8:44-47 introduce us to an interesting concept. In John 8:44, Jesus says: *"Ye are of your father the devil..."*, and in John 8:47, He says: *"He that is of God heareth God's words..."*. Most would be confused by these statements, for we are to be of God. We are told on the surface that the devil is our father. How can that be? This is directed toward those that believe in the ego self rather than the higher spirit self. We are pulled by the physical world and that is the devil – nothing else. Those that are of God focus on the beauty and love of life. They do not seek to control or own more than they can use for themselves, for if they do, they have their reward already. Worship the physical only, and you have all that you will get. When you pass on, it is all left behind – and that is your reward. You left it – it did not leave you. We also must learn to realize that the Christ said we should be single in purpose. Can we be, if we believe in duality, such as the devil and God? They are two opposites and we may believe in one or the other. If we believe in both, we will be split in our thinking. The fact is that we are all split in that area, while Jesus told us that we do not have to be. Choose one and go with it. **John 8:51** validates it: *"Verily, verily, I say unto you, If a man keep my saying, he shall never see death"*. This is distinctly single in purpose for you cannot and should not believe in the two opposites. We are to hear and heed the words of the higher nature, not just the physical, and we shall never see death as portrayed by contemporary myths. The Master repeats this quite often, yet we do not hear.

We have already discussed or made mention of the word **karma**. Now we have it depicted in **John 9:2-3** as something we must work out in our lives. Spirit will assure that we will accomplish this task. *"And his disciples asked him, saying, Master, who did sin, this man, or his parents, that he was born blind? (3) Jesus answered, Neither hath this man sinned, nor his parents: but that the works of God should be made manifest in him"*. Those are the works we must all endure. It is what we have earned in life as the spirit deems, in order for spiritual accounting to balance out our lives. The question from the disciples stemmed from one of the Master's inner teachings. They wanted to know what had been done to deserve such fate. Jesus' answer was about the understanding of the aspect of karma. We are told that it is of the spirit, so that a person would know of the higher nature of the Self, or to remember that which had been ignored and must now be balanced out in this person's life. When we come into life, it is with all of us a rectification of past deeds. Naturally, all depends on what we did during the last incarnation. Thus, it is merely a settlement of the spiritual debt that we have with God. There is no way out of this, and we must go through the process, as a moment of negativity can induce days of healing within us. A previous life of negativity will produce a new life of refinement. We may prevent this by being of a positive, truthful nature all the time. Life is far from being a negative thing. It is a blessing for us to enjoy and to learn. We are here to accept – rather than expect – the experience of happiness in the physical world. The Master told this man to wash himself in the pool of Siloam (John 9:7). This particular place has been mentioned in other parts of the Bible. You will find it in Luke 13:4 and John 9:7 and 11. In the Old Testament, you will find it in Isaiah 8:6 as *Shiloah* and in Nehemiah 3:15 as *Siloah*. The Metaphysical Bible Dictionary defines Siloam as: *"One sent, sending forth*, or putting away. "Go, wash in the pool of Siloam" means to deny away the false idea. We are to deny the universal race belief in the reality and power of matter, and to affirm the spirituality of all substance". In **John 9:8-9**, we see that the man had changed so much that no one could believe or recognize him for who he was. It represents the power of new ideas unfolding within the human. In **John 9:32-34**, we see the allegory of being blind very well defined: *"Since the world began was it not heard that any man opened the eyes of one that was born blind. (33) If this man were not of God, he could do nothing. (34) They answered and said unto him, Thou wast altogether born in sins, and dost thou teach us?..."*. This is an excellent example of the karmic nature of self and what one will be able to understand once a deed or an action is completed. As the knowledge expands, some begin teaching others, but no one will believe them, because we do not allow other people to change. We hold them in place and then rebuke them. Understanding removes blindness. In the first three verses of Chapter 9, we are told to appreciate and accept the work of the spirit so karma will be carried out through our higher selves. It will be implemented by our lower selves, but we all seem to avoid this because it is too difficult. It may be true, but once you have had the courage to overcome the obstacles, the path is smoother and your journey becomes easier. You may do the work of self, in union with the spirit.

We see more of this in **John 10:1-4**: *"Verily, verily, I say unto you, He that entereth not by the door into the sheepfold, but climbeth up some other way, the same is a thief and a robber. (2) But he that entereth in by the door is the shepherd of the sheep. (3) To him the porter openeth; and the sheep hear his voice; and he calleth his own sheep by name, and leadeth them out. (4) And when he putteth forth his own sheep, he goeth before them, and the sheep follow him: for they know his voice"*. This door is the inner entrance to your mind, where you can examine your own thinking, whether positive or negative. You must be willing to confront it, because if you try to ignore or deny it, you may have a thief within you known as the ego. So, one must not deny what is really there: the knowledge of self. Once you recognize it, you become the shepherd of the thoughts, and they will respond to you. You may control or own your thinking and types of thoughts, to improve them toward a more positive nature, but you may only do this within the strict parameters of Truth. Conversely, if you have negative type thinking, you may free yourself by herding it away from yourself or releasing it to the world. One does not play host to an unwelcome guest. As with anything else, it takes efforts, but it will be opened to you if you merely work with it. It is your mind and you may command it to do whatever you want it to do, rather than sheepishly doing its will. You must accomplish this yourself, for no one else can do it for you, even though you may try. In John 10:4, the spirit is in front, as the Ark of the Covenant, but initially, it will take everything you have to reach that point. This is so you may become inwardly clear. As you are told by the Master, your thinking will follow along, and it takes actually very little effort in the long run. Conclusively, do not avoid this task.

The Master expands on this idea in **John 10:9**: *"I am the door: by me if any man enter in, he shall be saved, and shall go in and out, and find pasture.* In **John 14:12**, Jesus said: *"...the works that I do shall he (man) do also".* Based on this categorical statement, we can be sure that the door is within us all. We all possess the Christ nature and must bring it forth as well as the spirit within for a better future. We may enter at any time to seek assistance not only in the spiritual realm, but also in the physical. The pasture mentioned in the verse is the symbol of happiness and fulfillment. **John 10:11-14**: *"I am the good shepherd: the good shepherd giveth his life for the sheep. (12) But he that is an hireling, and not the shepherd, whose own the sheep are not, seeth the wolf coming, and leaveth the sheep, and fleeth: and the wolf catcheth them, and scattereth the sheep. (13) The hireling fleeth, because he is an hireling, and careth not for the sheep. (14) I am the good shepherd, and know my sheep, and am known of mine".* These verses indicate the ability we have to control our mind. We must be shepherds of our thoughts and must herd them gently to the positive attributes of our lives. The Master is guiding us to the humble side of thought, and not to the aggressive nature we all demonstrate to force our way into and through life. If we follow His advice, we are the owner, and not the hireling. As the owner, we are being told to be responsible for what we do, because if we are not, we may lose all that we have. Our thinking will get out of control within us, if we allow it. And we normally do... If we live up to what we are, we find the inner truth of our being. No one may take it from us and we become the true owner of our being. It will be the cornerstone of our life, but not until we give in to the higher nature within us, making us a real and genuine point of power in life. We become the true cause with all the control, in the service of others. We can see clearly and are no longer blind in life.

In Genesis 3:5, we read: *"...and ye shall be as gods, knowing good and evil"*. In **John 10:34**, Jesus said: *"...Is it not written in your law, I said, Ye are gods?"*. Is the Master saying that, biblically, it is written that we are gods? The answer is simple: yes! How many other ways are there to confirm that we are in God's image and likeness? If this is so, Jesus' statement is correct indeed and we all miss the point. We are taught that to consider ourselves as such is a grave misconception, yet, the Master Himself recognizes the fact. He has expressed in many ways that we are just as He is. The fact alone that it is recorded in the Bible should be enough, considering the fact that we accept the rest as truth. Several religions tell us that we cannot be, that only the Christ is God and that we are too evil. The question is: why are we not able to accomplish or carry on His deeds? To be practical and realistic about it, we would probably kill each other in the process, because we do not know how to use such power. We could compare this situation to putting an irresponsible teenager in charge of the nuclear arsenal. In reality, this power comes from the ability to love, even in the face of adversity. We fall short of that quality and usually become angry. We are to be humble in our nature, thereby allowing others to be who they are in life. We are not to interfere and condemn them for what they do. Who are we to do so? Do we possess the spiritual strength to be as Jesus? It is rather safe to say that we are not without sin, therefore we should not cast the first stone unless it is in arrogance. And arrogance will never release the essence of love to another. It will create nothing but selfishness, and that will be our reward – not from the spirit. We do have a long path ahead of us...

John 11:9-10. These verses are a reference to understanding and the lack thereof: *"Jesus answered, Are there not twelve hours in the day? If any man walk in the day, he stumbleth not, because he seeth the light of this world. (10) But if a man walk in the night, he stumbleth, because there is no light in him"*. The Master tells us that there are twelve hours of light and twelve hours of darkness in a day, theoretically. It symbolizes the fact that when we walk with understanding within us, we do not stumble. However, if we walk without the knowledge, we will more than likely stagger and lurch in life. The stumbling happens only to assist us in gaining comprehension of matters that we know not. It is a natural part of life. The intent is for us all to walk in the light, knowing about and aspiring to the higher self. If we learn and work with that knowing aspect, no one will have to stumble in any way. We will have the knowledge and be able to see events clearly. "There is no light in him" is a metaphor depicting the non-acceptance of the spirit or higher self, therefore the absence of the light of understanding. Jesus advises us not to walk in the dark.

In the book of John, several unrelated accounts fall within the spiritual nature of its author. For instance, Lazarus has been shown in many a light through the different Gospels. In **John 11:1-45**, we have still another situation wherein the man is dead and the Master raises him. In the other books, Lazarus had sores or a variety of illnesses. Given a period of time, it would stand to reason that in this book, he had died and laid four days in the tomb for attainment purposes. Allegorically, he was not really dead, as Jesus stated in **John 11:11**: *"...Our friend Lazarus sleepeth; but I go, that I may awake him out of sleep"*. We see the symbolism of the man turning himself over to the spiritual aspect, as in **John 11:25**: *"...he that believeth in me, though he were dead, yet shall he live"*. He gave his life so that he could save it. He lost himself so that he could find himself in true reality. He had gone through the struggle of releasing material importance for the spiritual, thus saving his life. In **John 12:3-5**, Judas Iscariot is mentioned as the one complaining that Mary was being wasteful with oil and perfume, when these items could have been sold. In the other books, it is reported that the Pharisees made the remarks, but now we can put a name on the truth. It is placing the greed on the appropriate name rather than on a religious figure of the time. Thus, the ego is that part of us that is greedy. The same subject is found in **John 12:19**: *"The Pharisees therefore said among themselves, Perceive ye how ye prevail nothing? behold, the world is gone after him"*. We are being told that we are using the material aspect to manifest the physical. It is portraying the ego within telling the physical aspect that it is losing the struggle with the higher or soul nature. As we all know, producing the physical desire is difficult at times, but if we used the spiritual nature, it would become easier to accomplish. If we allowed it, it would come from within us, and greed is nothing more than our ignorance in how we conduct life. In **John 12:24**, we see the Lazarus issue carried a bit further: *"Verily, verily, I say unto you, Except a corn of wheat fall into the ground and die, it abideth alone: but if it die, it bringeth forth much fruit"*. This metaphor implies that we must be willing to give our lives in order to bear the fruits of spiritual enlightenment. If the seed does not die, nothing will grow. Imagine if a caterpillar did not retreat into its cocoon, it could not become a butterfly. It gives itself up so that it may fly rather than crawl on the ground. It metamorphoses into a thing of beauty. So must we. Jesus tells us further on that we each shall have our hour, when our time will come to declare our belief. This is our purpose for life.

John 12:35-36: *"Then Jesus said unto them, Yet a little while is the light with you. Walk while ye have the light, lest darkness come upon you: for he that walketh in darkness knoweth not whither he goeth. (36) While ye have light, believe in the light, that ye may be the children of light..."*. The Master is that light, as He predicted His death. That spiritual light allows us to realize all things with no limitation, for we must look to see. We can be what He was if we let ourselves be illumined in life and within. We will not walk in the darkness of spiritual ignorance. We will understand if we simply surrender ourselves and let spirit light our path before us. This is our legacy and the road to our destination, for He was the way of knowledge. We must learn to absorb these teachings within us, rather than externalize them the way we are conditioned to do. The external will fall away because it is merely a façade, but the inner being will remain for it is real. After all, our true self resides within a body that is simply a vehicle for the soul. In **John 12:40**, the prophet Isaiah said: *"...that they should not see with their eyes, nor understand with their heart, and be converted..."*. This is the perception that has already been discussed in this work. It is the sixth sense that we all have housed within us and the only true way to identify God in life and as a real entity. God is not a physical body. It is all things seen and unseen.

Love is the greatest key to life. We are not just talking about your immediate circle of family and friends. We are talking about the whole human race. **John 13:34-35**: *"A new commandment I give unto you, That ye love one another; as I have loved you, that ye also love one another. (35) By this shall all men know that ye are my disciples, if ye have love one to another"*. This one simple thing is rare for any of us to do. It is difficult only because we see solely the external nature, the actions. We judge others by what we think, not for what we feel. These actions then intermingle with our memories, and we merely see the repetitions of things past that now block the present moment – the real action. The present deed is now blocked from our reality for what it is. We see only what we think we see, not the real. To love is actually very easy to do, but only if we do not use it as a weapon, or let the clouds of the past block our vision. If we give it and take it away as punishment, it is a form of conditioning. We must overcome this trait and allow ourselves to flow with this love. The Master is suggesting a higher form of love, as opposed to our contemporary definition. Look around you, and you will conclude that we have tried everything else. We have used hate, lust, and greed, and they certainly have not solved anything. The physical nature is beginning to fail and the proof is overwhelming. Would it not be easier to love your neighbors than fight them? Frankly, for what reason do we fight in life? Is it not to be accepted? Common sense dictates that it would be simpler just to allow for acceptance, since fighting is the opposite of what we seek.

Fortunately, God knew what we would do, and in **John 14:2**, Jesus says: *"In my Father's house are many mansions..."*. Those are the many levels of existence offered to us to comprehend. The mansions are for those who have grown above the physical realm. At first, not everyone may enter them, until they have learned a higher way in the conduct of their lives. Their experiences help them to understand the other levels of being until they reach the status of the spiritual human they were originally intended to be. This occurs through knowledge only and not through ignorance, which we seem to prefer. In **John 14:3**, the Master leaves us this message: *"And if I go and prepare a place for you, I will come again, and receive you unto myself; that where I am, there ye may be also"*. We are to attain the Christ consciousness for ourselves as He did. Once we have reached our goal, we are in union, and again, spirit goes before us to prepare the way. It will let us know when it has, and we may journey forth with greater ease. **John 14:6**: *"...I am the way, the truth, and the life: no man cometh unto the Father, but by me"*. This is the merger of the higher levels being suggested to us. In the physical sense, we are not able to approach the Spirit and we may do it only through the Christ consciousness. This is accomplished just by knowing ourselves, and how we think and operate. "Know thyself" are the key words. We do this by meditation – looking within - - until we turn our thoughts into a living prayer. It becomes reverence of self, with the union of the spirit within us – and the bridegroom comes. Jesus says in **John 14:21**: *"He that hath my commandments, and keepeth them, he it is that loveth me: and he that loveth me shall be loved of my Father, and I will love him, and will manifest myself to him"*.

John 14:10-12: *"Believest thou not that I am in the Father, and the Father in me? the words that I speak unto you I speak not of myself: but the Father that dwelleth in me, he doeth the works. (11) Believe me that I am in the Father, and the Father in me: or else believe me for the very works' sake. (12) Verily, verily, I say unto you, He that believeth on me, the works that I do shall he do also; and greater works than these shall he do; because I go unto my Father"*. This is the true union with the higher nature. The Master is telling us about channeling, spirit communication, and doing it directly. He is communicating from His higher nature. It is a union we can all have, for only spirit may talk to spirit. He is also telling us that we are like Him. Should we simply believe it, His and our abilities would be the same, because of the realization that we are already one, and not dual in nature. It is a matter of bringing them together in one Temple, our body. Once we have achieved this union, then and only then will all things be given unto us in life, no matter what it may be – material or otherwise. He tells us this in **John 14:16**: *"And I will pray the Father, and he shall give you another Comforter* [helper]*..."*. The helper is self-realization, and we will only need our higher selves to do the works. This will be delivered to each of us, through the Christ consciousness, in our time, and we may proceed to the place that was prepared. This alliance is confirmed in **John 14:20**: *"At that day ye shall know that I am in my Father, and ye in me, and I in you"*. The key to our own selves could not be clearer. We are the holy trinity in one place: the human form. We are one and the same, with no real separation except for the fences that we built in our own minds. Our beliefs are more important, and they bind us. **John 14:27**: *"Peace I leave with you, my peace I give unto you: not as the world giveth, give I unto you. Let not your heart be troubled, neither let it be afraid"*. This is the gentle legacy the Master grants to those who earnestly attempt to reach spiritual enlightenment. If we would trust the higher nature, we would enjoy that inner peace. With the spirit before us, we should not act in fear or in troubled ways, because it knows what is best, no matter what we may think. We should not burden ourselves, for we know not where we really go in life (See **John 3:8**). He has already told us that like birds, we drift onto the wind.

John 15:1-4: *"I am the true vine, and my Father is the husbandman. (2) Every branch in me that beareth not fruit he taketh away: and every branch that beareth fruit, he purgeth it, that it may bring forth more fruit. (3) Now ye are clean through the word which I have spoken unto you. (4) Abide in me, and I in you. As the branch cannot bear fruit of itself, except it abide in the vine; no more can ye, except ye abide in me"*. Once again, we are told of the holy trinity, and the real question is: what is the Father without the Son? God would still be God, but It would be where It was eons ago, before we came into being. We are the ones who give God life through our realization of It and Its concepts. We need each other to sustain existence or at least to understand Its presence. *"I am the vine, ye are the branches"*. **John 15:5-7** are verses that vividly portray the importance of a necessary union. It takes place in our belief system, and we may do nothing without the soul of self. We will be more fruitful in life with this spiritual merger. It is the only way to be truly successful in the physical world. **John 15:10-13**: *"If ye keep my commandments, ye shall abide in my love; even as I have kept my Father's commandments, and abide in his love. (11) These things have I spoken unto you, that my joy might remain in you, and that your joy might be full. (12) This is my commandment, That ye love one another, as I have loved you. (13) Greater love hath no man than this, that a man lay down his life for his friends"*. Jesus tells us about the power of love. It is His only commandment, but He reminds us to abide – as He did – by His Father's commandments. We must have this element housed within us, not as a weapon, but in truth. This power will help us overcome many impediments if we just give it unconditionally. Conditions will only bind all those involved. We must learn to develop our hearts and the feelings associated with matters of the heart. We must reach for a higher level of openness and sharing, then we may have all things given to us.

The Master expands on this thought in **John 15:14-15**: *"Ye are my friends, if ye do whatsoever I command you. (15) Henceforth I call you not* *servants; for the servant knoweth not what his lord doeth; but I have called you friends; for all things that I have heard of my Father I have made known unto you"*. We go from being servants to life to living it fully, in alliance with our higher friend housed within, and this makes life subservient to us. Life becomes our effect, and we are the cause. The Master tells us that, as our friend, He has passed on to us all that He learned from his Father, making us equal in knowledge. It also implies that we should make the best of it. It is truly the safety net of the Father, and it is at our disposal, should we choose to use it. There is an interesting old maxim about life: "You cannot know what you now know". Jesus says it in a somewhat different way in **John 15:22**: *"If I had not come and spoken unto them, they had not had sin: but now they have no cloak for their sin"*. Once we have learned, we have no excuse. If we were to simply watch ourselves in life, we would recognize that we have the knowledge, yet we do not apply it. In that negative light, we now attempt to deny it. How can we? Once we know, the denying becomes a lie. Are we not to live in the truth?

John 16:25: *"These things have I spoken unto you in proverbs: but the time cometh, when I shall no more speak unto you in proverbs, but I shall shew you plainly of the Father"*. Many do not realize that the Master spoke figuratively on most occasions. He used metaphors to paint pictures of understanding. Today, however, we have a tendency to accept these proverbs based only on their literary value. Jesus tells us that when the time comes, He will speak more clearly to us. This could already be happening to many of us, on the inner level. In **John 16:33**, He tells us: *"These things I have spoken unto you, that in me ye might have peace. In the world ye shall have tribulation: but be of good cheer; I have overcome the world"*. Why would the world bring tribulation to us? It does this only for us to know our very own being. It is to teach us to overcome the physical distractions through the higher level or the soul. In reality, it is the only way to prevail and have all that we seek.

In **John 17:11**, we have a definitive statement that we are one with the Father: *"...Holy Father, keep through thine own name those whom thou hast given me, that they may be one, as we are"*. The Father, the Son and the Spirit in us... The lesson here is that the higher and lower natures must become one and the same, in the concept of the individual thinking of the person. We are to merge them by placing equal importance to both. This notion is emphasized in the works of John, and no place else is it offered. It is reiterated in **John 17:21**: *"That they all may be one; as thou, Father, art in me, and I in thee, that they also may be one in us..."*. It is an attestation to the fact that we are all the same seeds, with a like mind and interconnected consciousness. The only difference is in the choices we make and the paths we choose to follow. In that verse, we do know that the Son interceded on our behalf, encouraging us to attain spiritual wisdom.

We have now reached the point of the rapture, or the awakening of the reality of being and of life. The next chapter will be on the book of Revelations. This particular work is an experience in unfolding our selves and our lives. It is not the destruction that we have been led to believe will happen. It is a guide once all other processes have been completed, in preparation for this enlightenment. It is ours to have if we simply follow the guidance. If we apply the principles of self, the door will be open as was the promise. Still, you must be ready, because when the door opens, there is no turning back. **Luke 9:62**: *"...No man, having put his hand to the plough, and looking back, is fit for the kingdom of God".*

We will leave this chapter by bringing you food for thought. We offer **1 Corinthians 15:42-54** in its entirety. It is very moving, and it will tells us what we will have if we are on the right path: *"So also is the resurrection of the dead. It is sown in corruption; it is raised in incorruption: (43) It is sown in dishonour; it is raised in glory: it is sown in weakness; it is raised in power: (44) It is sown a natural body; it is raised a spiritual body. There is a natural body, and there is a spiritual body. (45) And so it is written, The first man Adam was made a living soul; the last Adam was made a quickening* [life giving] *spirit. (46) Howbeit that was not first which is spiritual, but that which is natural; and afterward that which is spiritual. (47) The first man is of the earth, earthy: the second man is the Lord from heaven. (48) As is the earthy, such are they also that are earthy: and as is the heavenly, such are they also that are heavenly. (49) And as we have borne the image of the earthy, we shall also bear the image of the heavenly. (50) Now this I say, brethren, that flesh and blood cannot inherit the kingdom of God; neither doth corruption inherit incorruption. (51) Behold, I shew you a mystery; We shall not all sleep, but we shall all be changed, (52) In a moment, in the twinkling of an eye, at the last trump: for the trumpet shall sound, and the dead shall be raised incorruptible, and we shall be changed. (53) For this corruptible must put on incorruption, and this mortal must put on immortality. (54) So when this corruptible shall have put on incorruption, and this mortal shall have put on immortality, then shall be brought to pass the saying that is written, Death is swallowed up in victory".*

CHAPTER 8

REVELATIONS

"...I am Alpha and Omega, the first and the last: and, What thou seest, write in a book, and send it unto the seven churches..."
Revelations 1:11

If we, as individuals, have completed all the tasks the four main Gospels have suggested, we are now ready for a spiritual awakening that, in the past, was limited to a very few. Today, the masses may also be the privileged recipients. Deductively, we have mastered the prescribed steps properly. These steps have been outlined for us in Matthew, Mark, Luke and John, telling us how to live life fully from the physical, mental, emotional and spiritual aspects of being. We should be at a point where we have learned to accept and not to expect anything life has to offer. The Gospels clearly chart the need for a greater acceptance of self, others, and of life. By now, we have learned to assume our own responsibility and we no longer blame others for the circumstances in which we find ourselves. We have now rested our inner issues regarding other people we have encountered along the way. We have forgiven all, including ourselves. We have come to realize that what we have done in this life was our path, our dharma. This path is exclusively ours and belongs to no one else. We may place the responsibility only on ourselves and point the finger in no other direction. We have gleaned our lessons. We now accept ourselves for who we are, not what we are. If all this is in place, we are ready to receive our reward, in the form of a very remarkable awakening to a relationship with spirit and life. It will come through the final tribulation: the crucifixion, if you will, of the physical self. It is the beginning of the spirit vibration, the energy of God flowing through us all. Awakening is coming whether we are willing or not, for this is the part of our own evolution that we do not accept. We cannot receive it, because we do not see this spiritual side of life. This development will be a transition to the higher nature, to commune with God on all levels of self and being.

Henry Drummond says it best in his work *"Natural Law in the Spiritual World"*: *"How is the soul to escape to heaven if it has neglected for a lifetime the means to escape from the world and self? And where is the capacity for heaven to come from if it be not developed on earth? Where, indeed, is even the smallest spiritual appreciation of God and heaven to come from when so little of spirituality has ever been known or manifested here?"*. This opening will be the arousing that propels all of us to the greater things we may do, as the Master has promised us we can do. We saw this in 1 Corinthians 15:42-54, as all will become one within our own being. We will no longer seek this from outside sources, because it will be realized within us.

We now begin the mystery of mysteries of Biblical texts: the rapture, or the awakening of the lower to the higher aspects of life. This is where we must lose our lives to gain them. This text tells us not only how to accomplish this task, but also what our experience will be. We must all awaken to the higher plane sooner or later in life. If we absorb all the biblical guidance, it is something we will all experience for ourselves and cannot avoid. To not be ready would be like telling the God of us all to wait a moment. This cannot happen, because we are told in the earlier works to not go back, even for our coat or anything else. We must be ready in that moment, and it will be in the blink of an eye. Those that are not prepared did not hear the call of spirit. No one knows when this time will come. Revelations plainly explains to us that we will experience this, belief or not, and it will most surely come.

Reaching the higher aspects is not a strange event in our way of life, and by the best calculation, it will be the fourth time it has occurred to humanity. The swing of the pendulum is uncaring and relentless. It will wait for no one. It will use whatever methodology is necessary for the lifting of the level of understanding, or the expansion of our reality with life. We are told in **Revelations 1:1** whence came this information. It relates that an angel came and told John of these events while he was on the island of Patmos in the Greek Isles. Revelations is the reporting of this message from spirit addressed to all of us.

John had learned to open himself to the higher forms of direct communication with Spirit. He had learned it from the Master who was the perfect channel of God, and who taught all His disciples not only how to prepare themselves to communicate, but how to receive the information. If we were to seriously accept the truth of this inner exchange, we could also understand how others have received this divine information through the years, which continues even today. All of us have this ability, no matter what we are told. Those who communicate on the spiritual level are the teachers of the future, for they hear the higher truths of life and share them. This is the reason Jesus told us that we would be ridiculed by others, were we to reveal to them that we are in touch with the Almighty. We must continue to bring it forth for all to know, regardless of the consequences. Imagine that Jesus decided the price of His persecution was too great. Would we now have the Bible or Christianity?

Most believe that Revelations is about the destruction of the world by humankind. Would God truly allow people to destroy Its creation? This does not stand true, unless of course, we do not change our present path. That being the case, God would do it for us. If we observed our present path, we would see that it binds us tightly to the physical and material aspects, and we must soon realize that it is not the only aspect to life. Still, our greed and egocentricity has taken over, and we do very little to really assist others in this life because we are preoccupied with being self-serving. We are too engaged in taking from each other, and we do not share ourselves truthfully with others either. We do things for our reasons - no one else's. Whenever we do something for others, chances are that we expect something in return, consciously or unconsciously. With this particular mindset, we will never really be of service to each other, nor will we rise to a higher level. It seems to this author that we are too busy attempting to take, instead of giving what we have. This is against all of the Christ's teachings as well as any other master's of old or present days. Unfortunately, it is a dominating aspect of our lives. Spirit knew this long ago, and it is time to be awakened.

The awakening comes, no matter what it is that we deny. None of us know when it will happen – at least the spiritual part – even though we may think we do. We cannot know, as long as the material world is the domineering factor in our lives. In the first chapter of Revelations, we find many confirmations as to who we are. **Revelations 1:6**: *"For [Jesus] hath made us kings* [kingdom] *and priests unto God and his Father…"*. This kingdom is within each and all of us, as we were told in the four Gospels. We are the temples to all that is and are in the exact image of the spirit. Genesis, the very first book of the Bible, tells us that.. On the other hand, do we treat ourselves and others as though we were temples? We are a sacred place in the material realm, because we are God's house. We are the priests living within this kingdom, for control and teachings. The rapport could be compared to an automobile. We are the driver of the vehicle, but we are not the vehicle. So is the soul in relationship to the body. The body is merely the vehicle used to get us where we wish to go. Spirit made us this way to have dominion in the physical aspect, allowing us to operate within this world. **Revelations 1:10**: *"I was in the Spirit on the Lord's day…"*. John tells us that he had gone into himself. We see this type of biblical reference on many occasions. "Being in spirit" is opening one's being to the higher nature. This communication method is taught in the Far East and is considered very normal. The Master, having been in the lands of ancient knowledge, brought it back and taught His students how to accomplish this task for themselves (See Acts 1:8). To "be in spirit", one has to awaken to the higher forms of thought to establish a connection with the energy centers that, we are being told biblically, exist and are with the body of the human: the seven trumpets of God.

These seven energy centers, as mentioned earlier, are known as the seven **chakras**. They will begin to function as centers for the transformation of psychophysical energy (mind and body) into spiritual energy. When the spiritual energy becomes functional, the **Kundalini** – fluids contained within the spine – absorbs all the other energies or elements as it rises to meet God. In the process, it cleanses the physical self for a higher presentation to Spirit. Our behavior is influenced by these energies, to wit, the mind, the intellect, the ego, and ultimately the physical. Although the energies change the obsessions of the mind, the ego will compel the intellect to constantly think about the desires that occupy the mind – things that have been done by us before. We must remember that the mind creates the individual's world. It could be disrupted – and generally is – as a person is being transformed, thus the formation of a struggle. This is why most do not continue the journey. Ego decides what is important or not and what we will or will not accept. Intelligence finds the ways to act and methods to use in order to achieve goals fed by ego. In this way, we eventually understand that the world we know is not the outside world, but rather the one with which we mentally associate. As we travel through them, the energy centers will teach us exactly that: our mental associations. At this point, we will let **Harish Johari** [1] give us his definition of "chakras": *"Chakras can be thought of as wheels of the mind that dwell in the forest of desires. And desires, like wheels themselves, are great motivating forces. Each chakra is a stage-by-stage playground of desires, exhibiting its influence on the persons who are attached to the enjoyment of that particular chakra. Throughout life, one dwells in this forest and thinks and understands life's situations from the standpoint of the chakras in which one normally feels most comfortable"*. This might explain the old saying: "one cannot see the forest for the trees". The real struggle will occur to those attached to the carnal aspects only. Realistically, any personal attachment may have this affect, even a person we love. Consequently, there will be behavioral characteristics associated with each of the chakras. These will be cleared and broken as we grow. It is a process of shedding, as Abraham at Sodom and Gomorrah pleading with God not to destroy the cities, and Lot's wife longing for the past. She became frozen in time, and the cities were destroyed.

As the kundalini rises from the baser aspects, it will pass through the different energy centers, and the shedding occurs, bringing new light to under-

---

[1] Harish Johari (1934-1999) was a painter, sculptor, and composer of Indian music. He authored twelve books on Eastern spirituality, one of which being "Chakras".

standing. Various spiritual experiences will occur which are the explanations offered in Revelations. We will also see how the above will change us. We will be born again, giving up our lives as we have created them. We will not be weighted down by past desires, but will have more than ever in our spiritual and material lives – all we ever dreamed of having.

Biblically, most of these centers have been translated from the ancient names they held. They are outlined in **Revelations 1:11** and are as follows: Ephesus, Smyrna, Pergamos, Thyatira, Sardis, Philadelphia and Laodicea. All seven are in the sequence in which they reside with the body, from the first – or root (Ephesus) to the seventh – or crown (Laodicea). The crown is the one we see setting about the Master's head. It is the symbol of the activation of knowledge, filled with wisdom. It is the realization and acceptance of the power of the wisdom in union with self. The cities mentioned above are not cities of the old world as we are taught to believe. They are not material at all but are truly parts of us, regrettably not perceived by all. We are told that we are a kingdom wherein lie the seven churches, the Menorah of God or Spirit. This is because all seven candles (chakras) are lit for direct communication to God, within one's own being. This form of spiritual contact concerns all aspects of life and what their impact can be on the internal kingdom. This impact is a type of education from our higher selves, the path to guide us toward working in union with all the energy centers and ultimately with spirit. We are to work with them in perfect harmony for them to take action within us. This action is the higher forms to life, and we are to pay attention to the higher impressions, more so than to those of the physical or lower impressions. We must remember that the kingdom is us (Re: Revelations 1:6). These energy centers are the individual churches within us, representing the kingdom of God. God is not interested in the external nature of Its creation – only the internal nature, or the inner churches which we all could control if we desired. Those with the knowledge will know what is being said.

Revelations 1:12: *"And I turned to see the voice that spake with me. And being turned, I saw seven golden candlesticks* [lamp stands] [2]*"*. The "lamp stands" are the energy centers or Menorah, being mentioned for us to know and to use through realization, since they are a part of us. In **Revelations 1:13-16**, John recalls a vision he was given of the future as he was in deep meditation with Spirit. In **Revelations 1:13**, he tells us: *"And in the midst of the seven candlesticks one like unto the Son of man, clothed with a garment down to the*

---

[2] In the course of this book, you may have noticed that there are several words in brackets. It is to emphasize the difference in interpretations and translations, while hopefully making the dissertations clearer for the reader.

foot, and girt about the paps with a golden girdle". Visualize the human body, if you will. In your mind, place an overlay of the seven unseen but very real energy centers from the bottom of the spine to the top of the head. You now have a complete picture of the son or daughter of man. **Revelations 1:14**: *"His head and his hairs were white like wool, as white as snow; and his eyes were as a flame of fire;".* White is the symbol of wisdom for all of us to behold and of which we can be a part in life. If you recall, Jesus told us in Luke 11:34-36 that the eyes are the window to the inner self. The portrait painted above is how true wisdom would show itself. Our eyes would shine very brightly, as though aflame. A truly enlightened being is being sketched for our eyes to enjoy. On this journey into light, we must rightly know ourselves before we can rightly know another, and not until the first aspect is done. "Know thyself"! In **Revelations 1:16**, John says: *"And he had in his right hand seven stars: and out of his mouth went a sharp two-edged sword: and his countenance was as the sun shineth in his strength".* Those of you familiar with the Bible may have noticed how often the number seven is used, especially in Revelations. This number comes up in many works other than the Bible and all pertain to the subject of spiritual enlightenment. In fact, it is in every religious text known to human kind and it is considered to be the symbol of fulfillment or the number of attainment. It is offered in relation to these energy centers, because one must use all seven – not just the one root chakra which is the material or base need in the world. This particular root center assists us in the physical aspect of understanding only. Unfortunately, this is where the majority of us are stuck. Fear may also be an attribute of this center, and fear will bind us, as it always does. How much money can we make? That seems to be the only concern most of us have, and it is caused by fear of the lack thereof. The root chakra is the survival center from which we operate, and we have allowed it to become dominant in too many ways.

The seven stars in the hand are knowledge that is to come from the psychophysical shift ready to take place. It is not within us yet, but it will come into play as we operate in the higher aspects of self, life and our energy centers. This verse also tells us that our communication will become much more important (the two-edged sword). We will be held accountable for what we say. What we externalize will be sharper for us and will only be the truth of what we have nurtured within our hearts. It will no longer be hidden from view. All will know our motive, no matter what we do. We will struggle with the truth – as we should – for the lie will be exposed if we deviate from that path.

Another important point that should be brought up is that in biblical times, there was a different meaning to words. We have advanced in intellect and technology, but have we advanced in understanding? We may have in some respects, but those are limited. John saw the awakening to come. We cannot perceive or predict when this will happen to us in life, for the Master said that it will come like a thief in the night. However, the eleventh hour has come, and the window opens for us to become all that we dream to be, to become what is within our hearts. Nothing may be hidden and nothing is truly worth hiding – unless it is not the truth. Why would truth hide, for it is innocent, is it not?

Everything in John's vision becomes clearer in **Revelations 1:20**: *"The mystery of the seven stars which thou sawest in my right hand, and the seven golden candlesticks* [lamp stands]. *The seven stars are the angels of the seven churches: and the seven candlesticks which thou sawest are the seven churches"*. The seven angels are kinder forms of thinking about ourselves, others and life in general. They are the keys of new knowledge that will be exposed to us as we awaken. It indicates that a purer level of understanding will be given to us by these angels. They will also produce higher levels of energy with which we will be able to operate.

Each center – or chakra – has a different usage of energy for our material world and for attaining higher aspects with life. You may have noted that the stars were specifically in the right hand. That hand works with the left brain functions, or the logic side of life -- a side that requires the higher understanding. The Bible also points out that our creative or higher functions emanate from the right brain. In seeking a better spiritual life, the logic side will be raised to a higher level of feelings and thoughts with which we can work, matching and working with the right side of the brain for a balanced mind function. It further explains the illumined head or halo of the Master. After all, Einstein once said that we only use ten percent of our full capability. This transfiguration will bring more into play for us to use, should we choose to do so. We are to become more sensitive, because of the fullness we are to experience in our interactions with all of life – once the change has taken place. Imagine being able to use one hundred percent of the mental capabilities that are at our disposal.

The second chapter begins the true journey of the higher nature merging with us into one entity, one being, steeped in the path of the spiritual truth about the reality of life. We will now begin to awaken and it will not be an easy crossing, because the material desires clash heavily with those who wish to become a spiritual human. Regardless of the arduous trek, we can reach that destination through the Book of Revelations.

As it has been for eons, it will be difficult for us to learn to balance both spirit and physical, for spirit may be sensed – not seen – unless we accept the fact that spirit is in all things. Most must not believe in this, because they are constantly seeking signs and proofs. For the rest of us, God will have to prove it through what will befall us on this journey of life and disclosures. The first message concerns the first energy center, the Church of Ephesus. This center is there to assist us in the physical aspects and interactions of life, as mentioned earlier, and how we handle them.

THE FIRST CHAKRA

Before we begin, we would like to point out that some of you may already be familiar with the chakra concept. There are many publications pertaining to this subject. The next few segments will merely translate the verses of the Seven Churches into their metaphysical meanings and how it applies on our journey to spiritual attainment.

Revelations 2:1-7: *"Unto the angel of the church of Ephesus write; These things saith he that holdeth the seven stars in his right hand, who walketh in the midst of the seven golden candlesticks; (2) I know thy works, and thy labour, and thy patience, and how thou canst not bear them which are evil: and thou hast tried them which say they are apostles, and are not, and hast found them liars: (3) And hast borne, and hast patience, and for my name's sake hast laboured, and hast not fainted. (4) Nevertheless I have somewhat against thee, because thou hast left thy first love. (5) Remember therefore from whence thou art fallen, and repent, and do the first works; or else I will come unto thee quickly, and will remove thy candlestick out of his place, except thou repent. (6) But this thou hast, that thou hatest the deeds of the **Nicolaitans**, which I also hate. (7) He that hath an ear, let him hear what the Spirit saith unto the churches; To him that overcometh will I give to eat of the tree of life, which is in the midst of the paradise of God".* The main indicator in these verses is found in the word "Nicolaitans" (followers of Nicolas, name which coincides with the Hebrew name Balaam). Metaphysically, it means that we are apt to form wrong combinations of thoughts, or mixed thinking; in other words, a house divided. This is created by the pull, the influence of the physical nature and the distractions of the outer material world. One can easily see the reasons for it. The two-edged sword mentioned in Revelations 1:16 is the pure Truth in all matters. Most of us do not listen to it because of the heteroclite thinking that clouds our minds -- minds that are allowed to do whatever they desire in the physical realm, and because of our egotistic nature. This is due to the pull of the first chakra toward material and carnal cravings of the mind. We place entirely too much importance on those subjects. By the same token, it happens because it is the first of the seven energy centers, and it is a must for the survival of physical nature.

We are told we abandoned the spirit of our own being, and of course we did by becoming the physical outward shells that we have today. In addition, we also forgot what we really are. We left our first love, which was that of the spirit or higher nature, and we do not remember this attribute of self: the real power of being. We are asked to reawaken our first love and become aware that it will be done by spirit. We must be prepared for this event, and if we are, it will be much easier for us to work with the shift because the light of spirit will be upon us. Those of us who are conscious of this will taste of the tree of life. We will have what we desire in life as we overcome the physical nature that pulls us so far from the spirit within us.

In truth, we must admit that we are indeed enamored with the body. We are all engrossed in it and do not give our inner nature its due. The Master alluded to this in Matthew 23:26: *"...cleanse first that which is within the cup and platter, that the outside of them may be clean also"*. In the Ephesus message, it is stated that Spirit also hated the Nicolaitans and their deeds. Why would It feel that way since we are all Its creation? For God to hate anything, it would have to be a huge misdeed, and this is simply not the real intent. God does not like mixed thinking, which in itself cannot be clear thinking. The Creator is alluding to this, and not living creatures. The issue is our style of thought, our confused thinking. The Master told us to be single in purpose, and the Spirit is telling us we must focus on the spiritual rather than the material side. To achieve that, we are to eliminate the dual thought process with which we all tend to operate. This original intent dualism is taught us in life by all people and systems which we encounter. We perpetuate this concept in our thinking through the physical forms of teaching. Except for the few who seek the true form, we do not teach or instruct in higher systems, even in meditation. Ironically, it is taught in most countries of the world, but not in the United States – at least not formally. Mixed thinking can be described as combining or confusing the higher with the lower, the good and the bad, God and the devil. Sadly, we tend to prefer the lower aspect(s), simply because we enjoy the physical or lower form, when compared to the spiritual. It seems to be the vibration in which we operate out of desire. The natural pull from both sides will occur and the physical will win, as in Cain and Abel. On the material side, we can see the impact of our actions immediately. On the higher side, it takes a little more time for results to appear.

In Matthew 7:7, Jesus said: *"Ask, and it shall be given you; seek, and ye shall find; knock, and it shall be opened unto you"*. This statement does not proclaim that whatever we desire will just come to us. We must take the first step ourselves, like ask, seek or knock, before anything takes place. Spirit will not come to us first. We must journey toward It, and It will meet us on the road – nothing less. In a way, it is telling us that we must prove ourselves to the higher nature before it will come to our assistance – after we ask. We must ask and seek first before anything is given to us on any level.

The first chakra is there for us to overcome the physical side of this life, to assist in our working with the lower aspect. Without it, we could not function very well in life. In fact, we must overcome all those energy centers. The first three are more difficult than the last four.

THE SECOND CHAKRA

Revelations 2:8-11: *"And unto the angel of the church in **Smyrna** write; These things saith the first and the last, which was dead, and is alive; (9) I know thy works, and tribulation, and poverty, (but thou art rich) and I know the blasphemy of them which say they are Jews, and are not, but are the synagogue of Satan. (10) Fear none of those things which thou shalt suffer: behold, the devil shall cast some of you into prison, that ye may be tried; and ye shall have tribulation ten days: be thou faithful unto death, and I will give thee a crown of life. (11) He that hath an ear, let him hear what the Spirit saith unto the churches; He that overcometh shall not be hurt of the second death"*. The next quote is from the Metaphysical Bible Dictionary: *"**Smyrna**: Substance (myrrh, "but thou art rich") – the substance center in the body, located at the pit of the stomach"*. The mention of "them which say they are Jews, and are not" symbolically refers to false beliefs or false thoughts occasioned by the pull of the negative mind. The negative mind includes such traits as envy, jealousy, greed, restlessness, destructiveness and anxiety, to name a few, and it influences the second energy center. This pressure may create great anger and frustration with the external life, if one is filled with negativity.

In Verse 2:10, the devil is a metaphor representing ego and ignorance, and the jail is the confinement of doubt and negativity within your own self. You are to be tried by tests that will remove those burdens and you are told not to fear those tests. Further, we read about ten days of tribulation. These are ten degrees of attainment in an individual's knowledge, and each will be tested. It is a verification of our progressive understanding of the nature of being. It could be compared to Jacob's ladder. Our inner spirit gave us first seven roots to learn and comprehend. They are: Mother-Father, Earth, Life, Joy, Sun, Water and Air. They are the channels of nourishment, our foundation to life, or our "Cephas" if you will. The tests of understanding come through the seven virtues of self: Cosmic Father, Eternal Fluid, Creative Force, Peace, Power, Love, and the most important: Wisdom. We are tested by the higher aspect for our level of comprehension and the proper use of the knowledge which is to be combined with patience of practice. It is to be performed on the inner nature, where Satan or ego will be tested. The last three assessments are the symbol of the pyramids, the Trinity. They represent Father, Christ and Human or, as we know them, the Father, the Son and the Holy Ghost. Jesus said in John 17:21: *"That they all may be one, as thou, Father, art in me, and I in thee, that they also may be one of us"*. It clearly states that we are all one and the same. Once we reach that state and understand, we eliminate the last illusion of the dual mind and see only one. Perhaps we should now understand why we get a feeling "in the pit of our stomach" when something unpleasant is about to happen to us. It is the second energy center that tells us this or that is not correct.

If we were to accept and learn to appreciate the seven tests of spirit, we would not do wrong things. This feeling would then go away and we would be at peace. After all, it is the power center of the spiritual self. It is warning us that something is not right and we must learn to trust it with our feelings, no matter what the event may be. In some parts of the Orient, it is known as the "Don Tian", the power center of the body. We store our energy there, then give it away to external matters. Its purpose is to help us obtain what we want in life, hence the reference to the "rich". We all have the ability if we use it properly and do not squander our energy.

In Verse 2:9, we are reminded of the physical form in the mention of the "synagogue of Satan", where the Ego of self resides and to which too much importance is given in today's teachings. Satan does not exist, except in our own thoughts, and only if we allow the ego to continue to jump the way we do. We decide the direction and purpose of our lives, and no one else. The task would be much easier if we were to earnestly work with Spirit. As long as we formulate mixed thinking (See the first chakra), we give credence to the mixed style of thought, thus the "synagogue of Satan". Verse 2:11 tells us that "he...shall not be hurt of the second death". That is tied in with what the Master said in Mark 8:35: *"For whosoever will save his life shall lose it..."*. We must be willing to turn ourselves over to the higher nature and give up the shallow focus we place on the physical aspect. It is painless, but if we are successful, we may have all that we require or want in life. We reach this status through the higher nature – not the lower.

THE THIRD CHAKRA

Revelations 2:12:17: *"And to the angel of the church in Pergamos write; These things saith he which hath the sharp sword with two edges; (13) I know thy works and where thou dwellest, even where Satan's seat is: and thou holdest fast my name, and hast not denied my faith, even in those days wherein Antipas was my faithful martyr, who was slain among you, where Satan dwelleth. (14) But I have a few things against thee, because thou hast there them that hold the doctrine of Balaam, who taught Balac to cast a stumblingblock before the children of Israel, to eat things sacrificed unto idols, and to commit fornication. (15) So hast thou also them that hold the doctrine of the Nicolaitans, which thing I hate. (16) Repent; or else I will come unto thee quickly, and will fight against them with the sword of my mouth. (17) He that hath an ear, let him hear what the Spirit saith unto the churches; To him that overcometh will I give to eat of the hidden manna, and will give him a white stone, and in the stone a new name written, which no man knoweth saving he that receiveth it".* By now, you should have noticed that, for each church, the opening is different. This is because dissimilar areas of the body are being offered, along with various levels of being. A different form of experience is taking place as the person overcomes the issues contained within a particular energy center. We must learn to accept that the energy centers interact with the thinking processes of the person. As this takes place, the unresolved attachments – be they positive or negative – will come to the forefront for resolution, as desires or fears of the past. It may be difficult, depending on the lifestyle of the person. We must prevail over all the past experience stored within us, especially if it is not of a positive nature. We now move to the subject of personal truth, and for that, we must explain some of the terms found in this specific lamp stand of the body. The first is "Antipas". Metaphysically, Charles Fillmore defines it as: *"Faithfulness to Truth ideals, even to the point of becoming against all that does not measure up to these ideals. This resistant attitude of mind leads to martyrdom".* This includes the people around us. We see this attitude today in personal relationships, because they follow the ideal and not the truth. The next is "Balaam". It represents the mental sense plane in human beings. Again, the wisdom of Charles Fillmore helps us understand this biblical reference: *"This discernment that Balaam represents, however, being of the sense man and reaching no higher in its expression than the phase of the psychical that is governed by the sense mind, is deceptive".* He also defines "Balac" or "Balak" as follows: *"An empty, void, destructive, wasting thought... that rules the carnal mind".*

The third chakra may bring us to a higher or lower aspect, depending on what we think of ourselves, as we can see by the words originated by St. John. We are being told that we do not live in the Truth of old which is about the nature of the higher realm. Due to the confusion presented by the second chakra and the pull of life itself, this may be difficult to reinstitute within us. We do not realize the truth of life, even though we originally did not deny the faith of what we knew. Through the centuries, we have become so ingrained in material life that we do not remember our first love which is Spirit. During those years, we have talked ourselves out of this blissful state. As a result, we have the pull of ego to stop us in the area of attainment. Verse 2:14 explains that it produces a stumbling block with which we must contend.

Once we have passed through the third lamp stand, we will advance to the higher realms – or centers. They will lead us to deeper emotions and understanding. Verse 2:16: "[I] will fight against them with the sword of my mouth". The truth will come and will be exposed to us. As a world, we are beginning to see and experience this observable fact in the form of the many current struggles inside every walk of life. When we learn to understand and accept the spirit nature, we receive greater levels of energy or comprehension of our existence. The white stone and the new name are the new perception given to us from above. This goes back to the seven stars held in the right hand of Spirit. If you remember, the Master was renaming all the apostles, hence, why would we not fall within the same purview? It is reasonable to assume that if we are changed in the process of reaching for spiritual attainment, the old self no longer fits. On this journey, the transition from the lower forms of thought to the higher is a fascinating inner climb.

We are now moving closer to the heart center, and we are somewhat afraid of that area because we will have to feel our way into this one. Most of us consider feelings as painful to some extent because of our previous experiences. We do not wish to remember them, yet we must, so that they may be flushed or removed. We take this position because so many people in our lives have raised havoc with what we feel, from our parents to our friends, to our loves of life. Love has been used as a weapon all too often. It is given and taken away by the people we say we love and the people we believe love us. Much conditioning has taken place over the years, and we have all the memories of the events. We avoid the deeper aspects of these emotions and they stack themselves in our self-visualization, hurting our self-worth in the process.

THE FOURTH CHAKRA

This is the heart center of the human body, the chakra of Thyatira, the fourth and the first to the higher aspects of self, and the balance point of life. It is the balance point because it is in the center of the seven chakras and can be the very block that will not allow us to travel any further, based on the fact that too often, we ignore what we really feel about ourselves and life. Biblically, it is lengthy because it covers the mastery of self and life.

Revelations 2:18-29: *"And unto the angel of the church in Thyatira write; These things saith the Son of God, who has his eyes like unto a flame of fire, and his feet are like fine brass; (19) I know thy works, and charity, and service, and faith, and thy patience, and thy works; and the last to be more than the first. (20) Notwithstanding I have a few things against thee, because thou sufferest that woman Jezebel, which calleth herself a prophetess, to teach and to seduce my servants to commit fornication, and to eat things sacrificed unto idols. (21) And I gave her space to repent of her fornication; and she repented not. (22) Behold, I will cast her into a bed, and them that commit adultery with her into great tribulation, except they repent of their deeds. (23) And I will kill her children with death; and all the churches shall know that I am he which searcheth the reins and hearts: and I will give unto every one of you according to your works. (24) But unto you I say, and unto the rest in Thyatira, as many as have not this doctrine, and which have not known the depths of Satan, as they speak; I will put upon you none other burden. (25) But that which ye have already hold fast till I come. (26) And he that overcometh, and keepeth my works unto the end, to him will I give power over the nations: (27) And he shall rule them with a rod of iron; as the vessels of a potter shall they be broken to shivers: even as I received of my Father. (28) And I will give him the morning star. (29) He that hath an ear, let him hear what the Spirit saith unto the churches".*

We must learn to balance all activities of the heart. The higher centers must maintain equilibrium with the lower centers, and vice versa. This is important because we have all learned to overly store things in the area of the emotions. That in itself is not prudent, and the Master Himself said: *"...first be reconciled to thy brother, and then come and offer thy gift"*. Excessive storing – as mentioned above – does not allow one to do this. On the contrary, it denies, it hides, it ignores, and it is a major issue in our present society. It leads to mistrust of others and even of our very own self.

In order to bring a little more clarity to the heart chakra, let us cover the Jezebel allegory. First, as stated earlier, this energy center is the balance point between the lower and the higher aspects, as well as the seat of the ego. Because of our past, the ego is driven through the misuse of what we feel. The Metaphysical Bible Dictionary describes Jezebel as follows: *"The animal soul, unbridled passions of sense consciousness. When the union of the ruling identity in the intellect and the licentious desires of the body is complete, the whole man is involved in error.....Jezebel could also be called the ruling emotions on the physical plane of consciousness*". She is the image of carnal self and passionate desires run amuck. We seem to have not let go, and the energy centers of desire will make us hold on to the old ways more tightly, creating the type of stumbling block cited in Verse 2:14. We have allowed this to dominate because of the fascination we have with the physical gratifications. We give in to our carnal nature, rather than the higher aspect of love in its true sense. We seek release only, and that is misuse of what we feel. It is the adultery mentioned in Verse 2:22 and the immorality we commit on ourselves. For most of us, in the course of our material life, there is no focus on the higher purpose of the emotions. This is why spirit searches what is in our minds and hearts. It wants to know whether we have an inner balance between our higher and lower natures. If we accept the reality of these natures, it occurs in our minds and hearts as they work in union with each other, toward the higher good of all. Those who are "balanced" properly are the ones who are truly in the service of others, and they tend to give us a glimpse of that stability. This is a status that should be reached by all of us, not just a few.

We are all destined to be of service to humanity, rather than be self-serving. When one reads the penalties reserved for the church of Thyatira, it indicates the difficulty level attached to the fourth chakra. We must persevere and stay single in purpose, single in nature. We may do this by not only being in service to others, but also by achieving our inner balance through maturity and moderation. That is how we can bring out how we really feel and think about ourselves. If it is of a positive nature, Satan will not enter and we will find no evil in our lives. We do know, however, that it will be lurking in the shadows, looking for a home, and there are many who will give more importance to self-gratification than to their better qualities. We are not to judge them in any way for what they do.

"...To him will I give power over the nations...". This is not about ruling other countries. It is about us and the centers of the body. Each of us is a "kingdom". As we rule these centers, we will be given the morning star, which is the wisdom associated with attainment. It is the halo of the angels and the Masters, which we perceive rather than see. It will also be ours.

As we progress further up the ladder to spiritual consciousness, we begin to see – even in the wording – that we are reaching a certain level of attainment. The verses are now being written in a totally different fashion and are addressing higher issues. We have gone beyond the balance point, and it is assumed that we understand more on the deeper level. We begin our journey into the fifth chakra, the Great Teacher of communication to self and the outer world, with enriched sounds and spiritual rebirth. Here, we can be "harmonious", or we can be the opposite – which is what most seem to choose. "Harmonious" defines the sound of the person, what emanates from him or her, and what is in the heart will be made known. Remember, it is not what goes into the human that defiles it. It is what we express toward others, what we say to or about them. If there is disharmony, it will show through judgment and downplaying of others. This will not be hidden either.

THE FIFTH CHAKRA

Revelations 3:1-6: *"And unto the angel of the church in Sardis write; These things saith he that hath the seven Spirits of God, and the seven stars; I know thy works, that thou hast a name that thou livest, and art dead. (2) Be watchful, and strengthen the things which remain, that are ready to die: for I have not found thy works perfect before God. (3) Remember therefore how thou hast received and heard, and hold fast, and repent. If therefore thou shalt not watch, I will come on thee as a thief, and thou shalt not know what hour I will come upon thee. (4) Thou hast a few names even in Sardis which have not defiled their garments; and they shall walk with me in white: for they are worthy. (5) He that overcometh, the same shall be clothed in white raiment; and I will not blot out his name out of the book of life, but I will confess his name before my Father, and before his angels. (6) He that hath an ear, let him hear what the Spirit saith unto the churches"*. As can be seen, we are moving upward in the spiritual framework of the physical human, and departing from a dual nature reality can be a struggle.

We are reaching a higher level of understanding within the consciousness of the mind, and communication with the higher aspect is much clearer. It tells us that we are almost there and to persevere a little longer in this growth. "...that thou livest, and art dead" may sound confusing, but is really is not. It simply means that we have not yet reached the crown of being, or complete understanding of the nature of life. We are to wake up and strengthen the remaining aspects of our selves because we are not quite complete as a single entity uniting body and spirit. The reference to those who are "worthy" seems to define the fact that we have climbed this far, and some have completed the journey. Assumedly, we have tamed and controlled the lower physical nature, yet its pull will be greater at this point than at any other. The Gospel of St. Thomas in the Nag Hammadi Library says: "The closer we come to God, the greater the pull of evil". Evil, in this instance, is the pull of the material world, nothing more. We are almost home and we are tired from the journey upon which we embarked. We had to deal with much of ourselves. Not only do we have the temptations of the material distractions, but we also have this pull on our emotions and the higher aspect – or God. We must find a better way to express ourselves, because expressing our truth is very difficult, based on the fact that others will judge us for what we feel. When we articulate these feelings, others may tend to use them against us later on. This includes hearing them from loved ones, in which case we, for the most part, will simply let them fade away. If so, it will undoubtedly create another set of situations. We cannot unlearn what we have already learned, nor can we deny it. The Master said, in Luke 9:62: *"...No man, having put his hand to the plough, and looking back, is fit for the kingdom of God".*

As we begin to fully understand our own individual nature, we start to share this truth, yet, we have the fears of our past hurts. Still, spirit urges us forward. We must share what we truly are. We cannot share what we are not, simply because we want to avoid the judgment of others, and that can be symbolized by the "defiled garments". If we were to proudly, unconditionally reveal our real selves, others would accept us for what we are – no matter what that may be. These trials are designed to strengthen, not weaken. We must learn self-acceptance, and that includes weakness as well. Do not hide it. Let others think and do as they wish. As we accomplish this, the last aspect of this chakra comes into being. "Clothed in white raiment" refers to having absorbed the understanding of life and of spiritual matters concerning life. Achievement on the path of life and its experience will show us the way, if we are flexible. The tree will fall if it is unbending, no matter its age.

THE SIXTH CHAKRA

Revelations 3:7-13: *"And to the angel of the church in Philadelphia write; These things saith he that is holy, he that is true, he that hath the key of David, he that openeth, and no man shutteth; and shutteth, and no man openeth; (8) I know thy works: behold, I have set before thee an open door, and no man can shut it: for thou hast a little strength, and hast kept my word, and hast not denied my name. (9) Behold, I will make them of the synagogue of Satan, which say they are Jews, and are not, but do lie; behold I will make them to come and worship before thy feet, and to know that I have loved thee. (10) Because thou hast kept the word of my patience, I also will keep thee from the hour of temptation, which shall come upon all the world, to try them that dwell upon the earth. (11) Behold, I come quickly: hold that fast which thou hast, that no man take thy crown. (12) Him that overcometh will I make a pillar in the temple of my God, and he shall go no more out: and I will write upon him the name of my God, and the name of the city of my God, which is new Jerusalem, which cometh down out of heaven from my God: and I will write upon him my new name. (13) He that hath an ear, let him hear what the Spirit saith unto the churches".*

"I have set before thee an open door". When a dedicated person reaches this chakra, the door opened by the Spirit allows the use of the **intuitive senses** that are within us. That same door remains closed for the majority of the population, for reasons stated numerous times in this book. In fact, others would have you believe that intuitive senses are evil, yet, they are given to us by God Itself, to use as a means of communication between ourselves and the higher realms. Once opened, this door cannot be shut. It means that we can only ignore this sense system and what it can give us. In the second chakra, or the church of Smyrna, we talked about tests. The test that is to come is to see who may withstand the higher realms, and to determine what the mind – working with spirit – may produce and see. Our reality may change, and as the Spirit said: *"thou hast a little strength [power]"*. It is "little" only because we do not let the influence of the Spirit assist us in what we wish to know. It may help to quote John 10:34-35 when Jesus said: *"...Ye are Gods? If he called them gods, unto whom the word of God came, and the scripture cannot be broken"*. The truth is that we can exercise the full power of the spirit, but we do not put it into focus, to use properly with life and other people. In Verse 3:11, we read: *"...Hold that fast which thou hast, that no man take thy crown"*. Metaphorically, the crown is your knowledge and belief system. This belief must be deep and complete, for it is then that the knowledge will be known by all. It is the last bastion that will keep the "not so serious" out of the higher realms, considering the fact that this is not a playground of life.

One must have that crown to come this close to the Father. Christ was tested and so shall we, for no one is above the law of knowledge. If we maintain steadfastness, the crown will be passed on to us. It will happen in an instant, thus we must be prepared. We must be prepared so that we can stand up under its glow and use it in the service of others. It is its purpose, and it is close to the intended destination. *"He that overcometh"* is the key, because most falter at this point in the spiritual journey of life. There is always a fear to face one's conscience or one's past, but we have already reached a cleaner plateau. So, why the fear, when all we seek is to know if God is a truthful and just reality? From my personal experience, believe me, God is. It is real not only to myself, but to others that have worked with the Spirit. "Overcoming" is merely rising above the physical nature of self, to the higher aspects. Those tests are there to expand the belief system that we have. *"...and he shall go no more out..."*: once you have attained the blessings of the sixth chakra, you will be with spirit, always. In that time, you will overcome death.

THE SEVENTH CHAKRA

We now have reached the last and greatest of all energy centers of the body: life's crown of knowledge. One may attain this level only through the activation of all the centers. We are to use them all at the same time, rather than one or the other, as we normally do. Selective activation tends to let one feel incomplete. We are to combine the higher and lower natures, for one is nothing without the other. They are like the two hands of a single body, the two eyes of one face. They are like the wind and the sail, the sword and the shield, for one is only half of itself if the other does not exist. They are night and day and must work in union, with not one overpowering the other. This must come to pass if you want life to be what is promised as heaven on earth.

Revelations 3:14-22: *"And unto the angel of the church of the Laodiceans write; These things saith the Amen, the faithful and true witness, the beginning of the creation of God; (15) I know thy works, that thou art neither cold nor hot: I would thou wert cold or hot. (16) So then because thou art lukewarm, and neither cold nor hot, I will spue thee out of my mouth. (17) Because thou sayest, I am rich, and increased with goods, and have need of nothing; and knowest not that thou art wretched, and miserable, and poor, and blind, and naked: (18) I counsel thee to buy of me gold tried in the fire, that thou mayest be rich; and white raiment, that thou mayest be clothed, and that the shame of thy nakedness do not appear; and anoint thine eyes with eye-salve, that thou mayest see. (19) As many as I love, I rebuke and chasten: be zealous therefore, and repent. (20) Behold, I stand at the door, and knock: if any man hear my voice, and open the door, I will come in to him, and will sup with him, and he with me. (21) To him that overcometh will I grant to sit with me in my throne, even as I also overcame, and am set down with my Father in his throne. (22) He that hath an ear, let him hear what the Spirit saith unto the churches".*

First, it is obvious that we can all do what the Christ did, as mentioned in nearly all the chapters in this book. He confirms it right at the very end of this chakra dissertation by sitting those who persevered successfully upon His throne. The condition is that we must do this ourselves, by answering the knock and opening the door. Of course, if one desires to do these works as He did them, one must learn how. The only way to accomplish this is to rise up through complete understanding and acceptance. This acceptance also means that only through our very own being can we have a true relationship with spirit. It cannot be obtained through others or through material things. The difficulty is that we are unable to commit to this because we do not want others to think that we have sunk into a mentally challenged status. We may also have a fear that people and organizations will condemn us for what we seek and will accuse us of being evil. However, we are told that if we are lukewarm – or indecisive – we are not completely pledged to the ultimate goal, to wit, commitment to self or the Spirit. We must believe firmly in our decisions and our actions, and we must equally believe in the goal we have set for ourselves. Without this kind of determination, you are bound to go nowhere. To reach the final destination is not any different than the efforts we put into climbing each rung of the ladder of spirituality and knowledge. The majority of us has a propensity to gloat over our greater individual achievements, but it is not prudent to be arrogant upon arriving within the warm rays of the crown. We are reminded that we are human and we must approach quietly, in all humility. Were we not told in Matthew that what we say to the Father is in secret, and it should remain in secret?

The buying of the gold is the acquisition of the wisdom of the ages. You may recall that gold was given to Jesus at His birth by one of the Magi. It is that same gold, refined by the fire of spirit. We too can possess it, but not as money, for it is indeed the symbol of knowledge gained to assist us, so that we may be ready to help others in life. If we are to accept this metaphorical gold, we must also accept the white garments. They are a sign of purity or understanding, so that we may not do evil deeds as we did before. We are to be above all this, because now, our united inner being will manifest itself from the inside to the outer world, and we are spiritually richer. It is as it should be, and we are born again into spirit. No matter what anyone may tell you, there is no other way to be born again. Now, you are born of the Spirit – not of man. We have much higher purposes than we allow ourselves to share.

In Verse 3:19, we are told that we will be disciplined by the spirit itself, because we know the difference, we know better. Only the spirit can offer this to us, so that we can retain and maintain what we have gained. This is simply clarity and purpose. Again, when we operate out of the higher centers of the body, we allegorically hear the knock at the door, and at that time, we open it for spirit to enter, to dine with us for all time in life. Then, "I and my Father are one" applies to us as well. It is our heritage. We must remember that we are creation still in the evolving process, and we may not know where this evolution will take us. This is exactly what Jesus meant in John 3:8: *"The wind bloweth where it listeth, and thou hearest the sound thereof, but canst not tell whence it cometh, and whither it goeth: so is every one that is born of the Spirit".*

Creation is constant and perpetual with all of life. It has been unfolding for many years, and we are now finally becoming the spiritual human, a God in the making (John 10:34). Our obligation is to overcome the physical pull of life and work with the higher nature – that of spiritual self. The paragraphs that follow are intended to bring knowledge about the experience of opening the energy centers of the body. Thus far, with the help of the seven churches, we have only given a brief introduction to each of them. There are many great works written about these centers, and if one were to seriously wish to study them in more details, one would discover the truth of creation. These intellectual and spiritual discoveries will defy your belief system. They will leave you in awe of the divine span of God and the power of it all.

Until now, we have shed a certain amount of light on the energy centers, at least on what they are fundamentally meant to do and what they can be for us on our spiritual journey. It is time to share what to expect with those who chose or will chose to let themselves unfold, so they can reach for the God of eternity, the Creator of all things, the One that defies all understanding or acceptance by the mortal mind of human kind. We can qualify ourselves as finite beings when we consider the way we live our lives. How can we truly comprehend infinity, when our definitions are from a finite point of view? In fact, any of our definitions will confine whichever subject to a limited perspective. It will apply only to the person who defined it in the first place – unless we agree with it. This book offers an understanding, as opposed to a definition. This understanding will allow for expansion, rather than an answer, since an answer is a conclusion, and a conclusion is the end of the subject. That is not life. If it were, it would be the end result of all things, and it certainly is not.

"Being in spirit" comes up again in **Revelations 4:2.** Having attained that state, John was taken to a higher place for him to behold, a place where the physical form cannot journey – only the higher aspect. His consciousness went before him, as the Ark of the Covenant does. This place is the connection of the physical mind lifting or opening itself to the "super-conscious" for communion and understanding. **Revelations 4:5** reads: *"And out of the throne proceeded lightnings and thunderings and voices: and there were seven lamps of fire burning before the throne, which are the seven Spirits of God".* Here, we have a better description and verification of the seven spiritual energy centers of the body. They comprise all things so that they may have a physical form – even the rainbow that we admire in the skies, a rainbow that has seven colors in it. This is from the least to the greatest.

THE SEVEN SEALS

It brings us into the **book of life** that is each human being upon this earth. We each have the right to open this book, and the right to understand ourselves with deeper significance. The book – or the individual – has seven seals. Anyone who opens them all shall know the book of life – the true book of self. In fact, we are challenged to open these seals. According to biblical texts, no one has been successful, except one. It is depicted in the midst of people warring against it, attempting to force their way – and this is not permitted. **Revelations 5:6-7**: *"And I beheld, and, lo, in the midst of the throne and of the four beasts, and in the midst of the elders, stood a lamb as it had been slain, having seven horns and seven eyes, which are the seven Spirits of God sent forth into all the earth. (7) And he came and took the book out of the right hand of him that sat upon the throne"*. And he proceeded to open the seven seals of the book of life. We must go about this gently, because if we approach it with a rebellious attitude, we are attempting to force our way, and that, we may not do. Gentleness is the issue of life. Aggressiveness will only create struggles. So far, this has been the case. For most, is life not a struggle? We may possibly be too aggressive in our physical nature, too demanding. This self-imposed task has nothing to do with the physical, and we must move toward it from within our own spiritual nature. The undertaking cannot be approached assertively because it is as gentle as the lamb. It is truly the lamb of God. We will now begin to discuss the opening of these seals. It will be better for us to realize the experience we will have, before we begin the actual journey.

You now have the book of life. It is only a matter of opening the seals, and Chapter 6 of Revelations begins the guiding process. In this area of the Bible, we must once again use our perceptive nature, because the words are written in metaphorical style. If we were to read the Vedas, we would find references similar to those offered biblically.

THE FIRST SEAL: **Revelations 6:2**: *"And I saw, and behold a white horse: and he that sat on him had a bow; and a crown was given unto him: and he went forth conquering, and to conquer"*. The white horse is the good, pure energy put forth by Spirit. Symbolically, it is the coiled serpent known as kundalini, about to rise and cleanse the human and the energy centers of the past hurts or misconceptions unto which we hold. The bow represents the preparation for inner war, a war meant to overcome the adverse effects of the physical pull. We must be sharp and penetrating in our work through the journey of the centers. The work must be genuine and gently firm with the self-realizations we encounter – so that we can remove them from ourselves. The crown is the knowledge of the seven stars mentioned earlier in this work. It is the picture of a determined human being, armed with knowledge, in search of spiritual truth. It is the true awakening, the kundalini within the spine of every individual. It begins to rise in each of us as we start the journey with spirit. All that we know will be changed in the twinkling of an eye. The words "Come and see" in Verse 6:1 are for us to move forward in our pattern of growth. We must travel toward spirit and no longer away from it. We will find these words with each seal being opened – at least the first four – and it is designed as a progressive encouraging statement. When we reach the last three centers, it appears that we no longer need encouragement. It is due to the understanding we have been gathering in self-knowledge, strength and perseverance. Persevere until the end! God knows that as we do this and speak to others about it, they will condemn us. They will refer to us as evil, judged by the human mind that is steeped in fear of the truth. However, this is the true path. We should listen to the encouragement of spirit while letting the mind of the human pass its erroneous judgment. Our spirit within will whisper the word to come, not the outer shell.

THE SECOND SEAL: in **Revelations 6:3-4**, the lamb opens the second seal: *"And when he had opened the second seal, I heard the second beast say, Come and see. (4) And there went out another horse that was red: and power was given to him that sat thereon that they should kill one another: and there was given unto him a great sword"*. Red – as in the red horse – is actually the color of the first energy center. This red energy is now rising, moving forth through the body. It is the destruction of the carnal nature and the desires of the lower aspect. Red is the color of the passions and the anger upon which we have been conditioned to rely. They encompass greed, control, manipulation, stealing, lying, all the despicable things we have been doing to each other. Ultimately, they will be gone. As the energy moves, it takes away the alleged inner peace of the worldly things in life. Our thinking will begin to fight itself. Ego and intellect will enter the struggle. The war between the higher nature versus the lower will begin and increase, as we attempt to move away from the desires of the physical self. Add the condemnation of others, and the confusion will truly set in. At this point, most will retreat when faced with the unleashed difficulties. Remember Luke 9:62: *"...No man, having put his hand to the plough...".*

The sword is the symbol of truth being wielded to shred our belief system. Consequently, it is wise not to hold on to the belief of the material world, if you do not want to increase your level of personal difficulty. All who open this seal must now create an inner balance. It is the balance between the material attractions – which they seek to shed for a higher purpose – and the spiritual attainment. At this point, our past conditioning is still strong, and the task will be hard, but do not be dismayed. We must understand spirit needs protection from us, because it is pure and we certainly are not, until we clean the inside of the cup. Only then may we enter God's house.

THE THIRD SEAL: **Revelations 6:5-6**: *"And when he had opened the third seal, I heard the third beast say, Come and see. And I beheld, and lo a* *black horse; and he that sat on him had a pair of balances in his hand. (6) And I heard a voice in the midst of the four beasts say, A measure of wheat for a penny, and three measures of barley for a penny; and see thou hurt not the oil and the wine".* The rider of the black horse carried scales. They are the scales of spiritual justice, the scales of judgment. As in previous paragraphs, and for our own stability, we must create that inner balance as we travel the path to the crown. When we gradually gain spirituality, it is evident that we must shed more attachments to the material side of us, to provide a certain equilibrium. Once we take the first step, we should be prepared to release all that we mistakenly consider important, so that the balancing effect may take place. This is what the Master intended for us to realize when He said in Mark 13:16: *"And let him that is in the field not turn back again for to take up his garment".* Nothing should be more important to us than our very own alliance, our bonding to spirit – for the Bridegroom comes. The wheat and the barley are references to tangible and physical things that we have done to ourselves and possibly others. The mention of the penny is simply to indicate how cheap these actions are considered. The oil and wine are our fluid and soul natures and will not be harmed. We are told that in that hour, we should not be afraid.

THE FOURTH SEAL or the heart center: **Revelations 6:7-8**: *"And when he had opened the fourth seal, I heard the voice of the fourth beast say, Come and see. (8) And I looked, and behold a pale horse: and his name that sat on him was Death, and Hell followed with him. And power was given unto them over the fourth part of the earth, to kill with sword, and with hunger, and with death, and with the beasts of the earth".* This is the true battlefield of spiritual attainment. We are at mid-point, feeling equal pressure from the lower and higher aspects. Having progressed this far, we must shed the old beliefs residing in the first three charkas, to replace them by the new acquired knowledge, while maintaining our inner balance. As stated earlier, the fourth chakra – the fourth part of the earth - is the heart center and the seat of the ego. **David Pond**, in his book "Chakras for Beginners", explains it quite simply: *"It is through this Fourth Chakra that you begin to merge with collective levels of reality. The lower three chakras deal with individual energy, separate and distinct from all others. The upper three chakras are the collective aspects of the self, increasing the connection with the universal energy. The Heart Chakra is where these two aspects of self meet and merge".*

In order to understand the metaphysical importance of these verses, it is essential that we not look upon the allegories therein as depicting the end of the world through malevolent calamities – as we have been conditioned to believe. We must sense them as the tribulations perpetrated by the ego not wanting to release the old ways, thus creating a struggle with the higher nature. That is the battlefield. The only death involved in this segment is that of negative physical traits found in the first three chakras – or a spiritual cleansing if you prefer. The energy of the kundalini can be compared to the fires of Hades burning our past adverse actions and thoughts in a process of transmutation. Did Jesus not warn us that we would be tested by fire? We may also recall that, according to God, we are a kingdom onto ourself. We are in the fourth energy center, and the power over the "fourth part of the earth" suggests that it should overcome the lower three, because the sword of truth is now being raised against them. As a result, our lower nature is being seriously modified. There is nothing wrong with removing greed and other lower aspects from our path in life... Once they have been released, you will find that life becomes much simpler, because it will use the sword of truth, given by God. Hunger, death and wild beasts are allegories referring to the starving and demise of material desires, as well as the overcoming of the ego, so that it can be put to more positive use. The rise toward spirituality slays the needs for material distractions. Even though we now recognize them as illusions, we are reluctant to relinquish their superficial convenience. Nevertheless, we will be gaining more influence over our lives, without the ego's necessity to control our physical whims. Without the need to be controlled by other things, we will be able to journey toward acceptance of life as it should be. A life without negativity, but filled with the true understanding of love, has to be a thing of sheer beauty, taken from dreams to reality. However, the work is not yet complete.

THE FIFTH SEAL: **Revelations 6:9-11**: *"And when he had opened the fifth seal, I saw under the altar the souls of them that were slain for the word of God, and for the testimony which they held: (10) And they cried with a loud voice, saying, How long, O Lord, holy and true, dost thou not judge and avenge our blood on them that dwell on the earth? (11) And white robes were given unto every one of them; and it was said unto them, that they should rest yet for a little season, until their fellow-servants also and their brethren, that should be killed as they were, should be fulfilled".* The biblical climb to the higher realm is quite different in its explanations than those found in other texts. With its insistence in the absolution of "sin" or the attainment of a "state of grace", it presents a harsher awakening, in no uncertain terms – and in many ways, it is. It is difficult for anyone's ego to suddenly realize that it was on the wrong path, that it had unceremoniously created problems for self or others. But spirit is relentless, and it demands that in the fifth chakra, we complete the task of the cleansing that started in the fourth.

And so, the fifth chakra is now opened for us to examine our own past for what we have done that was not in the interest of others. It is represented by the souls crying out from under the altar. The "word of God" is the symbol of truth. The metaphor relates to the past hurts we have inflicted upon ourselves and others. It must be addressed so that it may be cleared for us to receive forgiveness granted by the higher level. The white robes could be considered as a reward for truth and purity, but there is still further clearing to take place. We are to be patient, for our hour has not yet come. We may even say that our previous burdens are now gone from us. Our karma has been balanced within, and our path – dharma – is being freed of obstacles, making our path straight. This process will make us face what we have done to others, and we will not be able to ignore it.

THE SIXTH SEAL: **Revelations 6:12-17**: *"And I beheld when he had opened the sixth seal, and, lo, there was a great earthquake; and the sun became black as sackcloth of hair, and the moon became as blood; (13) And the stars of heaven fell unto the earth, even as a fig tree casteth her untimely figs, when she is shaken of a mighty wind. (14) And the heaven departed as a scroll when it is rolled together; and every mountain and island were moved out of their places. (15) And the kings of the earth, and the great men, and the rich men, and the chief captains, and the mighty men, and every bondman, and every free man, hid themselves in the dens and in the rocks of the mountains; (16) And said to the mountains and rocks, Fall on us, and hide us from the face of him that sitteth on the throne, and from the wrath of the Lamb: (17) For the great day of his wrath is come; and who shall be able to stand?*

To most of the readers, the sixth seal may seem to be one of absolute tribulation. It is indeed quite a departure from the other seals – which are not exactly gentle either. Perhaps, if you were to return to **Matthew 10:34**, you would realize that Jesus issued a warning: *"Think not that I am come to send peace on earth: I came not to send peace, but a sword"*. The sword of truth inflicts pain, the pain of renouncing the shallow pleasures of the material world. If you read **Matthew 10:35-42**, you may catch a glimpse of the hardship, the anguish of unconditionally giving your inner spirit for the greater glory of God. This seal will bring on what is known as the "dark night of the soul". We will cover this in greater detail in the last chapter of this work.

Thus, the metaphors in the above verses are of cataclysmic proportions, a continuous death of the old sense system and the opening of the new. For most, it will be quite a shock, because in the blink of an eye, they will perceive life as it really is. In such a sudden change, there will be a point in all of infinity with no place for reference, and all that they have known will be made anew. That moment defies all physical comprehension of what we have seen and experienced to this point. It can indeed be compared to a great earthquake that will shake every belief you ever held, and now descending into the darkness of oblivion. The mountains of greed and the islands of carnal desires, along with other negative physical traits, will be involved in a major shift and they too will fade in the forgiving mist of spirituality. All that we perceive as our present physical reality will be moved to a new position. We will see ourselves and all that surrounds us in a different light. This marvelous metamorphosis will eventually happen to the powerful, the rich and the poor, and that initial, spiritual earthquake will undoubtedly unleash misconceived fears. But their minds will open, as "heaven departed", to reveal the light of truth. The seven stars held in His right hand will shower them with knowledge, while making the unwanted past burdens fall to the ground as so many "untimely figs". Jesus said in **Mark 8:35**: *"...but whosoever shall lose his life for my sake and the gospel's, the same shall save it"*. It implies that if we give all, we may have all, and the sixth seal shows us the way.

As the shift happens within us, our material reality will also be affected, because mental definition will be completely changed, as logic no longer will work. This particular seal may be perceived on a more global aspect. The great earthquake and the lands being moved can be indicative of the polar shifts discussed in the Book of Genesis. The inner turmoils will release outer ones as well – and vice-versa. However, it would be better if we initiated this, since most of us have been ready for eons for the catastrophes to take place. If the outer aspect was to shift first, it would indeed unleash great destruction. On the other hand, it could very well happen that way. The reason this is said is because, as we shift to the spiritual nature, we will shed the physical mass which would have to apply to our beloved Earth also – as mass will also shift for a lighter nature. This new environment would still be able to support or sustain us as a finer human form.

For a moment, let us move away from the seven seals to look at Chapter 7 of the Book of Revelations. This unique chapter is one of the greatest mysteries of the Bible, for it unfolds the aspect of spiritual growth and also what will happen to our planet, to our world. At some point, there is to be a correct number of people to witness these events. They are those who attain the knowledge and understanding of the God nature. Once this is accomplished, all will unfold, but not *"till we have sealed the servants of our God in their foreheads"* (Revelations 7:3). Compared to the masses, the number itself is quite small. Through the higher nature, they are to verify that we are ready as humanity, nothing more. We are almost at that point in our history, but history is merely the recorded past, hence ours is before us – not behind us. The awakening has begun and its signs are all around us. We may observe or deny them, but it will not change the tide reaching our shores with the turmoils of life. Those waves will raise us to a higher understanding and acceptance.

To assist us in the appreciation of physical shift, may we offer a few simple principles of electromagnetism. Most of us understand the concept of electricity and magnets. If we were to take a piece of steel and wrap a wire around it from top to bottom, and if we were to apply an electrical charge to the coil of wire, the piece of steel would have a receiving end and a repelling end – in other words: a magnet. Now, if we were to apply the electrical charge to the other end of the wire, the two poles would shift, and the receiving and repelling positions would be reversed. Before the shift takes place, there must be a pause for the current to flow from the opposite direction. This same concept applies to all things that have this function, this possibility. It includes the human form and mind. It would also pertain to our world as we now know it. Because of its recurrence, this phenomenon has been and is being geologically recorded. A 180 degrees shift would almost be unnoticed, unless one was to specifically look for it. At the same time, there is no one today who has experienced this, therefore, no one can confirm it. However, in **Joshua 10:13**, we find this quote: *"...Is not this written in the book of Jasher? So the sun stood still in the midst of heaven, and hasted not to go down about a whole day"*. The Mayan texts also recorded a lengthy period of darkness, and the Hopi legends have two sunrises in the same twenty-four hour period. The latter would not be that unusual except that each time, the sun rose from a different direction – and that is the Legend of the Two Suns. It obviously indicates a shift, and all were recorded at approximately the same period of earth history. It is also the swing of the pendulum as we mentioned earlier. This is only a possibility – not a fact. Yet, documentation will support this theory, including the biblical texts in Genesis and Revelations, among many others. These records range from the sciences to religion, along with myth, and seem to predict both a geophysical and a geomagnetic pole shift. No one knows the day or the hour when the Bridegroom will come, and Revelations expresses symbolically the preparation for this anticipated period. As an act of perseverance, we must have enough oil in our lamps so they may stay lit, up to and during that time.

If we were to apply this concept to Chapter 7, we would possibly see these indicators on a global basis – only when the number is correct. In fact, from a numerological viewpoint, the number 666 added together come to 9 – which means end of cycle. In **Revelations 13:18**, John says: *"Here is wisdom. Let him that hath understanding count the number of the beast: for it is the number of a man;* **and his number is Six hundred threescore and six**". The verse seems to depict one person, but it is not perceived as such, for it applies to all of us as we reach the end of the cycle or the number of attainment, therefore beginning a time of renewal.

When one reads Revelations 7:1, it tells us that the four winds of the earth were held. According to the laws of physics, there is really only one way that the winds would not blow: the earth had stopped its rotation as related in Joshua 10:13, prior to reversing said rotation. A shift had occurred, and when the next one happens, we will shift with it as we must. It is quite possible that such an event could engender the moving of the lands, huge earthquakes, material upheaval and great fears, as well as living in caves and striving to find protection. **Revelations 7:3-4**: *"...Hurt not the earth, neither the sea, nor the trees, till we have sealed the servants of our God in their foreheads. (4) And I heard the number of them which were sealed: and there were sealed an hundred and forty and four thousand of all the tribes of the children of Israel".*

The next verses show twelve thousand people chosen from each of the twelve tribes. It does not represent the number to be saved, but rather the number of those to witness the shift of the ages. This is confirmed in **Revelations 7:9**: *"After this I beheld, and, lo, a great multitude, which no man could number, of all nations...".* This had to be indeed a huge crowd, all wearing white robes – the color of wisdom – that they had attained. They were from every land, tongue and color. This vision reveals that all the people of the world will be included, thus we will all be involved if we let go and allow God within us. **Revelations 7:14**: *"...These are they which came out of great tribulation, and have washed their robes, and made them white in the blood of the Lamb".* The presence of all these people gathered together is the symbol of individual purification.

We now move to the opening of the seventh seal, our final shedding, our opening to wear white robes and reach the crown of spirit and knowledge.

THE SEVENTH SEAL: **Revelations 8:1-5**: *"And when he had opened the seventh seal, there was silence in heaven about the space of half an hour. (2) And I saw the seven angels which stood before God; and to them were given seven trumpets. (3) And another angel came and stood at the altar, having a golden censer; and there was given unto him much incense, that he should offer it with the prayers of all saints upon the golden altar which was before the throne. (4) And the smoke of the incense which came with the prayers of the saints, ascended up before God out of the angel's hand. (5) And the angel took the censer, and filled it with fire of the altar, and cast it into the earth: and there were voices, and thunderings, and lightnings, and an earthquake".* Silence will softly blanket heaven and fill the sky. Your minds will become hushed in their way, in a reverent true prayer. A higher communion will replace the discordance of your inner noise and you will hear God speak. This silence has been offered for you to experience true bliss within, a bliss so complete that it will almost surpass the comprehensive capabilities of the mortal mind. You will feel the kingdom of God within, and all things will be made known. Following this divine communion, even for a moment, you will never be the same. You will henceforth be in a constant state of prayer, for God will hear, and so shall we. You are at the true altar of the spirit, and as Aaron's staff in Genesis, the golden censer will be your own. The smoke of the incense will be your prayers being lifted, and now they will surely be heard by the Father in heaven, because many others will join you, and all things will be given. The saints are the pure thoughts, for you have settled all that you held against your brothers and you have forgiven. You have cleansed yourselves of the past events.

The seven trumpets represent our centers – which are indeed shaped much like a small trumpet. And they will resound throughout the land – your kingdom – for all to hear. You will have no need to say anything, because it will surely show, as light makes darkness disappear and nothing will be hidden. The Ark will truly go before you and light your way as you reach the sacred union.

As this spiritual development makes its way through not only the physical being but across the globe, much takes place within the human. Our perceptions change from the heavy material outlook to the finer aspect of the inner world, through a spiritual mind and eyes. We will begin to see things as they really are, and it will create the unrest being portrayed in the Book of Revelations. It appears after the opening of the sixth seal of the book of life – the intuitive seal given to each of us by the Father. It unleashes pure creative energy and, combined with the seventh seal, all power through Spirit is realized. We reach our own self-realization as the physical merges with the spiritual. The respective knowledge of the higher and lower natures is unified. The inner conflicts experienced prior to this soul-saving unification can indeed be compared to thunder, lightning and earthquakes as the shifts take place.

We are told that there will be great destruction, that only 144,000 people will be saved who will be chosen individuals from the original twelve tribes (Revelations 7:4). Incidentally, this number is also the exact same number of petals that adorn the symbolic chakras that are with each of us. It reveals that all energy centers will be fully activated to give us complete understanding of not only what but who we are: in the image of Spirit, as we were created to be.

In Revelations 7:9, we see a different variation presented as a great multitude too large for anyone to count, all of whom are wearing white robes before the throne of God. If those who are to be saved are limited in number, who are these people wearing white? They are those who have attained. They have overcome the physical ego nature of the human being. They have cleared themselves of all the karma that has built up. They have achieved the opening of the seven seals to their book of life. This metaphorical destruction is the release of what we had perceived as important things, what we say we own, or people we attempt to control, and the belief systems onto which we have held so dearly. This is symbolized as destruction for the very same reasons Abraham was seeking to save Sodom from annihilation. He, like us, pleaded for the toys of life, the outer world things we think give us great joy and perfection. No matter how much we plead, these things will be of no value when the time comes. Only what we have within us will be of value. This is what Abraham attempted, and so do we now. We struggle against our own self to maintain what we have of the material realm, making the transformation more difficult. The lesson is to learn to let go and let the Spirit prevail, for It knows what is in our best interest. We are told, however, that we will not be able to let go, thus the destruction is depicted in symbolism, but can become reality if necessary. It behooves each of us to take heed of the warning signs, but if we break out of that material prison, our spirit will say: *"Riches profit not in the day of wrath: but righteousness delivereth from death"* (Proverbs 11:4).

THE SEVEN TRUMPETS

We now have the seven angels with seven trumpets unleashing what appears to be great destruction. These are the same seven energy centers of the body letting loose all that we have been hoarding within ourselves. We must travel through the illusions of the mind and the devious temptations offered by the ego. These are regrets, the unfinished business we have with others, the matters we did not wish to face. They are all stored within these centers, at different levels, from the lower to the higher aspect, from the first to the seventh. **Revelations 8:7**: *"The first angel sounded, and there followed hail and fire mingled with blood, and they were cast upon the earth: and the third part of trees was burnt up, and all green grass was burnt up"*. Metaphysically, this is the initial ascent of the kundalini – or serpent energy – rising from within to reach the crown, or the seventh angel, to be in alignment with the higher purposes. The allegories are at earth level, symbolizing the burning of the old growth forests of the mind – the burdens of the past. **Revelations 8:8-9**: *"And the second angel sounded, and as it were a great mountain burning with fire was cast into the sea: and the third part of the sea became blood; (9) And the third part of the creatures which were in the sea, and had life, died; and the third part of the ships were destroyed"*. As we progress on our upward journey, we can feel the release of the higher nature into our system. The mountain is the dross of life, its heavy obstacles being burned so that spirit can course through our veins. The creatures and the ships are metaphors painting more of the impure temptations and distractions stored at that level and being eliminated from our belief system. We are beginning to come as one with the higher nature. **Revelations 8:10-11**: *"And the third angel sounded, and there fell a great star from heaven, burning as it were a lamp, and it fell upon the third part of the rivers, and upon the fountains of waters; (11) And the name of the star is called Wormwood: and the third part of the waters became wormwood; and many men died of the waters, because they were made bitter"*. On a more earthly note, you may not be aware that there is an herb used all over the world, known as wormwood, a.k.a. absinthe. It is used to assist in clearing the body of certain impurities we tend to ingest, and even in the preparation of certain wines. Ironically, it has a bitter taste, as described in the above verse. The truth, which can be harsh at times, fell into the rivers and fountains of our thoughts, our beliefs. On this spiritual path, the matters related to the physical now leave that bitter taste within us. In fact, it has already begun in most of us today. We are starting to understand and realize that there is more. As we move higher within our inner selves, the physical will no longer satisfy our wants. **Revelations 8:12**: *"And the fourth angel sounded, and the third part of the sun was smitten, and the third part of the moon, and the third part of the stars; so as the third part of them was darkened, and the day shone not for a third part of it, and the night likewise"*. We are at the heart center of the human, where lies the power of the ego. We have heard the sound of the first three trumpets, and to this point, everything has been expressed in thirds. Our time for achieving is being shortened. We are halfway into our journey. The pull of the physical may still be there, but it has begun to lessen. There is a resistance to the higher or lower aspects, depending on the direction of our thoughts. They may become darkened through fear of the unknown self. It also alludes to the quickening or higher vibration for which we are destined. Time will appear to move at a higher or faster pace. Look around you. Does not time seem to be moving at a quicker rate?

We hope that our readers will not consider this too long of a dissertation. That far into the book, you must understand the importance of clearly exposing the metaphysical meanings we find in the Bible. Our primary concern is for you to comprehend the guidance, the lessons, the warnings that are contained therein, for the benefit of your spiritual awakening.

Revelations 9:1-3: *"And the fifth angel sounded, and I saw a star fall from heaven unto the earth: and to him was given the key of the bottomless pit. (2) And he opened the bottomless pit; and there arose a smoke out of the pit, as the smoke of a great furnace; and the sun and the air were darkened by reason of the smoke of the pit. (3) And there came out of the smoke locusts upon the earth: and unto them was given power, as the scorpions of the earth have* *power"*. Contrary to religious credence, the bottomless pit is not necessarily the depths of hell. However, it can be your own individual hell if you allow it. Metaphysically, it is a glimpse into our own sense of infinity, where old definitions are now changed. When this occurs, we have the feeling of no longer knowing ourselves. The Master implied it when He said in Mark 8:35: *"...but whosoever shall lose his life for my sake...the same shall save it"*. It is the process of giving up your worldly aspirations. The pit is also the storage place for our physical past, our erroneous thoughts and beliefs, our unfinished business – all related to the material world. As we open the door, the smoke rises out of the darkness. It is the illusion of corporeal life. It is the dark night and what we have seen of self no longer applies. The locusts, inhabiting the shadows of the black smoke, are allegories referring to egoistic thoughts, temptations, carnal excess and misdeeds. Even though they are released, they will pursue us in our journey. Unless we persevere, they will create ravaging damages to our spiritual garden. With the sound of the fifth trumpet, we step into the infinite consciousness. Following the inner cleansing, we can begin to communicate in a loving way, rather than be influenced by the fear nature. This is where the focus of the self really comes into play, for our minds tend to play tricks on us as our experience begins to deepen. It is exposing us to the dark night of the soul, and this dark night is a necessary attribute of the rise in consciousness. It assists us in removing the illusions of the material parts of life to which we hold on tightly..

Revelations 9:4: *"And it was commanded them that they should not hurt the grass of the earth, neither any green thing, neither any tree; but only those men which have not the seal of God in their foreheads"*. You may find it interesting that in Revelations 8:7, all the grass and one third of the trees are destroyed by fire. Deductively, there should be no grass left. The sensible implication would then be that all fertile creations must be left alone because they open, grow and continue to assimilate the energy of spirit – and the locusts are simply a metaphor. The seal of God on the forehead is the use of the sixth energy center – the third eye in Eastern philosophy. It is the means to communicate directly with spirit, hence the illusions are removed forever. **Revelations 9:5-9**: *"And to them it was given that they should not kill them, but that they should be tormented five months: and their torment was as the torment of a scorpion, when he striketh a man.. (6) And in those days shall men seek death, and shall not find it; and shall desire to die, and death shall flee from them. (7) And the shapes of the locusts were like unto horses prepared unto battle; and on their heads were as it were crowns like gold, and their faces were as the faces of men. (8) And they had hair as the hair of women, and their teeth were as the teeth of lions. (9) And they had breastplates, as it were breastplates of iron; and the sound of their wings was as the sound of chariots of many horses* *running to battle"*. One must admit that the vivid portrayal of those rather large locusts is rather gruesome. Again, there are seven comparative descriptions. Did John, in his vision, face the ugliness and corruption of covetousness, pride, lust, anger, gluttony, envy and sloth? Are we not facing our own swarm of locusts in today's society?

We will stop here because it is believed we have grasped the point. The concepts of the human mind make us very frail indeed, even though we have the understanding. Now we must accept our illusions of self because of these frailties. **Revelations 9:11**: *"And they had a king over them, which is the angel of the bottomless pit, whose name in the Hebrew tongue is Abaddon, but in the Greek tongue hath his name Apollyon"*. The Metaphysical Bible Dictionary defines **"Abaddon"** as follows: *"...a very destructive belief of man's...So Abaddon must stand for the error belief in utter destruction of life and form...The true life principle can never be destroyed; only the outer form of man's belief in materiality is destructible. So long as man believes in materiality or destruction, the outer destruction of forms will take place"*. You will find "Abaddon" mentioned in Exodus 10:14-15 and Joel 2:3-10, and it is meant in the same terms. Are materiality and destruction not transpiring as we write these words?

We now hear the sound of the sixth trumpet. **Revelations 9:15**: *"And the four angels were loosed, which were prepared for an hour, and a day, and a month, and a year, for to slay the third part of men"*. This is to take place through a series of plagues, and if you keep up with current events, you may realize that they are upon us now. They are being produced as the physical is eaten away from us. It eats at us each and every day, merely because of our desire to hold fast to materiality. We are also informed that we still will not be able to trust the higher realm, that the material world will still have the greater pull upon our very beings. The majority of us will not let go of the illusionary importance of the physical. Close your eyes for a moment. Are not the four horsemen of the apocalypse riding now? Are fire, famine, flood and pestilence not creating devastation all over today's world? It is not symbolism. It is real. Are we yet not aware that our fears, our own thinking, are creating the reality of these plagues? The mind indeed gives us the things we see. If the inner is in turmoil, so must the outer be!

In **Revelations 10:2-3**, the seventh angel spoke: *"And he had in his hand a little book open: and he set his right foot upon the sea, and his left foot on the earth, (3) And cried with a loud voice, as when a lion roareth: and when he had cried, seven thunders uttered their voices"*. The "little book" is our own personal book of life. The fact that it is open would imply that we are most surely aware of all aspects of our nature. The angel had one foot on the land – symbol of the physical, and one foot on the sea – the symbol of the spiritual, portraying the balance between the two natures. The seven thunders are the awakened seven energy centers of the Spirit coming to life. We have finally opened the seventh seal and those are the sounds of spiritual achievement, as we arouse from our physical slumber to the larger realization of greater things of life. They are cries of joy, as we free ourselves from the corrupted bonds of the material world. In Revelations 10:6, we have arrived in the everlasting arms of infinity, time without end. In Revelations 10:9, the eating of the little book is another allegory of the sweet taste of spirit and a reminder of the bitter aspect of physical life that we may have given up, but still lurks in the shadows of the material realm.

Before we step off the path of Revelations, you may be interested in the statement expressed in **Revelations 11:8**: *"And their dead bodies shall lie in the street of the great city, which spiritually is called Sodom and Egypt, where also our Lord was crucified"*. Metaphysically, Sodom is a concealed or obscure thought, a habit of man, and the lowest sense desire. On the other hand, Egypt is substance and life in body consciousness, the darkness of ignorance, obscurity. The bodies are the angel's two witnesses that were decimated by the beast of the abyss. Are we to understand that Jesus was crucified in Egypt? Is Sodom merely a metaphor, as implied in the American Standard Bible that replaces "spiritually" by "mystically", and "their Lord" for "our Lord"? Or is it telling us that Jesus was crucified because of an obscure thought – the habit of man – and the darkness of ignorance? The seven seals being opened, would the concept of the city of Sodom and its destruction be only within the human form? John's vision is indeed disturbing, and its meaning can only be elucidated through our higher nature, through the opening of all our energy centers.

We have come a long way, on a tortuous and arduous road. We have learned much about the understanding of life and human kind, but we are still in the process of development. This unfolding may only take place as we face ourselves - individually – and not others. After all, are we not to be born again in the likeness and image of the Spirit? Were we not presented this priceless gift in the Book of Genesis? We are to rise from the ashes of self, out of all that has been burned and removed from us, in spite of our own lower natures. As you have read, to reach that point is not an easy matter. It takes courage, conviction, self-determination, diligence and perseverance. The Bible is more on the spiritual, mystical aspects of life, but very few give it any significance. In fact, most of us do not seem to give life much significance either. It is either too deep or not important enough.

The Bible is not a book to be read with the left brain function, but rather with the creative spiritual thinking of the right brain. Of course, it is abstract esoteric thinking, and most of us do not want to plunge into that task because it is "too much work". Yet, this style of thinking would be the seat of growth for all of us to enjoy. We would learn more of life and what it has to offer, and we would certainly learn more about our real inner nature, as well as the power to work with the spiritual aspect of life. If we were to allow for just a few moments of inner reflection, we would realize the true depth and nature of life, including our own. We have encountered many tribulations in the course of this book, and the struggles portrayed in Revelations are a very personal matter. We must journey through them, and we will do it alone, no matter who is around. Ironically, we do this with each and every moment, in very tiny increments, consciously or unconsciously. Eventually, these tiny increments catch up to us. They have the nasty habit of generating the struggles and misunderstandings of today. However, they are truly meant to destroy the mental egoistic aspect that controls us, but it must be done a little at a time. If it were applied all at once, it would be overpowering. This is not to say that it will not be instantaneous, because it can occur in the blinking of an eye. Ultimately, spirit will descend upon us, and realization will take us by surprise. As it is stated so often biblically, the truth shall be revealed.

As it is true in all beliefs, religion has become too strong a conviction, with very little flexibility. It then becomes ingrained in all those involved, not allowing for the faith of the mustard seed and the enlightenment of the spirit nature. With this flawed concept, if you do not believe, you are wrong. So goes the individual nature we all have. For the dragon of the ego will surely devour the lamb nature of the human form, and the inner war will continue. We will be tormented until it is all wrested. What will we have in the end? Pure physical egoistic nature, and someone attempting to control it all, because at that time, we will not know what we do or what to do! All of gentleness will be thrown away, and no love will exist in the true sense of the word. Fear, hate, anger and frustration will feed upon themselves.

In Part 2 of this book, we will offer for your understanding the true spiritual human. We will portray for you an individual free of the shackles of life and love, one who offers all things in freedom, the freedom of sharing who we are and being open with no fear of retaliations by another. The truly enlightened human is one of acceptance and selflessness. We hope that the final part of this work will provide this understanding. As you have learned, we should be releasing, looking forward to all matters that we seek and that Spirit has promised us we may have. If we are looking forward, we will know where we are going and how to get there. If we are continually looking over our shoulder, we are sure to stumble as we do now – because we are still blind to the truth of life. Aspire to be great, but not at the expense of another, for whatever you step on in your path may someday step on you.

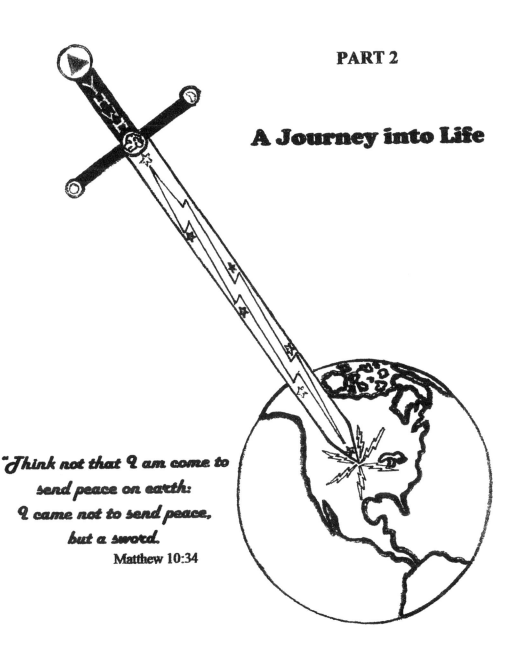

PART 2

A Journey into Life

"Think not that I am come to
send peace on earth:
I came not to send peace,
but a sword.
Matthew 10:34

PART 2

A Journey into Life

INTRODUCTION

Part 1 of this book has depicted the more significant parts of the Scriptures with a unique metaphysical perspective. We hope that the readers have enjoyed and understood a message that is quite different from that taught traditionally by the numerous religious organizations of the world. We should apply these new concepts to our lives, to our own selves, to gain a higher purpose.

It has not been the intention of the author to downplay these organizations in any way, even though it may sometimes give that impression. The honest intent has been to show that, within the pages of the Bible, there is a different level of understanding available, especially in the teachings of the Master Himself found in the four main Gospels. It was His desire to bring people to another level of self-appreciation, and to bring their thoughts and actions to a higher plane. It was His intent to expose a higher vibration to all those who could hear and comprehend His message. This is how He healed them. My own purpose is to paint a clearer picture of His words. His teachings were actually quite succinct. In **John 10:34**, He said: *"...Ye are Gods"*. In this book, we have attempted to explain and confirm these deeply significant words, and we all realize that this blessed individual never told an untruth. It was His intent to be the example of the persons we may all become, should we but have the faith of the mustard seed. It was also His purpose when he stated that "I am the light, I am the way", as if to say: "Do what I do and follow my example". As He so aptly put it, we can, but only if we follow the path of true understanding and acceptance.

The following chapters will be to assist you in a brighter illumination of the path, and a deeper study of the meanings from ancient times. Today, these old messages have become confusing because of the way they are being taught, and we do not try to deepen the accepted form of the teachings. We have mentioned that such messages tend to point at the physical part of life only. This should never have been the case, because the physical is not the reason that we are here in the first place. Granted, life has its purpose, but we are here for all the metaphysical reasons established by Spirit for our betterment. We are here to climb the spiritual ladder - Jacob's ladder - portrayed by the Master as a very real possibility. He lived it Himself and demonstrated it by His actions. So can we, should we choose to do so. It is simply a matter of choice.

If we were to take a moment and look around us, we would see a growing interest toward the spiritual nature on the part of most of today's society. There is a greater level of acceptance and curiosity about the higher aspects than ever before. It is also the reason for the struggles that are so prevalent in the world today. We are beginning to realize that there is more to life and to self than just the body. Now, it is time for all of us to carry this even further than in the past by taking a new look at the very ties that bind us to a less rewarding belief system. We must ask: why have we fenced ourselves in by the limiting of the mind? By doing this, we are limiting ourselves in the material sense as well.

"Ye are Gods" is a very bold concept, yet we are told this is the truth, in both **Genesis** and **John**. The question is: how do we reach this heavenly goal? It cannot be easy, in light of the fact that most of the information has been hidden from us through many centuries. We must learn to subdue the fears of the mind into which we fall each and every moment we have available. We truly lead ourselves to them so that we may rid ourselves of the preconceived notions of limitations. True freedom in all respects is what the world is now considering.

We will begin to portray the higher spiritual aspect of life and the path leading thereto. This journey is through our ego-based fears, toward an upper level of self-acceptance, for the power of the cosmos is contained within each of us. However, we may not use it until we have rested all our issues with life. This is not an easy trek, but it is well worth the trip, should we decide to make that choice. It is a journey intending to develop the true purpose toward the blessed silence of the crown. It is a decision we all will face at some point in our lives because there must be a better way.

We will attempt to apply what has been perceived in the first part of this work from a scriptural point of view and try to fit it into our everyday lives. We cannot intellectualize this concept. Living it is the only way. We must experience it to make the difference. That path must be walked by any of us who seek this level of being. It is not for the weak-hearted, and the Master said: "You must persevere until the end". There will be many pitfalls along the way, but they are the downside of the egoistic mind. These stumbling blocks are on the very path to attainment, and that makes them merely stepping stones. They are the areas that must be accepted, understood and corrected. They cannot be ignored or avoided because they will not go away. We must learn to work through them, since this path is about shedding the lower carnal aspect for a higher, finer way of life. It can be attained only through diligence and persistence. There is no other way to achieve it. We will be tested at every step, but these tests are easy if we are self-observant and conscious of our interactions during these events. We must be open to them.

We must also realize that the more aware we become, the more powerful we become. We are not talking about muscle strength, nor is it for the sake of power itself, because that will certainly never work, since it is purely ego-oriented to fill the need to control. This path is for grace and humility alone. It is for all of us to become one – or to recognize it – for it is already that way with life. It has been said in the Nag Hammadi, in the Gospel of St. Thomas: "The closer we come to God, the greater the pull of evil". In other words, the closer we come to the higher nature of spirit, the greater will be the pull of life. This progressive growth is to overcome the war between the spiritual and the carnal. It is an inner fight with which we will have to deal on this path.

Part 2 of this work consists of a guide on how to live with and within our higher nature. We even speak again about the dark night of the soul that we will all certainly encounter along the way. There is a difference between being involved in a situation about which we know nothing, and one about which we know the substance and the reason. Even though one will be easier than the other, it does not mean that it can be avoided. To the Zen, it is chopping the wood and carrying the water; in other words, it is a necessary matter. It is the experience that is the path of knowledge, and nothing less. It is the true teacher of all things.

We will cover the true Holy Trinity of life. We will guide you in unifying the three aspects, to bring them together in all respects. It will require much more inner reflection than most are willing to give. The most difficult act in life is to look into one's own eyes, the window of the soul. Truly, we may not like what we have been doing. By peering into that window, we may easily shift ourselves into something we do like and learn to enjoy. We may learn to respect ourselves for who we are and have been. We should not fear, but rather take pleasure in the experiences that life will bring forth. At that point, by healing the mind and emotions, we can heal the physical form and bring all things to a state of perfection. Perfection is an inner choice and should remain secret, because it is between us and the spirit that has given us life. If one were to shout its achievement from the roof tops, all others would indeed attempt to destroy it. We must learn to live and love in great humility, with respect for all things because they have as much life in them as we do.

We are all in this experience together, by spiritual choice. We have chosen to be in this era for the shift of the ages that is to come, a shift to a much higher reality of life and form. May your journey be safe and fulfilling in all respects. May you travel in peace and love throughout life. Be free of judgment so you will not be judged.

CHAPTER 1

THE WAY OF THE LAMB

*"Life is truly filled with virtue, yet it becomes distorted
by the frailties of the perceptions and concepts of the human mind"*
Steven Hairfield, PhD

Now it is time to shape all of this biblical information into an understandable, conclusive format, so the reader may fully comprehend the data that has been offered thus far. If we are to become that spiritual human, it will take internal realization and much effort on our part. A true effort will be required as we shed the beliefs of what we deemed important in the past. This is the accumulation of concepts, doctrines, thoughts and deeds that we have collected through our years of life, and known as **dross** [1]. The Master tells us that we are to persevere to the end, and the journey is well worth it. It is the journey of the self, to a place most of us have never been. It is an inner journey for which no road map will be of service to us, simply because there is none. This is due to our individual nature wanting to travel its own path, yet the Bible is considered the best guide, because it is written about the one person who completed the voyage.

Each of us is a unique being, and regardless of the distinctive traits, we are about to embark in uncharted waters. We must now earnestly learn the messages from the Master, because we know we may all be like He was – only if we endure the hardships of the path. He did say to us: *"Ye are gods... "*, and God Itself described us as such in the Book of Genesis. This august state of being is not ready-made! We can reach this virtuous status only if we apply the understanding of the principles that were offered not only by the Father and the Son, but by many others in time eternal. We should merely accept that we are first born of spirit, then we come into physical reality. This becomes the true first and the last, only through recognition that we are this – and nothing less.

We are born on this world to be finite, one lifetime after another, to learn the extent of our being, so that we may use all the attributes the Crea-

---

[1] Dross: defined as a heaviness of being and the part that binds us where we find ourselves, living the past over and over in our minds.

tor has given us since time immemorial. These attributes are the quintessence of the higher and lower natures, and we have been granted complete use of both. This now stated is "as above, so below", or the true spiritually thriving path of life. It is purely the acceptance of the real natural human, built with the capacity to love all things unconditionally. It must begin first within each of us and no place else.

This journey not only comprises the mind of the human, but also the feelings, the memories, and the influence of the higher nature of the person on the physical attributes of life. These all come together to form the tapestry of our full thinking nature. We are the only living entity that has the complete comprehensive ability of creative independent thinking. Is not the concept of creation what life is all about? Do we not create with each moment we experience? The only obstacle interfering with creation is the mind of humankind, our unwillingness to let go of the yesterdays that we have already experienced. Our past is the one burden that holds us from growth. It is not creation. It is not the present. It is memories of another day, another time. It is truly an illusion of the mind that does not allow us to be in perfection. It is the yesterdays and the situations that did not work the way we expected. We see too many things wrong with our own self because of the past that has ensnared us and held us in place.

All things take place in the mind of life, within each of us. With the exception of the mind of the individual, everything else forever moves forward in time. Each new day, a little more is added with each new experience – or re-experience, and it is a choice we all make. It is up to us to either move forward or stagnate in the past.

Our physical form is the meeting place for the past and the future, and each exercises its own pull. We are in the middle of both. We operate on what we have done and what we would like to do, but seldom on what we are doing. We are to meet the unknown tribulations or bliss of the future. The mystery of what lies ahead and what it can bring is a better option. If we were receptive to it, it would probably diminish the potential difficulties. Our minds create certain dreams, and when they do not materialize, we are disappointed. Could these dreams be expectations? Still, the future may be seen. We need only to look forward and build on the events of the present. It will insure the realization of the dream. With flexibility, we will allow for the changes or lessons necessary for the achievement of the envisioned desire. We only need to understand what we do in the moment, and we will know what returns we can expect from the future. If the foundation is solid, we may build – one brick at a time.

The most solid foundation is one of self-love, not in a self-serving arrogant sense. No conditions should be attached at any time. Any conditions that we may place will surely erode any sturdy base we think we have built. Where conditions exist -- which are merely fears – there can be no love. Love is a choice of conscience. The fears really stem from the past events involving something we think others have done to us. In reality, love is not a thought. It is an experience of self, a true feeling of the heart. Unconditional love shouts its existence down to the smallest atom of life, whereas hatred denies itself and may not be embodied except in the mind. Hatred is the opposite of spirit, because it is not love. It may falsely bear its face, but it is not love. Still, love is beneath that mask of fear – fear of past experiences. Please understand that we are not talking about love in the physical sense, or the carnal, selfish gratification of baser instincts. We are bringing into focus the radiant beauty of spiritual love, including the pure feelings one may have for a spouse, for family members, for good friends or even for the splendors of nature. We are talking about the kind of forgiving love manifested toward those who may have hurt us in different ways. You see, love is the true reason for the existence of all that we know and see, and it goes on for all eternity. Anything else must meet an end, because it is steeped in disharmony. We must come to the realization that love is all-powerful, and forever so. We could say that the heart of the human is the seat of eternal power.

How can another love you if you do not love yourself first? This is a very basic concept that we should all apply, because life is a direct reflection of what we feel about ourselves. If we truly desire to have love in our lives, it must definitely begin with and within us, in an open, humble way, without arrogance. Self-love in any other sense is merely a façade of conceit, vanity, deceptions and untruth. A truly spiritual human has no fear or mistrust of life because of the aforementioned acceptance of self. Conversely, if we harbor those doubts, such a negative mindset will normally anticipate that life will take from us and not give. This is not a spiritual concept. Only another human may take from us, but not life itself. Were we to ask in the true sense, all would be given, providing it came from the heart. In the book of Matthew, the Master said that "your Father knoweth what things ye have need of, before ye ask him". We must be able to envision this, to imagine it. To envisage it is to place the image of what we desire in the mind's eye. Subsequently, we must use the power of the heart to feel the creation of the desire we seek, and we must be willing to receive it without conditions. You may remember that we were told to knock, and the door would be opened for us. All that is left for us to do is to enter. Too many times, however, our fears of "what if" block that entrance.

The Master also told us in the book of Matthew that if we are to enter the kingdom of heaven – or reach the crown – we must have the mind of a child, the acceptance of self. We must revert to the delightful innocence of the little children, not the "better than" approach we all seem to adopt at times as adults. To arrive at the blissful state of mind of our young friends, we must live in the moment as they do. Simply because it did not go our way before does not mean that it will not be better in just a little while. All things will be given in spirit's time, generally not our own. We must stay our course, persevere, and we will overcome. The price and effort are minimal. We simply release the negativity onto which we hold, and release our fear of the unknown self. The true beauty of each individual – including our own - will surprise us. In most circumstances, we must lose or bury our old self in order to enjoy the beauty of our true self. We have to give up all preconceived notions and illusions, and only then will we have the truth of our very own being.

So that we may read and understand the perceived truth within its pages, we must now take another look at the dissertations we offered about the biblical texts. We will present it now in a spiritual perspective, and how to live and walk that path. This is a record of life for us to realize and carry out personally. We are that little book the last Angel of Revelations held open. We are to read our own records, for there are no blank pages between these covers. To myself, the Bible is a perfect set of operating instructions, if we allow for the metaphysical use of all allegories and metaphors.

If the texts are taken literally, as printed, it will make no sense, and dogma will have to be used. Dogma is human. We are human and spirit combined, hence we must allow both as one. Spirit does not need an authoritative point of view without adequate grounds - only human control does, for the purpose of inciting fear. If we are to teach about spirit, it must be in a harmonious way, not through inflexible laws. We must move beyond the religious mind, break down the dogmatic approach and live through our hearts and minds operating in union with each other. We must leave this unbending method to the doctrinaire minds of the zealots. For the most part, this is the way this invaluable information is taught to us as religion. Through the years of translating and editing the Bible, we have changed the real purpose of this great book. It has been veiled so that others, qualified or not, may teach what has been printed. It is interpreted for the physical mind rather than the spiritual self. Because of this, the truth has been hidden, and we are led further into the abyss of darkness – darkness only in the sense that we are not allowed to comprehend it for ourselves, thus we have the blind leading the blind. Of course, this does not apply to all religious organizations of the world. There are many attempting to bring the divine guiding words to the light, so that we may accept the truth without being controlled. Truth comes to us like any other force. It occasionally offers itself with so much intensity that it will not be for all ears to hear. In most instances, spiritual truth must be perceived, felt – not spoken for only the ears to hear. This is why the Master so often used the phrase "let those with ears hear". He knew that not all would be able to absorb His most important deeper teachings – only the few.

We are this book of life, as mentioned above, for where else would it be written, except on our own soul? We attempt to hide its very pages from another's view, as we write them each and every moment of our lives. If other people were to know our past, perhaps they would not like us or love us as we are. We must learn to accept this as their own judgment of us – not ours. It belongs to them only, and on that premise, only they will suffer through what they judge. It is their thought process, not ours. We must not fight them, because if we do, we then become something we are not. We live our life based on another's superficial point of view. It is no longer our own life. You see, we have recorded these pages during each passing moment. We know our past, our experiences and their circumstances. It is not for anyone else to qualify our past as a good thing or a bad thing. Most of us would rather forget the past, nor do we wish to speak of it, because when we do, others may condemn us for it. When they do, it compounds the situation, leading us to hide from it or change it to a more acceptable status. At this point, the events recorded in our inner little book are no longer the external truth. Our book of life is like a diary that should be shared with no one. It is secret until someone finds it, opens it, and we become angry for what we believe may be discovered. Others have seen us physically for what they think we are. Now they have pried into the center of our inner distress and will turn these wounds on us through manipulation – so it may seem. This may enhance the very fears that bind us. We hide the truth because we will not let go the reality of the past. How can we forget the past, when others will continue to downplay who we are for what they think we were? The events of the past should be used as a tool for self-understanding. Once the lessons are absorbed, they do not plague us again on any level. We must focus only on the experience brought on by these events. It will give us a different view of the past and present. The wounds will heal on their own through understanding.

When we allow our fears to modify our inner being because of the irresponsible judgments formulated by others, we step off the path of spiritual, collective love. Under these circumstances, most of us will feel unlovable, or that we may not be accepted for what others believe went on in our lives. This reaction will attack our self-worth and will become more damaging if we let it continue. We must release this feeling, for it will harm our inner selves, as we begin to accept as true what other people tell us we are. As the Master said: "They will not know you and will persecute you".

We must remember that the more we evolve, the more power our thoughts have to create our reality. Hence, we must realize a greater responsibility for these thoughts of self. Do we not understand that we merely tell others what we think they are, and not what they really are? If we may see the God in us, will we not also perceive It in others? As equal creations, how can we condemn them, unless we see first what we really are? Now we will have truth, rather than the illusions related by others as to what they see or think. If we are truly the spiritual human, so will all others be, for we may see them in no other light. This principle is repeated throughout the Gospels: "Let your light so shine before men", or "put your candle on a candlestick – not under a bushel" – so that all may see. Emanating from us, it will show itself to the external world as the "city on the hill".

Were we to not accept the guiding light of spiritual life, we would tend to push away the very things we desire the most. At that point, we would blame others for our fate because, in general, we have an amazing propensity for pointing the finger in the wrong direction. Letting our inner light shine is letting ourselves know who we are – not whom we think we are. The truth lies beneath the rubble of self, a self shaped by what others have led us to believe we are. In fact, they may be just as confused about self as we are. In that case, untruth will engender untruth. How can others know what is best for our higher good when they do not accept the truth of their own life or who we are? And truth can only promote more truth...

Once more, we must revert to the Beginning, and Spirit is the only entity that knows for sure when and where this all began. As for us, we need only concern ourselves with the Now. In the scheme of things, whether the chicken or the egg came first does not seem that important. They are both here and so are we, filled with life, with the ability to love unconditionally should we choose to do so. Life is a very wonderful gift, laced with virtue. Too often, we all look for or are attracted by the negative aspects of life, but eventually, we find there is no virtue in this – only heartaches. We cannot live on this earth and avoid harsh lessons. Yet, we have the capability to accept them easily and with joy, rather than struggle and sorrow.

Heartaches will also create a period of healing, in order to help us get over the experience of negativity. Some of us never reach that point, out of the fear of pain. Sadly, many of us do not necessarily allow for the soothing effect of positive things that are so much more enjoyable to have and experience. In reality, it is a simple matter of choice. Positive or negative forces do exist – as they must – for the undeniable application of polar opposition. They actually create an easier way of learning. If not essentially easier, it is much faster. We have choice because of it.

We must offer at this time another look at the concept of Satan. This dark image is not a being, not even a spirit. It is the hidden energy of the universe, merely the power of differentiation. It is the dark breath released upon us so we may choose. It is the collective thought forms of those who experiment with destruction. It is there for us to compare, so that we may become builders of life rather than its wreckers – as we have become. It is less a force to fight than it is for us to go beyond by learning its messages. This Satan, whose name has become too familiar, is nothing more than egoistic density. Everyone born of this earth automatically dons the heavy cloak that will weigh down forward progress.

The relevant point in the subject of choice is not the experience itself, but how we are to receive it and how we decide to perceive it. This alone is the lesson being taught. We may smile or frown, but we will go through it, for it may not be avoided. The Tibetan philosophy says that the best we may hope to do is to either speed the event or slow it down, because what is written is written and may not be erased until the experience becomes reality. When it occurs, we have the opportunity to heal the hurtful memories of the past, or we may hold on to them through choice and deception of self. It is best not to put it off for another day. If we do, it will surely come again in the apparent cycles to which we are all exposed, for the unlearned lessons that are always on our path. We do not see most of these because we are busy looking in the wrong direction – that of past memories. We tend to overlook the present in most respect, and it should not be. We are in a hurry to go – where?

In the process, we create within ourselves the illusion of a cleaner house, when in reality, we have merely swept the unfinished business under our spiritual rug, along with Satan who really never left. Why is that dark shadow still there? It is simply because we did not complete the task at hand originally, thus the event will recur until we work it out completely. This is true healing in action, and the factual origin and growth of the body's ailments and illnesses come solely from the negativity that emanates from the heart of the person. If we heal the heart, the body will follow. It has no choice, but we do.

Through the positive and negative natures, we experience two sides to all matters. Even a simple battery has both of these poles, and when both are used in unison they supply the energy necessary for proper use – to get the full charge. Because of this, most of us understand and mistakenly accept the principles of dual nature created by positive or negative events. We should learn to use both for definite gains in knowledge. However, we must learn that duality is really an illusion of the mind, and the Master said that "a house divided against itself will not stand". He also reminded us that we cannot serve two masters, especially opposing forces. We simply choose one, but we must allow for both. Regardless of the event or subject, we must try to comprehend the pros and cons of it, at each end of the spectrum. Wisdom tells us that we should accept both ends, thus we may bring them together to enable us to grow. This acceptance will generate harmony and union for the creative principle to take place in our lives. The human element advises us to choose between the two. All we need to do is pick one and allow it to come to us, or we can pick the other for what it may bring. Either way, we do learn from that process. We choose the direction in which we will learn. Each of us must decide whether our experience will be positive or negative. We indeed have the gift of choice, not necessarily free will, because avoidance is not possible. Memories of how we perceive our past offer us that choice, yet, contained within is an opportunity for the past to be balanced or healed in our minds. The balance or the healing may take place only if we decide to learn from those memories, rather than merely hang on to them. Once healed, we may let them go. Without that remedial release, they will return to us again. If we insist on holding on, for whatever reason, we become trapped in that aspect within ourselves and only carry the memory of the hurts. We do not retain the lesson and potential growth they brought us. As mentioned earlier, this will resurface until the true lesson is attained. It will reappear because it is uppermost in our conscious thoughts, even though we may wish to not repeat the same thing.

The power of the mind is incredible. It is virtually unlimited. Imagine, if you will, that spirit heard everything we thought and considered it as a request to be granted. Would you change the way you think? The Master said that we need not ask, for what is in our heart is already known. Does this not tell us that every thought is a request? Will it not be granted for us to experience? The mind is the operation center for the physical kingdom of the body, making us the controlling priests of our corporeal domains – as mentioned in the book of Revelations. It is as a magnet on polar opposites, one that will accept or repel any subject about which we may think. You see, the mind of the human has the true responsibility for the outcome of our decisions. It must be, since it is where the exchange of positive and negative energies takes place. It is the field where the transmutations of the forces happen, regardless of their nature. No matter what we may think or believe, we are the sole proprietors of our thoughts and must accept responsibility for them.

With every act, we create the next experience from which we will grow. It will occur through an original deed that has not been inwardly settled. It may also happen because of the thought we give a particular subject, especially if it is deeply emotionally based. This is what the Master intended for us to absorb when he mentioned "from the highest to the lowest" and "nothing is above the law". We are responsible for the perpetuation of "evil" in our lives, not another being, or some dark creature hidden in the depths. Those depths are merely those of our mind, the steering mechanism for our lives. No one seems to realize that the only concealed creation therein is our own ego. It cleverly masks itself right in front of us, through our thoughts and reactions toward life. As a result, we lose control and must fight or struggle to achieve stability – or so we believe. If Spirit is truly the higher inner nature, it would stand to reason that it is also the seat of the "evil one". Once this is understood, it again becomes a matter of choice. We can opt for the higher spiritual nature or the lower carnal nature. Both are there, ready to be accepted. Whatever the personal preference may be, each will carry its own type of seed.

We must anticipate life's growth as the balancing effect the creator – our soul - gave us, merely to keep things in union, rather than the continual discord many of us find on a daily basis. We cannot base this choice on what others have expressed about us. We have to base all things on what we know ourselves to be. We must find out for ourselves, not for others. The next experience – which will surely come – will help in the search for who we really are. When it does return, we should blame no one for it. Unfortunately, we probably will place the culpability on what others do or did, and suddenly, we believe we are no longer accountable…In this fashion, we think we do not hurt ourselves. This is an illusion. The truth is that we are the creator of our life, unless of course, we have willfully allowed to be controlled by someone else, simply because we did not want the responsibility. This will only lead to heartaches, because now we cannot be who we really are – or want to be. We are living our life for another or others – not for ourselves.

The intent of this book is to assist us in changing the way we consider life to be, not only for ourselves, but also for those around us. Further, if we truly want to influence another person, the most effective way is to modify our impressions about them and our interaction with them. They will automatically respond to our changed behavior, but it is up to them to accept or reject the example we provide. In this instance, we again have choice. We can present a conduct based on the positive side of life and not the other.

It is quite possible, providing we understand our own spiritual aspect first. The first ideal is to not point our finger in another direction. If we do, it will give us further excuses and freeze us in place. We generally base ourselves on the past that we know, feeding on memories and not realizing that if we were to merely release them, there would be a change in personality and a change in our lives, at that moment. And the moment will give us what we desire for ourselves – a point of creation to build on.

This brings us to the birth of thoughts. Creation began with a very simple concept of individual thought or consciousness taking place in the moment. Subsequently, separation toward individual nature began and creation became a physical reality. At that time, we left the Garden of Eden with our newly acquired shape, which Spirit dressed with coats of skin. Corporeal form became reality as we now recognize it to be. We thought ourselves into physical form and gave life to all physical creation. Life was given tangible appearance for our comprehension in order to learn. If we are physical, the lessons must be physical as well. Consequently, we are subjected to events that occur for our edification, depending on the choice we make. If it did not develop at the physical level, all occurrences would be for naught. If the lessons were not physical, how would we know what the teachings were intended to be? In the very real sense, the lessons we are to learn are for esoteric matters that we mostly ignore. If our being was purely physical and nothing else, this learning could not take place.

CREATION

We were derived from the original timeless concept of infinity, and meant to know and understand all things, with pure intelligence and purity of our emotional nature. The physical transformation from an infinite being to a finite status had a personal and collective goal: to learn how to use the absolute creative power that we all have. An act of faith and belief is the only requirement. Most of us are convinced that this absolute power is indeed in the sole care of the Creator, yet we are in Its image. We are a product of this awesome might, and in our spiritual form, were declared equal in the development of that power. There were monumental limitations set upon us when our dual nature came into being. Without these limitations, and because of our dual natures, the acquisition and use of such might could prove to be catastrophic. This is not saying that a human being could not reach a certain level of power. The Master comes to mind at this point. Looking at this subject objectively, we know that Spirit is already aware of the limitless universe, and It realizes the availability of limitless power in the cosmos. Our rather rudimentary physical mind can barely comprehend the subject of simple physics, much less the idea that with absolute power, we would have no need for a physical body or a tangible life. Obviously, we chose. As a civilization, we have not yet grasped this concept, nor shall we, if we limit the scope of our knowledge to the material only. We work with only what we are able to accept and prove to ourselves, based on the precept that if it cannot be touched, it is not real. Further, we have been taught to be skeptical of most things – even the truth. This is part of the illusion of life and mind.

Because we are not yet ready to truly accept and love all things without conditions, our experiences in life will definitely create doubt and a myriad of questions. Again, our high level of expectation normally leads us to disappointment. A truly spiritual human accepts even that which he/she cannot see or understand. If uncertainty exists, allow it to show itself for what it is – and it will. Uncertainty comes because we do not have enough information on a particular subject. That is natural. It shows us what we should learn from any given situation we face in order to increase our knowledge. Deductively, we should welcome uncertainty for what it can bring us. Question what is before you for the answer, using a reasonable amount of discriminatory balance if need be. If we were to proceed in this fashion, we would not carry things around in the form of old baggage because we would be in balance. If we doubted the subject once and received no answer, we will doubt it again the next time – even if it were the truth, no matter what the subject may hold for us. In that case, it could possibly spill over into other areas of our lives and we will become "Doubting Thomas". We will be suspicious of anything that is dissimilar from us, and to resolve any differences, we will all try to be alike – a rather tangible trend in our society. That is not possible, and we should acknowledge and attempt to understand the differences. How boring would it be if we were all the same?

People's individual ego would love to see the rest of us as it is. Do we not all wear similar garments? Do we not all aspire to live in the same manner? Are we not all taught the same things in our educational system? Is this not carefully orchestrated so that we can all be on the same page? Where is individual nature in any of this? Are not all persons and the Spirit's creations unique unto themselves? This is the true beauty of life and the way acceptance works, if we allow it. Without a doubt, Spirit made us individual thinkers, and that right alone allows each of us to develop our own brand of thoughts, whether it corresponds to others or not. Were we to simply acknowledge the differences in thought and action, we would advance to a higher appreciation of life. It could even end wars, or at least belligerence and disagreements. It could be so, because of a universal acceptance of the rights given to the different perspectives of life. It would remove certain levels of mistrust created by doubts. It is a question of inner balance, one of inner clarity.

Originally, from nothing came everything. Who can really explain this incredible concept? Biblically, it had to be written in a way the minds of the time could indeed comprehend how it all began. Today, we have a much greater ability to expand on the subject and enhance our knowledge, yet there is no flexibility in the way it still is presented. Its current explanation is roughly 1,700 years old, with only words being shifted, reinterpreted or inserted for better intellectual definitions – certainly not for clarity. The records have been kept so we could learn, but in religious formats, they reflect a final, irrefutable conclusion: this is the way it is, because that is how it was. Where is the growth or the creative capabilities in this style of terminal thought or teaching? It is mainly due to the rigidity of the religious mindset and agenda of that bygone era. That same rigidity has been verbally and academically perpetuated ever since. Editorially, however, it has most certainly been changed if not for a more physical approach, at least for the sake of convenience in ecumenical discoveries. The texts of the Old and New Testament were originally intended as a philosophy of life – not as a religious doctrine intended for control. On the other hand, rigidity rhymes with inflexibility and is not conducive to growth, nor is it philosophical. The Bible was written in metaphors so that it could be interpreted by all people because of their individual thought process. Hence, it could fit all readers throughout time. Spirit is not a vengeful concept. It is a loving one from which we could all learn and therefore grow.

Even as young children just entering school, the system attempts to teach us to act like everyone else by having us compare ourselves to others, thus insuring that lifestyle. We are herded into a robotic societal production line that creates physical and spiritual obstacles on the path of individuality. Even at that early age, we begin to compare, and it sadly leads to discrimination. Can anyone deny that? Why would Spirit diminish Its own creation through comparison? It would not. The egoistic human would and a spiritual one would not.

From the beginning of time, evolution has been going on as creation in process or forward movement as we know it to be. It was born of the unseen – the spiritual or conscious nature of self. We were shaped as a thought from Spirit, with our own individual awareness. Each of us at that time had his/her own concept of what he/she wanted to be. Consequently, based on the original idea, we choose our experience each time we come into life. We have been experimenting with this ever since the dawn of time. With each new life, we have experienced a deeper understanding of our own being. With each incarnation, we are to apply what was learned during the last time we had a physical form, to bring us further on our chosen path. We pick up where we left off, and will continue to add knowledge to our already complex being and to resolve the unsettled matters of the past. We are not to undo them, but rather balance the old events in the present time we have in our current life. However, we must move through all existing situations as they present themselves. We must learn to solve things now and not another day. It will be more difficult the next time. The primary goal is to grow in a spiritual aspect instead of the material one only. Most of us are not aware of this or we totally ignore it. For those, there is no gain. The lack of awareness does not mean that this does not happen.

Think of it this way: are we given life and consciousness to be thrown into a black box so we never rise again? What kind of a loving Spirit would create, only to annihilate forever? Many others before me have expressed this very same thought so we could understand and accept life. Our true nature is eternal as spirit. Nevertheless, we do not accept the inner truth because we do not want to be condemned by others for our differences in beliefs. By some people's standards, anyone who believes in what is discussed in this book is not normal. In too many cases, we hide from it all instead of finding out for ourselves. This is the dogmatic way of life, not the truthful way.

For many of us, it is difficult to comprehend that upon passing, we just shift or transition from a heavy vibration to a much finer one – so, in reality, no one dies as we know or understand it. Analogically, we shed our skin much like snakes shed theirs, for new growth and a new way of enjoying life. What we will truly have then is a life not as heavy as the old, and a much finer state of being. We become a form built in true spiritual perfection and return to the real aspect of life. We leave the illusions behind. We spend much longer periods of time as spirit than we do as embodied beings by ten fold. After all, how can energy die and dissipate into nothing? Are we not all energy based? We merely continue in another higher form that the physical eye may not necessarily see. Simply because we do not see it does not mean it is not there. Imagine for a moment that our planet was always covered by a layer of clouds. Would we not be unaware of the sun and the stars? And when the clouds disappear some fine morning, would it not be a pleasant surprise to behold? It would be beyond our comprehension. Using this analogy, we just need to look around us today, to see the different stages of human development and perhaps experience that pleasant surprise: all of life in its true form, climbing the spiritual path for greater attainment, learning to blend the physical and spiritual as one.

Some people appear more advanced than others, only because they may have been here more often in the cycles of reincarnation. This is the way it has always been. It is the growth of the spirit that drives all things of life. Ultimately, we will all have learned and accepted the same information, the same principles at a future moment in time. At that point, we would be able to use that wonderful manna for the benefit of everyone around us. The ideal situation would call for us to grow together. Some prefer to grow apart, individually. The latter method begs for someone to be in control, in power – and that is the way it is now. In spite of it all, we still grow through what we learn about ourselves and life. In growing together, we would discover free thinking, and no evil would exist, except possibly the few who would still wish to control and manipulate. Today, we see much of this are all around us. We give them the power to do what they do for gain or profit. By doing so, it also implies that we do not have the ability to think for ourselves or to do what is right for all concerned.

Whenever other persons feel bad or depressed, it is not wise to give away or drain your own energy by willfully transferring their problems onto you. Maintain your own spiritual strength, not in an ego sense, but in a pure sense. Of course, help heal their wounds, but bring them to your level. Do not go to theirs. "Render to Caesar the things that are Caesar's". Let those in power be in that position and do not fight them. Their power has nothing to do with you on a personal level. Besides, we are all meant to work together, not against one another. **Sonaya Roman** and **Duane Packer** say it best: *"The only way you can truly love and support others is to support their aliveness and growth, and one of the best ways to do that is to support your own aliveness and growth".*

Creation continued with our individual thinking pressing itself into physical life so we could enjoy the experience of it. It came to pass so we would have form with which to work and to educate ourselves. Spirit knew, however, that we would become enamored with the physical body and the material world. We wanted this corporeal experience for ourselves, and Spirit allowed it. Ever since, through Its loving patience, It has been slowly showing us the way home, a home we all desire. The clouds being removed, we were to learn to rise above, to reach to the heavens for the highest possible concept of self.

We were created from a concept that was planted in our mind by Spirit for us to envision, and for us to carry out. It began to imagine a material reality, a reality that would hold or support physical form. It held this notion in consciousness until It became Itself the concept It was witnessing through Its awareness – and life began. This was intended to give life to thought, to give thought substance, form and animation. Once It had the notion firmly established within Its realm of thought, It began the process of pressing it down into form. This form was not as the human we know today, but rather an ethereal form, not quite physical because we had to match the original primordial soup that was called life. As the materialization took on a more physical nature, so did we, simultaneously. Within the text of Genesis, we find in essence that Spirit created the human to tend the garden. As It pressed downward, everything had been placed in divine timing. We must also appreciate the fact that we were not quite the advanced specie we are today. It simply could not be, since we had no experience as to what or who we should be – only the concept.

When we think about all this, we should understand that when we have an idea about anything, it is merely in the mind, and not a reality. When we begin to work with any idea, it very seldom works the first time, and we should allow ourselves to make periodic adjustments so that it will fit the original concept of such idea. At that point, we begin to shift the idea so that it matches the initial intent. We will make these adjustments as we go along, thus we may improve upon the idea itself. We do it this way so it can expand and become an enhancement of the dream we first had. So it is with life.

Spirit had to undergo the same process and to this day, It is still working on the original ideal we call life. It is still seeking the perfection for what Its vision was initially intended to be. It is still looking for the spiritual human, a creation that can operate within the realm of all reality, seen and unseen. Its objective was for us to be like Spirit, a God. We may remind you once more that both God and Jesus the Christ clearly stated that intent which was recorded biblically, so we could understand and accept it. Upon deep reflection, it implies that we are the creator of the initial notion of self, the individual nature that we have been shaping ever since toward independence.

To the mortal mind, this independence seems to have backfired. We have an internal sense of isolation. After all, what is independence? It implies that we work alone and, deductively, we apply the rule of separation. Yet, as complex beings, we fight for that independence, but cannot reconcile this controversial issue because of the feelings of loneliness we experience. Hence, the inner war continues – as a dog chasing its tail. We can only blame it upon ourselves because we have been steadily moving away from Spirit's original concept. At least, that is what we are led to believe. This type of teaching could not be further from the truth. In reality, we can never move away from spirit, for it gives us life. We have been so much in that frame of mind that we are restricting ourselves to be only the physical humans we are today. We have become progressively more steeped in the body, because of the initial pressing down of thought. Paradoxically, it is also what spirit had in mind on our path of growth.

Today, the swing of the pendulum of life has reached its bottom position. It will now begin to rise the other way – as we have done before. This situation repeats itself so that we may learn to combine the lower and higher aspects and to be the spiritual human being, in the image of the original concept. Through individual efforts, the graduation – or attainment - bestows upon you the bliss of the Master's crown, the status of a living God. We should learn to accept this for ourselves and begin to prepare for this process in our minds. Remember that this must be done in humility, a virtue that is the next step in the gaining of spiritual growth. Unconditional love is the first. Remove all conditions that have been placed upon you by self or others, and see what is left. You will discover much personal freedom, resulting in a true spiritual life, with no burdens of the mind and an effortless form in respect to all life.

People living in other parts of the world will tell you that an American is not a very humble person. How can one be humble when there is nothing patient about him/her? On the other hand, we must consider how we view humility in our country. Somehow, in our culture, we erroneously see it as a weakness. This "weakness" is truly an illusion created by an arrogant mind. We are taught from birth to be "number one" and that we must win at all cost. Is there humility in that concept? Absolutely none. It does not stop us, however, from acting as crazed gladiators in schools, sports, business, government or the military. But this is not the time to talk about misguided pride... Sometime in the future, humility will be rediscovered – perhaps not in a gentle way. We have simply been conditioned to be "number one" and have made it a credo in our belief system.

We are a land-locked nation, away from other cultures that now come to us to be accepted – and we need not list the reasons. Of course, many of our citizens do not agree with such behavior. Why? Did our forefathers not migrate to this continent for the sole purpose of freedom? Was it not so we could have a more meaningful experience with individual belief systems? Obviously, we have forgotten. We have become arrogant, with a desire to undermine the very foundation the forefathers have built. In the process, we do not appreciate or respect other cultures, and of course the spiritual aspect has been completely left out. The trend is to dominate and, as a nation, to be a "super power" only through materialism – at the expense of all else. On the subject of a national soul, are we now better than those who create war? This is a beautiful country, and it was meant to be a wonderful place in which to live. Does not the same apply to the rest of the world? How can any one person or group own this, unless we all allow this "number one" obsession to take place, through ignorance of being. We cannot afford to continue the engendering of beings without humility or spiritual grace.

We must consider Spirit in this because, had It not been humble, we would not be sharing space with Its pure nature. It could have remained as It was before the beginnings of life. Once creation was set in motion, it turned into creative evolution, and it was intended to be as perpetual as its Creator. Life will always be in a state of forward movement through continuous change, not only of the physical, but of everything about us. It includes the way we think and feel about all things in general. It could also explain the concept of extinction. Certain species had reached their highest purpose in the lower aspect, so they could develop in a new direction. This new direction will ultimately be to reach for its highest granted purpose, and to eventually give itself up for yet another direction. Had the seed not died, would we have the plants or the flowers? We see this when a tree falls in the forest, and from it, new growth springs into existence once again. It is all part of that forward movement, from very rudimentary beginnings. This progressive motion is working at the pace of the original concept, not our own pace. We have developed a pattern of resistance to the Divine plan. With or without our acceptance, forward movement is the only direction creation is able to travel. Everything has a vibration, down to the smallest atom. If only one of these microscopic atoms was to cease its vibration, it could have the power to destroy the entire universe. Our tapestry of life is woven from the smallest to the greatest...

THE ART OF BEING PATIENTLY HUMBLE

We must all begin to realize that every idea contains a particle of spiritual life within its vibratory pattern. In that vein, let us take a brief look at what matter truly is. Creation is this simple: it is a myriad of particles of life that have been magnetized by the force of a persistent controlled concept. As matter, spirit and force are one and the same. Like the simple atom, if we do not continue to move forward, we enter a self-destruction mode while attempting to stay in place without an onward vibration. Humility is the act of accepting that nothing is permanent. It is the one virtue that will persuade you to give yourself up for the new forward vibration or movement. Consider this. If water were to become permanent in its present form, would it not simply stagnate in place? If this is true, it stands to reason that everything would follow the same fate. This includes any individual who chooses to say: "I like who I am, so I will not change". There, you have found the true meaning of stagnation. Notice all the "I's" in what was suggested. These people are now trapped where they are – with no movement – as they attempt to hold the past in place as the present. That just is not possible if evolution and growth are one and the same. In order to produce their own motion, these same people will probably tell you to change since they cannot, or they refuse to allow for the evolution of self. They are frozen in place – and there are many today. That is the beginning of their inner destruction, and they will point the finger without really knowing why or realizing that it is them and not the other person. The finger will point in your direction, rather than theirs. Is this not based on their own decision? Should we not allow them to experience it for themselves? The point is that we must, otherwise we become tangled in their cycle and render a judgment on what they wish to do. Perhaps it is best if we allow them the grace to learn through their methods, because now, only their choice and their ego are involved.

The human is the only specie that is aware of this yet, we somehow manage to hold ourselves in place and resist change. Resisting change is in reality resisting growth. By its very nature, anything that grows – including us – is organic. It must grow or it will surely die. As Paul said in Romans 8-6: "...to be carnally minded is death", and anything carnal is physical – and that too will surely die. It is another reason why we tend to struggle in order to reach our physical goals swiftly, as opposed to concentrating on spiritual attainment. We are in a hurry for the anticipated results. Being in a rush is obviously not being humble, nor does it show an inclination toward patience. Humility will breed patience, but if we are filled with ourselves from an egoistic point of view, there is no room for either, or the guiding light of spirit. This further indicates that we do not believe in the spiritually divine principles. Those who are in this state of mind would have great feelings of aloneness or condescension, would they not? We are pretentious and impatient enough that we do not want to wait for spirit to assist us in what we are seeking at the moment. The moment is where the past and the future collide to give us the present. In reality, it is the only place any of us may be. The instant is ours, and nothing else. It is the true principle of creativity, as it is the point and the moment where it lies. When we are truly filled with awe and humility, we are rewarded with that precious moment.

We have all been working on this improvement of self, yet for most, it has not been a conscious endeavor. This refinement is pointing us toward a union of the higher and lower nature of being, and we often refer to this in this text. Humility will be our greatest virtue, as mentioned in Revelations, for we egoistically created conflicts against the seven seals of our book of life. They could not be opened because of our spiritual state. Then entered the lamb, and it broke the first seal. The lamb is this true, humble and gentle nature that we all have, yet very few externalize it for others. We must travel gently in our awakening. If not, it will become a rather rude one – if we awaken at all. Were we to look back in time, we would see the Neanderthal man, the caveman, none blessed with any humility as we understand it. We would see a human with a very rudimentary mind and energy set. We have progressed beyond that concept into a more refined human, in the physical sense. However, we still manage to act the way the cavemen did, especially when we consider the sum total of the planet's inhabitants.

Today, we seem to be working on the mental, emotional aspects for deeper enhancement of acceptance. These are being worked on to learn humility, leading us toward a higher spiritual growth. It appears that spirit is using Zen techniques by showing us the opposite, explaining why we are so aggressive today. We must first become tired of this belligerent nature, so that we may allow for the other – the peaceful nature. All of us already have that, but we chose not to use it because of the fear of not being assertive enough to take what we want, the fear that someone will take advantage of us at any moment. We will wait for the others to be gentle and when they are, so shall we be – but they must do it first. With this approach to life in general and humility in particular, we might just have to wait a long time... This is actually the path of arrogance and selfishness.

We do not need to learn in this harsh fashion, if only we give in to higher thinking and allow for the acceptance of others just the way they are. Until we do, we will travel the wide road rather than the narrow one. Of course, the narrow path is much harder to follow. It is barely perceptible. Our continuous warring against each other has placed us on the wide, easy road of ego and erroneous thoughts. This is obviously not acceptance, and it has not been working well for us. As you can see, the stumbling block has been our ego nature, a nature that is the combination of the mental and emotional, linked with the past, to protect the physical from harm. This leaves us stagnant in the first energy center which, in our belief, is the most important. It definitely shows that we tend to place our focus on the baser needs of life. Sadly, we have not reached the level of trust in Spirit demonstrated by plants and fauna.

This ego has grown with us, but the spiritual human has no need of this adverse attribute, at least in the way it is used today. Ego creates great insecurity within us, because, for the most part, we are unable to release the need of it. It has been with us from the beginning, originally as the physical protection necessary for survival. Today, we apply the same levels of protection, but from a mental and emotional front. In the genetic makeup, this is life and death. It now creates high levels of stress in the present day human. The protective mechanism still works to the very same degree, and we have no real, effective release in our times. We see the pent up attitudes all around us, only because we hold on to entirely too much. We must remember that our own thinking is creating us in the daily developments of our lives. In essence, it is attempting to create higher levels of spiritual acceptance within our thought process, and we ignore it. Inexorably, we fight, making excuses to maintain this physical experience we call life and living. We are really perpetuating the way things have always been, which logically will not allow for the newer aspects of self and a more gracious being. This being no longer lives in caves, except for those whose minds still live in the dark ages. We have quite a history of growth and struggle with and against each other. Do we not realize yet that it has not been working? Our way will never work, for its intentions are destructive. Spirit will let us do what we wish. It has eternity in which to work. We certainly do not – until we overcome death. The Bible tells us we shall do this also, but we will not reach that stage under our present attitudes, for we live in fear of destruction.

The day we entered this life, we were given all the tools needed to love unconditionally. We still have them within us, no matter what our age may be or the experiences we encountered. This is a gift to share with others. In turn, it will breed humility and compassion in all of us. It will also grant us great levels of patience, for there is no hurry. Imagine living for all eternity! Would we not become patient merely because of this prospect? If we were to apply unconditional love to self, we may not even age, at least not as rapidly as we do. In the Old Testament, look at the ages of the patriarchs. They lived many hundreds of years. So could we, if we did not burn ourselves out so quickly, through the constant worry and stress we create as our experience. The external, carnal human has given us what we now have, including the stress that goes with it. We can understand why this is mistakenly given so much importance, since the eyes naturally do look outward and not inward. We see it, therefore it must be real…The problem is that we tend to believe it. We do not gaze inward to know ourselves because of this very same concept.

We were created in a spontaneous action, an instant expansion of consciousness into reality. As a result, we too are to be spontaneous in what we do in life, physically and spiritually. The Master told us not to concern ourselves, for in that hour, we will be told what to say and do. Spontaneity – if allowed – would also bring us humility, but everyone else would consider us eccentric, therefore we believe we would accomplish nothing. This deed occurs only in the moment, and that in itself is spontaneity. We could create great things for life, unselfishly, only if we are truly in that moment we face. It is now or never in all respects of life. Do not all true creative ideas come to us in the moment? This should provide the proof, yet it does not. We will say: "I have struggled with this for a long time, and this is how it came". It really came because we released the grip. The mind, through spirit, delivered the idea or inspiration. We allowed it to happen and nothing more. We relaxed to let the real influence of spirit come to the surface, to grant our inner desire.

This spontaneous aspect is once more halted by the yesterdays of the mind. These may be humbling events that we may not have accepted. The pull of our memories creates the stumbling blocks as the Master tells us in Matthew, but especially those we have not settled and closed within ourselves. They are the open doors of the past from which we hide. Those that we have left somewhere as unfinished business will return to us for resolution. Think back and honestly notice the cycles of your very own life. Ask yourself why the same thing continues to occur. It could be an invaluable lesson.

Now we are told that we should plan nothing, that in that hour, we will be told what is necessary for us to say, and what action we are to take.

Does this not sound like spontaneity? This will come to us from spirit, if we but listen – as the Ark is always before us. We are too impatient. We must do things now. If we were to wait, the right idea would show itself to us, 100% of the time. There is an old Zen philosophy that says: sometimes, the best thing to do is nothing, and the path will appear. When it does, we are to act upon the instructions we receive from the higher authority, our spiritual input. To the mind of the mortal, it will not work. We are conditioned to establish a plan to reach the goal. Ask yourselves: how could even Spirit know the outcome, when creation was spontaneous? It knew where it was headed, but not quite how it would get there. So should we – to a point – because we can only control the immediate moment, not those that have not yet come. They may be seen intuitively, but not executed until the proper time arrives. We operate more on the premise of things that have not come. This diminishes the importance of the present that, in reality, is the only place in which we can operate. If we were simply to wait, we would not be blindsided as we sometimes are in life. We may think that life dealt us a strange hand, without thinking once of our egoistic, excessive interference before it is time to act. We think we know best, do we not?

Creation is a permanent guest within us. Unfortunately, the efforts of spirit are not always noticed. Designs toward higher planes do enter our mind, and I would like to say that we turn them into different forms for our enjoyment, yet, it is not always an enjoyable experience, merely because of the way we contemplate life. Further, our perceptions are based on previous events. We can readily understand the truth of the Master's deeper teachings when He said: *"There is nothing from without a man, that entering into him can defile him: but the things which come out of him, those are they that defile the man"*. It is indeed what we do with it once it has entered. Whatever interpretation emanates from us is the problem. It is our form of expression, whether it is in words or in actions – and expression is creation in process. In most cases, it is filled with judgment, because of past events devoid of humility. We must admit that the human element tends to guide our decisions, our lives, from what we have done to others and what others have done to us. Our past is our witness. In the midst of living our lives the way we see fit, we may hear the voice of spirit, but we seldom follow it. We do not allow for the necessary changes it may want us to institute, simply because our ego convinces us we are right in what we do. Change was the original and subsequent concept for creation. We fight or ignore these potential changes, thus our flow of life is interrupted. Not only has this flow been disrupted, but we will now corrupt any spiritual suggestion that we receive in that moment, just because our thoughts are filtered through our past. In too many instances, we give more credence or power to the ghosts of our yesteryears than to the input of spirit. It influences the present moment we have to enjoy, and we are in that precise moment because we can be nowhere else. We must realize that the past has no hold on us, unless we allow it. Our thoughts are the experience and creation of life itself. The spiritual human will not be affected by the negative thinking that may come. Fearing or disliking them will only give these thoughts more power over you. Who ever said that a negative thought was a bad thing, unless you decide to make it so? When one recalls the law of opposition, it is logical to conclude that if positive thoughts exist, so must the negative ones. Both aspects, both poles are within each of us so that we can function in and with all of life

Because of past events, the ego will remind us to trust no one. Whatever may have happened yesterday should remain in that time frame, and we need not give it another thought. This constant looking back will eventually create a serious obstacle on our path of forward motion. We should realize that the mind cannot really think of two things at once or focus simultaneously on the past and the now. Physics tells us that two objects cannot occupy the same space at the same time. This theorem also applies to the thinking process. In that moment, we either think the truth or the lie – not both. It is not possible. However, we must know that in order to lie, we must think the truth first. Without the truth, we cannot formulate the lie, and the lie will be born out of ego's fear of the truth. Truth is an integral part of our spiritual being, while the lie is purely carnal insecurities.

It was once told me that life is about thought experiencing its own self. It has been found to be very true, for what else do we have, except our thoughts and the personal experience associated with them. They make us exactly what we are. If we have the thoughts of a criminal, we are a criminal. By the same token, if we have loving thoughts, we will be loving persons. *"Blessed are the pure in heart: for they shall see God"*, and Spirit knows what is in our hearts. As we think, so we become. There is no way around this. Anything we think about long enough will come to the surface, will become a part of our reality. It may create security or insecurity within our own selves, depending on how we consider the situation. The Tibetan philosophy teaches us that if we gaze upon anything long enough, we will eventually become that upon which we gaze. If we look upon Spirit or God's creation, the same will stand true. Somehow, we remain as we are, because we are told through a lower system of belief that we cannot achieve this. Let us take a moment to contemplate this subject, and we will discern a divine hand in all that we have experienced – and the truth will appear. We have created whatever it is that we are, as well as the surrounding ambiance.

We may attempt to deny it, based on the results of the situation. Spirit is very literal and It has a sense of humor. It will give us what we ask for and nothing less. How can we possibly deny it? Once we have learned and know, how can we "unlearn", or "unknow"? We may try to reshape it into something else, but the truth is still intact within our own thinking.

THE PHYSIOGNOMY OF HUMANKIND

Each new day is a creation. It does not come with old days attached to it, except in our minds. Did not Spirit have seven days of creation? Did It not create new wonders each of those days? This is why each day is offered to us in moments, for all things are done in a moment and cannot be removed by the next. It took that long to create all seven charkas, one for each day, so that the physical can function. The first, or base, began as a rudimentary starting point, and progressed to the seventh, or crown. This last one turned out to be Sunday. It also brings the opportunity of the Christ within us, the expression of wisdom from all given experiences. In the Far East, it has been stated that whoever attains permanent contact with his/her seven energy centers will no longer be bound to the world of matter. It is the crowning moment of a spiritual human who has mastered the spiritual laws and is now anointed a true master of self and nature. The Book of Revelations depicts the hardships involved in attaining this exhilarating status. It also portrays the potential events involved in the shedding of the old belief system we held, while it rearranges our value structure as we climb the ladder of attainment.

Undaunted, creation continues to unfold. For countless reasons, our mortal minds and bodies attempt to stop this forward movement by whatever means. We are still in the infancy state of being. When spirit began the process of human development, it needed different energy centers to draw mass together. Since all the planets were formed this way, so had the human. Each planet began as a swirling mass of gases, until the aspect of gravity started to condense and solidify into matter. These small swirling pools of energy, created by polar opposites in harmony, are the element that attracts said energy to give us life as we know it. Spirit needed points of gravity, if you will, to draw the necessary ingredients to give us a physical form – the baser aspect of being. The energy centers were turned into the desired body, and they still operate today so we can experience life and its tribulations. They draw onto us that upon which we focus, with the intent to gratify the wishes we believe should be granted. Dual thinking will tend to interfere. As an example, if we want wealth but our focus is on poverty, it will bring poverty. We simply should focus on one or the other, then apply great emotion on our chosen path. It will give the power necessary for the realization of the goal we seek. We have yet to truly understand the powers of the positive and negative aspects of life. We have learned that both are necessary for life to even exist, as long as we apply them in a unified manner. Our general consensus is to use only the one, because we see the other as undesirable, thus initiating a struggle. Positive and negative poles are both equal and necessary, even for thought.

Once we get passed our pretentiousness and observe a moment of humility, we learn that our bodies consist of all the elements of Mother Earth. We add about eighty percent water, and we have our present form. Something was needed to attract the elements into a single package of living spirit. The energy centers were needed to allow form for the soul. It had to draw what was necessary to craft thought, so that human beings could survive on earth. The human had to be a source and a store for learning, and to do this, it had to think for itself. It had to have reasoning so that it would learn not to destroy itself. It had to know the difference between life and death. It had to taste of the tree of knowledge, so that it would live and reach the level of spiritual attainment God had intended. We must learn to realize that a true spiritual human can create as the Creator does.

The magnetic process that formed the swirling centers is just as active today as ever. The centers are about to lift us again to higher levels whether we want it or not. The lesson is to accept these same centers as reality. At this point in time, they sadly emphasize our internal division, simply due to the fact that we know not they exist. We divide ourselves because we attempt to add only that which derives from the physical realm, an aspect that offers no growth. Growth occurs only if the seed is planted in rich soil... Further, we see only good or bad, win or lose. Even though we think and feel greater things, we regrettably fear only for material failure. Desire has become pervasive, but it assists solely in the control of the physical world. Whatever we may add has no vitality. It only consumes. This power now reigns over us. Our present collective desires even bring on addictions as we give the sentient control to impulse or compulsion. It has led us to a very compulsive society, with no constraints applied. It now seems to overrun us at every turn. All the Masters have advised us to desire nothing. This is not my suggestion. You may have whatever you wish. In truth, desires run us and we do not realize yet what we do to each other. Physical desire is now in control of our minds and hearts, which is why we seek external gratification only. Eventually, we will understand this, but not until we learn that what we truly seek is within us. The distressing part is the number of lonely people around us. It can be expected when we look outwardly for fulfillment and watch the inner burdens accumulate – the burdens of debt to the material aspect. Far is the well mentioned by the Master in John 4:14.

Next, we will venture into the concepts of overcoming the material world as we understand it. We will discuss the idea of survival in the material sense and what it means to each of us. We will dig a little deeper into the laws of opposition, laws that in reality give us life. All this will help us on our journey toward spiritual growth and attainment. We might discover that we can all achieve a less stressful, more fruitful life.

CHAPTER 2

THE WAY OF THE HUMAN

*"Man is to himself the most wonderful object in nature; for he cannot
conceive what the body is, still less what the mind is,
and least of all how a body should be united to a mind".*
PASCAL, Pensees (1670)

What would a God be without anyone or anything to recognize it? For God to be real, It needed us as we need It to survive and continue on. Since we require each other in life, it is a symbiosis of sorts. It is also why we are one and the same. Would this not be the true acceptance of the biblical statements made on that subject – if properly read and understood? There are many texts older than the Bible that will verify much of what is being offered here for your consideration.

On the same subject, much of the Bible was related from a pagan, non-intellectual origin of life laced with a certain amount of superstition. You can easily detect this style intertwined within its pages, down to the symbol of the cross. All things considered, we are necessary to the Creator. In fact, we have the greatest significance of all on this planet in relationship with Spirit. In Genesis, we are told we are over all things, because the Creator made creative or cognitive thinking available for our use, so that we may learn and grow through difficulties and challenges. This would imply permanence, would it not? All else may perish, yet our individual thinking remains. We are given the ability to survive through reason – should we use it properly.

To use reason properly always seems to be the very issue. Are we not in the habit of asking for the wrong things, or asking the wrong questions? It stems from the dual nature of the mind, because we seek the win and lose, or the good and the bad, when each of these can be seen separately if we look hard enough. The real key to mind and thought is to accept the entire concept. On the other hand, how many of us accept anything as it is stated? Further, how can we, if we see only a way to win or a way to lose? We must merely change it to: it is as it is. If we do this, there is no win or lose since it is already in a balanced state of being, both internally and externally. At that point, we are in agreement with all matters, with nothing to rectify. To explain this somewhat complex philosophy, let us assume that it is raining. Some see this natural event as dreary, and others do not. Rain produces growth – along with the sun – so why should it be bothersome or dreary? The truth is, it is just raining – nothing more. Why the issue? It is due to the way it affects some people. It may bring sadness to some, but we all have the choice to retain the experience any way we wish. The dark clouds may revive a sad memory that has not yet healed. We have a perfect opportunity to grasp the moment and proceed with the healing. We must learn to not ignore these instants and recognize them as prospects in becoming whole. It must be viewed as a real chance rather than an oppression. This is an external impact, one that has now taken the control of the emotions away from us. We tend to believe that we cannot do anything about it. We may, however, by changing how we view ourselves. The event is not personal. It is just raining. We can change it by looking at the impact, to see what in our past contains the cause. The proper use of reason is to clear it.

SURVIVAL

"As life is, I may lose"…This type of thinking keeps some of us in a survival mode. It breeds fear of and to life. It does not encourage us to accept it either. By its very nature, fear is certainly not acceptance – nor is it humble. It will have a person become very reactionary to life, not in harmony with it. As a result, life will continue its control over us. As mentioned before, it gives life the cause, thus making us its effect. We must learn to break this pattern of thought to become the spiritual human we can be. This is done through humble control with life. We could surmise that life is filled with lessons on the subject of the humble nature. If we were in a state of acceptance, life would not be so humbling. Ask yourself: why do we have so many humiliating experiences come our way? It happens as a balancing effect for the arrogant moments we had prior to the humbling lesson – nothing more. The lesson is that "humiliating" is a derivative of "humble", and real humility will never engender humiliation in any form. It all depends on how we look at the events of life for what they bring. If we see them just for what they are, the lesson contained therein will be very clearly shown to us. The spiritual human does not get caught in the trap laid by "you did this or that". The only true way this can be accomplished is to see the event, the moment, as it is. We must look upon it as a set of circumstances we created for ourselves for the sake of our growth, to further our self-knowledge. If we deem there is no message for us, we simply should release the event rather than hold it in our minds and hearts. It has to be done with an unbiased approach, without an ego involvement of the mind. If the ego enters the picture, we will tend to blame from a defensive posture. It will be of no value because we will seek to place the blame on someone else. Once this occurs, we will have to deal with another balancing process. We all must learn to be honest with our own selves first, for here the truth resides.

Survival is an inbred aspect of the human form that tends to make us somewhat reactionary. We have survived much through the eons of time. It is an instinct we have, all the way down to the cellular level of our being. It was given to us when the saber-tooth tigers walked the earth along with us. We learned to conceal and protect ourselves for personal safety reasons, however rudimentary it may have been. Over the years, we carried this character trait a bit too far. Today, we hide from all things, including our very own selves. The instinct of survival is buried within us, down to the center of our being. It is so prominent that as events happen, we internalize them, we personalize them. Our physical form does not distinguish the difference and it becomes inner stress, caused by the hiding of the personal self. Needless to say, it has a serious negative impact on the creation of spirit, to the point where we now become lepers to our own being. The result is not pretty as we witness the increase in road rage, gangs, divorce, moral decadence and incredible levels of discontent in our lives. It happens because of all the things that tend to eat at us each and every day. We leave an audit trail of our lives as we struggle to move forward within our own selves. The problem is that we struggle only with our own being, because we have learned to draw and restrain much of life within ourselves, thus making it too personal.

At first, you may find it odd because we all believe that life is indeed personal. In reality, it is not. It is the way we take it – nothing more. We, as spiritual humans in training, are actors in or witnesses to events that we promptly absorb and file internally. We are under the impression that they are personal. Even the five senses have the same effect within us. Once the events are internal, they become personal. These particular invasions of our inner selves are normally generated from the external world. They become embedded in our minds and we now think about them, not as they really were, but rather as we believe they occurred. We have changed them to match ourselves in order to establish a balance. What if they had nothing to do with us? How would we know? We have already made them match us, and they are now personal. This is why it is so important for us to see things as they are and not just react. We must see the truth of the event. If this is done, it will never be personal, for we see truth in action and we will have more clarity because of it.

Have things really changed in the arena of survival since the days of the dinosaurs? Do we fully realize the difference between being attacked by a saber-tooth tiger and heavy traffic? We may – in a mental sense – but apparently not in the cellular makeup, because our survival instinct reacts instantly. If we really understand and accept all these concepts, why are we so violent? Why are we so frustrated, not only by the traffic but by people around us? We are always on the defensive. We could even say that we are not a very tolerant society. We are not even tolerant of our own nature, much less someone else's. At a glance, we are still operating on some levels as though we were still living in caves – at least in the subconscious sense. Whatever it is we allow to eat at us is precisely what creates our dubious actions and reactions. That is being reactionary. Life, or the external realm, is in control – not us.

In passing, it must be stated that you will become the very thing you dislike. "Reactionary" is reacting to certain or all events rather than acting upon them, and there is a distinct difference. To act is to be in control. To react is acting on an event after the fact, depending on our analysis of it – right or wrong. It further means that we are not in control of ourselves vis-à-vis what goes on around us. In any case, we are interrupting creation through our concepts and beliefs pertaining to the way life is. It is not really as physical as we would like to believe. If we were to accept this, we could enjoy relaxation in the true sense of the word. Today, even if we have the intention to sit and relax, the mind will be too busy thinking of all it did not do or could be doing. If we learn to be patient and unwind our minds, our bodies will follow suit, as they must.

If we just relax the body but do not turn off the mind, how can we ever hear spirit when it speaks? Were we to relax the mind, we would have much less stress and would live longer, happier lives. It can be attained through spiritual acceptance of being – without conditions. In that state of mind, we would follow the natural law instead of the unnatural one we created. Basically, in our own ways, we have been attempting to remove ourselves from life while building and living in our own little world of materialism. We have tried to insulate ourselves from the perceived troubles of the world. We must realize we are the world and cannot insulate from it. We have lost touch with true life, and as a civilization, we have chosen to embrace one of our own making, devoid of spirituality and love.

We have a fear. That fear is that there is something at work greater than all of us, something that has a mission, and we do not know what that mission is. It is actually very simple, since all it wishes is to produce love in all of us – a pure love, unconditional. If we want to embrace this wonderful concept and be part of it, we must let go of the things onto which we hold so tightly, change our beliefs and release memories that bind. We must also realize that life being personal is an illusion of the mind, coupled with a desire for it to be more personal than it is. We must learn to have a flexible belief system so life can continue in the physical and spiritual sense. When we believe in something – under our present physiological makeup – whatever it may be becomes chiseled in stone as we fence ourselves within our minds. We have a tendency to resist change in our beliefs. It may be so strong that even if we are wrong, we are unable to shift to something new. If we believe it strongly enough, we presumptuously assume that it is correct, even if it is in error. Allegorically, we are an old bottle in which new wine cannot be poured, for it will spoil. We must acquire a new bottle. Sadly, we seldom allow for change in the arena of our thoughts, therefore we stop our growth.

Paradoxically, we find a high level of mental flexibility in many other parts of the world. In the western world, we are indeed too rigid in this very concept. This is not to say we are off the path, because that is not possible. We walk spirit's path and not our own, no matter what we believe. A long time ago, it became part of creation, and it is still here for us to follow. "...[T]he man is become as one of us", said the Creator. Could it have been a mistake on Its part, or even Jesus, or are we that rebellious in our nature? We are still the original concept in process of growth and thus far, we have become what we are today. We have drifted in a direction that will change as quickly as light travels because we have not really grown spiritually. We have many subjects to learn before graduation. Have we not yet realized this? Are we not able to accept, based on what we are taught on this earth and led to believe? Are the blind still leading the blind in life?

The difference in each of us is merely the level of understanding or acceptance. Where do we get our understanding? Does it not come, for the most part, from what other people tell us, or during the course of a study? This only feeds the mental power of the person. However, experience comes in to breed wisdom, intellect in physical action, to produce knowledge. It is what we do with what we know, and we carry it out to see for ourselves. Experience, combined with intellect, is the path to wisdom. It is the true path to knowledge and self-discovery. We show a certain propensity toward staying away from this for fear of failure or fear of rejection. In reality, failure is not negative. It is the one teacher that can show us what we need to understand and do in order to accomplish the dream or reach the goal. Somehow, we give up too easily. We then become frustrated because we wish to be as successful as everyone else in all respects. We must look back into our own childhood to find where it all began. We must reflect on this period of our lives and see our insecurities as learning tools rather than possibly painful memories.

Each time we wanted to do something as a youngster, someone told us we could not do what we were about to learn. It grew from there. This concept of experience is done to and for us from the time we are born. It has expanded until now, and we have become so inhibited that we are unable to move forward without someone's approval. So, almost traditionally, we seek this endorsement from others. Most of the time, approval will come from a like mind, from someone who thinks as we do. Conversely, disapproval does not always mean that we are wrong. It may simply indicate a disagreement and nothing more. Find out for yourself, and then decide. Another facet of approval is that the other persons may want something we have, and to get it, they must agree. That is deception at its best. We cannot let ourselves be manipulated by the illusion of approval. We must decide for ourselves, seek our very own approval – not someone else's. We should let our own conscience be our guide – and it will not steer us wrong. It is the angel on our shoulder. If we listen to the entity on the other shoulder – and we know who that is – we will have to walk a different, uneasy path. Once the conscience approves, it should be all right and it would hurt no one.

There are many who really do not allow conscience to be a guide. They are too logical, and that means very little emotion. If they continue in this direction, will they not destroy a thing of great value? It will be what awaits them. Their lives will surely crumble and they will blame others for their sad situations. Those are not the feelings the spirit seeks for us. If we act without signs of emotion, how can we love anyone or anything? Our opportunity to become a spiritual human will dissipate because we will lack in compassion for life. We will be just a thinking body. It would destroy one of Spirit's greatest creations. The Eve within us would be dead or nonexistent. We would become cold and impersonal as was Adam's original nature until Eve entered the picture, according to Genesis. It proves that we should have both attributes on the inner plane, and we should use them equally. We should never allow one to override the other, to avoid an internal or external imbalance.

We are to be whole, and the spiritual person strives to maintain that delicate stability. One must be inwardly complete to reach higher levels. It means that we must use all the attributes spirit gave us - not half, not partially – if we hope to attain enlightenment. If we were to travel on that narrow path, we would experience a fulfilled life, not just part of what it can be. All things will be given and we can become a true master of all things, because we will know our inner selves.

In reality, we have become rather frivolous with our thoughts. It seems that they are always overpowering us. This is not the way because we have learned to rely only on the mind, which is a very complex thing. Based on this approach, we allow the self to drift into various situations because of the style of thinking we pursue. We do not need to force our thoughts. We should simply allow them to be what they are. When we force them, it takes entirely too much energy from us. The solution is to not expand them as in the past, but merely accept them and release them. This means we are not to fight ourselves, but regrettably, that is what we usually do. A fight denotes a winner and a loser, does it not? And most of us do not even know why or what we fight... In the process, we may lose what we wish to keep. It could be the person we love or the career we built – or even all of the above. We must first establish what we desire to keep and determine what can be safely discarded, then we can work toward what we want to retain. We must be sure before we begin. If a fight does indeed occur within – or without – we should wait patiently for the direction to show, and it most certainly will in its own time. At that point, we can move forward gently, without aggression. It is the hardest part of the fight, because we want all things now, rather than tomorrow.

When does anyone ask Spirit for approval? If we do, does It say yes? Or do we proceed under the pretense that It did? A follow-up question would be: does anyone hear Spirit when we ask anything of It? Most of us will say no. The reason is that no one waits to hear the answer. It is not something we will hear with the physical ear, but we will hear voices in our mind, varied thought groups. If we relate the event to other people, we will undoubtedly be considered mentally challenged and advised to use modern drugs. The truth is that some do hear the voice of Spirit, but others do not want to know or admit to what was heard. It is especially true if we present a deep belief in that voice, in those words. Our contemporaries will try hard to convince us that we are in need of a psychiatric evaluation. Those are the doubters we find in the Gospels. Is it fear, or jealousy? Their usual retort is: "What makes you think you are so special?". What standard do they use to measure us – other than their own? We must remember that our personal communication with Spirit should be done in secret and should remain as such. We were told this in the Book of Matthew, and the Master was quite serious about it. He knew that once we get the onslaught from others, we will begin to doubt. When this happens, we lose or let go the very solid connection we had with the higher aspect.

If we adopt this behavior, we will begin living our lives for others and will seek their approval for anything we do. If we really trusted our own nature, we would know the proper path to follow. We would not need the endorsement of others unless we were wrong in our intentions. If conscience is our guide, it should be known immediately, with no question. We should know, for there will be a feeling associated with the thought. The union of thought and feeling is our conscience.

We do know right from wrong, do we not? If we are to actually hear Spirit, it will come to us through the conscious nature of mind – not the thinking nature which is logical, devoid of feeling. Our thinking attribute is more a responsive nature, as opposed to thought which is an outpouring of the mind to self. It is what comes out of us, hence if it is going outward, it is not hearing or receiving anything. It is generating words or actions within our mind. With all the mental generating we do, how can we actually hear Spirit if It spoke with us? As we stated in the Book of Mark, the Buddha once said that "the mind of the human is much like a tree filled with chattering monkeys". Within this den of internal noise, how can we hear anything other than our own thinking? With much practice, we can master the art of inner hearing. We do this by ridding ourselves of one monkey at a time, one thought at a time. We release our thoughts and learn why they were in our tree in the first place. If we were to take this approach, we would discover that most thoughts were given to us by the outer realm. That being the case, we further discover that we are not ourselves, or we do not truly think or feel for ourselves. External input is important, but not more important than the inner human nature. According to Genesis, the human is the reason for the external, and not the reverse.

Through this process, we will truly find inner peace – enough so that we may hear Spirit when It speaks to us. We would know the difference in our thoughts and those of Spirit. The Master did tell us that before we come to Spirit, we must first settle our issue with our brother. We are to be clear, so that we may hear the conversation with the Spirit that lives in all of us. Our evolutional process takes us toward the embodiment of spiritual realization. These communications may go on each and every day, but the line is so busy with life that we may not even notice. Spirit does not give up, for It shall endure until the end, or until we meet It somewhere on the road of life, merely by surrendering ourselves to It, learning to trust what we already know.

Creation only happened once. Now it evolves through Spirit, as It learns of the physical attributes of life. We will also learn and change with it, unless of course we hold on too tightly to the belief we already have, with no flexibility. In this development, Spirit grows and so do we, one way or the other. We may not outgrow Spirit, but It will certainly outgrow us, if only for a short time. It is then a matter of catching up with It, to see where It will lead us with the new understanding we gleaned in the previous lessons. We do not know where the wind comes from or where it goes. That is the way of the higher spiritual nature. Acceptance and new understanding are associated with change that is being suggested by the words of the Master. We do not know initially where or how to place the new events or the budding appreciation within ourselves, and so fear may surface and we return to the road most traveled. It turn, great confusion may arise, and we may not understand the reason.

Confusion occurs because we are not yet willing to release the past – which we know – nor are we familiar with the new. We are momentarily uncertain. It is at this time that we must employ the Zen technique and do nothing – until we do become certain. If we do not, an inner struggle will surely ensue. We must begin progression toward blending the old and the new, in an attempt to find a point of balance or reference. However, we must furnish a word of caution because the old understanding may contaminate the new. We must once again emphasize that you cannot put new wine in old bottles, new thinking among the old, because one will pollute the other. The key is to always allow for the new and have that as a priority. The old, the yesterdays, are indeed outdated by the shear concept. Our common sense should tell us that if our hands are filled with the old, it certainly cannot accept or hold onto the new or anything else. The only way to solve the problem is to simply release the old and enjoy the fruits of the new.

We all have a tendency to seek the secrets of life, without realizing that there are none. Somewhere in this world, there are Masters who may guard these secrets in their deeply dedicated ways. Those in everyday life who may have approached us to divulge such secrets are not telling us the truth under most circumstances. Conceptually, we have all been given equal knowledge since the original creation. Over time, many of us have buried this knowledge or parts thereof deep into the abyss of our physical being. It is covered by layers of material superficialities, with the help of ego. These layers are removed one at a time with each spiritual or physical experience we may have, and each time, our spiritual knowledge expands.

Even Einstein said that we only use ten percent of our mental capabilities. That means we can expand into the other ninety percent at some point. Why not now? We can determine that for ourselves. Full consciousness only comes through acceptance of every facet, every side of self. Do the carefully crafted facets not make the diamond what it is? Does not its beauty radiate through those facets? Consciousness includes the sensory perceptions that we all have: the five that we know, but also the higher or unseen aspects – that of the intuitive sense. The original five senses were to assist us in the lower physical aspect of life. An example of this unseen perception might be the inferred spectrum of color. We did not witness this until the technology allowed us, yet we knew somehow that there was more to behold than our sense of vision could detect. Now we see it, and it proves that such technology assists the physical nature only. The higher nature already knew it was there. We did not, hence the higher led us to its discovery. As another example, we believed that the earth was in the center of the galaxy and the sun moved around it. In fact, people almost lost their lives over this, because churches of the day proclaimed the true information as heresy. Thank God we have grown to accept the truth in some physical respects. Why can we not have the same acceptance of new things learned, or the possibilities of things learned about the higher or spiritual matters? All too often, we want some physical proof for the benefit of our physical mind, even though we all know that the true concept of spirit is not a corporeal thing that can be seen with the naked eye. It is the pure unseen behind it all – the metaphysics of it. We do not see television or radio waves, yet they are there. We do not see the sunrays until they hit the earth and bounce off, then we have light – but not until then. We do not question these things because we know they exist through the laws of physics. Now they are accepted as common sense and knowledge. In reality, we have difficulties accepting the higher aspects because it does not match the material beliefs onto which we hold so dearly. If we can touch it, it is there... At the same time, we are all touched by Spirit and we will deny this because we cannot see it or touch it.

As we have often reminded you, creation began in the twinkling of an eye. That original creation was the formation of formless consciousness only. Since that time, we have been attempting to join the physical consciousness with the spiritual one, as we work toward preparation for a full union of the higher and lower states of being. With so many other thoughts in the way, very few realize it. This merger is related to us in all the ancient texts that have no interest in control. They were intended initially as philosophies for life. Only the human will seek to control through the intellect and the concept of winning or losing. That is definitely not spiritual philosophy, nor is it in the ancient texts.

From whom do we attempt to take the control, or to whom do we give it? If we try to control another, are we not ourselves being controlled? We give it and take it away from one another because we impose too many conditions, with little or no acceptance of each other as we truly are. If we were more tolerant of our fellow humans, we would realize that if we do not need to be controlled, no one else does either. This giving and taking is a win or lose effect, is it not? If we do not win, we lose – or so we have been taught to believe. We tend to agree with this principle of physical life. It seems to be the only thing we see or understand. We believe it will be easier, that it will tell us where we stand, and we will be considered normal.

What is normal? We are all individually unique. Our own personal fingerprints tell us this. Still, we desire to be like everyone else, in line with societal edicts. It does appear on the surface that people are "having fun", and we wish this for ourselves. That is considered normal. If we were to really examine this normality, we would detect great differences in our viewpoints, but we do not take the time. Our varied viewpoints will be what will separate us later in life. Most of us fear to be different, on the premise that others may laugh or ridicule us. This is one of the very reasons we wish to control. We want others to follow our way rather than their own. Reality, common sense and consideration dictate that what is easy for you may not be for another, but we will expose those who do not comply with our ways as being below our status.

We have just compared each other, have we not? This is not exactly what Spirit had in mind. Its intention was the celebration of our differences or uniqueness. "From the highest to the lowest". It seems that we are unable to work with this natural metaphysical law. What was and is intended is quite simple: no two things are exactly alike – even the snowflakes, or twins. Each is unique. We know this, but we insist on comparing everyone and everything to ourselves. When this is done, we destroy the special aspects of people and self. It is what happens to personal relationships. We attempt to make our partner fit our mold, instead of allowing for his/her own distinctiveness. The result is a struggle for both people, who eventually are no longer their own selves.

Conversely, the spiritual human will lean more toward the acceptance of others as they are, and gaze in wonder at the beautiful nature of all our distinctive aspects. Being in tune with Spirit, he/she will see only the higher aspects of others. What we truly see, no matter who we are, is the reflection of self, as taught us thousands of years ago. If Spirit is in us, is it not also in the other person? Whatever you see is in you first.

The struggle we see in our present era is nothing more than a mass of individuality fighting against itself, desiring to be noticed as separate individuals. We are presently in the process of shedding more of the psychophysical attributes, moving toward the true aspect of truth in each of us. Today, individual nature is magnified to a heightened state. On this plane, we may shed the past, so we can move forward with a great leap in personal consciousness, should we choose to do so. Our true state of mind is at this point of the struggle, a struggle that will increase and will represent the efforts we must put forth if we want full fruition in our growth. This is what the book of Revelations is telling us to understand. In the twinkling of an eye, all shall be changed and born anew. All we can do is speed up this process or slow it down, but it is inevitable. The question is: are we ready? It is the consciousness of Spirit, but not yet our own. If it were, it is believed that we would do this willingly. Why willingly? Because it would give us what we seek – not just money and toys – but all things. As often mentioned, we may have all things, but only with the strict condition of seeking first the spiritual aspect – not the material.

Growth is part of the original concept of creation, a growth that will enhance the mind of the human and bring it peace. Old belief systems must be discarded to make room for our new selves. If we were able to visualize, as an observer, we would perceive that creation began in a state of turmoil. This apparent turmoil began to take form and became life as we know it today. This same tumult is now being portrayed in the form of the human mind and emotions, to point us in a higher path for life. The physical has already achieved a certain state of perfection. The next phase is to bring the thought and feeling aspects into the same state. Because we have worked so long on the physical side of life, we find it difficult to now reduce its importance. Still, this will be done by us or to us, and we have to choose how we will experience it. It means that it will occur as it has before.

About every 2000 years, a higher vibration comes to take us to the next level. We may do so willingly or unwillingly. One will be easier than the other. We can choose how to reform into higher states of consciousness for the individual nature of being, and it will occur more in our inner selves than in our physical form. Having said that, let us look at today's world. We must admit that, in our present direction, it follows a sure road to insanity, along with the weather. It is more chaotic than ever. How many of us, upon deliberation, will believe that we are the creators of this external turmoil because of the inner struggles we have within us? Probably very few – yet it is the truth of things.

THE LAWS OF OPPOSITION

There are many facets to the process of the original creation, one being the laws of opposition. Thus was born the concept of God and the Devil, two great entities conflicting with each other, as we are taught. The laws of opposition are the sole reason for physical life, but they appear in all things, physical and spiritual. They are from the least to the greatest and are necessary for learning and acquiring knowledge – which is what creation is about. They support the basic law of physics that states that for every action, there is an equal and opposite reaction. This establishes a counterbalance that would automatically advise us of the opposition we may encounter in life, no matter what we do. We must learn to realize that we will be confronted by oppositions on a constant basis, in the search for our true self. Acceptance of the law of opposition is one of the greatest dilemmas in life. Opposing forces pull at us continually, no matter what the circumstances may be.

We will experience this on the outer and inner levels of being. It is why decision-making may become difficult at times. We question our own selves as to whether we are making a good decision or a bad one. Deductively, after most of us make a decision, we begin to question whether it was the right thing or not. Only time will reveal the answer, but we must go for the experience and gather what we can learn from it. These experiences are what allows us to expand and it will further our knowledge of either right thought, error thinking or both. Choices and subsequent decisions have their basis in this very same law. If we were to observe the process of choices, we would recognize what would be returned to us by the chosen act or action, and nothing is above the law. You see, once we make a choice, we will automatically tip the scales of these opposing forces. We will have a counterbalance that will now come into our lives, due only to the very choice that we made originally. Afterward, we must ready our own selves for the counteraction that is to come. It usually is the exact opposite of the initial choice, meaning that resistance will enter into the conflict – for education purposes – to assist us in what we need to know to accomplish the task we seek. It is not put in our path as an obstruction, but rather as a learning tool to use for gathering more knowledge, and to assist us in the new direction our choice put us.

For a moment, we must examine the concept of resistance. Even electricity requires resistance in order to flow. We must never allow inner resistance to become too great. If we do, the very thing we are opposing will most assuredly occur in our life. The classic example is the process of material wealth. When we seek to acquire and enjoy this status, we tend to resist the lack of it, and the lack of it is what we will more than likely receive in our lives. The reason is that we are putting our inner focus in the wrong direction, or on the opposite of what we seek. There may be only one outcome. On many an occasion, the Master reminded us to be single in nature. It is extremely important, because if we desire wealth and simultaneously worry about the lack of it, we certainly are not "single". We have created an inner division. Our house is divided, but ultimately we will have that to which we have given the most power and the emotion: wealth, or the lack of it. Here is a more simple example: if we get a headache and we resist it, what happens? Will the headache not grow in strength? Do not resist it. Change the focus and simply give it a color, then focus on the color. The headache will diminish and eventually disappear. Why? There is no resistance, since our focus has shifted direction. Resistance is a much greater energy than almost anything we do. Anytime we attempt to resist anything, it will grow in strength merely because of the natural laws of physics. It must. When we resist, we transfer power, thus the strength that returns is equal to the resistance. If we observe a smoker or a heavy drinker resist a cigarette or a drink, we might be surprised at what occurs. The same applies when we attempt to lose weight and try resisting eating... The opposite will always happen, only because we furnish it with greater strength and power. We must learn to accept the right direction and it will become easier. True ability lies in acceptance, since there is nothing to resist.

Our growth should be graceful. Resistance is far from either grace or humility, because both of the latter imply acceptance. All natural things – except us – give the radiance of grace. Of course, we are talking about kindness, dignity and blessings. Somehow, we manage to do very little gracefully, yet we have the greatest opportunity to grow spiritually through grace. **Henry Drummond** says it well: *"How are we to grow in grace? By what thought shall we add the cubits to the spiritual stature and reach the fullness of the perfect human? And because we know ill how to do this, the old anxiety comes back again and our inner life is once more an agony of conflict and remorse. After all, we have but transferred our anxious thoughts from the body to the soul. Our efforts after spiritual growth seem only a succession of failures, and instead of rising into the beauty of holiness our life is a daily heartbreak and humiliation".* Do any of us see ourselves in these words? If that is the case, we should accept those words and become graceful with ourselves as we touch reality. Once we accept that reality, we can grow freely. By its nature, realization cannot be negative. The key is to simply accept, and it will surely lead us to grace, along with the wisdom. To refuse the gift of self-knowledge will lead us in the direction whence we came – or the path most traveled.

"Creation is in essence God generating the pure concept and the Devil is the anchor which holds it in place": **Greg Braden**'s "Walking Between the Worlds; The Science of Compassion". Any building requires a foundation. An anchor is quite necessary for life, since it will give a foundation upon which all physical things can be built. This even affects the physical thinking we emanate in life, since it too must have a foundation from which to operate. In reality, it is the pull of oppositions. We see it in all areas of life because they must work in union. If they do not, we have turmoil, struggle. If we look into science, we find that the beginnings of creation were a primordial soup composed of oppositions learning to work in union. As they learned, the union began to work in harmony and life became more defined. In essence, it was the ethers condensing down into finite form through the action of energy vortexes – or centers – to draw us together through opposition. Ultimately, it condensed down to what we now have, and that is physical reality or life as we know it. That is the concept of Adam and Eve. They are the reality of the oppositions of creation: male and female. Thoughts and feelings took place at the same time. Since they are inner oppositions, they are very seldom in agreement in life. The result is that we have the obvious external opposition and the internal laws of opposition in present day life – as it has been from the beginning.

Now we have life. Until now, we have lived it in the external sense of the word. Everything we do is for the outer aspect of life. Through the eons, we have been steadily drawn to its opposite: the internal nature. It is becoming more obvious as each day passes, witnessed by each struggle with the physical external world. This forward movement is attempting to make us look inward rather than outward.

SPIRITUAL GROWTH

Today, most of us would rather point the finger at another instead of assuming responsibility for our own actions. The inner cause for the act becomes defiled by the outer expression of the cause, as it becomes corrupted through the selfish use of the ego. Jesus told us of these struggles, yet we still ignore the events around us and insist that we are not the cause.

We are the cause. Our life, our own conscience, is here now because of Spirit. It produced us in its image. Were we ever to endorse this true mantle, we would not be so destructive and wasteful toward life and ourselves. Today, Spirit is trying to get our attention to alert us about a devastating behavior that we base on a focus misplaced on the external egoistic nature.

As told in Genesis, we are special and above all things of life, and it was never intended that we should destroy any part of it. Sadly, we do, because we tend to compare ourselves to others, thereby demolishing our unique nature and disrupting other lives in the process. When we compare, we put the worse of ourselves into others. It is not celebrating our unique or special self. Logic would tell us that an apple is unique, but so is an orange. There is no comparison. We were put here to learn to accept – not to expect. However, our comportment shows that we mostly expect and do not accept. Expectancy is mental and acceptance is emotional. That is another example of our inner opposition. To expect is to follow the path to disappointment, especially if we have chiseled our expectation in stone. We expect the outside world and all its distractions to match us and what we want, when all the higher aspect wants is acceptance. Because we anticipate things to be a certain way, we will try to force them to be equal to what we expect. Now force enters the picture and will undoubtedly generate a struggle. When we accept, we allow, and when we allow, we are forcing nothing. As a result, there is no struggle. This is the true humility the Master mentioned 2,000 years ago, and we still do not understand or accept it. We do not agree to our circumstances on a personal level, and that engenders our daily fight – which in turn triggers expectations. If we expect so much of life, why do we not use our creative energies instead of our logic? We must realize that logic and creativity are two different matters. In all frankness, we really create nothing. We merely remove the veils from what is hidden from our view, to expose the realization of what already is.

Creativeness comes into play through acceptance, following the removal of the veils of the mind. Acceptance is not really giving in to circumstances, but it will allow us to work with them, to learn from them, so that they will become better or easier to handle, without a fight. If life is truly about thought experiencing its own self, we are indeed the embodiment of our thinking and nothing more: thought in physical form and action. Thought pressing into life is meant to be the full understanding of cause and effect, which in turn would give rise to a more proper form of thinking. This will naturally be reflected in the right use of speech, form and measure. Form and measure are the judgments that we were inclined to pass on others in the past. This practice will stop because we now accept and understand the principle of cause and effect.

Acceptance is easier because it does not present a struggle, and we will think clearly as situations develop. Acceptance is not pretentious, because it cannot be. Of course, if we resist, there will be a struggle, and it will impair our thinking during these events. Give up resistance and accept. Give in but do not give up. The surrender will assist in clarity and will offer a renewal and greater strength from within. It will breed new forms of thought that will be clearer and cleaner, without preconceived ideas born of expectations.

As the readers probably begin to realize, the aspect of creation is very difficult to explain. It goes much deeper than what has been written, yet the concepts that are presented are valid and can be proved by anyone who is willing to research on his/her own. When we become an observer of life, the task grows to be easier. The process of becoming a corporeal form out of the void of time and space is a separate subject defined in many texts already available. There are two works that could assist the serious student today. One is "Thinking and Destiny", by **Harold Percival**. The second is titled "Cosmo-Conception", offered by the Rosicrucian Society, which is an offshoot of the original family of Essenes. We must also realize that creation is still in progress. We have so stated on many occasions within these pages, as all things are in a progressive forward movement to this day.

We are here and are still learning about what we have been or whence we came. As each year passes, we expand this knowledge in various ways, but our curiosity leans toward the physical sense only. For instance, we want to know whence the first physical human came in life. It actually came from the higher or spiritual self known as God. This occurred because we wanted to know our own being, and we had to separate from universal consciousness for this particular task. We fashioned individual consciousness for self-knowledge. There is no real missing link, and this physical illustration may never be found, since we are the link. This will not come to resolution until we learn to blend metaphysics into the evolutional equation. When this is done, we may find the true answers to life and creation, because creation was not a physical process. It was metaphysical and still is to this day. The real point is that we are still learning to understand our nature in the physical sense of the word. That is why some answers simply do not fit the puzzle. Physical did not originally create physical. How could it? We are not yet able to do this, except through the mechanism we have been experiencing: the act of intimacy. This is why

Spirit created male and female. We create life through the blend of the two, as polar opposites come together in union to procreate.

In the concept of true creation, we must apply the knowledge of the One, that is to say the non-duality of spirit and matter. All of creation is at once spirit and body. We could say subtlety and density. This was granted us so that we can function in all realms – not just the physical. However, we insist on concentrating on the separate function of the physical and the physical thinking mind. This does not allow for the first cause – that of the higher spiritual nature. If we did, we would be the Alpha and the Omega, the first and the last. We must learn to transmute the lower to the higher, giving up the harshness of the physical nature, but we must know that such transmutation will always remain the greatest barrier or the hardest task for the human. Must we not lose our lives to gain them? The true master is in the heart of the eternal, and it will be the one who is able to blend the grains of life of the divine spirit with the atoms of their own flesh. It is not an easy task, unless we really do apply the faith of the mustard seed. With the truth of self, we may exercise our thoughts, will power, and love toward a much higher purpose. In fact, we could become living spiritual human beings, with the ability to project ourselves into the power of spirit, as so many of the biblical masters did.

Life is what we have been given through the intervention of the spirit bringing the breath of life into each of us. It is this breath that comes to us in a constant state of perfection. Sadly, we change it to something else. This personal expression is contaminated by the voice of experience and memory. The mind of the individual will establish the success or the failure, since we are the co-creators of life. Still, we are unable to accept this very simple concept. Within the spiritual human lies the force of the cosmos, but also the weakness of being human. The true revealing sign that will be given is in the union of the two characteristics in the authentic human path. All else is just the illusion of the physical mind. Our lack of acceptance continually gets in our way. We need proof for everything, and proof is purely material. We have erroneously learned to accept material facts over people's faith.

What we possess denotes our self-worth, or so we think. These are egocentric principles upon which we have come to rely, and we give them our power. If these things are taken from us, we have no power of self, for what was is now gone. It was taken by those superficial principles, yet, what is truly gone is only the illusion of power – nothing more. To the mind of the average person, power is represented by those who bow to the will of another. What would happen if no one bowed? The power would be drained from the one seeking it. No one, at any time, would have undue power, if we chose not to give it away.

The Tibetans taught me about the power of the human thoughts. This power will grow when we apply the true power of self, that which comes from the heart of the spiritual human. They teach that we should give our will power, our hands, over to our heart, from where we may manage this force with the thoughts we have. We would be able to direct it with the mind, to control any wave or vibration of life, but we must be life's eternal lover to do this. We must do this by not looking behind, for if all is truly done in the power of love, there would be no need to do so, and we would naturally look forward. By the same token, if anything was somehow left behind us, it would indeed be undamaged. Life has proved to me that these learned Teachers are correct in what they teach. Once the thought is expressed, it will be fashioned for us in the exact manner that it was externalized, down to the letter, and it will become our next experience. To repeat an example mentioned earlier, if we want success but worry about the lack of it, the lack of success is what we will receive, simply because we placed our focus on it. Spirit is not interested in the lack or abundance of anything. It does not know the difference, but we do. Deductively, we will have whatever it is we consider important. We have allowed life to be the cause and we are merely its effect. That is philosophy spelled backward. We are co-creators, and that means that we are the cause of all that befalls us. Not until we accept this premise will we be able to generate the changes we seek. To produce these types of changes, we could easily believe that it would have to be magic. Magic is nothing more than a technique that would enable any spiritual human with a strong loving will to dominate the laws of nature, for everything is nothing more than a vibration.

Being the cause is taking control with spirit and being responsible for the outcome, no matter what it may be in reality. Working in union is the "as above, so below" concept offered by the Master. It is the acceptance of our acts and actions. "From the highest to the lowest" is having all the energy centers in full operation and agreement. It is the unification of the spiritual principle of self-recognition. "From the crown to the root" or vice-versa, is what has been offered for all to understand and accept. The power of self comes through this idea. We have the power, but the majority does not realize it. How can we attain this power of self if we give it away to material matters that certainly are not us? We can do this by not being the cause. We are the effect by the way things operate in life at this moment in time. We may generate change by using all our attributes, not just the obvious ones that we accept because they have proved to us they are there. These are the five senses. We do not journey any further than these because they have been good to us. We can see, hear, taste, smell and touch. We have been led to believe that this is the final end result for each individual, and the physical proof has been our experience. This is a very limited use for very unlimited beings. The limitation comes from a very finite point of view because we seek too much in the way of definition. We feel that everything else has to be finite in nature. We see the world as finite, and we conclude that we too must be finite, therefore able to understand and manage the planet. This does not allow us to comprehend the bliss of spirituality in the truest sense of the word. Even our earthly definition of infinity is a limiting aspect of life. Were we to truly grasp this, the impact would be staggering. We would be dwarfed by the whole concept.

Insanity, as an example, is merely the definition of those not knowing themselves in the expanse of infinity. They have no point of reference with which to work. Their mind is lost in that unfathomable void. They have no boundaries of recognition in their mind. Instead of teaching them, we drug them because we do not understand how to reach or teach them. How can finite teach the subject of infinity? Would this not be odd in the first place? These unfortunate people must be taught the power of the mind. How can they be taught when we do not understand its full use? Unknown to us, they could be using the ninety percent that Einstein says we do not use…We, on the other hand, only use the other ten percent. Imagine if we could use this great tool in its entirety. Some may doubt it, but we can if we do not limit it by restraining it within the fences we have built through the need of definition.

We do not listen to the spiritual part. We listen to our minds, and they react according to the physical interest of the moment – not to the whole. The spirit evolves in a realm of tangible thinking, and it laughs at our world of logic, for logic is the very fence that binds us in place, with no spiritual growth in the physical sense.

We have covered much in the way a spiritual human can operate in life. The subsequent chapter will show us how to walk the spiritual path as portrayed by the principles not directly mentioned in a biblical sense. There are tools available in the next phase, to offer guidance in our everyday lives. These tools are the seven Essene mirrors of relationship, the seven virtues and the seven branches. They address the true trinity of being and ways to enhance the relationship of self in union with the higher nature. They teach us how to open and how to gracefully shed the inner war between the material and higher spiritual nature. This inner war is the very thing that has held us in place. We have all seen it and experienced it. The unseen spirit has a softer, gentler way that we find difficult to trust because of the physical events that occur. Nevertheless, it is there if we are truly interested in the path to enlightenment. It always shows itself at the most appropriate moments of our lives.

CHAPTER 3

THE WAY OF THE SPIRIT

"Truly understanding the self is to accept the illusions we have created for our own reality"
Steven Hairfield, PhD

We sincerely hope that, thus far, the readers have understood and enjoyed the dissertations explaining the higher and lower natures of the human. We have discussed the fragmentation of self – the integral inner parts we have given away – and how we have attempted to fill these self-inflicted voids through external means and other people. We have offered this philosophy in the form of dual natures, so we may know and realize the separation we have created through the way we conduct our lives in this present era. Today, life is very complicated, and we have no one to blame but ourselves. We have learned that we can change this any time we so choose. We can enhance our existence by living with and through spirit. These changes occur one person at a time, one step at a time, by being bold enough to step away from what is considered normal to a more spiritual way of life. We must have the courage to step away from the way we have done things in the past. As it was told us biblically, we may then become what Spirit has always intended for us to become: a human that can attain the virtues and benefits of the higher realm. Our experiences merely attempt to give us this gift through self-realization and acceptance.

In reality, this is the only path in life. It is a very difficult path, upon which we must face the illusions we have built during our years of life. These illusions are our own past hurts, our rejections, our fears, or the regrets for giving away individual controls, in fields we may consider important.

We may not realize that these are indeed illusions, especially if we know no other way to do things. How can we recognize them if they are truly illusions? We have thus reached the point where "normal" is now the illusion, and we accept it as reality. All of this will be addressed by each of us during some segment of our life, through the exposure to the "dark night of the soul" which we will all experience with the purpose of self-purification, clearing us of illusions, with the intent of facing the truth of our own self. It will be easier if we face this while being aware of those inner pains. Henceforth, they may no longer hurt as they did before. They will be cleared. We will see ourselves and life in a clearer, bluer sky, creating great love – a love that will surpass understanding because no conditions will be imposed on anything. We will be in acceptance of all that has been created. We will be living in grace, with the true power of choice – a choice that will wield the truth. We will now live a life of the purest truth, knowing ourselves to the very center of our being. We will be in harmony with all of nature, using it to benefit all life from the heart of love.

This book is humbly offered to assist us in the path that leads to this type of growth. Its primary goal is to teach us to unify ourselves with the inner nature, to grow into the spiritual part of being. The achievement is a true unification of being and the innumerable potentials of life, rather than the illusions we have faced on a daily basis. We will be single in nature, and confusion will not even be a memory. We will all have clarity of mind and knowledge that will defy comprehension.

We have spent much time looking at both sides of life's coin, and what we do to ourselves and others. In truth, what we do to others, we really do unto our own self. We do it because of the laws of cause and effect: Karma. We either do not understand yet, or we choose not to accept this very natural law of life. Each thing that we do – the dharma of our choice – will open an alternative path in our life. We give away control to the external power through the inner choices upon which we act. Spirit leads us as it presents us with these choices. It is up to us to decide. Through time, these alternative paths may create great confusion when we are faced with them. It leads us back to the path reserved for rectification of past deeds, and it will do this repeatedly until we formulate a proper resolution. This explains the repetitive cycles we find in our lives. When we finally grasp this principle and reach for the higher aspect, the cycles will be broken automatically. Subsequent acts will come from the true position of compassionate love. The mind offers us the real illusions of life. It is the only thing that can – and it does. The reason is that we have built a world of material illusion out of that very same mind, through our thoughts. This phase of growth, about to be offered, is to remove these bewildering illusions from our lives and replace them by the simple truth. For each and every one of us, it is a lesson in the control of the mind and the sense system. The results are that we become really consciously aware of the choices we make and the consequences that will surely accompany them. We will become single in purpose in our emotions and our hearts. We will develop a unified feeling of unconditional love, so that it can be generously and equally divided upon all aspects of life. This brings us to consciousness and feeling. Feelings are not illusions. They are truth and they make no decisions. Those are left to the mental part of ourselves, in combination with the impulses given by our hearts.

The last phase with which we must work is true unconditional nature. With pure love, spiritual growth can be here for all of us to enjoy and share. Imagine a genuinely loving world instead of the material reality we have all created through the misuse and violation of the first two principles of self: thought and feeling. We have developed a true heteroclite structure for our path. We have filled it with many side branches that are demanding an equitable resolution now or later. Sadly enough, some of us will never resolve anything because of poor or cowardly choices. We must allow them to travel their own journey of life. It is their choice, and we certainly cannot assist them while we are blinded by our own light. We must remove the cinder from our own eye before we can help them in any way. The best help is through what we do ourselves, and the understanding it can bring to us. It has been said that one person can change all things. It has been done many times in our past history. It is really done by example. It is a dedication to unconditional allowance and reverence to all of life – and we call it the spiritual path.

In the last phase, we must first work with the outer material world, primarily because it need not own us the way it does. This is the greatest stumbling block that we all will face on this journey of life. We have been taught that the Christ was the only human who has surmounted this obstacle. It is not really the case, because many – before and since – have managed this wonderful voyage. They do so in silence. As each of these masters attained the ultimate goal, they left us a path to follow, and it is our choice to take it or bypass it. Once found, it must be traveled by the individual for understanding of self first. It is a very delicate path and at times almost imperceptible, yet we will know it is there if we but respond to the inner nudging of the spirit. To us, the path can become imperceptible because these inner nudges are sometimes difficult to follow, and the ubiquitous ego is a very slippery thing that has troubles accepting, seeing or understanding. To attain this non-ego oriented spirituality, there will be many lessons we will have to learn in order to overcome.

The spiritual nudges and the ego will form a paradox for us along the way. These contradictions are there for us to glean valuable lessons rather than be confused by them. At first, however, we will become very confused. The confusion itself has the spiritual purpose of guiding us toward the proper choice. The struggle will stem from the improper use of the ego, which is normally in collision with the path of understanding. In that case, we should wait for clarity. This path is not one of speed. It is one of patience and the spiritual acceptance of its pace. It is called Divine Timing. If we are in a hurry, we may circumvent the most important aspect of the truth of self. If we are in too much of a rush, we will have to do it again. Repeats are what we should avoid, because each time, the lesson is harder than the previous one. It will always come down to the choice between material or spiritual self. Which to choose? Which way do I go? We may choose love of life or the material aspect of life. It is a difficult choice at first, but not really in the long run.

The greatest difficulty will be the pull from other people who do not wish us to "throw our lives away" - or from various material matters. We must also consider that the "lives" viewed by others are only a reflection of their own. We should ask ourselves: how can we possibly throw our lives away? Actually, this would be quite difficult, if not impossible. Upon consideration, is this nothing more than the judgment others placed on our lives? Do we not have the freedom to decide what to do with our own existence? It would help to understand that, for the most part, these very same people are the ones who say they love us… If this is true, they should be happy to the end, witnessing how truly peaceful we will become toward them and toward life. Once we start on this narrow path, we must be willing to let go of all preconceived notions of self and of life. At least, we should be willing to dedicate ourselves earnestly to this growth. Once we accomplish this, we gain all things. We must recognize that they who love us will become one of the largest stumbling blocks we will encounter, for we believe we return their love. It will be the biggest lesson of love we could ever imagine, and it is always right in front of us. It may be quite trying, because these types of situations reveal who we truly are. They are the reflections of what we have created for ourselves.

The pull of this emotion of love will be great upon us. We must know that as we grow, things tend to change in this particular arena. When changes take hold, our circle of people and circumstances will shift to match what we are becoming. The old, the past, will no longer work for us, since we have agreed to this metamorphosis. To hold on to our old environment will bind us in place and atrophy our growth, unless the others choose to grow with us. A struggle will now arise between the choice to continue on and the choice of returning to our past. Most will journey back to the past and will not know it until the same type of event recurs and comes upon them once again.

People that have begun upward changes come and go based on the truth or the deceit of self. Their personal struggle will be the releasing of old ways, of old beliefs, thus allowing the unrestricted acceptance of spiritual concepts by being open to them. This is the budding unification of the old and the new. We must realize through this journey that great adversity may arise as a potential challenge. If it does, it is merely for the recognition of the truth. Adversity is detrimental only to our inner selves and our old precepts, simply because we are not willing to let them go. On the positive side, it comes masked as the single greatest gift that we may have, because of the awareness it brings us. We should not fight adversity until we know all aspects of it, then use it as a tool for growth.

Spirit itself does not recognize adversity. It sees the lesson. Only we humans will see the physical situation because we are the ones caught up in it. It must be said that the only reason adversity shows up in the first place is for Spirit to get our attention. Something must be changed. If we acknowledge it and choose judicially, it will lessen the pressure that will eventually fade away. If we do not acquiesce, the pressure will increase, or it will come from a different direction to create the necessary change.

As we mentioned, know before we enter the path that, for the first time, it is the journey of self. It is as unique as each of us is. If we do not appreciate it already, it will show us our uniqueness. At times, it will appear to be a very lonely trek, because we are moving out of selfishness into selflessness. It is the ego crying out for entertainment. It wants us to be distracted. It will give the appearance of loneliness merely because of the full realization of our special unique nature. It should be a celebration rather than sorrow, for now we will truly journey into our inner selves and become the persons we were intended to be. It is a very magnificent path to travel. Upon completion, we will no longer feel outside controls. We will experience true freedom of self-expression – the spiritual perfection of the human.

The inner God self – which we all have, whether we believe it or not – is now truly resting there. This must be realized and accepted with great humility. Without unpretentiousness, it is pure egoistic arrogance, and we will have nothing more than we had before. Our God self has been there for all time and waits to be recognized by us. This consciousness comes in reverence. It is not a religious worship of the external God whom we are taught is out there, somewhere. It is within us and it is us in all respects. This very statement was passed on to us by the Master Himself, in the Book of Matthew, and we know deep inside that it must be true.

Those of us who walk this upward and painstaking path will achieve incredible results with our lives, as we unify ourselves with the higher spiritual nature. This will occur of itself whether we assist or not. The path of intent will surely speed the process. Paul said in **II Corinthians 3:18**: *"But we all, with open face beholding as in a glass* [mirror] *the glory of the Lord, are changed into the same image from glory to glory, even as by the Spirit of the Lord"*. It is the same message that the reader will find in other parts of this book. This one comes to let us know that spirituality is not "new age" but as ancient as the old texts. Two millennia later, we still do not grasp the meaning of it. Life is a mirror that does not lie and we should look into that instrument of truth. It is before us all and we are not willing to gaze at its reflection. We do not face it squarely because we may not like what we see, and we live in fear and illusion. If we do look, the truth of all things will become real and will help us to grow. When we look at ourselves frankly and honestly, we may find no one else to blame. What is done is done to us, by us, for us to help realize our real strength in life. This strength is needed to assist us in our personal relationships. We were intended to live life in joy and love, to share our experiences if only for a period of time. The individual person alone can own the experience, and nothing more. This principle will help us realize what we do. *"...but lay up for yourselves treasures in heaven....for where your treasure is, there will be your heart also"* (Matthew 6:20-21). We will begin now with what is termed as the "pointing finger" – a reflection of self, a concept of blame and one of self-responsibility.

When we look in the mirror and point, are we not pointing at ourselves? Even while looking into our own eyes, we seem to ignore the thoughts and deeds that are very easy to deny because of the temptations to which we succumb. How could we believe that we are the ones who inflicted the pains of life, or the types of relationships that seem to enhance pain? Relationships are actually chosen by us for what we ultimately learn to accept about ourselves. These liaisons, good or bad, tend to create physical or spiritual adversity. It will awaken several of our sensitive areas. These wake-up calls are to learn to take the status of various situations off the other person, and place it where it belongs: on our own shoulders – in terms of spiritual growth. If we choose to consider it a burden, it may become too great for us to carry. This is why the Masters have been here throughout time. They have helped to lighten the load that we have ignored by trying to teach us about life with their words and example. They have shown us that we are the burdens, but through the self-perceptions that we carry around with us. We are given – or choose to subject ourselves to – the kind of relationships we have, so that we may see ourselves for what we are but attempt to deny. We simply should cherish all personal bonds for the gifts of growth they bring to us. If we blame or condemn, what can we learn of self? Blame never teaches anything other than imposing more conditions on the event. Our puzzle will be more complicated than ever before because we do not place our focus on the situation. We place it on the person. If we were to focus on the situation, it would lend to a more friendly solution. If we were to become angry, let it be at the situation and not the person. On the other hand, if we became angry with the person, it would only bring bitter arguments. Too often have we seen the hurt, the pain, the words that cannot be unsaid as the outcomes of such altercations. Placing the focus on the situation may bring it to a resolution, and if there is a dispute, it should be with our own self and no one else. This would reduce the pain on either side. More times than we care to think, people do create these situations. They are there for us to learn and not point out that another "did this to me". Remember that we create the lessons, but are not necessarily to blame for them.

Next, we are going to offer something that is thousands of years old – older than the Bible itself. It may also be found – veiled – in the contents of said Bible. Today, this knowledge is used in most true monastic studies. It will encompass three separate areas of being. People, such as myself, have looked all over the world for this information. It will be offered here in the most understandable way possible. As mentioned, there are no real secrets to life. Most people do not use time wisely by looking for them. If there were a secret, it would be to locate the truth of our own being, and not someone else's. We should not even seek the hidden formula used by other individuals. Just because it works for them does not necessarily mean that it will work for us. We do not mean to say that there is no solid information contained in the formula, for there certainly will be.

This is so simply because their particular formula is the one they have found for themselves. It worked only for them. It is wonderful that they are willing to share their "secrets", but we must realize that it only applies to them. We must learn to take only what works for us and move ahead in life. If we attempt to take it all, we will surely find that it will be frustrating, and we will scrap the whole concept, thus gaining nothing. There is nothing wrong with taking only the parts that fit and use them, since all pieces to a puzzle do not fit in the same place. All the pieces, however, make up the whole.

These sensible principles are taught in Zen monasteries as "You may ask anything you wish, or read anything you seek, after which you must forget it". This sounds absurd, but their point is to get all information that applies to our unique self and release the rest, since it is of no value to us. The way to perceive what does apply is through inner reflection, not over-thinking. This concept is very old and quite easy to implement, yet we may feel that if we do not use all the secrets, it may not work. We may also very easily believe that we are in error by thinking: it worked for others but not me, so something must be wrong with me. This may turn into error think-ing, and it will certainly grow into feelings of inferiority. The truth is that no one is inferior. We all have the same abilities. Some just use them with-out fear, and others do not because of fear or insecurity. These are the sim-ple choices.

Any information in this work will be made flexible enough for all that want to walk the path. This is not really a formula for success. It is an understanding only. True spiritual growth is as individual as we are – as it must be. It is about attainment or enlightenment. Both equate to making our being lighter – by the removal of our burdens. It will occur through our experiences of such burdens and what we learn from them. Again, we must not deny but rather accept with no preconceived ideas or notions. The in-formation is offered because of its age and wisdom, and because it work through its flexibility for all those who apply it. It is used in most monaster-ies the world over. It considers each person as an individual nature. It is efficient because it allows us to think for ourselves, in view of our personal relationship to life. We are taught to become one with it, to no longer sepa-rate ourselves from all the natural wonders of life. We must admit that, to a very high degree, we have separated ourselves. We continue to do this on a daily basis by our reactions to life and to people we encounter. A Zen would tell you that the most important part of the journey is the path itself. No one may become enlightened without that path of knowledge, living life in all respects.

We have many subjects to cover, outlined not only in the biblical texts for growth, but in every ancient text known. It will be offered from the experiential point of view all the way to the point of crucifixion of the per-sonal being. We will all face the latter at some point. In reality, we do cru-cify ourselves without realizing it, then we mask it from our view because of the hurt it brought us. If this is done, the events of the past will surely raise their head to irritate us once again. We must not avoid the true lessons be-cause they will become much stronger each time they surface. We can find those teachings in the Book of John. We will cover this situation in detail at that point.

In the pages that follow, we will cover the true holy trinity: body, mind/emotion and spirit. We will show how to bring them together as a single point of unification. To become single in all regards will lead us to be single in purpose. We will portray the seven Essene mirrors of relationship to see our reflection before our very eyes. We will offer the seven virtues of life and the illusions they may create along the wonderful path of attainment. The illusions are the small tests along the road to enlightenment and knowledge. We must all pass these tests one at a time. Remember that even in the halls of education, we are tested to earn our degree. These assessments are obvious, and the spiritual ones are not. In fact, we may not know that it is taking place until after it is over, and we have the outcome before us. We either have to go through them again, or we are allowed to move forward. Our main choices in life are to live the truth or the lie – nothing less.

We will also look at the seven branches of life that coincide with the seven virtues. The branches will be covered as the third aspect toward attainment. We will not know these branches until we accept the virtues first and complete the tests they will bring forth. Notice that each of these has seven parts. This is the number assigned to attainment, and it appears in every religious text written and in almost every spiritual work. It indeed coincides with the seven chakras of the body so that we may operate through them for our growth. All of these are designed to bring the Holy Trinity together as a unified entity. Each of the seven works with one aspect of the trinity. The mirrors are for the body, the seven virtues are for the mind/emotions, and the seven branches are for the spirit or higher aspect of self.

Once these are gained, we become extremely powerful as an innate consequence to nature itself. We will be in harmony with – and not in opposition to – life. This ability brings power over all things material or spiritual in our lives, and that again is related to us in the Bible. Another natural consequence will be the capability to heal others through our practical demonstration with life, for we will have healed ourselves. We will have removed the cinder from our own eye and will see very clearly the true power of a love that may withstand the test of time and matter. This will turn out to be a personal choice we will all make, once we rid ourselves of the fear and the lie we have to live. These will no longer have influence over us.

We will begin with the reflections of life and what they reveal to us. We will also incorporate the concept of the pointing finger in a true sense, to assist in the path of self-knowledge. We must remember that life did not ask us to be here. We asked personally, spiritually, to be placed upon this earth.

It was our own request. Life owes us nothing. We are its true care givers and we already have dominion over all things. As care givers, we are the ones to give to life, but we must first have dominion over ourselves. Subsequently, all things will be given through this realization.

Spiritual growth is finding one's way home – nothing more. It is our personal path, and the first step is to no longer point the finger. Succinctly, this practice symbolizes refusal to accept the responsibility for what we do, for our own cause and effect, or karma. We believe it is easier to blame another for the circumstances in which we find ourselves. If we were to really believe this concept, but were to ponder upon it, perhaps we should ask ourselves a question: what has this "finger pointing" ever given me? Do we not live in a "What's in it for me?" style? If we were to state that it has given us this or that, can we not also realize that it is our personal ego at work? The truth is that this irresponsible practice has brought nothing but heartache and mistrust. It is obvious that people afflicted by this nasty habit do not recognize the first step toward spiritual growth: responsibility of self. If we find ourselves pointing the finger for any reason, we should have the fortitude to ask: Is this the truth? It seldom is. When we point that finger, we are finalizing a judgment of the situation, refusing to accept what we created out of our own insecurities. We become blind to the dishonesty of that judgment. It will undoubtedly cause us to stumble, because any conclusion we formulate shouts its condescension and we think everything else is beneath us.

If we point the finger in any direction other than toward ourselves, there is no self-recognition or acceptance. Instead, we hide behind the blame. In reality, we do recognize ourselves, but in the physical sense only, through our body or our things. In that manner, we know what we are but not who we are. In the long run, this will not assist us in any way. That is why we must lose all physical things to gain spiritual growth. In fact, the material aspect may even become a burden, especially if we hold on too tightly to what we have. This excessive hoarding will surely suffocate the very thing we love as a person because, at that point, we have stopped our growth. We become bound in place because we have an anchor holding us down. If the situation involves other persons, we will certainly suffocate them as well. They will eventually stop loving us or even liking us as they, in turn, are stunted in their lives. We will not allow them to be their own selves and grow in their individual ways. They must, and so do we.

We become entirely too busy identifying ourselves with others. We go one step further and attempt to live in the style of others... We progressively lose what we may think and feel about who we are. All this happens because of the "what" we are through our accumulation of possessions. We may own things, but certainly not people, and now we are slaves to both material goods and other people, merely because there is no responsibility for act or actions of self. Paul's message was that when we look in the mirror of life, we should see things as spiritual – not just physical. It is the removal of veils hiding our inner selves. We must learn that life is our mirror and reflects what we already are. It is the next step on the road of spiritual growth. Etched in this mirror are the lessons of self-acceptance.

These mirrors of life are the second step leading us to attainment. The first was the pointing finger. The mirrors are to show us where we point the finger, and to let us see ourselves as we are. In short, their purpose is the truth of self. You must understand this principle and it will grow more subtle as we progress. It may also become more difficult if we do not accept the likeness that we see before us as the reflection of self.

In Corinthians, Paul tells us that we are a mirror image of God, the ideal state of perfection we want to become, while not realizing that we already are. Somehow, our physiological nature will deny it in all respects. As a result, we become a reflection of the weakness of life. If we cannot accept our responsibility for act and actions, cause and effect or karma, we leave ourselves no other choice. It creates the path we must walk and from which to learn. This path is ever changing because of what we do. It explains the long and winding road.

Each and every event in our lives defines our image all the way down to the types of relationships we choose. The more personal the liaison, the greater the reflection with which we will have to work. These personal liaisons will give us a much greater impact than expected through what we see and feel about them. They actually will show us what our own insecurities are or what they have become. To use a more contemporary expression, they are the "buttons" to which we react when pushed, and we promptly blame others for pushing them. If we accept these "buttons" for what they represent and do not blame others for their meaning, we have an opportunity to heal such insecurities and understand our real self. Once they are accepted and understood, they become healed, and no longer will they affect us the way they did in the past. We stop being reactional and become truly in harmony with life as one and the same. Anytime a "button" is being pushed by the reflection and it is recognized, it now becomes a blessing rather than a feeling of anger or hurt. It is a lesson on clearing the past aches that we believe life has dealt to us. They are generally created at a very early age, and we never learned how to express them. They are carried into adulthood, buried beneath our conscious thoughts, and rear their head in different ways as we get older. This explains why we are so defensive and lash out at others.

THE ESSENE MIRRORS OF RELATIONSHIP

There is an old teaching that should help us understand. It was offered by the Essenes even before the times of the Master. It is called the seven Essene Mirrors of Relationship. It pertains to what any relationship tries to reveal about us, not others. However, it is true for either side of the affiliation. Each party will have his/her own reflection. Both must glean their personal lesson from what they see before them. They should not concern themselves about the other person's lessons nor bother to point them out. This considerate gesture will give more meaning for both, with no unnecessary further pressures on either party. If they do, they obviously are not working with their own.

The reflections show us that with which we identify ourselves, how we see or think of ourselves. Most of these are subconscious in nature. They are the missing pieces we left on the trail of life. They have become subconscious because we mostly do not work with the reality of the inner pain we experienced. We mask it. We do not believe that it was our creation, or at least the circumstances leading to the events. Simply because we ignore them does not mean that they will go away. They become deeply embedded within only to surface again in the next relationship we choose as part of our experience. It will not matter whether the bond is personal or professional.

We will share the seven mirrors with you, and how we may use them to assist in understanding the process of growth – spiritual or otherwise. If we learn what these mirrors represent, it could help us in all matters. We would acquire knowledge of ourselves, our frailties, our strengths. We would also be more willing to share ourselves without fear, as it would be done in truth. These mirrors are designed for the realities of external life, in the form of relationships that we have established. We must also come to realize that spirit will put these in our paths, not as stumbling blocks, but as stepping stones to a higher learning experience.

Ironically, if we were working through spirit, we would already realize the lesson to be gained. We could make a conscious choice on how to hold the experience and with whom we choose to share it. This would surely make it much more enjoyable for us, since we would know the lesson in advance and not after the fact – if ever at all.

We must take this opportunity to let all readers know that the rest of this chapter will be one of the most significant teachings we may ever have in respect to the journey toward enlightenment. We would also like to advise them that there will be three separate segments: the Essene Mirrors, the Seven Virtues and the Seven Branches. All of these actually work simultaneously, so that we may clear the lower and higher natures at the same time. In truth, they work in union, so that all three of the aspects – body, mind/emotions and spirit – are totally working together in cleaning our temple. Proceeding in that fashion, nothing can interfere, except our very own fears – that which we would rather avoid. We must point out that these concepts can assist us in clearing away those fears. We should not run from them, but rather acknowledge and work through them in humility and gentleness. We should never be aggressive with them because, in fact, it is inner resistance, and in a way, denial.

REFLECTIONS OF THE SEVEN ESSENE MIRRORS

1. REFLECTION OF THE MOMENT

The first mirror is the reflection of the moment. In the Nag Hammadi, it is written as follows: *"You read the face of the sky and the earth, but you have not recognized how to read this moment"*. We are talking about the first energy center of the body. It is to be noted that each of the mirrors interacts with its corresponding center (chakra). In Revelations, this is the first church of Ephesus, and the reflection contains the same effects, the same impact as portrayed in the biblical text.

No matter where in the world we may physically be, the moment is the only place in time and space in which we can locate ourselves. It is the definitive place wherein we will ever find ourselves at any given time. The only thing that may distract us is where our thoughts may be, and that is why we do not necessarily pay attention to the events that are right in front of us at the time. Our mind pulls us from where we are, nothing more. We must learn to insert our entire being in each instant. This is truly the point of all creation, where everything begins. Anything past and already started is "after the fact". The moment is the perfect opportunity to create or formulate what we desire to have next in our lives. When we are able to do this on a consistent basis, we may become a more powerful being in all of life's respects. It is proved to be true because we will tend to be more observant of the events taking place in that particular moment in time. If we were in a positive light in that instant, we would have no time for past regrets. We would have a greater sense of fulfillment with all things around us. We would be able to enjoy more of what life has to offer as the true gifts of spirit.

This must be why we call it the "present", for it is a gift. Since we do not see the ribbon and the bow, we miss it and give it no importance. We should. If we were to handle all moments properly, no forgiveness would be necessary and we would have nothing to settle with our brothers or sisters. All would be managed in that very tiny allocation of time.

The moment has no definition, so we do not necessarily see it until it has become defined. It now becomes the past or "after the fact". If this occurs, we will spend much effort in rectifying the past since it has now gone from us. This is where regret will enter because we may have hurt someone or some thing and that instant is behind us. We now will have old issues bound to return, especially if we deny them. The moment is always the point of the truth. It is one of the only truths in life. If we truly open ourselves, many lessons may be understood in each point of time as it occurs. We may learn after the fact, but most would rather ignore and bury the memory. If we choose to understand after the events occurred, it will require much analyzing. As we have said before, analyzing is not realizing. We attempt to figure out the situation, or to place the blame elsewhere. We should allow each moment to be a blessing for us and allow its virtues to be as they are, but we must be squarely in the moment to have this opportunity. If we earnestly do this, there will be nothing adverse about it because the true lesson is already known. This will create greater ease within, for we have no past from which to work, adding to the inner aspect of knowledge. We are more trusting when we are more accepting of events. It becomes true awareness of being, where there may be no more conditions we have to apply on our own selves. If we place them on ourselves, we would automatically place them on others for there is no choice in this. We must use all moments wisely. It is all we have. We must seize that moment as our true gift.

2. REFLECTION OF JUDGMENT

The second mirror is the Reflection of Judgment. It is the second energy center of the body and it shows us why we judge what we and others do. It corresponds to Smyrna, the second church of Revelations. It also works and agrees with what John had to say in his biblical dissertation. The

Nag Hammadi states this: *"Recognize what is in your sight, and that which is hidden from you will become plain to you"*. If the mirrors are indeed correct, the reflecting entity to recognize is ourselves, for it is in plain sight. The mirror is showing us who we are in any particular moment. We have the opportunity to live the truth or the lie. In the case of the lie, the arrogance of self is blinding us from our reflection. If this occurs, humiliation will undoubtedly challenge that arrogance, as it must. This is what is portrayed in Revelations with the appearance of the second horseman. It also tells us that we are in denial concerning what we are doing and have been doing for most of our lives. When this is identified, we would automatically realize the consequences that certainly await us, based on the judgment we have passed. We will experience that same judgment for ourselves as the next deed entering our lives. Once we have a thought, we must experience it. If we are critical of another, we will have a taste of it for the sake of our own knowledge and expansion. If we learn our lesson, it will be released. If not, then it will grow even greater. We can be assured it will happen because of the denial, blame or excuses we put forth and place on another.

We do not necessarily realize that, when we judge a thing or a person, we must first make a type of comparison between us and the subject, even though nothing can ever match us in any way – for it cannot. Remember that we are truly unique in all respects. Spirit built the individual nature of life for the path of wisdom. When we judge another on beauty or the lack of it, it should automatically let us know that we are not in acceptance of the reflection. If we feel or think we are more attractive, we are placing ourselves above others and we will eventually suffer humiliation because now, we think we are better than they are. If we think they are better looking than us, we should realize that we have issues with our self-worth, based on physical appearance only. This would not happen, had we simply restrained ourselves from making this vain, arrogant comparison that distinctly exposes the difference. Ironically, when we see the true difference, we may become somewhat insecure because of what we see. We perceive the reality that we are not the same, and this may bring forth potential shortcomings within us. If we persist on this behavior for too long a time, it will unavoidably turn into an inferiority complex. We must learn to appreciate all things just for what they are. If we do, we will no longer experience any great degree of separation.

If we see a person being deceptive, it is because we recognize it from our own inner repertoire. The only way that we may see this in another is because it is within us first. We cannot accept this, since we ourselves have probably done it, and we do not wish to be deceived. This implies that we cannot accept ourselves for what we have already perpetrated. This is the reflection of karma, in which we now must see our own denial of self. Thieves cannot trust anyone because they know the wickedness of their actions. They will be overly cautious in words and deeds in order to protect themselves. In most instances, a person having an affair will not be able to trust the person with whom the affair is carried in the long run, merely because they are equally guilty of the act. Everything returns to us, no matter the significance or the lack thereof. It returns because of the reflection we project. It must come back so we can see it and realize it. We call it karma, cause and effect, and we express it by "what goes around comes around". No matter how it is stated, it amounts to the same.

The power of this mirror is one of self-recognition, but we must have the courage to look into it. It will reveal our very own weakness, something we will not generally choose to accept. The real issue lies in the acceptance of what we see in the reflection. What does it tell us about ourselves? How did this image become what it is today? This goes on in our lives continually because we are the ones that set it in motion. No others should be to blame, nor should they be the target for what we tend to deny. This denial will surely bring the matter back in a future relationship so that we may settle it, unless we grasp the message of the present moment. If we do, we will have the occasion to clear old issues through the acceptance of the reflection we face. We will be able to identify our self through what we judge things to be.

If we were to truly work with this mirror, we would lose all forms of judgment, because we would become conscious of the fact that we are the ones being judged. It is self-judgment in the strongest sense. It also masks the insecurities that we have and do not wish to know. It is a form of willful ignorance while placing these weaknesses on someone else's shoulders, a place where they do not belong.

3. REFLECTION OF LOSS

The third mirror is the reflection of loss. It corresponds with the third energy center, the storehouse of power for the difficulties that it may place upon us. This power point may produce the negative or the positive for the next experience. It also is in conjunction with Pergamum, the third Church of Revelations, and the pressures that it may generate, from which we have to work. We find the scales of spiritual justice of the third Seal as well, to create the necessary balance – a balancing of the past deeds that we created.

We will offer an Essene parable in the way of a description. Many times, we may not even be aware of the loss of anything until we move into the next moment. At that point, we attempt to reach back for it, and all it can do is pull us from the present. It may bring us to discover that whatever we try to retrieve is now out of reach. It is too late. The parable from the Nag Hammadi reads as follows: *"The Kingdom of my Father is like a certain woman who was carrying a jar full of meal. While she was walking on a road, still some distance from home, the handle of the jar broke and the meal emptied out behind her on the road. She did not realize it; she had noticed no accident. When she reached her house, she set the jar down and found it empty"*.

Even though the example given in this segment refers to a marriage or a partnership, the principles of loss apply to many things. Of course, our first thought focuses on people, such as spouses, relatives, children, friends and partners. However, we can also have a feeling of loss when it comes to a pet, an automobile, a house or even a business deal. The pain may not be as deep, but nevertheless, it is there. By the same token, this reflection not only covers physical disconnection, but the inevitable final parting – death.

All too often, this mirror places us in a mode of survival with life. We have a regular tendency to give in because we believe in "change yourself to match the loss". We must learn to plot a course through the loss and what it can bring us rather than take away. This loss tends to show us the judgment and the moment, and it may be too difficult for us to endure. We now find ourselves in the survival column of our book of life. Things are unbearable and we begin to react. These events are the perfect opportunity to understand our own nature. We cannot go around, under or over the impacts brought by them. We have to journey through them and detect the inner messages. This way, we will learn about the points of sensitivity that will cause us to run in fear of such episodes. Again, it is a blessing in disguise that we may not ever see, as life's relentless cycles continue to repeat themselves.

If one loses a deep, personal, loving relationship, there will be many "buttons" that will be pushed in the future, because we tend to ignore or deny the reality of the events and our own involvement. Remember the pointing finger... It takes two in this type of situation. If we are open and honest with ourselves and face the truth, it will bring forth a greater level of understanding. This is how a bad experience can become worthwhile. We can discover the very triggers that set it in motion in the first place. If we turn our backs on this mirror, we will create a void that will need filling.

Could that be the root of the word "avoid"? The way we may fill it is with the complementary parts brought on by a new romantic love, those that will match our void only – the truth of the illusion. The deed will certainly repeat itself simply because we have given our power to another person and now we think they are our other half.

Let us look at the concept of the "other half". Does that mean that we are not complete in the first place? If we let it, it will show us the inner parts we have left behind on the trail of life. We can then gather the pieces that were lost and become more complete than ever. Once we are whole again, we can be happy and secure in what we feel. We can move into another relationship where there are no strings that would have to be cut at a later time. It will offer true freedom of the expression of self because of the gained knowledge of same. It is not to say that the hurts are not there. They are, but we now understand and accept them for what they were – not for what they are. They no longer have any power over us.

4. REFLECTION OF FORGOTTEN LOVE

By now, you may have noticed that these mirrors become more subtle in how we must handle them and ourselves as they appear before us. We have reached the heart of the body or the balance point as related biblically. In Revelations, it is the Church of Thyatira. From here on, the mirrors may also interact with each other and become more complicated. We presented this difficulty in Part 1, Chapter 8 of the book. We now encounter a multiple of inner events we must absorb if we are to remove our internal points of sensitivity, as we move into the fourth Essene mirror, the reflection of our most forgotten love. It is portrayed in the Nag Hammadi as: *"That which you have will save you, if you bring it forth from yourselves"*. These are truly very wise words.

Of the seven mirrors, this might very well be the most powerful, because what we may possess will undoubtedly be taken away if it is built or acquired on falsehood. This is why most of us have lost a very significant love of our life. Having ignored our true reflection in the mirrors of physical life, we have blamed that love and we have lost it. Based on our normal behavior, it is easy to imagine that we did not see the reality of the reflections offered in the relationship we have before us in the moment, what it has to show us of ourselves, what we do to others. If ignored, this mirror can cause all sorts of behavioral patterns and different forms of addictions. We will use these addictions – we think – to fill the self-inflicted voids, or cover the grief we more than likely brought upon ourselves. We are under an absolute illusion, and the masks will grow if we suffer the addictions of our compulsive nature. We are still working on self-denial of the truth and we will not see the reflection if we are on this type of path. We hide it from plain sight. The pain will become more ensconced and will surface at a later time, when we take another look at the reflection offered. If we have chosen this course, we must wait in anticipation of its return for the exposure and acceptance of self.

When we meet a new person, we should use the first mirror of the moment and ask ourselves this question: What is in this person that I may have lost along the way? We would all be quite surprised at the variety of answers we would reluctantly hear. Some may bring the pain of memory which we can either clear or bury once again out of fear. If we use the first mirror, we will not bring the same events back into our lives. It would only increase the level of inner pain that we are attempting to avoid. We must do this in truth. It would be unwise to fill our void with deceit or untruth. The cycle stands a good chance of repeating the original loss we have not fully cleared or accepted as our own responsibility.

All things do return to their creator. The Master told us that whatever we mete will be returned to us ten times greater. This mirror is to help us realize that those are not just words. If it is accepted, we may move to a higher understanding of life. If not, we will return to the road most traveled. We perceive this as the easy way and we mistakenly believe that some events cannot happen again. Unfortunately, it most certainly will unless the parts we once lost are recovered and returned to their original places within us. They are ours, and when we have the pleasure of having all of them on board, we have a feeling of wholeness. These missing parts can even generate an obsession or a compulsion within our natures. That being the case, we experience the opposite of what we seek. The physical is once again in control of us, negating whatever lessons we may have had with the mirrors of life.

In reality, we never have anything. We only think and believe that we do. This affects our relationships on a daily basis. We believe we have these liaisons, then we tend to ignore the great lessons they can teach us as the moments advance. We share time and experiences only. We share what we feel and think of our lives. If we live the lie, it is obviously what we have to offer, but the truth will surely come upon us at some time. This may come at the end, when we would not have the time to correct anything. If we choose the truth or the lie, either of those will be the only thing it will bring to us in return. We will enjoy the true reality, or we will suffer incredible levels of deception in which we can barely discern the truth. The path of deception always makes the truth of error much more difficult to realize. Eventually, we all will turn it over at some point in time, one way or the other. Hopefully, we will turn it over until we can all attain the higher levels life has to offer, so we can use them for greater, more purposeful endeavors.

5. REFLECTIONS OF THE CREATOR

We are now gazing into the fifth mirror of the Essenes. The creator may be our father or our mother, whom we consider our physical creator, along with the infinite. This is the fifth chakra or energy center of the body, where we find the harmony or disharmony in expression of self. It also equates to the fifth Church of Sardis, as presented by John in Revelations. The point of true well-balanced expression will arise from our inner harmony of being, only if we live in the truth of life rather than deceit. The deceit will create disharmony. Both will have the associated impacts outlined in this and the biblical texts we have been reading.

We offer another parable adapted from the Nag Hammadi: *"Whoever does not hate his father and mother as I do cannot become a disciple to me. And whoever does not love his father and mother as I do cannot become a disciple to me. For my mother gave me falsehood, but my true mother gave me life"*. This is the perfect example of a Zen "Kuan". They offer those riddles for deep inner reflections of self and of life. It seems that the parable is unthinkable on the surface, but it carries many thoughts at the same time for our own meditation. We may hate our mother and father, still we may invent a variety of reasons. All of those are a façade, or illusions. We should hate no one for any given reason. If we think in that fashion, nothing will be learned. Hate is the opposite of love and will have its repercussions which will come in the form of lessons about unconditional nature.

Why is this parable worded in such a way, especially in light of the statement made at the end of the allegory? It is about a willingness to let go of what we believe is important to us, to wit, the people that are the closest to us. They may stand in the way of the spiritual attainment that we seek without realizing it. It is suggested to us so that we may establish a true spiritual value system for life. We believe we have the same reverberating frequency as the rest of the family. Life being energy based, we seek harmony with its vibration, or a quality that matches. It must be said that all things will have a resonance, even the lie. The old adage is: "birds of a feather flock together" — there is no other way around this. We are attracted by that with which we believe we resonate, even to fill a void.

In many cases, family relationships ultimately create the opposite of what we were born to have. They do this inadvertently by imposing upon us a path that may be contrary to the one we choose. Our inner inhibitions grow from these relationships while we are still very young. As children, we did not have the defensive or argumentative tools, hence we accepted whatever the guidelines were. In our innocence, we did not know the difference. Once we are able to determine the difference, there are regrets or resentment, and so it goes.

On the surface, these disparities seem to balance out as we get older. Do they really? These childhood unwanted guidelines are ingrained and give us our reactions to people and situations. The fifth mirror is designed to show us where our personal inner disharmonies lie. At the same time, it may generate a tremendous dissonance to what we consider significant within us – our self-worth.

These reflections may hurt. Most of us do not get past this particular mirror because we will not settle old issues out of fear or blame. That is the wrong approach. Blame will not resolve anything since it is nothing but a finger-pointing escape. We must recognize what the reflection shows us and learn from it, in order to avoid the fate of Lot's wife. Blame will not bring our reactions to a firm and final resolution. We must accept what has been done and accept the responsibility, wherever it may lie. Once we endorse this behavior, we will no longer load anything on the shoulders of others.

This mirror advises us to be aware of that to which we hold on and why we give it such importance. It may cause us to stumble or divert us from the path we choose to travel, thereby keeping us from our goal. Our true purpose is to establish a relationship with our spiritual part from which sprung life. The last part of the parable informs us that our natural mothers gave us physical birth only. That is the falsehood, when compared to the spiritual aspect that gave us the eternal life of being. It tells us that we should not ignore this simple fact, while treating all of life with great reverence and appreciation.

Family relationships were mentioned in Matthew 12:46-50 by the Master Himself, when His family was outside the temple and wanted to see Him. In essence, He acknowledged His mother and siblings, but He pointed out that all those around Him were also His family. He was letting us know that we are all family, and that we should choose no one above another, in order to avoid favoritism. This is not easy to do. We are not saying that relatives are not important, because they are, but so are all people and things around us. We are not advising against having a special relationship with one person either. However, if we make it more important than ourselves, it will control us. We will not be able to express who we are freely. The truth is that each individual is the most important person in the world. If we were to see life this way, it would be very humbling because this cannot be done in arrogance. We would see the face of Spirit: us.

This mirror also reflects our own ego nature, the falsehoods we have established through personal relationships. We do not imply that all relationships suffer the same fate, but the majority of them do, especially those of our younger days. As we grow older, our patterns are set by the events of childhood. This reflection becomes invaluable as a tool to assist in the establishment of the defensive nature of the ego, the damage it may do to us and to others we know. We can correct this by understanding the reasons justifying our actions in life.

6. REFLECTIONS INTO DARKNESS

The sixth Essene mirror of life corresponds to the sixth center of the body. In Revelations, it is the one that suggests we must lose ourselves to gain who we truly are, and to help us further in the relationship we have with spirit and the love of life. This is the Church of Philadelphia, the seat of the higher intuitive nature of being, the place where we shed the illusionary importance of the material world and the last of old significance. The Essenes offer another parable to describe this reflection: *"All are born and must walk in the two spirits that the 'One' has created in man, the spirit of light and the spirit of darkness"*. This particular deep thought can be taken many ways, as all metaphysical statements can do. The first is that of understanding, represented by the light. The second would be the darkness, depicting the lack of comprehension. This may also be traced back to the Garden of Eden, the forbidden fruit and the earthly discovery of good and evil. Allow us to expand on this most important mirror, as it is the last bastion before we can reach attainment, thus giving us the understanding of internal interactions and the purpose of relationships with all that life has to offer us.

This reflection is the mirror of fears that must be addressed. It is where we may no longer hold our preconceived notions of life. Now we must prepare ourselves for direct higher communion and communication with our common and individual spirit. Here, we must know and understand completely the true nature of the concept guiding total unconditional love, without the obstructing effects of our prideful ego. Our soul will become entirely exposed for spirit to view. It is the place of judicious choice, knowing what we will choose and why. We will clearly see the outcome and effects of all the choices we have formulated, in advance of the decision. This opportunity will be heaven or hell in one stroke.

It is the point of the crucifixion of the flesh, because now, anything to which we held on tightly will be released, willingly or otherwise. In all the ancient texts ever written, this has been called the "dark night of the soul". It has been described in a variety of ways. In the Christian Bible, it is the sixth horseman. One merely needs to read the appropriate segment of Revelations, the letters to the Church of Philadelphia and the sounding of the sixth trumpet. We have covered these subjects in Part 1, Chapter 8 of this work, and there is a distinct, direct correlation with the reflection of darkness. The dark night is really the balancing effect of all past deeds we have inflicted upon our very own being. We experience it more often than we think, as a safety valve for true spiritual release, each time we give of ourselves to spirit.

The sixth reflection is our opportunity to affirm or deny all of life for ourselves. Truth or deception is the choice. The mirror is to protect the higher aspects from the lower carnal nature of humanity. Of course, it is to protect humanity from itself as well.

In his book "Walking Between the Worlds", from which we have borrowed some of this information, **Mr. Greg Braden** gives us a very clear definition of the "dark night of the soul": *"Your 'Dark Night of the Soul' is a time, as well as an experience in life, wherein you may be drawn into a situation or circumstance representing, what appears to you, to be your worst fear. To experience the Dark Night of the Soul is to live the Mystery of the Fifth Essene Mirror of Relationship: Your Quest into Darkness"*. His corollary is as educational as his definition. It reads: *"You are capable of entering a 'Dark Night of the Soul' only when you have amassed all of the emotional tools necessary to see you through your experience, intact and with grace"*. It is indeed what it can bring. Further, it may not be for just one night. It can last over an extended period of time, due to the tools we have to use or not use. This relies strictly on our personal choice. It is not an occurrence that we can avoid, but it is never given if we do not have the proper tools with which we can cope. Some simply choose not to use whatever they have available. In that case, the dark night will reappear at a later time, but this time, greater than before.

We are nearing the end of a very long cycle of life. At this present moment, there are numerous signs that indicate consequential future events. As a civilization caught in the triviality of materialism, we are refusing to look at the results of our actions. It would not cost anything to just look around us and see the existing truth. Unfortunately, we are relying on all of our technological advances and not our sense system. This sixth mirror is to awaken us to the reality of the cause and effects of life. We all have much to balance out before this cycle comes to a close. On the other hand, the cycle will end whether we choose to achieve that balance or not. It is a repeat of our own unending circle of life, and it can be found in all texts available on the subject of spirit. This period will bring a dark night to all of humanity – not just the few. It will come in the blink of an eye, to address the truth of all life, to bring forth a much higher realization to mass consciousness.

7. THE REFLECTION OF COMPASSION

This is the last of the seven Essene mirrors of relationship. True compassion has no judgment attached to it. It is one of the greatest acts we can perform. It works in conjunction with the seventh energy center of the body, the crown chakra that illumined the head of the Master and all Masters throughout time. It is Revelations' Church of Laodicea and its biblical description matches the Essene version. We draw again from the Nag Hammadi Library: *"Show to me the stone which the builders have rejected. That one is the cornerstone"*. You will find that Jesus spoke the same words, as reported in Matthew 21:42 and Mark 12:10. The cornerstone is the most important anchor in the construction business, and we are talking about the construction of self. As we can see, the Master learned this from the Essenes. It was one of the biblical quotes attributed to Him. The cornerstone is that of the science of compassion for self and all that contains life. It is not sorrowful feelings, which is what we generally offer. In its truest sense, compassion is realization of events devoid of judgment. This has to be the case, no matter what the devastation may be. It is valid if only for the purpose of clarity, so that we may be of value to the person or persons involved directly with the events. Compassion is not about being sorry. After all, the events may have been self-inflicted as another step toward attainment. Being sorry could hold those we want to help from the value contained in the intended lessons. It will also bring us down to their level, when we should lift them to ours, by using the energies of the higher levels of wisdom, the crown of knowledge.

We must understand that we are not the experience, but rather the result of such. The events give us the opportunity to determine how we choose to see the experience, as well as the knowledge it will bring us. They are to assist us in the appreciation of our own being because of the truth within them. Again, we return to the concept of truth and lie, for either one of these will ultimately teach us all we need to know. If the concept of the oppositions in life is truth, then we must have a taste of both sides, so that we may choose the more meaningful and beneficial aspect of these experiences.

The last mirror encompasses all the attributes of compassion, the unconditional aspect to live and to life. This is the true builder of character, the cornerstone of being. It is the truth of love that we are to share with life, the truth of being in all things. This is the reflection mentioned by Paul in Corinthians: behold the face of Spirit. It is the innocent truth of loving without conditions because we now allow this for ourselves. We are innocent, for we do not yet realize the truth of life. How can we, when we do not see through the undistorted truth? We carry too many burdens with us, because of the unforgiving nature we all carry so selfishly.

We see life as very unforgiving because we do not cherish each and every moment we chose to have. The reason is that we do not recognize the view in the mirror's reflection. We do not accept that we are the reflection. This is pure denial, no matter how we choose to look at it. We have become closed to all things and are not in harmony with ourselves, much less with life. We are not living the spiritual concept offered to us by Spirit. The time is near, however, when what is in our hearts will come forth. If it is not love without conditions, we will find that we have nothing of substance at all to offer life. We will also face the deceptions we carry within us and may have for a long time. In other words, we have not grown the way we believe we have.

We are to give all that we are, and accept what we give as the truth of our being. Even if the truth is the lie itself, it will be recognized as such and will then be released. Once this occurs, we will no longer possess or live the deceit. What we know as choice will disappear forever, for there will be only one way to see or do anything. We will no longer have the levels of confusion we once had. Under these premises, there would be no concept of evil in this world. It would be eradicated from within each of us.

This is now taking place with one human at a time. To quote again the words of **Greg Braden**: *"Once you know the possibilities, those possibilities become a part of you. Once you have seen them, you cannot un-see them......Our relationships are not separate from our spiritual evolution. Our relationships are our spiritual evolution".* We may understand now why so many of them have become so difficult, almost intolerable. They will present us with the greatest opportunities for growth – if we do not run and hide from them. We must learn to stand to and with the most severe tests offered, even to the absolute point of crucifixion of being, through the Dark Night of the Soul. There must be a cleansing of all deeds. In the end, to lose one's old self is truly the very best gift one can receive. The gift is the true joy of self-recognition as a spiritual human, alive and well on this wonderful planet, sharing the experiences all of life has for us to use with infinite pleasure.

All of us search for the supreme happiness. We may never find it or share it until we have confronted our very own nature, our deceptions, our lies, that which we have taken for granted, all things we have abused and misused. Our house must be thoroughly cleaned and put in order for the real physical and spiritual union to take place. If we can accomplish that, we have happiness in the truth of being, that of a very complete self.

As simply as it can be written, this is the purpose of the seven Essene mirrors of relationship. It addresses all issues in the physical aspect of the Holy Trinity. It covers all material things in life. If we take the time to see our reflection in the mirror of life, we may become very accomplished humans in spiritual form. There is no value to be gained if we remain blind to the reflection. The journey of truth pertaining to our material nature is the most difficult part of the path to knowledge, simply because we cannot escape ourselves. We may have tried on many occasions, but it does not work. We may have attempted to fill the voids but to no avail. However, if we paid attention, we have come to know ourselves. We should use these mirrors wisely as a tool for attainment and we will improve in grace and humility, practicing unconditional love in all respects.

THE SEVEN VIRTUES

We have arrived at the seven virtues of this life. We will discuss how they can improve and accentuate our inner reflections of being. Let us then enter the world of mind and emotion, part of the Trinity of wholeness.

If we have traveled through the mirrors and understand their reflections, this part will be somewhat easier to follow, since we now know the physical implications of self, the actions and reactions that have originated from us. We now begin the more delicate portion of the journey. It will be the beginning of the tests that we must all take if we have chosen this path, to give us depth and great spiritual character. When we successfully complete these, we will attain incredible strength of being because of the depth we have gained. These seven virtues are also in alignment with the seven energy centers of the body, to help in the clearing process. They will be presented in the same sequence as the rest, beginning with temptation in the first or root chakra, to the crown, as the voice of illumination and wisdom.

TEMPTATION

In all of its definitions, it is difficult to imagine temptation being a virtue. What is truly sought is its opposite or a resistance thereto. No temptation will befall the person who understands its lessons. It is something that we must overcome with the literal world so that it has no hold upon us. It has been said that absolute power corrupts absolutely. This is the rational reason why it is considered the first virtue that we must face in life. The biblical texts will tell us that even the Master was tested several times on this very subject. We must also remember Adam and Eve and the serpent in the Garden of Eden, and the temptations offered therein. In fact, to this day and for 2000 years, people everywhere have been reminded by the Master Himself, within the daily prayer He suggested. In Matthew 6:13, does it not say: *"...and lead us not into temptation..."*? Could it be that our civilization is long on words, but short on action?

The creator gave us temptation so that it could craft our spiritual knowledge. It was not given as a pit in which we were meant to fall. It was conceived to learn about compulsive nature, so we can repel it and be free of it. It seems that we keep on falling into it constantly... This virtue is to help in overcoming the material world. As the thinking specie of this planet, it is apparent that we have not achieved this goal to any great degree, let alone on the individual level.

The teachers of the Far East say that in life, we should desire nothing. Desires are like any seeds we sow. They grow. We then become insidiously tempted to carry them out, no matter what they may be. They can be materialized from a positive or negative point. Either way, they will have their effects on our karma. Consequently, these will need to be rectified through our actions. The more ingrained these desires become, the greater the temptation that we must overcome in order to continue the journey toward our very own soul.

This is why, on the surface, temptation may appear not to be a virtue. It is, however, through its potential as a teaching tool, and how we can organize our priorities in life. It is about the strength of the law governing cause and effects. Of all laws, nothing escapes this one. Temptation is the creator of self-division unless thoroughly understood. It keeps us from the proper use of truth. It is a master of illusions, unless we accept that it is there for us to learn and grow rather than succumb to it and become enslaved by it.

It is there to reveal the areas of weakness that lead us off the spiritual path that is in front of us. It guides us away from the very loves that we so much appreciate. Temptations distract us from the pleasantries of life into delusions that we do not recognize – until it is too late. When we learn why we are experiencing temptation, we will realize the void we are attempting to fill. Once that is done, it will decrease in strength until we are no longer affected by the carnal nature of the desire. Henceforth, nothing will have a further hold and our experience will deepen, with a greater learning ability. Temptation is truly a gift in disguise for what it reveals and the character building it possesses. We must be passive with it. If we resist, the temptation will surely grow and become even stronger.

When the Creator asked for the seven seals to the Book of Life to be opened, everyone fought and warred against it – to no avail. Then entered the lamb, the symbol of gentleness and humility. The first seal was opened. We must take this approach with the temptations of life because we cannot afford to have them overwhelm our own selves. Giving in to them is quite different than learning why they are there, in that moment. If we yield, they will have us running and not enjoying the higher aspects, the greatest joy that we can all have: the wisdom of life.

Temptation is to be used to overcome the first energy center of the body. As mentioned before, this clears and cleans the illusions we face each and every day in our lives. We must be humble and loving and we must not resist, but rather allow for temptations, because they will be there in all respects. We must use them as a tool for the higher consciousness, not as a weapon against ourselves. As a weapon, it will undoubtedly win, but then, it may also turn into a weapon to test our self-worth. It may help us in what we really think of ourselves as individuals, as well as fill, in some way, the empty spaces we have not yet learned to fill.

SINCERITY

The second virtue brings us back to the truth or the denial of self. The Webster Dictionary tells us that sincerity is being free of dissimulation and adulteration, free from hypocrisy, and having genuineness and an honest mind. Those are rather large shoes to fill. Do any of us understand and accept the concept of sincerity? If we did, the world would be a much different place than what it has become. This is the second energy center of the body, as we move up the ladder of life toward wisdom. Sincerity stems from truly knowing ourselves, all the way to the deepest part of our being. If we offer this virtue to the outer world through our actions, it will be the only thing that returns to us. We must explore the difficulties in being sincere from our own personal perspective. So far, our fears of the past have kept us from this level of honesty.

Since it begins with us, we must be sincere with ourselves. In this period of introspection, we must insure that our scrutiny is steeped in the heart of truth, and we must do this at all costs. This means that we must observe the laws of our inner genuineness and find our openness for life, with great joy and happiness, knowing no harm will come to us on the way. When we speak with our hearts, we are normally sincere, and we will see the same in others, but most importantly, we will see various situations in a different light. That is the beauty of speaking the higher truth. We realize in those moments that we should not tear down another for our own insecurities. If we mistakenly do so, we will find ourselves immerged in the delusion that we understand all things, that we are above others. On the other hand, if we are open, there are no preconceived notions, and we will not tear another down.

Sincerity is the opposite of deceit. If and whenever we use deception, it will be used for self-serving reasons, and deceit hurts many people no matter how it is used. What purpose does it really serve in life? Sincerity is honesty with great heartfelt respect. Deception is the expression of the lie that comes from the mind of the human – not the heart of truth. When we speak and act from the heart, we honor the message of the Master. When He said that nothing was above the law, that is what He meant.

Anytime we deceive, we justify the words or acts by thinking that they are a minor or major way to protect the other person's feelings. In the long run, the deception will hurt, even if the protection theory was well intended. The act itself is actually very hypocritical – even of one's own self – because we merely mislead ourselves and no one else, even under the guise of protecting another. In reality, we are protecting ourselves from the truth, or for fear of reprisal, or to avoid the hurt. When we deceive, we obviously have learned nothing about truth, whether it is a white lie or a large one. This aspect is not quantitative. It is qualitative. What good quality can you find in the act of deception? It is doubtful that you will find one.

Sometimes we refrain from making sincere statements because we do not want to hurt other persons' feelings. Why do we not let them decide? Whatever gave us the right to choose for them? Could it be our own insecure ego? Are we hiding some deep dark secret, or are we trying to boost our physical image? Whatever is said or done must be a part of their own experience. Sincerity will never interfere in this, simply because it is the truth. All of us would like to believe that everyone is indeed honest with us in words and deeds. If we are receptive and opened, we may come to realize that there are certain differences and nuances in presentations, but once accepted, they will not sting as much. We accept their insecurities and will not judge them. We will know this comes from their past hurts and will not condemn them. In fact, it may even help them heal these hurts. Sincerity in a person comes into play as a great inner resolve of the truth of things. It is not only refreshing and beneficial for ourselves, but for others as well. Honest beings operate from the greatest of strength: the true nature of the self. They are able to behave in that manner because all other burdens have been cleared from them, and their inner truth shines as the city on the hill. The inner light of knowledge glows for all to see, without the necessity of becoming a harlot to life. There is no longer a need to sell the soul in exchange for petty material possessions or an insignificant status symbol.

JUSTICE

Once again, the Webster Dictionary informs us that "justice" is the maintenance or administration of what is just, especially by the impartial adjustment of conflicting claims or the assignment of merited rewards or punishment – to be just, impartial or fair – conformity to truth, fact or reason. Justice is generally connected to laws, and in Matthew 5:18, the Master tells us: *"For verily I say unto you, Till heaven and earth pass, one jot or one tittle shall in no wise pass from the law, till all be fulfilled"*. It could be concluded that we, as human beings desiring to become spiritual and reaching for the higher aspect of the soul, would be wise to abide by such laws by behaving justly, impartially or fairly.

For the most part, we feel that this upward growth becomes too difficult. It is actually very simple and becomes more so as we grow. Moreover, is it not stated in the Bible that we must persevere to the end? Perhaps the reader can understand now the veracity of this statement. We are confronting many different attributes of self and life. We have progressed this far on this arduous journey and we may have become weary because of the anticipated hardships. We cannot afford to give up. At least we must know that the battle to overcome the carnal mind is over. Hopefully, the lessons of the seven Essene mirrors have been absorbed. The rest of the path is merely observational and knowing exactly how far we have come. As we put one foot in front of the other, we are using all the tools offered by Spirit simultaneously. It is true, because all these teaching aids automatically work together.

Justice is the third virtue. In the Book of Revelations, it is the third horseman that rides forth and carries the scales in his hand. The subject of balance comes to mind again. At the same time, we cannot forget the law of retribution – or karma – that will inexorably reappear now or later, and we know that it is indeed impartial. Based on these premises, we must learn not to strike back at those who may have acted unjustly or even violently toward us, at least in our estimation. The earthly enforcement of human laws can very well adjust whatever infraction may have been committed. Our spiritual health and growth, however, dictates that we leave the perpetrator to his/her own fate, without judgment or condemnation on our part. This behavior confirms our belief in the reflection of compassion.

It is not difficult to stay within the boundaries of justice. If we have followed the path assiduously, the ego has been put to bed and will no longer interfere with any aspect of the nature of life. When we stand in the radiance of love for all things, we no longer have the retributive temptations we had in the past. As a result, we have shed the need to retaliate just to prove a point. We must understand that words and deeds directed against us may be the result of our own verbiage or actions. In that case, turning the other cheek is not so much out of line, is it? Even if it is not of our own doing, we have learned that there is little we can do to prevent all events from happening. We cannot, nor should we control others. We must therefore learn to accept whatever comes our way as another lesson on our path to wisdom. In grace, and justly, we let others do what they wish, because we now fully understand the laws of spirit. What they do, they do unto themselves, and it will be duly noted in their book of life. We must do nothing. The laws of the land will handle the physical side, and Spirit will most certainly take care of the rest. Even though we may find this unjust toward ourselves in the physical aspect, it is a matter of balance and justice for all concerned. Our path is now cleared, and we can complete the unconditional nature of life. We are totally free of all the bonds that held us in place.

The excursion into spirituality is not over yet. The climb, even though steeper, becomes easier. We have created a sensible balance and our inner strength will be greater for it, on the continued journey through life. We will now begin to face varied situations with greater ease. We are slowly reaching the point of self purification in a knowing, loving sense of compassion.

FAITH

Faith is the belief, the trust in and loyalty to Spirit and to the higher aspects of life. It is a firm belief in something for which there is no physical tangibility. It is a strong word, a strong feeling that lies in the heart of every human, and it is located in the fourth energy center, where we also find the seat of the ego. The Master told His disciples that faith can move mountains (Matthew 17:20). It is indeed very influential, and it always guides our footsteps in the right direction, in the Spirit's hand. In John 3:8, Jesus said: *"The wind bloweth where it listeth, and thou hearest the sound thereof, but canst not tell whence it cometh, and whither it goeth: so is every one that is born of the Spirit"*. This could be a description of our own spirit, for there are times when we have no idea as to where we are going. Without absolute faith in life, it would be easy to be lost. It would behoove us, then, to fully accept whatever comes our way, because it is offered for the good of all. Faith is asking Spirit for guidance on our more than likely self-inflicted predicaments. It is also knowing how and when to silence the ego while waiting for the answer. That can be called a true leap of faith, the highest form of trust available. We must learn how the ego operates within ourselves, and the adverse effects it brings to our lives. It keeps us away from true faith while creating nothing but fears.

Faith is demonstrating absolute trust in everything spiritual and in nature's laws. As a result, we will be much more open to life and whatever it may hold for us. We must have the faith of the mustard seed (Luke 17:6) to spring forth new life, to expand in any direction we choose in our present and future endeavors. To those of great faith, all things will be given, no matter what form it will take. This is so because there are no more expectations to life on any level.

To arrive at this height of enlightenment, we know that there will be tests on just how much faith we have. When they come, we are not to force anything. If we do, it will merely prove that we are not ready, that we have no real faith. To demonstrate our belief, it is best to simply allow the situation to take place without our interference. It is knowing that the proper guidance will arrive when it is time, and not before. Under certain circumstances, we will find that it is not easy, because the ego wants to take its own action. That is why we must have the faith of that tiny mustard seed and wait patiently. The right direction will undoubtedly appear. We do not seem to be successful in this test because we believe we know what is best and will have a tendency to get in the way. We should let go of all preconceived notions and openly trust what is before us in that moment. Acting in this fashion, we can only gain in wisdom and patience – and pass the test.

Adversity is no longer on our path. Our constant questions are not as frequent as they were. We have complete faith and acceptance in ourselves because of the close liaison we have with Spirit. This union encompasses all the facets of our relationships with life. There will not be any more internal divisions or separation, because all is one within us. It is the end of the duality we previously endured.

Our faith allows spirit to travel before us, as the Ark of Covenant portrays. It will protect us at all times and warn us of any deceptions that are about to befall us on this journey of life. With faith in our heart, all relationships become a thing of wonder. They will be free of all pain and bonds that held us before. The guiding light is the willingness to test it out for ourselves, to know it is there. Faith is completely devoid of conditions. It is the motivation to be open, knowing that everything is as it is supposed to be. It is a simple matter of learning about higher aspects, nothing more. It is a state wherein we totally accept situations just as they are, without fears, realizing that they happen for our best spiritual interest, including others that may be involved. It is also the path of least resistance. We now know the value of unconditional acceptance.

SILENCE

In his book "Moral Sayings" (1ˢᵗ C., B.C.), **Publilius Syrus** said: *"I have often regretted my speech, never my silence"*. The Master said to the multitudes: *"Not that which goeth into the mouth defileth a man; but that which cometh out of the mouth, this defileth a man"* (Matthew 15:11). Silence is the true voice of spiritual communication. It is in the fifth energy center as presented in St. John's Revelations and the Essene mirrors of relationship. Silence is the art of knowing when to speak. It allows for spirit to guide what is said when the time comes. In that respect, the Good Teacher told us not to fear, because what we need to say and do will be given us in the appropriate moment. So advised, we will be operating from a much higher level, in a wise and harmonious way. It will not be from us, but it will be for us and all those concerned.

Silence is very difficult to observe, especially in a world filled with the noise of life. Above all things, we all wish to be heard, and when we are, we should speak and act in a well-balanced, loving way. We should add that in any situation, what we say should be without opinion and free of judgment. That alone requires a healthy dose of self-control and self-discipline. By expressing judgments, we can adversely block an otherwise impartial focus. They are too personal for a person of spiritual integrity and should not appear under any circumstance. Instead, we must communicate in the truth of loving words, with the utmost respect accorded the listener. Our speech and actions will show harmony or discord from an inner point of view that others will certainly detect. If we expect a just and proper return, we must speak only truth.

That is harmony in action, but we cannot forget that truth can also become a shocking offense, even when wrapped in considerate diplomacy. It is when the silent guiding of Spirit can be invaluable. If we do not intend to hurt, silence is sometimes the answer. Anything short of this is merely deception of the truth that will create disharmony for all. We should keep in mind that all things in our heart will be made known. We may hide nothing of what we feel. Hence, when we speak from the heart, we express our feelings. This is an area that cannot harbor any form of judgment. If it does, it will darken our image. The heart does not judge. Our mental side does this very well on its own.

Having learned about the higher nature of love, we find ourselves in moments of selflessness, with the ability to share our words of wisdom in truth and in a very simple way for the sake of collective happiness. Wisdom is acquired by the experiences we encounter along the way and, as other virtues, it should be absolutely free of judgment and opinions. Of course, this depends on how we have chosen to interpret the events. If we see them in a positive light, it will enhance harmony. If our approach is negative, we can expect disharmony. It is our choice, and whatever it may be, either of the two is a learning tool. The positive side has a bonus, since we can reach higher levels of wisdom to share.

Silence and being still is the opportunity for spirit to share the truth with each of us. Subsequently, we can share these moments with others, if we so choose. The feelings we have will never deceive us, yet the mask of the egoistic mind will. This is why we see so much deception going on around us at any time. The heart also will not deceive another, but again, the masks of the mind will. It comes out of the words we use to express ourselves to others. We have no other choice in the matter. We speak what we are. If we deceive ourselves, normally an action of the ego, we will certainly do the same to others. Sadly, we may not realize this until after the fact. This is the natural law of things, karma in action. When we activate our fifth energy center, we may speak only truth and harmony from the heart.

Physical silence, or the voluntary restraint of sounds, can be quite effective in our everyday lives. Its most important form, however, is the inner silence. It is the stillness of the mind. It is a step toward the elimination of the chattering monkeys mentioned by the Buddha. We have minds that are entirely too active, much more than necessary. We must shake the monkeys from the tree, to tidy the path for clear and calm thoughts, no matter what may take place around us. Clarity of self is the only way we can accomplish this, by releasing all negative thoughts and genuinely accepting who and what we are. The latter will result from filling the voids within us with our own missing pieces, rather than the pieces others attempt to give us. Our contemporaries may do this under the guise of making us happy. It is done with good intentions, but ultimately it will not work simply because we are missing the pieces, not the alleged donors.

As we quietly meditate in the silence of our mind, we realize that the guides to accomplishment derive from any turmoil we may have. This is really the personal path of attainment we have outlined for ourselves, and we could look upon the inner tumult as the opportunity for a blessing. If we find the cause, we have gained understanding and clarity. Of course, this stands true when we follow the course of our own confusion rather than someone else's. We must learn its reason for existing and whence it came. If we do this, we find the missing pieces through the awareness we have in the moment. We know why the inner buttons have been pushed. Once we arrive at the answers, our inner self will be calm in the mental sense. It will become still, free of burdens. We have achieved the purest of mental clarity, the innocence of the child. We stand in wonder of all things before us. The seas of our mind have become calm upon our inner command to be silent.

SOLITUDE

In "Discourses" (2ⁿᵈ C.), **Epictetus** tells us: *"When you have shut your doors and darkened your room, remember, never to say that you are alone; for you are not alone, but God is within, and your genius is within".* We now reenter the sixth energy center, or Revelations' sixth Church of Philadelphia. This time, we have a greater level of experience to handle what it may bring us. We have the opportunity to become very centered in life and the occurrences associated with personal and general liaisons or varied day-to-day events. We are starting to become aware that, to a very high degree, relationships are not personal, because they carry events with them that happen to be learning tools in all respects. We should consider these events only as the illumination of our growing understanding. It allows us to be the true observers of all actions, and in the same breath, it should make us detect the fact that we have become separated from others. We are on the outside, looking in. We see the situation only – which carries no blame – and not the person involved. There is no reason to point at another. We just observe to find our answer. It confirms the principle that we are unique, and at first it will be an extremely lonely affair. Initially, it may not seem to be a pleasant experience, but we will soon learn that Spirit is there for us – not a human. It will provide whatever assistance is needed. We will recognize that we have used others as a crutch in the past, therefore we have never stood on our own before. We have always been influenced by others but now, having advanced this far on the spiritual path, we must learn to rely on the unseen, on the inner guiding voice of Spirit. Feeling apart from others is not easy, and we must absorb the knowledge of that which is behind all things. We have reached the point where we no longer need a crutch. We will stand on our own and will feel solitude, even in the middle of a crowd.

We must return to the dark night of the soul because that is the test of our character, the test of our mental-emotional side. It is not the physical as we discussed, but it does occur at the same time. Do we have a strong will? Are we focused? Have we truly adopted the virtues of life? Have we taken heed of the daily lessons of self-worth with which we travel? If we do not meet or exceed the standards, we will continue to shed the build-up of illusions until we do. This dark night is not separate from the mirrors. It is the same. We have learned that it comes to all three aspects of the trinity of being. It will happen simultaneously with the mirrors, the seven virtues and the seven branches, on all levels of self. Nothing may be spared or ignored in the spiritual journey we have undertaken. Nothing is above the law. We must also realize that we will not really have a choice. It will come as a thief in the night. It is spiritually induced for our growth, and whether we are willing or not, it will come. Spirit is ready for us to have the experience. It knows that we have the tools to see it through. All the ancient texts verify that we are subjected to this for the benefit of our spiritual growth.

Being aware and forewarned, we know that the dark night is upon us. It is wiser for us to submit to this higher will. If we rebel against it or ignore it, it will become increasingly stronger. We must allow spirit to carry us through this part of the journey. It must be done in love, faith and openness. In the end, we travel alone through the adventures of life, especially in the dark night. We will be under the impression that no one understands the hardships of our chosen path and to a point, that is true. How can they? After all, it is not their experience – it is ours.

We are now working on the misconceptions of the mind for the final removal of all masks, in order to receive the ultimate mantle of truth. Spirit is guiding us toward that goal, and most of us will resist or deny because of fear. It may be painful. Spirit is very patient. It has all eternity to wait – we do not. When it is upon us, we should travel in grace, and love will assist us along the way, a love in the sense of non-arrogant, wholeness of self. This is what the journey is about. If we have learned this, true self-esteem will come forth from the center of us, from the very core of our being. We will arrive at the point of utmost confidence, for we know that we may really stand alone, in union with Spirit, able to face all things. Even though we may live in urban surroundings, among neighbors and crowds, we will be comfortable and at peace in our spiritual solitude, able to help ourselves and others. We have the real wisdom of life at our fingertips, the realization of the oneness of all things. We are all things and the reason all things are in existence. We have dominion above all else, the original promise given to us by Spirit in the Book of Genesis.

GRACE

According to Webster, this virtue covers "unmerited divine assistance given man for his regeneration or sanctification", or "a state of sanctification enjoyed through divine grace", or "a virtue coming from God". It gives us synonyms such as approval, acceptance, mercy, pardon, kindness and privilege. When receiving Holy Communion, the Catholic church insists that the recipient be in a "state of grace", implying spiritual purity, without sin.

We have passed the test, and now we find ourselves at the crown of being, as silence fills the sky. We have reached the seventh virtue, the last chakra, the Church of Laodicea. Our minds have become very still in the tumult of life, bathed in the grace of Spirit, enjoying an incredible inner peace, a peace that defies all things. That feeling is almost beyond the comprehension of the human mortal mind. We have totally lost ourselves as the bridegroom is now with us on the inner plane. This exalted status will now pour forth in the form of an astonishing power of being, as the holy trinity becomes ever so close to complete unification. "I and my Father are one" turns into reality. All metaphysical laws are becoming fulfilled within us and are us. Now we know the true significance of the teaching that tells us that nothing is above the law – from the least to the greatest. There is no separation at all. We come to realize that it just IS. GOD IS.

We now grasp that the experiences to which we once held with such willingness brought us to this place of true wisdom, a place that has no secrets to life. How can we achieve this level of grace for ourselves? We alone have the answer, through the events that life offers us.

Grace is a virtue that comes to us with each and every moment, every event, every decision, providing we accept and maintain it. We enjoy that choice if we follow the path of spirit. It depends on how we conduct ourselves during these moments. An experience can be good or bad, based on how we see it. If we are in a position where we can accept the gift of grace, we must see or hear the situations strictly as they are and devoid of judgment on our part. When we act as observers, they will become learning tools adding to our knowledge, thus we should not avoid these opportunities. It does not matter whether our personal viewpoint is right or wrong. We cannot know how those events may have been compounded by the previous episodes. What we witness becomes another lesson in the realignment of our own viewpoint. The grace bestowed upon us can indeed take the form of acceptance, mercy, approval, pardon or kindness. It becomes a blessing and helps us in attaining compassionate clarity.

This simple test is quite difficult. When faced with adversity, we have a tendency to not use the benevolent effects of grace in our actions. Instead, we stumble as we have in the past. When we have reached the seventh chakra, there is no need to stumble, because Spirit is there to help us in growth and wisdom. It is again a matter of choice.

Grace is a most wonderful gift and it is up to us to accept it and put it to work in our everyday life. It is the opportunity to advance on the road to wisdom, through our interactions with life and with our own selves. In that manner, we can see who we really are or what we are about to become. By earnestly applying the various sides of grace, we can shift our viewpoint to a higher level of flexibility, thus easing our physical and spiritual lifestyle. Having surrendered all illusions, we are at the door of the true fountain of life. Grace is Spirit. Spirit is love. We are learning to love all that is before us, and grace allows for a greater degree of acceptance and respect for what we know and see.

THE SEVEN BRANCHES

We have told you from the very beginning that the discovery of your inner spirit can be a complicated matter, normally irritated by the material pull. We are also talking about your eternal peace of mind in union with Spirit, and a rewarding and satisfying life on earth. As human beings, we have been weaving a tapestry of life with such complex designs that we no longer recognize the original concept. This book is a simple learning tool published in the hope that it will guide you toward a different path, perhaps narrow and strenuous in spots, but its final destination is filled with great personal rewards. We have attempted to disclose and explain the beauty and simplicity of what we have overlooked, and for our own sake, nothing should be overlooked. We have taught you new words and new ways to reach for the crown of spirituality. We now humbly ask you to enter the final phase of the holy trinity. The seven Essene mirrors were related to the body, while the virtues covered the mind and emotions.

That final phase is the ways of the Spirit, the last aspect of wholeness on the path of the spiritual human. **Anne and Daniel Meurois-Givaudan** wrote a book called *"The Way of the Essenes – Christ's Hidden Life Remembered"*. The following is an excerpt: *"Remember this: A human being is just one more variety of tree on this Earth. The Cosmos has endowed him with seven roots and seven branches. Now and then his consciousness suspects the existence of one or two of them, and a few buds open, but in what disorder!.....His seven branches grow and have consciousness in the transcendental ether....Thus you are like a tree that is still seeking a harmonious way to develop, one in which there are two tendencies that the trunk, because of its coarse bark is apparently unable to bring together...and for now, so that the earthly and cosmic saps may flood through you, here are the rules by which you will live"*. These words are attributed to the Master.

Spirit hears our knock. Behind the opened door is a gift waiting for us. We now need that leap of faith and all will be made known on the path of wisdom. We become the teachers of life and an ancient prophecy is fulfilled through us. This prophecy is found in Tibet. It states: *"The teachers of the future shall rise from the common human, from simple beginnings they shall all come"*.

Each of the seven branches has been given a symbolic name. They reside with the energy centers. In relation to their corresponding chakra, they are: Eternal Fluid, Creative Force, Peace, Love, Power, Wisdom and Cosmic Father. Because we know the physical and the mind/emotional connection within us, the last segment of our journey will be a short one. We will offer the higher levels of spirit. It will not be a lengthy dissertation, except where clarification is necessary. We realize that each of us may sense a different meaning, as has been the case during the moments we have shared. However, within the common thread that holds us together, there is a string of truth that cannot be denied.

ETERNAL FLUID

We are again in the presence of a term seldom used, and known by very few. Throughout this work, we have referred to water or liquid as the higher or the spirit nature of life. The same applies to the eternal fluid we are about to discuss. It is about the ethereal or the manna aspect of spirit, the unseen substance that permeates all that was, is and will be created. It is what gives us life and form, the creative power beneath and behind all things. We may use it once we have the proper focus and the necessary comprehension of its operation. It is an energy that the Master acquired because of His perseverance with His own being. Once we have overcome the purely physical aspect, we will vibrate to a higher rate of being. If you recall, Jesus once told us: *"...the works that I do shall he [man] do also; and greater works than these shall he do..."* (John 14:12). This alone should give us an incentive to persevere as He did. And if we do, we could tap into this unseen substance. To make use of perfection, we must be in faultless order ourselves, to bring it into form as the Father has intended us to do. We must learn from the wisdom of the Branches – the higher aspect – because we are entering the true realm of the creative power of being, the true nature and force of our focused thoughts. We have become the reality of the Creator's will. We are matching Its original intent and Its desire for us to be at one with It.

The eternal fluid is the deep well of life, a place of unlimited depth and resources, an unending supply offered as the gift of spirit to be shared with all things. It is the flow of spirit coursing through our veins. It is the spring of life mentioned by the Master. It is the deep well of infinite knowledge and experience, the one that flows with and through us all. It is the inner meaning of the endless surge of energy radiating from spirit, the heavenly bread of life, the manna discussed so often in the Bible. The eternal fluids have been around since the beginning of eternity. It is the fountain of all creation. It provides the real power we all wield in the material world. This level of energy is ours to use in all respects, as the controlling force behind the unseen nature. It is spirit's flow of energy given to us for the betterment of life. We cannot use it unless we have vanquished the adverse pulls of the material/illusion we have created.

It is the true reason we have been given birth from the womb of life. If we do not support our higher spiritual nature, we do not have the full use of the true eternal fluid. It is in its embryo form and cannot be used until we acknowledge the reality of our higher nature. It is there, but we do not have the control because the all-important ego interferes. The creative principle becomes unmanageable, and we turn into bewildered witnesses to events that are mostly less than palatable. We cannot deny this truth. We have denied too much of our self-reality already as well as some of our actions.

We must perceive that we have reached the third and most delicate part of the Holy Trinity. We are in the final stage of our spiritual growth journey. Life and its varied events have brought us the option to absorb and accept. These self-generated events should bring us no sadness at all and should be released. We created them as a means to learn, even if it was from the subconscious – which can be considered our higher nature. They took place because of our normal refusal to acknowledge our own true self. Life simply gave us what we asked and nothing less, since we chose to disregard the untapped energy source available within us.

The higher spiritual laws are very natural and unrelenting. The concept of eternal fluid encompasses the understanding and the appreciation of the reverence of all life. We should not use any of it for destroying any of its aspects needlessly, from the smallest insect to the greatest of emotion, because everything, including our most insignificant thoughts, is blessed with life. We should indeed respect life in all its magnificent forms.

The eternal fluids are the embodiment of the first energy center of the body, seat of the carnal aspect of life. Because of its unique position on the ladder of wisdom, it is also the seat of the creative principle that brings us procreation, through the union of the male and female. The masculine and feminine natures also reside on the inner plane of each individual as thought and emotion. Everything we create, from children to thoughts, becomes our offspring, and no matter what it may be – physical, mental or spiritual – we must lovingly nurture it until it comes to fruition. After all, did we not create it?

CREATIVE FORCE

All these creative principles work in union with each other for the foundation of life rather than its destruction. Creative force is the laws of opposition in motion. It is the positive coordinating with the negative. Without this coordination, we can expect turmoil, and that is what we see before us everywhere. This destruction exists because of the blatant misuse of the creative principles of life. We have allowed them to become the basis of greed. Once we understand this fact, it is not difficult to discern why the world is plagued with negative events. It is a result of ignorance or willful denial. If we do not comprehend the powers of eternal fluid and the creative force, and if we do not work assiduously and consciously with these energies, we are bound to encounter serious self-inflicted stumbling blocks. Maya – or illusion – stops us from proper use of these spiritually given energies. If we think clearly, we must admit that we have been blind to the truth – nothing less. The veils are being removed, allowing us to distinguish the realities of life and Spirit, providing we accept them and use them wisely.

The Master once said that we were free of sin until we had heard His message. Henceforth, we would be in "sin" because we refused to change. Does this not apply today? The real sin is in the omission or the denial. We have choices in life. It gives us at any time the opportunity to accept the truth of being.

The creative force of life sends us a distinct message. We must appreciate the fact that we are indeed the creative principle to all things. We are the true reason that life is here at all. What would it be without us? Nothing. We are the original spiritual entities that thought ourselves into physical reality, the original pressing down of thinking into the physical form. The creative force is here to assist us in remembering who we are and whence we came in the initial sense of life. It is pure realization of the meaning of self.

This has certainly been a long voyage, yet the journey has become lighter with each step. We have shed much of the excess baggage we carried and have traveled the path of the soul. We have come to the greatest experience a human can achieve: the true nature of self, the validation of the higher being within us. We are no longer divided. We are in union.

PEACE

It is the third energy center and the third seal, the level that in the past had created much in the way of our egoistic mind. It is the third horseman carrying the scales of justice in Revelations. We have reached an alignment of our inner self and a balance that we can enjoy. The material pull has no power over us and is no longer a hindrance in our endeavors. Peace is now the only thing that we may see, feel or realize for our own selves, therefore we see it among the people as well. We are willing to share it with all of Spirit's creations. We have lost the old selves and have gained the real selves. We are gazing upon the merger of the true trinity of life.

Being at the deepest part of our soul, peaceful nature has finally come forth into our hearts. Those around us will know and sense it. Ulterior motives of any kind have left us. We are a true leaf from the vine of spirit. There is no longer a conflict with the material world. We are in complete harmony within ourselves in all respects. When there is no inner conflict, it stands to reason that outer conflicts cannot exist. We have an inner acceptance and appreciation of the creative principles and we know that no harm will come – for it cannot. We agree to being the creative force underneath all things, having renounced all destructive thoughts at any level. We have become absolute living grace to all things.

This is the "Don Tian" center of the body, a powerful storehouse of energy that we now use with loving care. The ego has changed from a defensive nature to one of sharing and pure creativity. When properly guided, even the ego can evolve into that, and it hides nothing, therefore we have nothing to hide. Everything is in plain sight. Our actions in life demonstrate the purest of intents, always toward the higher good of all. We are not self-serving in any way, and selfishness has also left us. We are at peace with the world and with ourselves.

LOVE

Spiritual love, as that expressed so many times by the Master in the biblical texts, resides in the fourth energy center. It is Thyatira, the fourth Church of Revelations, the seat of our feelings. We have worked in other respects to bring our emotions to resolution with our thoughts. We have talked much on the subject of emotional healing, and great efforts have been applied. We have settled all previous debts brought on by past karmic events. We no longer see love as a purely carnal instinct. The physical is only the act – not the reality. The experience of love in a spiritual sense far surpasses the merging of two bodies.

We have entered this arena in the past to fill the voids that were created in us, and we have finally realized that true love does not reside outside ourselves. We know that it is within our very own heart. This particular kind of love cannot be given to us by others. It is very personal, and we can only share it. We cannot give it or take it away as has been done in the past. It now flows from us onto all the wonders of life, freely, without a price tag. No one may own the concept of love. It fits who we are. It is individual and unique to our own nature. Common sense tells us that owning is the opposite of sharing. Love is one of the greatest tests to which we may be subjected. We must be completely forgiving in our nature, and willing to share the love we have, as well as receive others' individual form of love. If we forgive, we must forget, because whatever it may have been should no longer matter. True exoneration will erase the memory of the events. Forgiveness is as unconditional as love should be and should be applied as such in all circumstances. If we are not able to forget the event, how can we possibly forgive? In that case, the cycle will repeat until we solve it and close it.

Love is offered from the heart, not from the mind. If it is in the mind only, it is merely a thought rather than a feeling. Love is the truth or seat of all feelings. It is turned into emotion through the mental machinations that we consider so important. We simply should move feelings out of the mind and put them where they belong: in the heart of the human. Love is harmony and the truth of our expression.

In "The Way of the Essenes" – by Anne and Daniel Meurois-Givaudan, the Master is heard saying: *"What do you want to love? The total love to which you aspire will never be vague and uncontrolled. It follows the lines of force whose ramifications spread across the whole universe. For now, you must learn to recognize these channels, to tame them so they may become an extension of your bodies".*

POWER

It is the fifth energy center of our body. It is the power to recognize our own selves and express the truth of being, knowing there will be no retribution in the process. It is creative wholeness, an evolved being in the flesh, an Avatar born onto life. It is the power to emanate truth and harmony from the center of being. It is the acceptance of who we truly are in relation to life. We accept that we are the living truth of all God's nature and are in the image and likeness of the Creator.

We have learned not to misuse ourselves on any level. We realize that all things are at our fingertips. We just need to ask and focus on the end results. We are no longer concerned with the methodology, for it does not matter. All things are given, because we know how to ask for the desire of the heart. The power of the heart center is with us in all respects. We are filled with the divine nature, for we know we are one and the same. All of life will respond to us in kind. We are an influence in all of life in a loving fashion. This is done from the purest point of self-expression, an expression that is not necessarily just the words. We give ourselves fully to our feelings and actions.

WISDOM

We are at the point of the true mystic, understanding absolute knowledge absolutely. We are in the sixth energy center of the body, or the third eye as it is known in metaphysical terms and in Eastern philosophy. We have the ability to see all things in a very learned light, the power of perception through all falsehood, no matter what it will be. Falsehood is the misperceptions of the egoistic mind. By now, it should have been shed completely, or it will be the last vestige of the influence carried by this kind of thought.

While we believe them to be very real, the ego presents the fears of being as fabrications. They are not, because they are the delusions of self. **John Muir** once said: "We must travel the journey of the trees before we may see the expanse of the universe". A very accurate statement indeed. These trees are merely the illusions of the mind, the fears we may still harbor on any subject. Spirit no longer allows us to hold on to these in any way because they will bind us in place as they have in the past.

For the last time, we must look at the "dark night of the soul", so we can have a full understanding of its purpose toward us. We will peer into it from a spiritual point of view, from the stance of the higher toward the lower. We have discussed this matter in the sixth mirror of relationship, with another level offered in the sixth of the seven virtues. We must now view it from the aspect of the seven branches.

We must remove all illusions so we can see the real truth to and of life. We offered the concept of solitude in the virtues and the overwhelming feelings of aloneness that will inexorably come to us as the natural laws of life dictate. Even the Master endured this in the symbol of His crucifixion, the crossroads of life when He uttered: "Eloi, Eloi, Lama Sabachthani". This is interpreted to mean: "Why hath thou forsaken me". In this dark night, we do feel the incredible weight of aloneness, and this is from a physical perspective only. In our case, we are truly carried by the spirit and it will assist us on our lonely journey. We are never cut off from spirit, and this is the point we are trying to present to the reader. It is with us particularly in this difficult part of the trek. It will watch over us especially in those moments because we are frail and susceptible to many confrontations from our selves and the illusions to which we hold. These frailties are exposed so they can be rectified or balanced.

Spirit never abandons us. It leaves us with our choices to either move forward or back to the places we have already known. We have that power. We either shed the burdensome baggage of the past, or we add new horizons to our knowledge. Spirit itself will become no heavier because of our decisions. It is above it all and it will not force us directly. It will guide us indirectly by bringing us back to the spot we know too well: the cycles to life, the road most traveled, the well-worn path.

Spirit has nothing to face. We, physical beings, do. We must face ourselves for what we do and have done. When we do, the situation becomes lighter in nature – unless we choose the old path. At that point, things will become even heavier than before and certainly will have a greater impact. We must accept that spirit, in its infinite wisdom, is always with us. We must always seek it and it will be made known to us. The purpose of the dark night is to bring a closer relationship and gain its everlasting wisdom.

COSMIC FATHER

Once again, we have arrived at the crown, or the seventh energy center, where silence is everywhere. It has been written: "Be still and know the voice of spirit". The Tibetans appropriately refer to it as the "roar of silence". It is the harmony of the universe that one will hear on the inner plane.

We find ourselves at the center of all there is, in complete union with all there is. The blissful hour has come, and the journey is now complete. The merger is over. In every respect, we have reached the stature of any master that ever lived upon the earth. This life is the path to attainment, through the journey of enlightenment and the parables and paradoxes that it brought us to gain full knowledge. We have a complete grasp of all things, seen and unseen. Nothing is hidden from us in any respect, since we have earned the promise given by the Cosmic Father that is everywhere before, within and around us.

We are the seat of cosmic power through the journey of life. The lessons were accepted and absorbed, and complete comprehension was achieved. All matters have been brought to fruition within us. We have access to the supremacy of the cosmos, to use within the power of wisdom. We are at the height of compassion in a very real sense while we sit in non-judgment and truly allow for things to be as they are: blinding, benevolent, everlasting Truth.

In the biblical sense, the messages of the Master portray all that is mentioned here. They are veiled in His use of allegorical language. In the Book of Matthew, we are told to be aware of our own inner reflection in the physical sense, what life will show us about our own nature. The Books of Mark and Luke offer us the seven virtues as He portrayed them. In the veiled words of the Book of John, we find the branches of life. We have added to our wisdom by respecting His advice: Seek and you shall find; knock and the door will be opened; ask and you will receive. We must do this in conjunction with all that life offers, no matter how it appears on the surface. Life is our teacher. It depends on what we do with the lessons and tests that are continually before us. We should present no excuses for any reason whatsoever. The laws are unrelenting in their nature. No matter how much we wish to deny, the scales will have to be balanced. We must recognize that it is our own creation and it will come back to us – as it must.

It is time to enjoy the true nature of life and the gifts it brings us, each in life's own way. We now have the intellect, but the real fruits come from the experience we gained and will share, and from the relationships we have established. We must use them in wisdom and love. Life will then be tranquil, peaceful and satisfying. In reality, nothing is wrong unless we think so. If we do, it will become our reality and we will begin the process of shedding erroneous thoughts all over again – our only "sin". We were told not to commit errors in judgment in any way. We should simply rise above so we may see clearly, unselfishly and lovingly, bathed in the light of the Cosmic Father. Be at peace with yourself.

We will leave you with this quote from 1887 by **Henry Drummond**, in his book titled "Natural Law in the Spiritual World": *"You can dwarf a soul just as you can dwarf a plant, by depriving it of a full environment. Such a soul for a time may have 'a name to live'. Its character may betray no sign of atrophy. But its very virtue somehow has the pallor of a flower that is grown in darkness, or as the herb which has never seen the sun, no fragrance breathes from its spirit".*

APPENDICES

COMPARATIVE CHART OF THE BIBLICAL
AND METAPHYSICAL REVELATIONS

CHAKRAS	CHURCHES	SEALS	TRUMPETS	PLAGUES	ESSENE MIRRORS	VIRTUES	BRANCHES
	Rev. 2	Rev. 6-7	Rev. 9-10	Rev. 16			
1st: Muladhara	Ephesus	White horse Bow & Crown	Hail, fire & blood	Sores upon men	Moment	Temptation	Eternal Fluid
2nd: Svadhishthana	Smyrna	Red horse Sword	Burning mountain into the sea	Blood of dead men in the sea	Judgment	Sincerity	Creative Force
3rd: Manipura	Pergamos	Black horse & scales	Star (Wormwood) into waters	Rivers of blood	Loss	Justice	Peace
4th: Anahata	Thyatira	Pale horse & Death	1/3 of sun, moon & stars darkened	The sun scorches the planet	Forgotten Love	Faith	Love
5th: Vishuddha	Sardis	Crying souls & white robes	Giants locusts Bottomless pit	Darkness	Creator	Silence	Power
6th: Ajna	Philadelphia	Earthquake & darkness	1/3 of the men killed	3 unclean spirits out of dragon's mouth	Darkness	Solitude	Wisdom
7th: Sahasrara (Soma)	Laodicea	Seal of the Living God	7 thunders & the little book	Earthquake & hail	Compassion	Grace	Cosmic Father

BIBLIOGRAPHY

BESSANT, ANNIE
THE SPIRITUAL LIFE. Quest Books, 1991

BHAKTIVEDANTA, A.C.
THE BHAGAVAD-GITA AS IT IS. The Bhaktivedanta Book Trust, 1972

BLAVATSKY, HELENA P.
ISIS UNVEILED. Theosophical Publishing, 1988

BRADEN, GREG
WALKING BETWEEN WORLDS. Radio Bookstore Press, 1997

CADY, EMILY
LESSONS IN TRUTH

CAYCE, EDGAR
THE SLEEPING PROPHET. Doubleday & Co., 1967

DRUMMOND, HENRY
NATURAL LAW IN THE SPIRITUAL WORLD. John Alden Publisher, 1887

EISENMAN, ROBERT & WISE, MICHAEL
THE DEAD SEA SCROLLS UNCOVERED. Element Publishing, 1992

FILLMORE, CHARLES, REFERENCE LIBRARY
THE METAPHYSICAL BIBLE DICTIONARY. Unity Books, 1995

FLACCUS ALBINUS ALCUINUS
BOOK OF JASHER. Kessinger Publishing Co., 1829

GOODSPEED, EDGAR J.
APOCRYPHA. Vintage Books, 1959

HEINDEL, MAX

COSMO CONCEPTION. Rand McNally, 1956

HELMS, RANDEL
GOSPEL FICTIONS. Promethus Books, 1988

HURTAK, J. J.
THE KEYS OF ENOCH. Academy for Future Science, 1977

JOHARI, HARISH
CHAKRAS. Destiny Books, 2000 (Revised)

KERSTEN, HOLGER
JESUS LIVED IN INDIA. Element Book Ltd, Longmead, England, 1986

KING JAMES VERSION
THE HOLY BIBLE. Thomas Nelson, 1976

LAURENCE, RICHARD, LL.D., Tr.
THE BOOK OF ENOCH. Wizard Bookshelf, 1976

LEWIS, H. SPENCER
THE MYSTICAL LIFE OF JESUS. AMORC, 1929

LOCKMAN FOUNDATION
THE NEW AMERICAN STANDARD BIBLE. Red Letter Edition, Broadman & Holman, 1977

MEUROIS-GIVAUDAN, ANNE & DANIEL
THE WAY OF THE ESSENES. Destiny Books, 1993

MOOKERJEE, AJIT
KUNDALINI. Destiny Books, 1982

PERCIVAL, HAROLD
THINKING AND DESTINY. World Publishing, 1946

PROPHET, ELIZABETH CLARE
LOST YEARS OF JESUS. Summit University Press, 1987

ROBINSON, JAMES M., Gen. Editor
THE NAG HAMMADI LIBRARY. Harper S.F., 1978

ROMAN, SANAYA & PACKER, DUANE
SPIRITUAL GROWTH. H.J. Kramer Inc., 1987

RORICH-NOTOVICH, NICOLAI
SAINT ISSA. Frederick A. Stokes, 1929

STEINER, RUDOLF
GOSPEL OF ST MATTHEW. R. Steiner Publishing Co, London, 1946

STEINER, RUDOLF
GOSPEL OF ST MARK. Anthroposophic Press, 1986

STEINER, RUDOLF
GOSPEL OF ST LUKE. R. Steiner Press, London, 1964

STEINER, RUDOLF
GOSPEL OF ST JOHN. Anthroposophic Press, 1940

UNKNOWN
SECRET INSTRUCTIONS OF THE SOCIETY OF JESUS. Kessinger Publishing, 1882

WILLIAMS, THOMAS D.
A TEXTUAL CONCORDANCE OF THE HOLY SCRIPTURES. Tan Books, 1908

If you wish to order a book for a friend or a family member, please send your request to:

Steven L. Hairfield, PhD
550 East Plumb Lane – Suite 305
Reno, NV 89502

Kindly enclose your check (payable to the above) for **$24.95** plus **$5.95** for shipping and handling.

You may also order through the Web Site
www.hairfield.com
or by Email to **steven@hairfield.com**.

The book will be shipped to you upon receipt of your check.